ADDISON-WESLEY MATHEMATICS

Robert E. Eicholz

Phares G. O'Daffer

Charles R. Fleenor

Randall I. Charles

Sharon Young

Carne S. Barnett

Addison-Wesley Publishing Company

Menlo Park, California   Reading, Massachusetts   London   Amsterdam   Don Mills, Ontario   Sydney

Illustration Acknowledgments

Frank Ansley 38–39, 228–229, 256–257, 266–267, 302–303, 322–323, 350–351

Ellen Blonder 2–3, 16–17, 44, 76–77, 86–87, 100, 103, 124–125, 154, 184–185, 212, 215, 240–241, 246–247, 260, 286, 312, 336–337, 360, 378

Sherry Balestra 18, 47, 84–85, 102, 155, 157, 160–161, 186, 226–227, 262, 306–307, 313, 338, 342–343, 361, 372–373

Elizabeth Callen 20–21, 30–31, 40, 78, 94–95, 104–105, 132, 142–143, 156, 216–217, 234–235, 242, 250, 290–291, 304–305, 348–349, 358–359, 364–365, 376–377, 380

Maxie Chambliss 4, 24–25, 46, 54–55, 79, 82–83, 116–117, 126, 172–173, 206–207, 214, 222–223, 238, 248–249, 274–275, 288, 310–311, 314, 324–325, 362

Randy Chewning 10–11, 97, 120–121, 146–147, 162–163

Barry Geller 36–37, 194–195, 224–225

Jon Goodell 88, 152, 174–175, 196–197, 296–297

Pat Hoggan 12–13, 112–113, 200–201, 213

Susan Jaekel 60, 74–75, 101, 114–115, 118, 130–131, 138–139, 164–165, 187, 192–193, 278–279, 289, 298–299, 326–327, 339, 346–347, 352–353, 368

Susan Lexa 56, 72–73, 90–91, 98–99, 140–141, 180–181, 190–191, 259, 272–273, 308–309

Jim McGuinness 6–7, 110–111, 210–211

Yoshi Miyake 14, 19, 50–51, 150–151, 168–169, 230–231

Deborah Morse 41, 45, 68, 70–71, 108–109, 127, 208–209, 220–221, 263, 268–269, 270

Dennis Nolan 26–27, 28–29, 34–35, 52–53, 64–65, 96, 136–137, 148–149, 166–167, 176–177, 202–203, 232–233, 252–253, 261, 272 (upper right), 300–301, 320–321, 332–333, 363

Valerie Randall 15, 66–67, 89, 122–123, 133, 144, 153, 170–171, 182–183, 204–205, 236–237, 258, 280–281, 282–283, 287, 318–319, 328–329, 334–335, 356–357, 370–371, 383–387

Doug Roy 32–33, 62–63, 92–93, 134–135, 178, 198–199, 254, 285, 294–295, 330–331, 344–345, 354, 374–375

Pat Traub 8–9, 42–43

Stephen Zinkus 1, 23, 49, 81, 107, 129, 159, 189, 219, 245, 265, 293, 317, 341, 367

Cover Photograph
© **Wayne Miller/Magnum Photos**

Contents

CHAPTER 5   DIVISION FACTS, 107

CHAPTER 6   MEASUREMENT: Metric Units, 129

CHAPTER 7   MULTIPLICATION: 1-Digit Factors, 159

CHAPTER 8   DIVISION: 1-Digit Divisors, 189

CHAPTER 9   FRACTIONS, 219

CHAPTER 10   ADDITION AND SUBTRACTION OF FRACTIONS, 245

CHAPTER 11   GEOMETRY AND GRAPHING, 265

CHAPTER 12   MULTIPLICATION: 2-Digit Factors, 293

ADDITION AND SUBTRACTION FACTS

ADDITION AND SUBTRACTION FACTS

1

Maria likes to watch the stars. Her grandfather knows a lot about stars. He shows her groups of stars called constellations. The constellation Orion appears in winter. A row of bright stars makes his belt. A red star is on his shoulder. It is called Betelgeuse. A blue-white star is on his foot. It is called Rigel. Maria saw 7 bright stars in Orion. She saw 8 of the fainter stars. Greek stories tell about Orion. He boasted about being such a good hunter. He was punished by the gods. The Scorpion was sent after him. The Scorpion appears in the summer sky.

Addition Facts

Joan is learning the names of some of her teeth. Her front teeth are made up of 8 incisors and 4 canines. How many front teeth does Joan have?

Since we want the total amount, we add.

$$8 + 4 = 12$$

Addend   Addend   Sum

$$8 \leftarrow \text{Addend}$$
$$+\ 4 \leftarrow \text{Addend}$$
$$\overline{12} \leftarrow \text{Sum}$$

Joan has 12 front teeth.

Warm Up   Read each equation aloud and give the sum.

Example   We read $9 + 5 = 14$ as "**Nine plus five equal fourteen.**"

1. $5 + 9 = n$ 2. $8 + 4 = n$ 3. $6 + 7 = n$ 4. $6 + 5 = n$

5. $2 + 8 = n$ 6. $1 + 9 = n$ 7. $3 + 6 = n$ 8. $8 + 7 = n$

9. $9 + 4 = n$ 10. $9 + 7 = n$ 11. $7 + 7 = n$ 12. $6 + 6 = n$

13. $5 + 3 = n$ 14. $7 + 3 = n$ 15. $0 + 3 = n$ 16. $6 + 4 = n$

17. $6 + 9 = n$ 18. $3 + 5 = n$ 19. $5 + 7 = n$ 20. $4 + 7 = n$

21. $8 + 3 = n$ 22. $8 + 6 = n$ 23. $5 + 0 = n$ 24. $8 + 5 = n$

Add.

1. 5 / + 6
2. 2 / + 3
3. 6 / + 8
4. 6 / + 4
5. 8 / + 5
6. 2 / + 0
7. 4 / + 4

8. 7 / + 8
9. 3 / + 6
10. 5 / + 2
11. 3 / + 8
12. 9 / + 8
13. 5 / + 3
14. 4 / + 2

15. 9 / + 3
16. 0 / + 8
17. 8 / + 8
18. 3 / + 7
19. 9 / + 9
20. 4 / + 8
21. 8 / + 2

22. 3 / + 4
23. 4 / + 9
24. 9 / + 7
25. 9 / + 2
26. 5 / + 5
27. 7 / + 4
28. 6 / + 8

29. 3 + 3
30. 7 + 2
31. 7 + 5
32. 9 + 5

33. 1 + 6
34. 6 + 7
35. 7 + 7
36. 0 + 7

37. Find the sum of 7 and 4.
38. Find the sum of 5 and 8.

39. Find the sum of 9 and 6.
40. Find the sum of 4 and 6.

Solve.

41. Jim's back teeth are made up of 8 bicuspids and 6 molars. How many back teeth does Jim have?

42. **DATA HUNT** Count your upper front teeth and lower front teeth. How many do you have of each? How many in all?

┌─ **THINK** ─┐

Shape Perception

Place 6 coins like the ones shown. Move one coin so you have 3 straight lines of coins with 3 coins in each row.

MATH

Subtraction Facts

Jack baked 15 large dinner rolls. There were 8 people at the dinner. Each person ate 1 roll.

Take Away

How many rolls were left?

To find how many are left, we subtract.

$$15$$
$$-\,8$$
$$\overline{7}$$ ← — Difference

$$15 - 8 = 7$$

There were 7 rolls left.

Compare

How many more rolls were there than people?

To find how many more (fewer), we subtract.

$$15$$
$$-\,8$$
$$\overline{7}$$ ← — Difference

$$15 - 8 = 7$$

There were 7 more rolls than people.

Warm Up   Read each equation aloud and give the difference.

Example   We read $12 - 8 = 4$ as **"Twelve minus eight equal four."**

1. $15 - 7 = n$
2. $10 - 5 = n$
3. $14 - 9 = n$
4. $13 - 4 = n$

5. $14 - 7 = n$
6. $13 - 8 = n$
7. $12 - 4 = n$
8. $16 - 9 = n$

9. $8 - 5 = n$
10. $17 - 8 = n$
11. $15 - 6 = n$
12. $6 - 6 = n$

13. $16 - 8 = n$
14. $7 - 0 = n$
15. $9 - 7 = n$
16. $14 - 8 = n$

17. $13 - 7 = n$
18. $11 - 4 = n$
19. $11 - 8 = n$
20. $12 - 9 = n$

21. $15 - 9 = n$
22. $10 - 7 = n$
23. $14 - 5 = n$
24. $12 - 5 = n$

Subtract.

1. 15
   − 8

2. 10
   − 3

3. 13
   − 5

4. 6
   − 0

5. 16
   − 8

6. 11
   − 7

7. 11
   − 5

8. 14
   − 8

9. 15
   − 9

10. 10
    − 4

11. 12
    − 9

12. 9
    − 9

13. 13
    − 6

14. 12
    − 8

15. 17
    − 9

16. 7
    − 5

17. 11
    − 9

18. 15
    − 6

19. 18
    − 9

20. 8
    − 3

21. 13
    − 8

22. 12
    − 5

23. 10
    − 6

24. 9
    − 4

25. 8 − 2

26. 10 − 5

27. 14 − 5

28. 12 − 4

29. 13 − 7

30. 16 − 7

31. 11 − 6

32. 17 − 8

33. Subtract 7 from 15.

34. Subtract 8 from 11.

35. Subtract 2 from 10.

36. Subtract 4 from 13.

37. Subtract 6 from 14.

Solve.

38. Janet made 12 cornsticks. Her family ate 9. How many were left?

39. Ted baked 16 muffins and 8 rolls. How many more muffins did he bake?

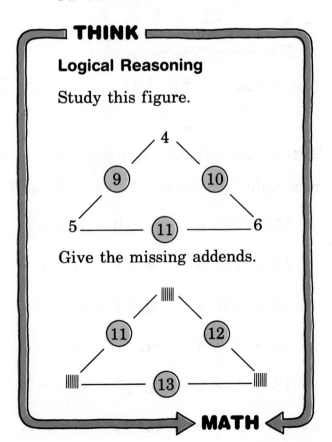

THINK

Logical Reasoning

Study this figure.

Give the missing addends.

➡ **MATH** ⬅

Addition and Subtraction

Addition and subtraction are related. For two different addends and their sum, there are two addition facts and two subtraction facts.

The fact family helps us see a special property of addition.

Addend	Addend	Sum
8	6	14

Fact Family

8 + 6 = 14
6 + 8 = 14
14 − 6 = 8
14 − 8 = 6

Order Property +

When the order of the addends is changed, the sum stays the same.

When 0 is an addend, the fact family helps us see some special properties of zero.

Addend	Addend	Sum
7	0	7

Fact Family

7 + 0 = 7
0 + 7 = 7
7 − 0 = 7
7 − 7 = 0

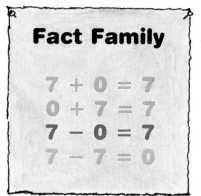

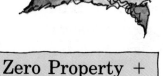
Zero Property +

When one addend is zero, the sum is the same as the other addend.

Zero Property −

When zero is subtracted from a number, the difference is the number.

Zero Property −

When a number is subtracted from itself, the difference is zero.

Find the sums and differences.

1. $6 + 7 = n$
   $7 + 6 = n$
   $13 - 7 = n$
   $13 - 6 = n$

2. $9 + 0 = n$
   $0 + 9 = n$
   $9 - 0 = n$
   $9 - 9 = n$

3. $\begin{array}{r} 7 \\ + 7 \\ \hline \end{array}$

4. $\begin{array}{r} 8 \\ + 6 \\ \hline \end{array}$

5. $\begin{array}{r} 5 \\ + 6 \\ \hline \end{array}$

6. $\begin{array}{r} 2 \\ + 0 \\ \hline \end{array}$

7. $\begin{array}{r} 9 \\ + 7 \\ \hline \end{array}$

8. $\begin{array}{r} 3 \\ + 8 \\ \hline \end{array}$

9. $\begin{array}{r} 15 \\ - 9 \\ \hline \end{array}$

10. $\begin{array}{r} 12 \\ - 4 \\ \hline \end{array}$

11. $\begin{array}{r} 18 \\ - 9 \\ \hline \end{array}$

12. $\begin{array}{r} 11 \\ - 3 \\ \hline \end{array}$

13. $\begin{array}{r} 8 \\ - 0 \\ \hline \end{array}$

14. $\begin{array}{r} 6 \\ - 6 \\ \hline \end{array}$

15. $\begin{array}{r} 6 \\ + 0 \\ \hline \end{array}$

16. $\begin{array}{r} 9 \\ - 3 \\ \hline \end{array}$

17. $\begin{array}{r} 12 \\ - 7 \\ \hline \end{array}$

18. $\begin{array}{r} 3 \\ + 4 \\ \hline \end{array}$

19. $\begin{array}{r} 13 \\ - 6 \\ \hline \end{array}$

20. $\begin{array}{r} 11 \\ - 7 \\ \hline \end{array}$

21. $\begin{array}{r} 14 \\ - 6 \\ \hline \end{array}$

22. $\begin{array}{r} 6 \\ + 9 \\ \hline \end{array}$

23. $\begin{array}{r} 0 \\ + 3 \\ \hline \end{array}$

24. $\begin{array}{r} 17 \\ - 8 \\ \hline \end{array}$

25. $\begin{array}{r} 8 \\ - 8 \\ \hline \end{array}$

26. $\begin{array}{r} 5 \\ + 9 \\ \hline \end{array}$

Write four equations for each set of fact-family numbers.

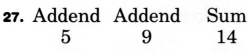
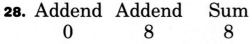

	Addend	Addend	Sum
27.	5	9	14
28.	0	8	8
29.	3	4	7
30.	6	1	7

THINK

Guess and Check

Find the hidden addends. Their difference is 1.

Addend	Addend	Sum
+	=	15

MATH

PROBLEM SOLVING ★ The 5-Point Checklist

To solve a problem

☆ 1. Understand the Question
☆ 2. Find the needed Data
☆ 3. Plan what to do
☆ 4. Find the Answer
☆ 5. Check back

QUESTION
DATA
PLAN
ANSWER
CHECK

Use the 5-Point Checklist to help you solve the following problem.

Jim's family had a garage sale. They had 14 old books to sell. Only 8 of them were sold. How many were not sold?

1. Understand the QUESTION
How many books were left?

2. Find the needed DATA
Had 14 books. Sold 8.

3. PLAN what to do
We want the number of books left. We should subtract.

4. Find the ANSWER
$14 - 8 = 6$ 6 books were not sold.

5. CHECK back
Read the problem again. 6 seems about right.

Solve. Use the 5-Point Checklist.

1. Paul took $10 to the sale. He spent $6 for books. How much does he have left?

2. Mary sold a lamp for $8 and a doll for $3. How much money did Mary make?

Solve.

1. Mr. Lambert had 4 bow ties and 8 regular ties for sale. How many ties did he have?

2. Mrs. Lambert had 15 glasses to sell. She sold 8 of them. How many were left?

3. Jim put a price of $8 on a ball glove. He put a price of $2 on a small bat. How much more money was the glove than the bat?

4. The sale lasted 3 hours in the morning and 4 hours in the afternoon. How long did the sale last?

5. An old chair was priced at $13. It did not sell in the morning. Mrs. Lambert took $4 off the price. How much was the chair then?

6. Jim had 14 comic books to sell. A friend bought 5 of them. How many were left after the sale?

7. Mr. Lambert sold a radio for $9 and a hand saw for $4. How much did he get for these two sales?

★ 8. Mary sold 5 records for $6. She was paid with a $10 bill. How much change should she return?

9

Practice the Facts

Add.

1. $\begin{array}{r} 4 \\ +5 \\ \hline \end{array}$	2. $\begin{array}{r} 7 \\ +6 \\ \hline \end{array}$	3. $\begin{array}{r} 3 \\ +5 \\ \hline \end{array}$	4. $\begin{array}{r} 9 \\ +8 \\ \hline \end{array}$	5. $\begin{array}{r} 6 \\ +6 \\ \hline \end{array}$	6. $\begin{array}{r} 4 \\ +6 \\ \hline \end{array}$	7. $\begin{array}{r} 7 \\ +8 \\ \hline \end{array}$
8. $\begin{array}{r} 6 \\ +3 \\ \hline \end{array}$	9. $\begin{array}{r} 3 \\ +7 \\ \hline \end{array}$	10. $\begin{array}{r} 7 \\ +7 \\ \hline \end{array}$	11. $\begin{array}{r} 5 \\ +8 \\ \hline \end{array}$	12. $\begin{array}{r} 4 \\ +7 \\ \hline \end{array}$	13. $\begin{array}{r} 3 \\ +2 \\ \hline \end{array}$	14. $\begin{array}{r} 4 \\ +8 \\ \hline \end{array}$
15. $\begin{array}{r} 5 \\ +9 \\ \hline \end{array}$	16. $\begin{array}{r} 8 \\ +0 \\ \hline \end{array}$	17. $\begin{array}{r} 9 \\ +2 \\ \hline \end{array}$	18. $\begin{array}{r} 4 \\ +3 \\ \hline \end{array}$	19. $\begin{array}{r} 9 \\ +1 \\ \hline \end{array}$	20. $\begin{array}{r} 8 \\ +8 \\ \hline \end{array}$	21. $\begin{array}{r} 6 \\ +5 \\ \hline \end{array}$
22. $\begin{array}{r} 5 \\ +8 \\ \hline \end{array}$	23. $\begin{array}{r} 7 \\ +9 \\ \hline \end{array}$	24. $\begin{array}{r} 0 \\ +6 \\ \hline \end{array}$	25. $\begin{array}{r} 9 \\ +9 \\ \hline \end{array}$	26. $\begin{array}{r} 8 \\ +6 \\ \hline \end{array}$	27. $\begin{array}{r} 5 \\ +5 \\ \hline \end{array}$	28. $\begin{array}{r} 7 \\ +5 \\ \hline \end{array}$

Subtract.

29. $\begin{array}{r} 14 \\ -7 \\ \hline \end{array}$	30. $\begin{array}{r} 15 \\ -7 \\ \hline \end{array}$	31. $\begin{array}{r} 10 \\ -3 \\ \hline \end{array}$	32. $\begin{array}{r} 12 \\ -4 \\ \hline \end{array}$	33. $\begin{array}{r} 7 \\ -0 \\ \hline \end{array}$	34. $\begin{array}{r} 16 \\ -9 \\ \hline \end{array}$	35. $\begin{array}{r} 11 \\ -2 \\ \hline \end{array}$
36. $\begin{array}{r} 13 \\ -6 \\ \hline \end{array}$	37. $\begin{array}{r} 10 \\ -4 \\ \hline \end{array}$	38. $\begin{array}{r} 17 \\ -8 \\ \hline \end{array}$	39. $\begin{array}{r} 18 \\ -9 \\ \hline \end{array}$	40. $\begin{array}{r} 6 \\ -2 \\ \hline \end{array}$	41. $\begin{array}{r} 12 \\ -7 \\ \hline \end{array}$	42. $\begin{array}{r} 15 \\ -6 \\ \hline \end{array}$
43. $\begin{array}{r} 16 \\ -8 \\ \hline \end{array}$	44. $\begin{array}{r} 12 \\ -0 \\ \hline \end{array}$	45. $\begin{array}{r} 11 \\ -6 \\ \hline \end{array}$	46. $\begin{array}{r} 9 \\ -4 \\ \hline \end{array}$	47. $\begin{array}{r} 10 \\ -5 \\ \hline \end{array}$	48. $\begin{array}{r} 14 \\ -5 \\ \hline \end{array}$	49. $\begin{array}{r} 7 \\ -2 \\ \hline \end{array}$
50. $\begin{array}{r} 13 \\ -5 \\ \hline \end{array}$	51. $\begin{array}{r} 14 \\ -8 \\ \hline \end{array}$	52. $\begin{array}{r} 11 \\ -8 \\ \hline \end{array}$	53. $\begin{array}{r} 8 \\ -5 \\ \hline \end{array}$	54. $\begin{array}{r} 10 \\ -3 \\ \hline \end{array}$	55. $\begin{array}{r} 12 \\ -6 \\ \hline \end{array}$	56. $\begin{array}{r} 10 \\ -8 \\ \hline \end{array}$

Add or subtract.

1. 6
   + 4

2. 11
   − 3

3. 15
   − 8

4. 8
   + 8

5. 9
   + 7

6. 12
   − 8

7. 15
   − 8

8. 13
   − 7

9. 2
   + 9

10. 0
    + 7

11. 11
    − 5

12. 14
    − 6

13. 5
    + 7

14. 16
    − 7

15. 5
    + 4

16. 16
    − 8

17. 7
    + 3

18. 15
    − 9

19. 8
    + 5

20. 7
    + 7

21. 12
    − 7

22. 13
    − 5

23. 10
    − 7

24. 11
    + 0

25. $14 - 9 =$

26. $8 + 9 =$

27. $6 + 6 =$

28. $18 - 9 =$

29. $6 + 0 =$

30. $8 + 1 =$

31. $11 - 8 =$

32. $9 - 2 =$

33. $14 - 8 =$

34. $5 - 0 =$

35. $15 - 6 =$

36. $6 - 1 =$

THINK

Patterns

Guess each rule. Then give the missing numbers.

Sara said	José answered
3	11
5	13
7	15
37. 4	▨
38. ▨	14

José said	Sara answered
10	4
12	6
9	3
39. 7	▨
40. ▨	9

Sara said	José answered
2	4
4	8
3	6
41. 5	10
	8	▨

MATH

Three Addends

Don planted flowers in a window box. He planted 5 short purple flowers, 3 tall purple flowers, and 6 tall yellow flowers. How many flowers did Don plant?

$$(5 + 3) + 6$$
$$8 + 6 = 14$$
Purple — Yellow — In all

$$5 + (3 + 6)$$
$$5 + 9 = 14$$
Short — Tall — In all

Don planted 14 flowers.

Grouping Property +

When you add, you can change the grouping and the sum stays the same.

Other Examples

$9 + 3 = 12$

$4 + 8 = 12$

$$(4 + 5) + 3 = 12$$

Adding Down

$$\begin{array}{r} 2 \\ 4 \\ + 5 \\ \hline 11 \end{array}$$

6 and 5 more make 11.

$$4 + (5 + 3) = 12$$

Adding Up

$$\begin{array}{r} 2 \\ 4 \\ + 5 \\ \hline 11 \end{array}$$

9 and 2 more make 11.

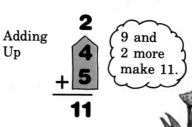

Warm Up Add.

1. $6 + 2 + 3 = n$ 2. $5 + 4 + 1 = n$ 3. $3 + 6 + 3 = n$

4. $\begin{array}{r} 2 \\ 4 \\ + 3 \end{array}$ 5. $\begin{array}{r} 5 \\ 5 \\ + 4 \end{array}$ 6. $\begin{array}{r} 3 \\ 6 \\ + 2 \end{array}$ 7. $\begin{array}{r} 5 \\ 4 \\ + 5 \end{array}$ 8. $\begin{array}{r} 6 \\ 2 \\ + 5 \end{array}$ 9. $\begin{array}{r} 4 \\ 4 \\ + 6 \end{array}$ 10. $\begin{array}{r} 3 \\ 5 \\ + 3 \end{array}$

Add.

1. $\begin{array}{r} 2 \\ 3 \\ +\ 2 \\ \hline \end{array}$	**2.** $\begin{array}{r} 4 \\ 1 \\ +\ 3 \\ \hline \end{array}$	**3.** $\begin{array}{r} 6 \\ 1 \\ +\ 7 \\ \hline \end{array}$	**4.** $\begin{array}{r} 4 \\ 5 \\ +\ 0 \\ \hline \end{array}$	**5.** $\begin{array}{r} 3 \\ 7 \\ +\ 2 \\ \hline \end{array}$

6. $\begin{array}{r} 7 \\ 1 \\ +\ 8 \\ \hline \end{array}$	**7.** $\begin{array}{r} 6 \\ 2 \\ +\ 2 \\ \hline \end{array}$	**8.** $\begin{array}{r} 5 \\ 4 \\ +\ 3 \\ \hline \end{array}$	**9.** $\begin{array}{r} 2 \\ 1 \\ +\ 4 \\ \hline \end{array}$	**10.** $\begin{array}{r} 6 \\ 4 \\ +\ 6 \\ \hline \end{array}$	**11.** $\begin{array}{r} 3 \\ 3 \\ +\ 3 \\ \hline \end{array}$	**12.** $\begin{array}{r} 2 \\ 8 \\ +\ 2 \\ \hline \end{array}$

Add. Look for tens.

13. $\begin{array}{r} 2 \\ 7 \\ +\ 3 \\ \hline \end{array}$	**14.** $\begin{array}{r} 8 \\ 1 \\ +\ 2 \\ \hline \end{array}$	**15.** $\begin{array}{r} 6 \\ 4 \\ +\ 5 \\ \hline \end{array}$	**16.** $\begin{array}{r} 5 \\ 3 \\ +\ 5 \\ \hline \end{array}$	**17.** $\begin{array}{r} 3 \\ 2 \\ +\ 7 \\ \hline \end{array}$	**18.** $\begin{array}{r} 9 \\ 1 \\ +\ 1 \\ \hline \end{array}$	**19.** $\begin{array}{r} 4 \\ 2 \\ +\ 6 \\ \hline \end{array}$

20. $5 + 2 + 5 = n$ **21.** $4 + 6 + 3 = n$ **22.** $2 + 0 + 8 = n$

23. $4 + 2 + 6 = n$ **24.** $7 + 3 + 3 = n$ **25.** $4 + 5 + 5 = n$

Solve.

26. Karen planted 6 yellow flowers, 3 blue flowers, and 4 pink flowers. How many flowers did she plant?

★ **27.** Jeff planted 3 red, 2 blue, 4 yellow, and 5 pink flowers. How many flowers did he plant?

SKILLKEEPER

Add or subtract.

1. $\begin{array}{r} 3 \\ +\ 5 \\ \hline \end{array}$	**2.** $\begin{array}{r} 4 \\ +\ 7 \\ \hline \end{array}$	**3.** $\begin{array}{r} 13 \\ -\ 6 \\ \hline \end{array}$	**4.** $\begin{array}{r} 5 \\ +\ 2 \\ \hline \end{array}$	**5.** $\begin{array}{r} 14 \\ -\ 8 \\ \hline \end{array}$	**6.** $\begin{array}{r} 17 \\ -\ 9 \\ \hline \end{array}$

7. $\begin{array}{r} 8 \\ +\ 8 \\ \hline \end{array}$	**8.** $\begin{array}{r} 12 \\ -\ 7 \\ \hline \end{array}$	**9.** $\begin{array}{r} 15 \\ -\ 8 \\ \hline \end{array}$	**10.** $\begin{array}{r} 3 \\ +\ 4 \\ \hline \end{array}$	**11.** $\begin{array}{r} 9 \\ +\ 5 \\ \hline \end{array}$	**12.** $\begin{array}{r} 10 \\ -\ 4 \\ \hline \end{array}$

PROBLEM SOLVING
Understanding the Question

To solve any problem, you must **understand the question.** You could ask an addition or a subtraction question about the data on the card.

> **DATA CARD**
> Amy earned 9 dollars for baby-sitting. She earned 5 dollars for doing dishes.

Addition   How much did Amy earn for both jobs?

Subtraction   How much more did Amy earn for baby-sitting than doing dishes?

Write an addition or a subtraction question for each DATA CARD. Solve your problem.

1.
> **DATA CARD**
> Larry had 7 dollars. He earned 3 dollars for mowing the lawn.

2.
> **DATA CARD**
> Molly has 8 dollars in her bank. She has 5 dollars hidden in her desk.

3.
> **DATA CARD**
> Hank earned 7 dollars for cleaning house. He already had 6 dollars.

4.
> **DATA CARD**
> Dora spent 6 dollars for a record. She also bought a book for 10 dollars.

PROBLEM SOLVING
Using Data from a Graph

Tina's class collected data about their pets. Then they made a graph to show the data.

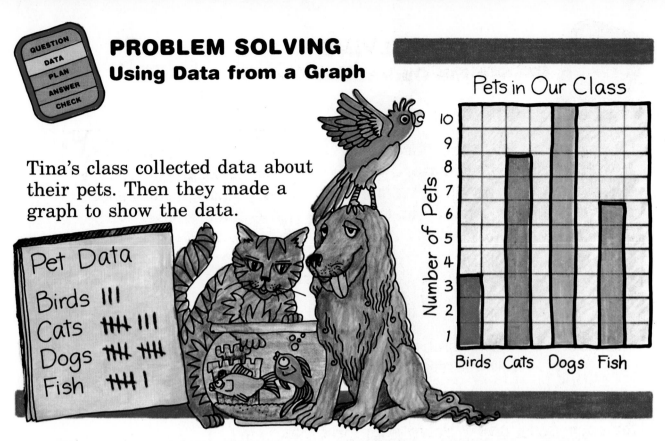

Pet Data

Birds III
Cats ₩₩ III
Dogs ₩₩ ₩₩
Fish ₩₩ I

Pets in Our Class

Number of Pets

Birds Cats Dogs Fish

1. How many dogs do the students in Tina's class have?

2. How many cats do they have?

3. How many dogs and cats do they have?

4. How many more cats are there than birds?

5. How many cats and fish are there?

6. How many more dogs are there than birds?

7. Three squares are colored for Sue's 3 dogs. How many dogs does the rest of the class have?

8. How many birds, cats, and fish are there?

9. Ben's cat had 4 kittens. How many cats does the class have now?

10. **DATA HUNT** How many pet dogs does your class have? How many pet cats do they have? Find the difference between the number of cats and the number of dogs.

PROBLEM SOLVING
Choose the Operations

QUESTION
DATA
PLAN
ANSWER
CHECK

SOME PROBLEMS CAN BE SOLVED BY USING JUST ONE OPERATION. FOR OTHER PROBLEMS, YOU MAY NEED MORE THAN ONE OPERATION. A STRATEGY THAT CAN HELP YOU IS SHOWN BELOW.

Try This Mary saved $7. She earned $6 more. She spent $4 to fix her bicycle. How much money does Mary have left?

CHOOSE THE OPERATIONS

To choose the correct operations, you need to **understand** them.

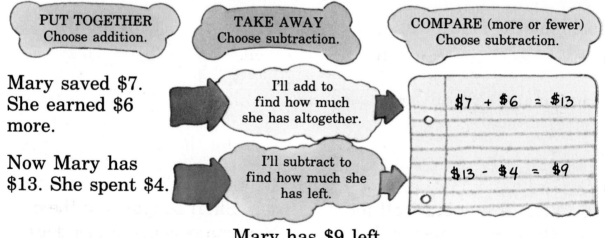

PUT TOGETHER
Choose addition.

TAKE AWAY
Choose subtraction.

COMPARE (more or fewer)
Choose subtraction.

Mary saved $7. She earned $6 more.

I'll add to find how much she has altogether.

$$\$7 + \$6 = \$13$$

Now Mary has $13. She spent $4.

I'll subtract to find how much she has left.

$$\$13 - \$4 = \$9$$

Mary has $9 left.

Solve.

1. Steve has saved $11. He bought a record for $5. Then he earned $7 more. How much money does he have now?

2. Jack has $12. Sue has $15. Sue spends $7. Jack does not spend any money. Now how much more money does Jack have than Sue?

Find the sums.

1. 3
   + 6

2. 8
   + 6

3. 7
   + 6

4. 7
   + 5

5. 2
   + 5

6. 7
   + 8

7. 4
   + 2

8. 5
   + 8

9. 5
   + 3

10. 9
    + 0

11. 3
    + 9

12. 3
    + 8

13. 8
    + 9

14. 7
    + 3

Find the differences.

15. 12
    − 8

16. 16
    − 8

17. 4
    − 0

18. 10
    − 3

19. 14
    − 6

20. 15
    − 6

21. 12
    − 8

22. 14
    − 8

23. 12
    − 5

24. 8
    − 4

25. 17
    − 9

26. 6
    − 2

27. 14
    − 7

28. 6
    − 6

Find the sums.

29. 6
    2
    + 4

30. 3
    2
    + 3

31. 5
    0
    + 1

32. 2
    8
    + 2

33. 3
    4
    + 3

Solve.

34. Sam sold a skateboard for 6 dollars and a baseball for 3 dollars. How much did he get for both?

35. Debra had 11 comic books to sell. Sheri bought 4 of them. How many comic books does Debra have left?

36. Brian made 8 dollars. Julie made 14 dollars. How much less money did Brian make than Julie?

37. The children in Ken's class have 7 dogs and 9 cats. How many dogs and cats are there in all?

The "doubles" may help you remember the facts.

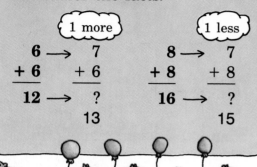

1 more		1 less	
6 →	7	8 →	7
+ 6	+ 6	+ 8	+ 8
12 →	?	16 →	?
	13		15

Thinking of addition may help you with subtraction.

13	6	15	7
− 7	?	− 8	?
	+ 7		+ 8
?	13	?	15
6		7	

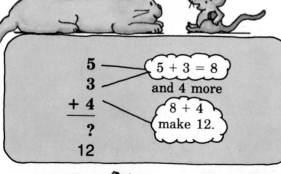

5	5 + 3 = 8
3	and 4 more
+ 4	8 + 4
?	make 12.
12	

Find the sums.

1.	8	2.	6	3.	7
	+ 7		+ 7		+ 3

4.	5	5.	9	6.	5
	+ 6		+ 8		+ 9

7.	8	8.	2	9.	8
	+ 6		+ 8		+ 4

Find the differences.

10.	14	11.	11	12.	13
	− 6		− 6		− 8

13.	12	14.	17	15.	10
	− 7		− 9		− 3

16.	13	17.	14	18.	9
	− 4		− 9		− 7

Find the sums.

19.	2	20.	8	21.	5
	7		1		5
	+ 2		+ 2		+ 5

Logical Reasoning

This game is for two players.

1. Use a figure like the one shown to the right.

2. One player uses the odd digits: 1, 3, 5, 7, and 9. The other player uses the even digits: 0, 2, 4, 6, and 8.

3. The player with odd digits goes first. Players then take turns writing one of their digits in a square. Each digit can be used only once.

4. The winner is the player who can write a digit that gives a sum of 15 for any complete row, column, or diagonal.

Here are some sample games.

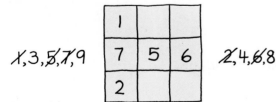

	1		
7	5	6
2		

1̸,3,5̸,7̸,9   2̸,4,6̸,8

	7	
	9	4
	6	

1,3,5,7̸,9̸   2,4̸,6̸,8

You have the even digits and it is your turn. Where can you place a digit to **win**? Try this game with a partner.

You have the odd digits and it is now your turn. Where should you place a digit to **block** the other player?

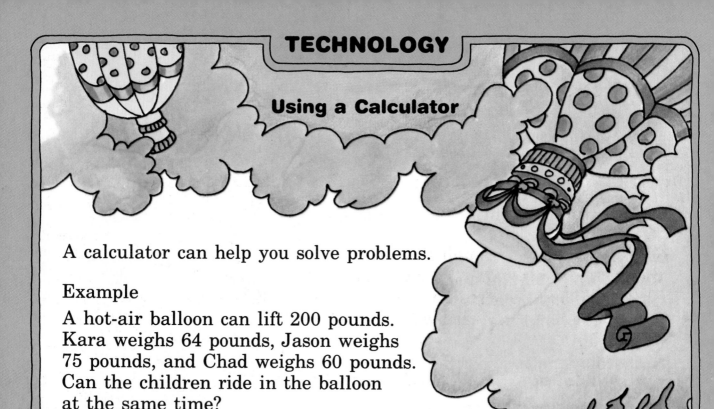

Using a Calculator

A calculator can help you solve problems.

Example

A hot-air balloon can lift 200 pounds.
Kara weighs 64 pounds, Jason weighs
75 pounds, and Chad weighs 60 pounds.
Can the children ride in the balloon
at the same time?

Plan the Solution Add the children's weights.

Write Out the Plan $64 + 75 + 60 =$

Carry Out the Plan Turn the calculator ON.

Press 6 →Press 4 →Press + →Press 7 →

Press 5 →Press + →Press 6 →Press 0 →Press =

The calculator shows 199.

Check the Answer

$$
\begin{array}{r}
64 \\
75 \\
+\ 60 \\
\hline
199
\end{array}
$$

The children together weigh less than 200 pounds.
They can ride in the balloon at the same time.

Remember to press CLEAR c before you begin the next problem.

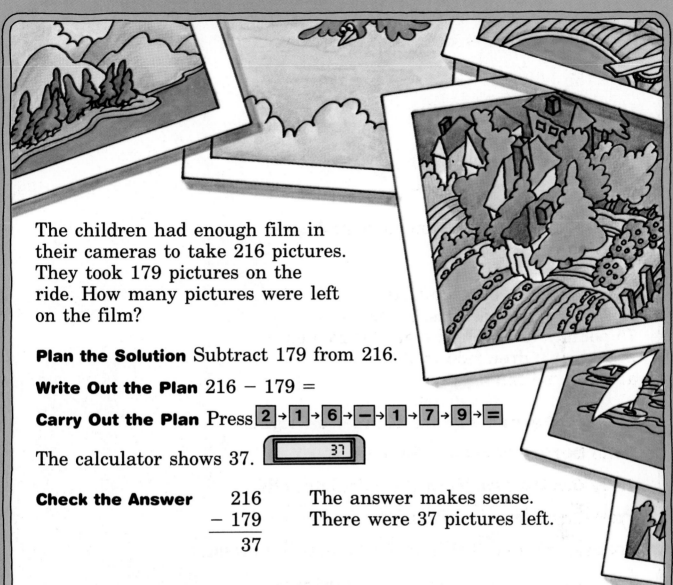

The children had enough film in their cameras to take 216 pictures. They took 179 pictures on the ride. How many pictures were left on the film?

Plan the Solution Subtract 179 from 216.

Write Out the Plan $216 - 179 =$

Carry Out the Plan Press 2 → 1 → 6 → − → 1 → 7 → 9 → =

The calculator shows 37. [37]

Check the Answer

$$\begin{array}{r} 216 \\ -\ 179 \\ \hline 37 \end{array}$$

The answer makes sense. There were 37 pictures left.

Plan the solution to these problems.
Use a calculator to help carry out the plan.

1. What is the sum of 392, 4,012, and 573?

2. Subtract 187 from 4,830.

3. Jody had 47 horses. She sold 24. How many were left?

4. Add 28, 999, and 1,407.

5. What is the difference between 592 and 386?

6. Is 100 dollars enough money to buy a coat for 58 dollars and shoes for 52 dollars?

CUMULATIVE REVIEW

Give the letter for the correct answer.

1. $6 + 2 = n$
- **A** 9
- **B** 4
- **C** 8
- **D** not given

2. $5 + 7 = n$
- **A** 12
- **B** 11
- **C** 13
- **D** not given

3. $9 + 0 = n$
- **A** 0
- **B** 9
- **C** 90
- **D** not given

4. $14 - 7 = n$
- **A** 8
- **B** 5
- **C** 6
- **D** not given

5. $8 - 8 = n$
- **A** 16
- **B** 8
- **C** 0
- **D** not given

6. $16 - 7 = n$
- **A** 8
- **B** 9
- **C** 7
- **D** not given

7.
$$\begin{array}{r} 8 \\ + 3 \\ \hline \end{array}$$
- **A** 11
- **B** 5
- **C** 10
- **D** not given

8.
$$\begin{array}{r} 6 \\ + 9 \\ \hline \end{array}$$
- **A** 15
- **B** 16
- **C** 17
- **D** not given

9.
$$\begin{array}{r} 5 \\ + 4 \\ \hline \end{array}$$
- **A** 1
- **B** 9
- **C** 8
- **D** not given

10.
$$\begin{array}{r} 10 \\ - 3 \\ \hline \end{array}$$
- **A** 7
- **B** 8
- **C** 6
- **D** not given

11.
$$\begin{array}{r} 18 \\ - 9 \\ \hline \end{array}$$
- **A** 8
- **B** 9
- **C** 7
- **D** not given

12.
$$\begin{array}{r} 15 \\ - 6 \\ \hline \end{array}$$
- **A** 7
- **B** 8
- **C** 9
- **D** not given

13. Travis sold a game for 2 dollars and a picture for 3 dollars. How much did Travis get for both?
- **A** $1
- **B** $6
- **C** $5
- **D** not given

14. Cheryl had 9 dollars. She bought a basketball for 6 dollars. How much did she have left?
- **A** $17
- **B** $3
- **C** $2
- **D** not given

Jason's family took a railroad trip. They crossed the whole United States. Jason had studied about railroad history. At one time eastern rail lines ended in Nebraska. They did not cross the West. America needed a railroad connecting both coasts. Jason learned how this railroad was built. Separate groups laid tracks from either end. Some workers started in California. They crossed the Sierra Nevada Mountains. They laid 1,110 km of track. Other workers started in Nebraska. They crossed the Rocky Mountains. They laid 1,738 km of track. The tracks were joined in Utah in 1869.

Hundreds, Tens, and Ones

These models are used to help you understand numbers.

ten ones → one ten (10)   **ten tens → one hundred (100)**

0, 1, 2, 3, 4, 5, 6, 7, 8, and 9 are called **digits.** We use digits and **place value** to write large numbers.

We see numbers in **standard form.**

243

The model below shows the meaning of 243.

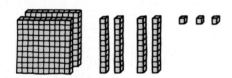

2 hundreds, **4** tens, and **3** ones = **243**
We read, "**two hundred forty-three.**"

Warm Up   Read each number. Tell the meaning of the red digit.

Example   456   four hundred fifty-six   The 5 means 5 tens.

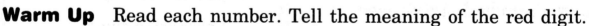

1. 362	**2.** 739	**3.** 19	**4.** 402	**5.** 924
6. 437	**7.** 806	**8.** 36	**9.** 791	**10.** 91
11. 520	**12.** 348	**13.** 143	**14.** 43	**15.** 500
16. 677	**17.** 908	**18.** 455	**19.** 380	**20.** 813

Write the standard number for each picture.

1.

2.

3.

4.

5.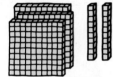

6.

Write the standard number. Be careful!

7. 5 hundreds
6 tens
4 ones

8. 3 tens
7 hundreds
9 ones

9. 6 ones
4 tens

10. 4 hundreds
0 tens
3 ones

11. 7 tens
0 ones
4 hundreds

Write the standard number.

12. two hundred sixty-seven

13. three hundred eighty-four

14. seven hundred three

15. one hundred sixty

16. four hundred ninety-nine

17. five hundred twenty

THINK

Logical Reasoning

1. I have three digits.
2. My hundreds' digit is the sum of my tens' digit and ones' digit.
3. My ones' digit is 3 more than my tens' digit.
4. My tens' digit is 2.

WHO AM I?

MATH

Thousands

The models below may help you understand larger numbers.

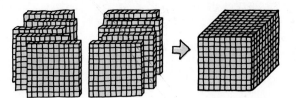

ten hundreds   **one thousand (1,000)**

The Great Wall of China is the longest wall in the world. It is 1,684 miles long.

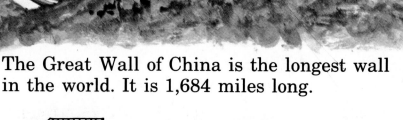

1	**6**	**8**	**4**
thousand	hundreds	tens	ones

We read, **"one thousand, six hundred eighty-four."**

Warm Up Read each number. Tell the meaning of the red digit.

1. 2,515
2. 4,612
3. 1,704
4. 5,061
5. 3,948

6. 9,323
7. 2,406
8. 6,280
9. 8,729
10. 5,952

11. 4,003
12. 1,691
13. 3,545
14. 2,130
15. 8,017

16. 2,336
17. 5,277
18. 4,094
19. 1,800
20. 3,563

21. 6,008
22. 1,408
23. 2,889
24. 3,070
25. 7,153

Write the standard number for
each picture.

1.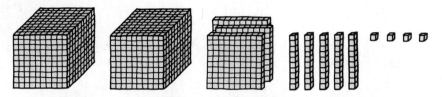

2.

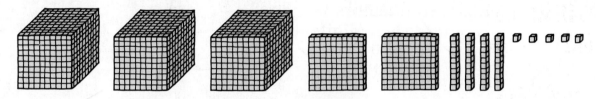

3.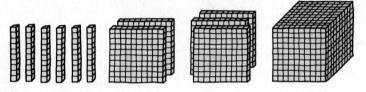

Write the standard number.

4. 3 thousand
2 hundreds
5 tens
9 ones

5. 2 tens
6 hundreds
4 ones
1 thousand

6. 5 hundreds
7 ones
0 tens
4 thousand

7. six thousand, seven hundred eighty-three

8. four thousand, two hundred three

9. eight thousand, five hundred thirty

═══ **THINK** ═══

Place Value

Write the standard number for:

      12 hundreds,   12 tens,   and 12 ones.

➤ **MATH** ◄

Comparing Numbers

Mt. Baker and Glacier Peak are volcanoes in Washington State. Mt. Baker is 3,285 m high and Glacier Peak is 3,213 m. Which volcano is higher?

To find which of two numbers is greater, you compare their digits.

Start at the left. Find the first place where the digits are different.	→	Compare these digits. Which digit is greater?	→	The numbers compare the same way the digits compare.
3,2**8**5 3,2**1**3		8 is greater than 1 8 > 1		3,285 is greater than 3,213 **3,285 > 3,213**

Mt. Baker is higher than Glacier Peak.

Other Examples

Remember: The "arrow" points to the smaller number.

486 is greater than 483
486 > 483

6,275 is less than 6,342
6,275 < 6,342

Warm Up Write > or < for each 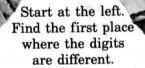 .

1. 426 ● 430

2. 715 ● 695

3. 867 ● 864

4. 3,269 ● 3,400

5. 5,280 ● 5,279

6. 7,563 ● 7,463

7. 4,082 ● 3,999

8. 3,794 ● 4,079

9. 6,280 ● 6,267

10. 4,000 ● 3,989

11. 3,756 ● 3,821

12. 4,987 ● 5,000

Write > or < for each ◉ .

1. 37 ◉ 41
2. 52 ◉ 48
3. 327 ◉ 347
4. 138 ◉ 135
5. 483 ◉ 476
6. 982 ◉ 892
7. 5,836 ◉ 5,841
8. 7,400 ◉ 7,398
9. 3,279 ◉ 3,280
10. 4,620 ◉ 4,618
11. 7,000 ◉ 7,021
12. 8,604 ◉ 7,987

Give the number that is 10 less. Example 8,975 Answer 8,965

13. 3,268
14. 1,347
15. 8,629
16. 4,308
17. 7,600

Give the number that is 1,000 more. Example 6,428 Answer 7,428

18. 4,268
19. 275
20. 3,640
21. 7,800
22. 6,999

Give the number that is 100 less. Example 3,950 Answer 3,850

23. 3,278
24. 4,629
25. 3,765
26. 8,036
27. 7,000

★ 28. Give these numbers in order from smallest to largest.
5,268, 4,975, 5,187, 5,099, 4,795

Solve.

29. Lassen Peak is 3,187 m high. Mt. Jefferson is 3,199 m. Which volcano is higher?

30. Mt. Hood is 3,424 m high. Mt. Adams is 3,751 m. Which volcano is shorter?

31. DATA BANK See page 384. Crater Lake is 2,486 m high. Which volcano is closest in height to Crater Lake?

THINK

Place Value

Use only these four digits. | 4 | 0 | 8 | 5 |

1. Write the largest 4-digit number you can.

2. Write the smallest 4-digit number you can.

MATH

Rounding

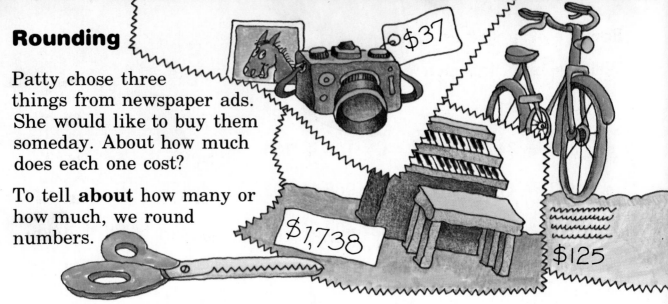

Patty chose three things from newspaper ads. She would like to buy them someday. About how much does each one cost?

To tell **about** how many or how much, we round numbers.

nearest ten	nearest ten	nearest hundred

30   37   40   120   125   130   1,700   1,738   1,800

37 is closer to 40 than to 30.

37 rounded to the nearest ten is 40.

The camera cost about $40.

125 is halfway between 120 and 130. When a number is halfway, round up.

125 rounded to the nearest ten is 130.

The bicycle costs about $130.

1,738 is closer to 1,700 than 1,800.

1,738 rounded to the nearest hundred is 1,700.

The organ costs about $1,700.

Warm Up

Round to the nearest ten.

1. 57 **2.** 33 **3.** 38 **4.** 45 **5.** 92 **6.** 75

Round to the nearest ten.

7. 356 **8.** 482 **9.** 794 **10.** 835 **11.** 279 **12.** 314

Round to the nearest hundred.

13. 2,467 **14.** 382 **15.** 4,625 **16.** 2,850 **17.** 325 **18.** 2,848

30

Round to the nearest ten.

1. 78   2. 72   3. 26   4. 69   5. 55

6. 43   7. 87   8. 71   9. 48   10. 36

11. 85   12. 64   13. 19   14. 35   15. 93

16. 154   17. 737   18. 382   19. 671   20. 345

21. 289   22. 703   23. 655   24. 277   25. 254

Round to the nearest hundred.

26. 3,271   27. 5,247   28. 466   29. 2,796   30. 3,806

31. 831   32. 5,489   33. 5,726   34. 7,055   35. 7,435

36. 4,463   37. 3,026   38. 385   39. 2,813   40. 2,860

Give the cost to the nearest ten dollars.

41.

42.

SKILLKEEPER

Add or subtract.

1. 4
  + 3
2. 9
  + 6
3. 8
  − 2
4. 9
  + 9
5. 7
  + 8
6. 14
  − 5

7. 7
  − 7
8. 5
  + 9
9. 17
  − 8
10. 2
  + 4
11. 16
  − 8
12. 7
  + 0

More About Rounding

Newspapers often use rounded numbers in headlines. Actually, there were 8,127 fans at the concert and tickets were $17.95.

8,000 FANS PAY $18 EACH TO SEE CONCERT

nearest thousand	nearest dollar
8,000 8,127 9,000	$17.00 $17.95 $18.00

8,127 is closer to 8,000 than to 9,000.

$17.95 is closer to $18.00 than to $17.00.

8,127 rounded to the nearest thousand is 8,000.

$17.95 rounded to the nearest dollar is $18.00.

Other Examples

nearest thousand	nearest dollar	nearest dollar
6,500 → 7,000	$36.49 → $36.00	$7.50 → $8.00

Warm Up

Round to the nearest thousand.

1. 3,247
2. 7,860
3. 5,702
4. 7,500

5. 1,487
6. 8,295
7. 9,142
8. 6,567

9. 2,600
10. 4,288
11. 8,167
12. 6,503

Round to the nearest dollar.

13. $27.65
14. $24.10
15. $7.50
16. $28.95

17. $15.20
18. $16.35
19. $28.49
20. $37.98

21. $8.56
22. $16.89
23. $2.49
24. $38.16

Round to the nearest thousand.

1. 2,426	**2.** 2,300	**3.** 5,675	**4.** 4,500
5. 6,521	**6.** 5,387	**7.** 7,162	**8.** 3,499
9. 8,568	**10.** 1,600	**11.** 9,208	**12.** 4,835
13. 5,162	**14.** 9,030	**15.** 8,278	**16.** 1,630

Round to the nearest dollar.

17. $16.08	**18.** $6.75	**19.** $14.49	**20.** $3.50
21. $78.16	**22.** $3.18	**23.** $37.50	**24.** $2.79
25. $29.88	**26.** $79.95	**27.** $5.26	**28.** $62.38

Write a newspaper headline for each story.
Use rounded numbers.

29. There were 3,918 fans at the game. Tickets were $4.95 each.

★ **30.** There were 3,124 fans at Friday's games and 4,897 at Saturday's games. All tickets were $6.90 each.

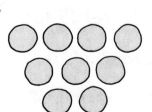

THINK

Shape Perception

Place 10 coins in a triangular shape.

Then make it look like this

by moving only the coins at the corners.

⟶ MATH ⟵

More About Thousands

Digits are grouped by threes to help us read and write large numbers. These groups of three numbers are called **periods.** The periods are separated by commas.

The arctic tern flies from the Arctic to the Antarctic and back once each year. The distance the arctic tern flies is 35,400 km.

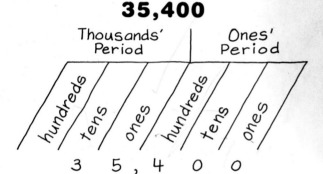

We read, **"thirty-five thousand, four hundred."**

Other Examples

462,350 —→ four hundred sixty-two thousand, three hundred fifty

136,249 —→ one hundred thirty-six thousand, two hundred forty-nine

27,036 —→ twenty-seven thousand, thirty-six

Warm Up Read each number aloud.

1. 37,275	2. 265,386	3. 13,431	4. 856,520
5. 19,600	6. 307,325	7. 480,486	8. 26,179
9. 951,000	10. 718,030	11. 60,426	12. 218,300
13. 39,005	14. 72,000	15. 300,385	16. 400,000

Match.

1. 42,658   2. 426,580   3. 456,580

4. 42,568   5. 400,300   6. 427,580

A four hundred thousand, three hundred

B forty-two thousand, six hundred fifty-eight

C four hundred twenty-seven thousand, five hundred eighty

D four hundred fifty-six thousand, five hundred eighty

E forty-two thousand, five hundred sixty-eight

F four hundred twenty-six thousand, five hundred eighty

Write the standard number.

7. three hundred sixty-seven thousand, two hundred sixty-eight

8. five hundred thirty thousand, three hundred fifty-one

9. one hundred six thousand, three hundred fifteen

10. eighty-six thousand, four hundred thirty-two

11. 375 thousand

12. 605 thousand

Write the standard number.

13. The diameter of Earth is twelve thousand, seven hundred fifty-six kilometers.

14. The deepest ocean on Earth is eleven thousand, thirty-three meters.

THINK

Place-Value Patterns

Find the number that is 1 less than
1. one hundred
2. one thousand
3. ten thousand
4. one hundred thousand

MATH

Comparing Larger Numbers

The table shows the cost of TV ads for different nights. Which costs more, the Thursday night ad or the Saturday night ad?

To find which of two numbers is greater, you compare their digits.

PRICE OF A 30-SECOND TV AD*	
MONDAY	$135,000
TUESDAY	95,000
WEDNESDAY	92,000
THURSDAY	115,000
FRIDAY	170,000
SATURDAY	112,000
SUNDAY	175,000

*Estimates for selected programs during prime time in a recent year.

> Start at the left. Find the first place where the digits are different.
> 5 > 2

$$115,000 > 112,000$$
↑ Check here. ↑

The Thursday night program costs more.

> Remember
> \> means "is greater than"
> \< means "is less than"

Other Examples

$$32,468 < 32,568$$
↑ Check here. ↑

$$172,286 > 96,857$$

> This number has more digits.

Write the sign > or < for each ⬤.

1. 32,468 ⬤ 31,568
2. 47,286 ⬤ 46,286
3. 57,419 ⬤ 67,419
4. 95,200 ⬤ 85,200
5. 110,215 ⬤ 98,215
6. 87,989 ⬤ 100,000
7. 86,493 ⬤ 386,490
8. 518,379 ⬤ 518,380

★ Which costs more

9. the Friday program or the Sunday program?

10. the Thursday program or the Wednesday program?

More Practice, page 391, Set B

Roman Numerals

The Romans used letters to write numbers.

Some Roman numerals are written by adding.

III	XI	VIII	LX
↓	↓	↓	↓
(1 + 1 + 1)	(10 + 1)	(5 + 3)	(50 + 10)
3	11	8	60

Other numerals are written by subtracting.

IV	IX	XL	XC
↓	↓	↓	↓
(5 − 1)	(10 − 1)	(50 − 10)	(100 − 10)
4	9	40	90

Look at these other examples.

X	III	XL	V	XC	II	M	DC
↓	↓	↓	↓	↓	↓	↓	↓
10	3	40	5	90	2	1,000	600
	13		45		92		1,600

Write the standard number.

1. XII   2. XXIV   3. IV   4. XXXIV

5. LX   6. LIX   7. MD   8. MC

Write the Roman numeral.

9. 7   10. 21   11. 61   12. 35

13. 40   14. 600   15. 1,500   16. 700

Millions

One million is 1,000 thousands.

1,000,000

The chart below will help you read numbers in the millions.

In a recent year, about 44,238,000 passengers used Chicago's O'Hare Airport.

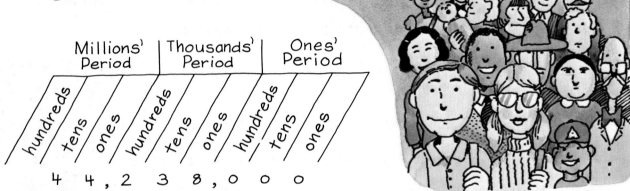

Millions' Period			Thousands' Period			Ones' Period		
hundreds	tens	ones	hundreds	tens	ones	hundreds	tens	ones
4	4,	2	3	8,	0	0	0	

We read, **"forty-four million, two hundred thirty-eight thousand."**

Other Examples

346,285,000   three hundred forty-six million, two hundred eighty-five thousand

7,360,500   seven million, three hundred sixty thousand, five hundred

27,469,000   twenty-seven million, four hundred sixty-nine thousand

Warm Up   Read each number aloud.

1. 75,342,000   2. 8,286,000   3. 216,415,000   4. 345,000,000

5. 124,700,000   6. 86,000,000   7. 7,287,000   8. 240,365,000

9. 36,720,900   10. 500,000,000   11. 18,283,000   12. 768,400,000

Match.

1. 28,375,000   2. 28,753,000   3. 2,837,000

4. 283,570,000   5. 28,573,000   6. 283,750,000

A two million, eight hundred thirty-seven thousand

B twenty-eight million, five hundred seventy-three thousand

C twenty-eight million, seven hundred fifty-three thousand

D twenty-eight million, three hundred seventy-five thousand

E two hundred eighty-three million, seven hundred fifty thousand

F two hundred eighty-three million, five hundred seventy thousand

Write the standard number.

7. seven million, three hundred eighteen thousand

8. twenty-nine million, four hundred eighty-four thousand

9. nine hundred sixteen million, three hundred thousand

10. 29 million   11. 375 million   12. 8 million

13. **DATA BANK** See page 387. Which airport served this number of passengers in the given year?

A 23,190,000

B 29,977,000

C 15,087,000

D 23,775,000

E 15,281,000

THINK

Ordinal Numbers

How many kilometers to the moon?

To find the answer, list the digits below in order from left to right.

fifth—8   third—6
sixth—4   fourth—2
first—3   second—7

MATH

Counting Money

We often use skip counting when we count money. How much are the nickels worth?

To count nickels, we can count by fives.

35¢
or
$0.35
35 cents

5 10 15 20 25 30 35

How much are the dimes worth?

To count dimes, we can count by tens.

60¢
or
$0.60
60 cents

10 20 30 40 50 60

Count this money.

$1.00 $1.25 $1.35 $1.45 $1.50 $1.55 $1.60

Warm Up   Count the money. Write the total.

1.

2.

Count the money. Write the total.

1.

2.

3.

4.

5.

6.

SKILLKEEPER

Find the sums.

1.	**2.**	**3.**	**4.**	**5.**	**6.**
7	2	7	3	5	2
2	3	0	2	4	8
+ 3	+ 2	+ 1	+ 6	+ 5	+ 2

7.	**8.**	**9.**	**10.**	**11.**	**12.**
6	3	1	0	6	3
1	4	8	9	3	4
+ 8	+ 3	+ 2	+ 1	+ 7	+ 3

Counting Change

A sales clerk must know how to count out the correct change. The example below shows how some clerks count change.

Jack sold a tape for $3.78. The customer paid with a five-dollar bill. This is how Jack counted the change.

Start with the cost.

Count the smaller coins first.

End with the amount given.

Warm Up Look at the money chart. Touch the money you would use as you count the change aloud.

1. You sold   Amount given

2. You sold   Amount given

3. You sold   Amount given

4. You sold   Amount given

Match each price tag with the change you
would give for a five-dollar bill.

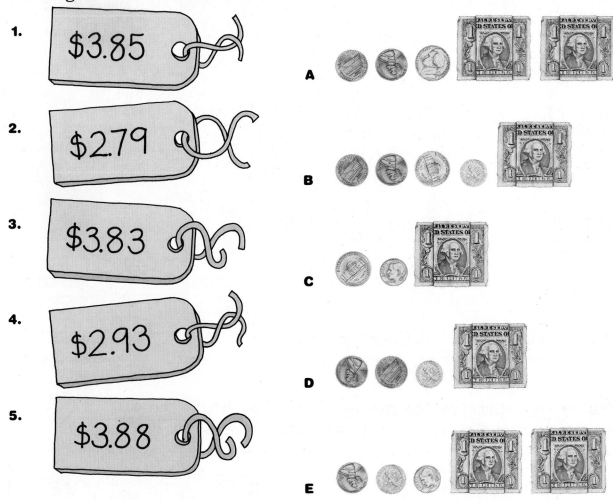

1. $3.85

2. $2.79

3. $3.83

4. $2.93

5. $3.88

A

B

C

D

E

★ Tell what coins and bills you
would use to make change for
$10.00.

6. $7.78

7. $8.82

THINK

Calendar Puzzle

Joan said, "Today is Friday,
December 22." Then she
asked, "I wonder what day of
the week New Year's Day
will be?"

Can you help her? December
has 31 days.

MATH

PROBLEM SOLVING
Draw a Picture

QUESTION
DATA
PLAN
ANSWER
CHECK

TO SOLVE A PROBLEM LIKE THIS, IT MAY BE HELPFUL TO USE THE STRATEGY SHOWN BELOW.

Try This Four boys are in line for tickets. Bill is ahead of Ted. Don is behind Ted. Bill is behind Sam. Who is first in line?

DRAW A PICTURE

FIRST, I'LL DRAW AND LABEL A LINE.

NOW, I'LL SHOW BILL AHEAD OF TED.

NEXT, I'LL SHOW DON BEHIND TED.

LAST, I'LL SHOW BILL BEHIND SAM.

SAM MUST BE FIRST IN LINE!

BACK   FRONT

BACK   TED BILL   FRONT

BACK   DON TED BILL   FRONT

BACK   DON TED BILL SAM   FRONT

Solve.

1. Terry is shorter than Betty. Fran is taller than Betty. Donna is shorter than Terry. Who is the tallest girl?

2. Sue is younger than Carl. Joan is older than Carl. Ed's age is between Carl's and Joan's. Who is the youngest?

44

Write the standard number.

1. 6 hundreds
   4 tens
   5 ones

2. 7 tens
   0 ones
   5 hundreds

3. 2 thousands
   9 hundreds
   0 tens
   4 ones

4. 5 tens
   6 ones
   7 thousands
   0 hundreds

Write > or < for each .

5. 525 ● 540

6. 761 ● 758

7. 6,921 ● 6,879

8. 5,724 ● 5,719

9. 6,834 ● 6,835

10. 4,600 ● 4,599

Round.

nearest ten		nearest ten		nearest hundred	
11. 68	12. 74	13. 375	14. 423	15. 2,472	16. 3,649

nearest thousand		nearest dollar	
17. 3,379	18. 6,500	19. $15.69	20. $28.25

Write > or < for each ●.

21. 121,000 ● 98,000

22. 653,497 ● 653,500

23. 29,887 ● 29,890

Write the standard number.   24. XII   25. IV

26. three hundred twelve million, five hundred sixty-seven thousand

Count the money.

27.

28.

29.

ANOTHER LOOK

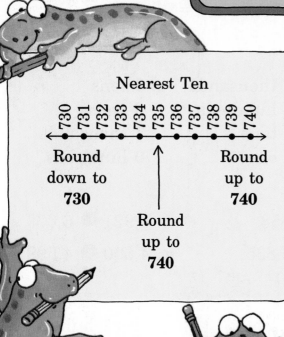

Nearest Ten

730 731 732 733 734 735 736 737 738 739 740

Round down to **730**

Round up to **740**

Round up to **740**

two hundred forty-six thousand, seven hundred fifty-three

Thousands	Ones
2 4 6 ,	7 5 3

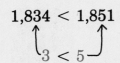

1,834 < 1,851

3 < 5

More digits Fewer digits

2,376 > 729

Round to the nearest ten.

1. 48 **2.** 74 **3.** 25

4. 367 **5.** 433 **6.** 755

Round to the nearest hundred.

7. 2,763 **8.** 3,548

Round to the nearest dollar.

9. $37.50 **10.** $24.49

Write the standard number.

11. seven hundred eighteen thousand, five hundred thirty-two

12. forty-nine thousand, six hundred seventy-three

Give the sign > or < for each ▓.

13. 546 ▓ 564 **14.** 387 ▓ 378

15. 63 ▓ 637 **16.** 480 ▓ 478

17. 6,524 ▓ 6,542

18. 376 ▓ 1,476

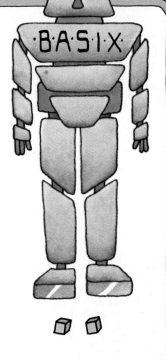

Place Value

Pretend you are on the planet Basix. On Basix, they group by sixes instead of tens for place value.

They use the digits 0, 1, 2, 3, 4, and 5 and place value to write larger numbers.

six ones   one six

This model shows the meaning of the Basix numbers. ——→

So on Basix,
    32 means 3 sixes and 2 ones.

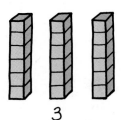

3
sixes

2
ones

The chart below compares Basix counting with Earth counting.

Basix counting	1	2	3	4	5	10	11	12	13	14	15	20	21
Earth counting	1	2	3	4	5	6	7	8	9	10	11	12	13

Write a Basix numeral for the number of objects.

Example

1.

2.

3.

Answer 24

4. Write the Basix counting numbers from 1 to 55.

CUMULATIVE REVIEW

Give the letter for the correct answer.

1. $3 + 5 = n$
- **A** 8
- **B** 10
- **C** 9
- **D** not given

2. $8 + 0 = n$
- **A** 0
- **B** 80
- **C** 8
- **D** not given

3. $6 + 7 = n$
- **A** 11
- **B** 12
- **C** 14
- **D** not given

4.   17
      $-\ 8$
- **A** 7
- **B** 8
- **C** 9
- **D** not given

5.   14
      $-\ 9$
- **A** 6
- **B** 5
- **C** 7
- **D** not given

6.   12
      $-\ 6$
- **A** 5
- **B** 8
- **C** 6
- **D** not given

7.   10
      $-\ 4$
- **A** 5
- **B** 6
- **C** 7
- **D** not given

8.   2
       4
      $+\ 5$
- **A** 11
- **B** 10
- **C** 9
- **D** not given

9.   3
       3
      $+\ 3$
- **A** 12
- **B** 11
- **C** 10
- **D** not given

10.   5
        3
       $+\ 7$
- **A** 13
- **B** 15
- **C** 14
- **D** not given

11.   1
        2
       $+\ 7$
- **A** 12
- **B** 11
- **C** 10
- **D** not given

12.   6
        3
       $+\ 6$
- **A** 15
- **B** 16
- **C** 14
- **D** not given

13. Allen had 8 dollars. He spent 7 dollars. How much did Allen have left?
- **A** $15
- **B** $17
- **C** $1
- **D** not given

14. Margo had 8 seashells. She found 5 more seashells. How many seashells does Margo have now?
- **A** 12
- **B** 13
- **C** 3
- **D** not given

ADDITION AND SUBTRACTION

3

Danny took his cat to the veterinarian, Dr. Li. The office seemed very busy. Dr. Li and her partner would see 32 animals that day. They had seen 28 animals the day before. They treat mostly dogs and cats. There are also veterinarians who treat birds and other small pets. Some of them treat farm animals and horses. Some work for zoos. Others work for the government. Many of them study and treat wild animals. There are veterinarians who study animals with sicknesses that people can get, too. Dr. Li learned to do all of these things at a college of veterinary medicine.

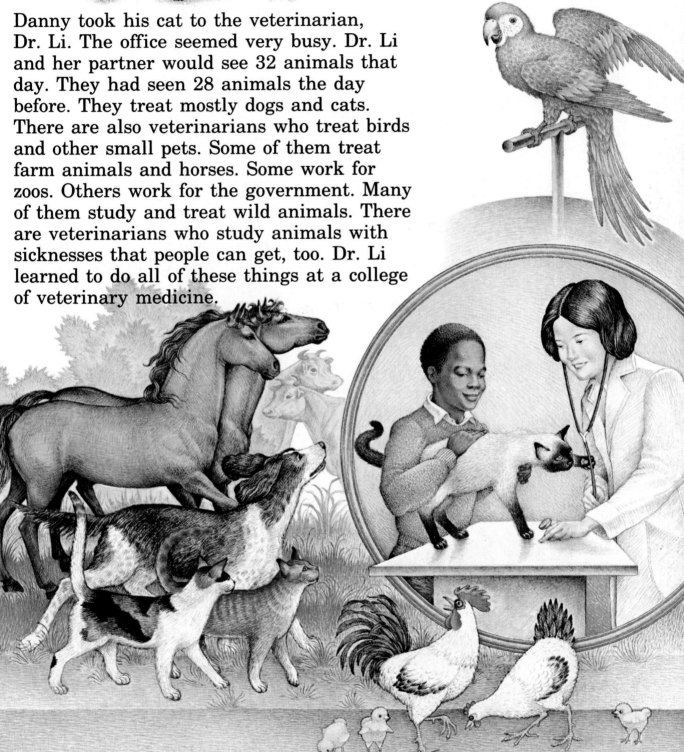

Adding: One Trade

Tara checked her breathing rate after running.
She counted 48 breaths for the first minute.
She counted 27 breaths for the second minute.
How many breaths did Tara take in the two minutes?

Since we want the total, we add.

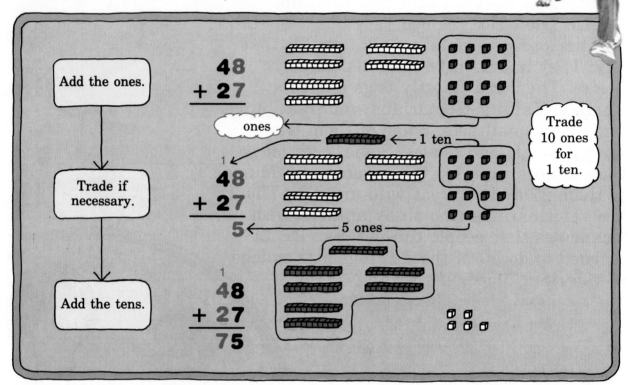

Tara took 75 breaths in the two minutes.

Other Examples

75	54	327	6	482
+ 53	+ 25	+ 146	+ 53	+ 136
128	79	473	59	618

12 tens = 1 hundred and 2 tens

Warm Up   Add.

	1. 26	2. 95	3. 175	4. 382	5. 654
	+ 38	+ 41	+ 281	+ 94	+ 820

50

Find the sums.

1. 39 + 46	**2.** 52 + 83	**3.** 24 + 35	**4.** 76 + 8	**5.** 9 + 24	

6. 352 + 180	**7.** 216 + 157	**8.** 324 + 912	**9.** 261 + 90	**10.** 365 + 121

11. 257 + 13	**12.** 762 + 824	**13.** 325 + 142	**14.** 281 + 346	**15.** 643 + 164

16. 64 + 82   **17.** 75 + 18   **18.** 26 + 52   **19.** 38 + 9

20. 356 + 125   **21.** 710 + 628   **22.** 381 + 125   **23.** 275 + 82

24. Add 27 to 59.   **25.** Add 917 to 830.   **26.** Add 261 to 56.

Solve.

27. Cindy counted breaths after swimming. She counted 39 breaths the first minute. She counted 24 breaths the second. How many breaths did Cindy take in the two minutes?

28. Kate counted breaths after bicycling. She counted 37 the first minute, 25 the second minute, and 18 the third minute. How many breaths did she take during the second and third minutes?

29. DATA HUNT Run in place for a minute. Then count your breaths for each of the first two minutes after running. How many breaths did you take in the two minutes?

More Practice, page 392, Set A

THINK

Patterns

What comes next?

1. AA, AB, AC, AD, AE, ____
2. AA, AB, BB, BC, CC, ____
3. AB, DE, GH, JK, MN, ____
4. AB, DC, EF, HG, IJ, ____

 MATH

Adding: Two or More Trades

Nina and Bert are circus elephants.
One night Nina ate 196 kg of hay and Bert ate 227 kg.
How many kilograms of hay did they eat together?

Since we want the total amount, we add.

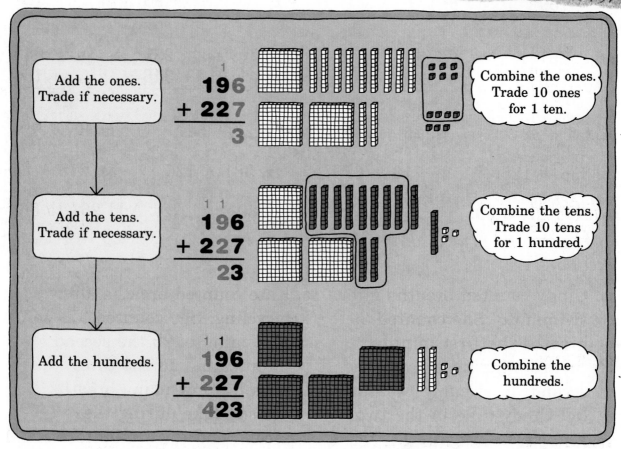

Add the ones. Trade if necessary.

$$\begin{array}{r} 1 \\ 196 \\ + 227 \\ \hline 3 \end{array}$$

Combine the ones. Trade 10 ones for 1 ten.

Add the tens. Trade if necessary.

$$\begin{array}{r} 1\ 1 \\ 196 \\ + 227 \\ \hline 23 \end{array}$$

Combine the tens. Trade 10 tens for 1 hundred.

Add the hundreds.

$$\begin{array}{r} 1\ 1 \\ 196 \\ + 227 \\ \hline 423 \end{array}$$

Combine the hundreds.

Nina and Bert ate 423 kg of hay that night.

Other Examples

14 hundreds = 1 thousand and 4 hundreds

$$\begin{array}{r} 1 \\ 627 \\ + 845 \\ \hline 1{,}472 \end{array} \qquad \begin{array}{r} 1\ 1 \\ 754 \\ + 489 \\ \hline 1{,}243 \end{array} \qquad \begin{array}{r} 1\ 1 \\ 987 \\ + \ \ 38 \\ \hline 1{,}025 \end{array} \qquad \begin{array}{r} 1\ 1 \\ \$6.87 \\ + \ 1.16 \\ \hline \$8.03 \end{array}$$

Warm Up Add.

1. $\begin{array}{r} 368 \\ + 137 \\ \hline \end{array}$
2. $\begin{array}{r} 649 \\ + 824 \\ \hline \end{array}$
3. $\begin{array}{r} 375 \\ + 980 \\ \hline \end{array}$
4. $\begin{array}{r} 695 \\ + \ \ 87 \\ \hline \end{array}$
5. $\begin{array}{r} \$4.75 \\ + 5.72 \\ \hline \end{array}$

Find the sums.

1. 728 + 659	**2.** 346 + 188	**3.** 695 + 28
4. 764 + 236	**5.** 416 + 807	**6.** 76 + 185
7. $2.25 + 1.50	**8.** $3.69 + 1.45	**9.** $2.98 + 1.29
10. $6.88 + 3.90	**11.** $8.95 + 3.60	**12.** $2.95 + 3.27
13. $3.57 + 0.88	**14.** $9.16 + 7.15	**15.** $6.75 + 0.98

16. 836 + 918   **17.** 296 + 175   **18.** 67 + 289   **19.** 315 + 909

20. 675 + 956   **21.** 374 + 187   **22.** 737 + 418   **23.** 89 + 596

24. $1.69 + $2.58   **25.** $3.88 + $1.75   **26.** $3.15 + $1.85

Solve.

27. One night Nina drank 188 L of water. Bert drank 232 L of water. How much water did they drink together?

28. Write a question that can be answered using the data below. Then solve the problem.

> Bert ate 196 kg of hay on Friday. He ate 184 kg of hay on Saturday.

THINK

Logical Reasoning

Find the missing digits.

1.   ▥ 2 ▥
 + 5 ▥ 7
 ─────
 8 7 5

2.   2 ▥ 9
 + 1 8 ▥
 ─────
 ▥ 5 4

3.   3 ▥ ▥
 + ▥ 4 8
 ─────
 7 5 3

4.   ▥ 6 2
 + 4 ▥ ▥
 ─────
 1, 0 7 1

MATH

Adding Larger Numbers

The deepest part of the Atlantic Ocean is 8,385 m. The deepest part of the Pacific Ocean is 2,475 m deeper than the Atlantic. How deep is this?

Since we want 2,475 more than 8,385, we add.

Add the ones. Trade if necessary.	Add the tens. Trade if necessary.	Add the hundreds. Trade if necessary.	Add the thousands.

1	1 1	1 1	1 1
8,385	8,385	8,385	8,385
+ 2,475	+ 2,475	+ 2,475	+ 2,475
0	60	860	10,860

The deepest part of the Pacific Ocean is 10,860 m.

Other Examples

1 1 1	1 1	1 1	1 1 1
5,697	$76.92	92,463	7,659
+ 1,843	+ 8.53	+ 43,572	+ 86,837
7,540	$85.45	136,035	94,496

Warm Up Add.

1.	2.	3.	4.	5.
3,742	3,867	$68.23	18,296	17,619
+ 5,924	+ 1,549	+ 75.91	+ 24,385	+ 9,285

54

Find the sums.

1. 2,369 + 1,358	**2.** 6,721 + 8,937	**3.** 6,598 + 276	**4.** 3,057 + 9,386
5. 2,856 + 14,728	**6.** 26,395 + 34,120	**7.** 78,265 + 49,141	**8.** 65,295 + 74,968
9. $38.95 + 19.88	**10.** $57.50 + 4.95	**11.** $69.95 + 27.50	**12.** $16.98 + 13.25

13. 7,268 + 6,471

14. 2,697 + 583

15. 1,358 + 9,672

16. $26.50 + $17.80

17. $16.95 + $7.75

18. $58.60 + $29.30

19. Add 1,566 to 1,890.

20. Add 379 to 2,658.

21. Add 483 to 1,456.

22. Add $37.45 to $26.98.

23. Add $27.89 to $1.35.

Solve.

24. The deepest part of the Arctic Ocean is 5,334 m. The Indian Ocean is 2,117 m deeper than that. How deep is the Indian Ocean?

25. The Mediterranean Sea is 4,594 m deep. If it were 422 m deeper, it would be as deep as the South China Sea. How deep is the South China Sea?

26. **DATA BANK** See page 385. The Gulf of Mexico is 3,452 m deeper than the Caribbean Sea. How deep is the Gulf of Mexico?

THINK

Using a Calculator

Show 306,458 on your calculator. By adding just one number, make your calculator read 376,458.

MATH

Estimating Sums

Sometimes you want an answer that is only close to the exact answer. To estimate, we round and add.

I wonder about how far it is between these two national parks.

$$\begin{array}{r} 541 \\ + 399 \\ \end{array}$$ nearest hundred > $$\begin{array}{r} 500 \\ + 400 \\ \hline 900 \end{array}$$ nearest hundred

It is about 900 miles between these two parks.

Other Examples

nearest ten	nearest hundred	nearest dollar

$$\begin{array}{r} 78 \rightarrow 80 \\ + 54 \rightarrow + 50 \\ \hline 130 \end{array}$$

$$\begin{array}{r} 387 \rightarrow 400 \\ + 129 \rightarrow + 100 \\ \hline 500 \end{array}$$

$$\begin{array}{r} \$6.75 \rightarrow \$7.00 \\ + 2.29 \rightarrow + 2.00 \\ \hline \$9.00 \end{array}$$

Warm Up Estimate by rounding to the nearest ten.

1. $$\begin{array}{r} 59 \\ + 32 \end{array}$$
2. $$\begin{array}{r} 87 \\ + 49 \end{array}$$
3. $$\begin{array}{r} 52 \\ + 19 \end{array}$$
4. $$\begin{array}{r} 65 \\ + 34 \end{array}$$

Estimate by rounding to the nearest hundred.

5. $$\begin{array}{r} 698 \\ + 315 \end{array}$$
6. $$\begin{array}{r} 427 \\ + 178 \end{array}$$
7. $$\begin{array}{r} 632 \\ + 778 \end{array}$$
8. $$\begin{array}{r} 309 \\ + 492 \end{array}$$

Estimate by rounding to the nearest dollar.

9. $$\begin{array}{r} \$5.65 \\ + 3.25 \end{array}$$
10. $$\begin{array}{r} \$8.98 \\ + 1.39 \end{array}$$
11. $$\begin{array}{r} \$4.25 \\ + 5.79 \end{array}$$
12. $$\begin{array}{r} \$6.95 \\ + 2.17 \end{array}$$

Find these special sums.

1.	30 + 40	**2.**	60 + 20	**3.**	80 + 70	**4.**	900 + 600	**5.**	300 + 500
6.	700 + 900	**7.**	600 + 800	**8.**	700 + 500	**9.**	$4.00 + 2.00	**10.**	$7.00 + 9.00

Estimate by rounding to the nearest ten.

11.	29 + 42	**12.**	56 + 31	**13.**	88 + 39	**14.**	26 + 53	**15.**	85 + 24

Estimate by rounding to the nearest hundred.

16.	395 + 206	**17.**	418 + 276	**18.**	750 + 342	**19.**	867 + 444

Estimate by rounding to the nearest dollar.

20.	$3.75 + 2.16	**21.**	$4.67 + 2.39	**22.**	$4.78 + 3.24	**23.**	$6.95 + 2.13

Estimate by rounding to the nearest thousand.

24.	6,284 + 7,869	**25.**	3,785 + 6,392	**26.**	4,195 + 6,500

Solve.

27. It is 598 miles from Rocky Mountain to Yellowstone and 370 miles from Yellowstone to Glacier. About how far is it between these national parks?

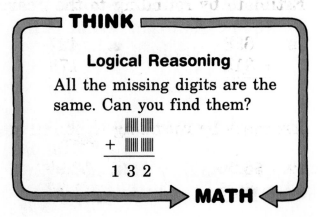

THINK

Logical Reasoning

All the missing digits are the same. Can you find them?

```
  ▓▓▓
+ ▓▓▓
─────
1 3 2
```

MATH

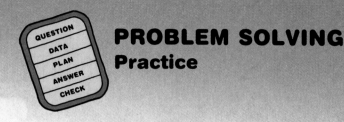

PROBLEM SOLVING
Practice

QUESTION
DATA
PLAN
ANSWER
CHECK

Yellowstone National Park is the oldest (1872) and largest (9,000 square kilometers) park in the United States.

Solve.

1. The average elevation of Yellowstone Park is 2,400 m. Its highest mountain, Electric Peak, is 950 m higher than this. How high is Electric Peak?

2. Mortar Geyser may erupt water and steam for as long as 15 minutes at a time. After it has erupted for 8 minutes, how long could it continue?

3. Splendid Geyser erupts water at least 29 m high. The highest it erupts is 21 m higher than that. What is the geyser's greatest height of eruption?

4. The limber pine gets as tall as 15 m. The whitebark pine grows to 9 m. How much taller is the limber pine?

5. Yellowstone Lake is at an altitude of 2,356 m. Mt. Sheridan is 783 m higher than the lake. How high is Mt. Sheridan?

6. Old Faithful Geyser erupts water and steam 52 m high. Grand Geyser erupts 9 m higher than that. How high is that?

7. The main road system is 225 km long. There are 265 km of other roads. Estimate the total number of kilometers in all.

8. **Try This** The Upper Falls plunges 33 m. The Lower Falls plunges 28 m more than twice the Upper Falls. How far does the Lower Falls plunge? Hint: Choose the operations.

Adding: Mental Math

Sometimes you want to add numbers "in your head" without writing anything down. You may need to find sums like **15 + 7** in your head when you add three or more numbers.

Here is a way you might think.

15 + 7

> THINK
> 15 + 5 = 20
> and 2 more make 22

17 + 8

> THINK
> 17 + 3 = 20
> and 5 more make 25

24 + 8

> THINK
> 24 + 6 = 30
> and 2 more make 32

Find the sums. Write answers only.

1. 12 + 9
2. 17 + 5
3. 19 + 6
4. 14 + 7

5. 23 + 9
6. 28 + 9
7. 13 + 9
8. 11 + 7

9. 16 + 8
10. 15 + 9
11. 12 + 8
12. 18 + 7

13. 24 + 8
14. 17 + 6
15. 22 + 9
16. 29 + 4

17. 13 + 8
18. 25 + 6
19. 15 + 8
20. 14 + 8

21. 27 + 7
22. 16 + 7
23. 26 + 9
24. 18 + 8

Column Addition

Jay bought a new shirt, slacks, and a pair of shoes. What was the total cost?

Since we want the cost of all three, we add.

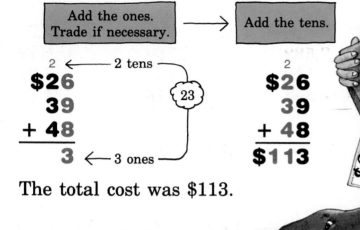

| Add the ones. Trade if necessary. | → | Add the tens. |

$$\begin{array}{r} {}^{2} \\ \$26 \\ 39 \\ +\,48 \\ \hline 3 \end{array}$$

2 tens ← 23 → 2 ← 2 tens

3 ← 3 ones

$$\begin{array}{r} {}^{2} \\ \$26 \\ 39 \\ +\,48 \\ \hline \$113 \end{array}$$

The total cost was $113.

Other Examples

¹ 35	¹² 635	¹² 349	¹³² 283	²³ $1.75
47	786	8	4,475	2.68
+ 22	+ 429	67	3,864	3.19
104	1,850	+ 123	+ 88	+ 0.79
		547	8,710	$8.41

Warm Up Add.

1.
```
  42
  69
+ 38
```

2.
```
  27
   9
+ 37
```

3.
```
  346
   78
  265
+  39
```

4.
```
   725
 6,348
 1,642
+   76
```

5.
```
  $1.49
   2.98
   3.56
+  4.75
```

60

Add.

1.	17	**2.**	27	**3.**	426	**4.**	7,692	**5.**	$2.79
	38		9		135		581		0.65
	+ 16		+ 38		+ 283		+ 1,273		+ 3.88

6.	62	**7.**	467	**8.**	3,624	**9.**	583	**10.**	$2.95
	43		73		2,582		2,764		6.79
	38		394		1,763		3,726		3.35
	+ 29		+ 6		+ 1,095		+ 78		+ 0.69

11. 26 + 32 + 45

12. 76 + 58 + 92 + 37

13. 365 + 78 + 214

14. 576 + 37 + 275 + 9

15. 3,842 + 2,675 + 1,038

16. 7,624 + 138 + 2,785 + 96

Estimate the sums.

17. Round to the nearest ten.
28 + 33 + 56

18. Round to the nearest hundred.
884 + 329 + 592

Solve.

19. Jean Winters bought some presents. She bought a blouse for $37, a skirt for $58, and a purse for $25. How much did these three items cost?

20. Scott bought some T-shirts for $17, some socks for $9, and a pair of shoes for $28. How much did he spend for the shoes and T-shirts?

═ THINK ═

Magic Squares

The sum of the numbers in each row, column, and diagonal of this Magic Square is 34. The sum of the numbers in the shaded part is also 34! How many other "squares" of 4 numbers can you find in the Magic Square that have a sum of 34?

16	2	3	13
5	11	10	8
9	7	6	12
4	14	15	1

➡ MATH ⬅

Subtracting: One Trade

A record age for an elephant is 61 years. A record age for a bear is 34 years. How much longer did the elephant live?

Since we want to find how much longer the elephant lived, we subtract.

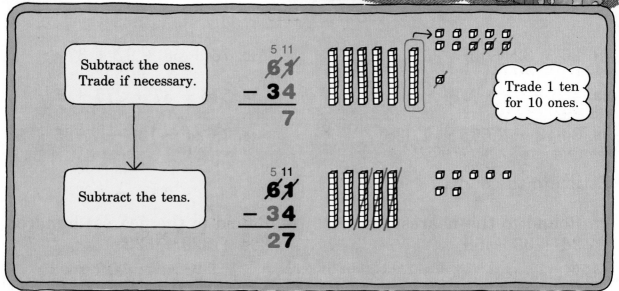

| Subtract the ones. Trade if necessary. | 5 11
$\cancel{6}\cancel{1}$
$-\ 34$
$\overline{\quad 7}$ | | Trade 1 ten for 10 ones. |
| Subtract the tens. | 5 11
$\cancel{6}\cancel{1}$
$-\ 34$
$\overline{\quad 27}$ | | |

The elephant lived 27 years longer than the bear.

Other Examples

Trade 1 hundred for 10 tens.

$$
\begin{array}{r} {}^{6\ 12}\\ \cancel{7}\cancel{2}\\ -\ 48\\ \hline 24 \end{array}
\qquad
\begin{array}{c} \text{CHECK}\\ \begin{array}{r} 1\\ 24\\ +\ 48\\ \hline 72 \end{array} \end{array}
\qquad
\begin{array}{r} 87\\ -\ 25\\ \hline 62 \end{array}
\qquad
\begin{array}{r} {}^{5\ 12}\\ \cancel{6}\cancel{2}8\\ -\ 552\\ \hline 76 \end{array}
\qquad
\begin{array}{r} {}^{6\ 10}\\ \$8.\cancel{7}\cancel{0}\\ -\ 1.34\\ \hline \$7.36 \end{array}
$$

Warm Up   Subtract. Check by adding.

1. $\begin{array}{r}84\\-\ 29\end{array}$	**2.** $\begin{array}{r}68\\-\ 17\end{array}$	**3.** $\begin{array}{r}739\\-\ 264\end{array}$	**4.** $\begin{array}{r}138\\-\ 83\end{array}$	**5.** $\begin{array}{r}\$5.24\\-\ 1.30\end{array}$

Subtract.

1.	72 − 25	**2.**	54 − 18	**3.**	67 − 24	**4.**	98 − 16	**5.**	70 − 26
6.	529 − 179	**7.**	615 − 340	**8.**	136 − 72	**9.**	148 − 95	**10.**	390 − 36
11.	482 − 58	**12.**	627 − 92	**13.**	$5.95 − 1.49	**14.**	$3.65 − 1.90	**15.**	$2.79 − 1.35

16. 73 − 36   **17.** 97 − 64   **18.** 729 − 63

19. 994 − 175   **20.** $1.29 − $0.75   **21.** $4.76 − $1.39

22. Subtract 58 from 92.   **23.** Subtract 327 from 475.

24. Subtract 82 from 146.   **25.** Subtract 284 from 729.

Solve.

26. A record age for a horse is 54 years. A record age for a monkey is 25 years. How much longer did the horse live than the monkey?

27. DATA BANK See page 386. How much longer did the hippopotamus live than the cat?

THINK

🖩 **Calculator Patterns**

Discover the pattern. Then find the next 4 numbers. 367, 734, 1,101, 1,468, . . .

MATH

More Practice, page 394, Set B

Subtracting: Two or More Trades

The albatross has a wingspread of about 356 cm.
The condor has a wingspread of about 298 cm.
How much less is the wingspread of the condor?

Since we are comparing the numbers, we subtract.

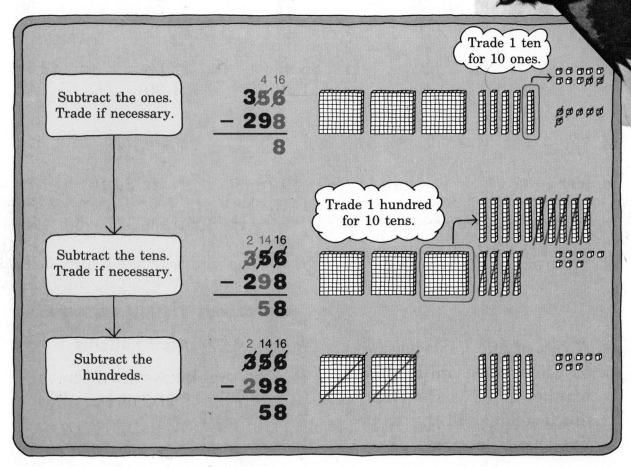

The wingspread of the condor is 58 cm less than the albatross.

Other Examples

$$\begin{array}{r} {\scriptstyle 5\ 13\ 12} \\ \cancel{642} \\ -\ 179 \\ \hline 463 \end{array} \qquad \begin{array}{r} {\scriptstyle 11\ \ 14} \\ \cancel{124} \\ -\ \ 78 \\ \hline 46 \end{array} \qquad \begin{array}{r} {\scriptstyle 5\ 12\ 15} \\ \cancel{635} \\ -\ \ 96 \\ \hline 539 \end{array} \qquad \begin{array}{r} {\scriptstyle 3\ \ 15\ 10} \\ \$4.6\cancel{0} \\ -\ 1.85 \\ \hline \$2.75 \end{array}$$

Warm Up Subtract. Check by adding.

1.
$$\begin{array}{r} 726 \\ -\ 149 \\ \hline \end{array}$$

2.
$$\begin{array}{r} 650 \\ -\ 283 \\ \hline \end{array}$$

3.
$$\begin{array}{r} 135 \\ -\ 97 \\ \hline \end{array}$$

4.
$$\begin{array}{r} 726 \\ -\ 58 \\ \hline \end{array}$$

5.
$$\begin{array}{r} \$8.50 \\ -\ 2.98 \\ \hline \end{array}$$

Subtract.

1.	632 − 365	**2.**	815 − 196	**3.**	741 − 478	**4.**	930 − 156	**5.**	850 − 279
6.	134 − 75	**7.**	156 − 98	**8.**	124 − 77	**9.**	628 − 79	**10.**	526 − 89
11.	640 − 95	**12.**	722 − 275	**13.**	$3.56 − 0.78	**14.**	$4.50 − 1.75	**15.**	$4.25 − 1.79

16. 624 − 278   **17.** 530 − 142   **18.** 762 − 95

19. 124 − 88   **20.** $7.35 − $1.49   **21.** $6.50 − $2.77

22. Find the difference between 620 and 288.

23. Find the difference between 427 and 712.

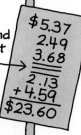

Solve.

24. The king vulture can have a wingspread of 310 cm. The bald eagle can have a wingspread of 244 cm. How much greater is the wingspread of the king vulture?

25. The white pelican can have a wingspread of 274 cm. What is the difference between this and the wingspread of the king vulture?

26. The sandhill crane can have a wingspread of 213 cm. Write a question to compare this bird with one of the birds in problems 24 or 25. Solve your own problem.

┌─ **THINK** ───────
🖩 **Using a Calculator**

Here is Mrs. Ortega's bill from the supermarket. The cost of the ground meat is marked out. How much was the ground meat?

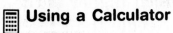

→ **MATH** ←

PROBLEM SOLVING
Using Data from a Table

QUESTION
DATA
PLAN
ANSWER
CHECK

HEIGHTS OF SOME FAMOUS TOWERS

Tower	Location	Height
Leaning Tower of Pisa	Pisa, Italy	54 m
Skylon Tower	Niagara Falls, Canada	156 m
Space Needle	Seattle, USA	180 m
Stuttgart Tower	Stuttgart, West Germany	211 m
Cairo Tower	Cairo, Egypt	225 m
Eiffel Tower	Paris, France	295 m

Use the table to solve the following problems.

1. How much higher is the Space Needle than the Skylon Tower?

2. The Moscow Tower is 222 m higher than the Eiffel Tower. How high is the Moscow Tower?

3. How much higher is the Cairo Tower than the Skylon Tower?

4. What is the difference in the heights of the Leaning Tower of Pisa and the Stuttgart Tower?

5. What is the difference in the heights of the Space Needle and the Cairo Tower?

6. The Washington Monument is 54 m shorter than the Cairo Tower. How tall is the Washington Monument?

7. The Statue of Liberty in New York is 54 m taller than the Leaning Tower of Pisa. How tall is the Statue of Liberty?

8. What is the difference in the heights of the tallest tower in the table and the shortest tower in the table?

9. The Great Pyramid in Egypt is 73 m shorter than the sum of the heights of the Leaning Tower of Pisa and the Skylon Tower. How tall is the Great Pyramid?

10. Which tower in the table is just 9 m shorter than the sum of the heights of the Leaning Tower of Pisa and the Space Needle?

11. *Try This* Tower A is shorter than Tower B. Tower A is taller than Tower C. The height of Tower D is between Towers A and C. Which tower is the shortest?

Subtracting Across a Middle Zero

Over one hundred years ago there were as many as 60,000,000 buffalo in the United States. A park ranger found a male buffalo that weighed 806 kg. A female buffalo was found that weighed 458 kg. How much more did the male weigh?

Since we are comparing numbers, we subtract.

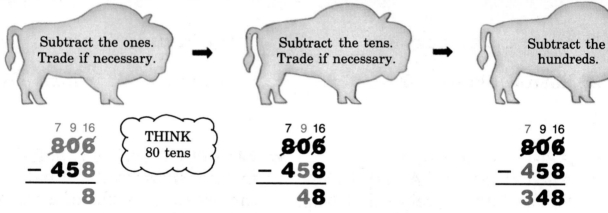

Subtract the ones. Trade if necessary.

```
  7 9 16
  8̶0̶6̶
- 4 5 8
───────
      8
```

THINK
80 tens

Subtract the tens. Trade if necessary.

```
  7 9 16
  8̶0̶6̶
- 4 5 8
───────
    4 8
```

Subtract the hundreds.

```
  7 9 16
  8̶0̶6̶
- 4 5 8
───────
  3 4 8
```

The male buffalo weighed 348 kg more than the female.

Other Examples

```
  8 10              49 13            9 14             79 10            59 14
  9̶0̶7              5̶0̶3̶            1̶0̶4̶             8̶0̶0̶            $6̶0̶4̶
- 3 8 2           -   6 8         -   6 7          - 7 6 4          - 2 5 9
───────           ───────         ───────          ───────         ───────
  5 2 5             4 3 5             3 7              3 6            $3 4 5
```

Warm Up   Subtract. Check by adding.

1.   503
   − 147

2.   705
   − 37

3.   900
   − 275

4.   601
   − 529

5. $7.04
   − 2.98

68

Subtract.

1. $601 - 259$	2. $602 - 123$	3. $400 - 176$	4. $706 - 324$	5. $501 - 56$
6. $803 - 75$	7. $805 - 726$	8. $601 - 537$	9. $900 - 254$	10. $403 - 231$
11. $702 - 356$	12. $902 - 87$	13. $\$7.05 - 1.47$	14. $\$9.00 - 3.34$	15. $\$9.03 - 7.98$

16. $504 - 125$ 17. $906 - 829$ 18. $500 - 275$

19. $603 - 56$ 20. $\$4.00 - \$2.98$ 21. $\$7.06 - \$1.49$

22. Subtract 247 from 705.   23. Subtract 124 from 406.

24. Subtract 39 from 604.   25. Subtract 727 from 801.

26. A very large male buffalo weighed 900 kg. A very large female buffalo weighed 504 kg. How much more did the male buffalo weigh than the female buffalo?

27. **DATA HUNT** Look up "buffalo" in your encyclopedia. Find the greatest weight of a male buffalo. How much more is this than the female buffalo in problem 26?

SKILLKEEPER

Add or subtract.

1. $7 + 2$	2. $18 - 9$	3. $8 + 6$	4. $13 - 8$	5. $8 + 0$
6. $6 - 4$	7. $9 + 3$	8. $1 + 5$	9. $15 - 6$	10. $5 - 4$

Subtracting Larger Numbers

While orbiting Earth, a communications satellite was 5,634 km from Earth at its farthest point. It was 956 km from Earth at its closest point in orbit. How much greater is the farthest point than the closest point?

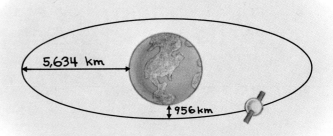
5,634 km
956 km

Since we are comparing, we subtract.

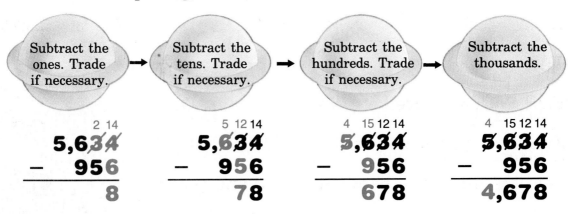

Subtract the ones. Trade if necessary. → Subtract the tens. Trade if necessary. → Subtract the hundreds. Trade if necessary. → Subtract the thousands.

$$\begin{array}{r} 5,634 \\ -956 \\ \hline 8 \end{array} \qquad \begin{array}{r} 5,634 \\ -956 \\ \hline 78 \end{array} \qquad \begin{array}{r} 5,634 \\ -956 \\ \hline 678 \end{array} \qquad \begin{array}{r} 5,634 \\ -956 \\ \hline 4,678 \end{array}$$

The farthest point was 4,678 km greater than the closest point.

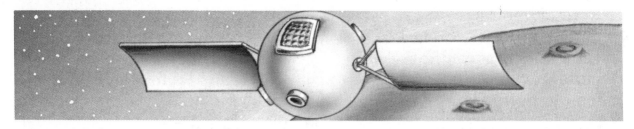

Other Examples

$$\begin{array}{r} 1,253 \\ -675 \\ \hline 578 \end{array} \qquad \begin{array}{r} 6,002 \\ -1,758 \\ \hline 4,244 \end{array} \text{(THINK 600 tens.)} \qquad \begin{array}{r} 62,573 \\ -24,728 \\ \hline 37,845 \end{array} \qquad \begin{array}{r} \$72.15 \\ -26.87 \\ \hline \$45.28 \end{array}$$

Warm Up Subtract. Check by adding.

1. $\begin{array}{r} 6,243 \\ -1,768 \end{array}$
2. $\begin{array}{r} 1,340 \\ -856 \end{array}$
3. $\begin{array}{r} 7,004 \\ -2,836 \end{array}$
4. $\begin{array}{r} 74,823 \\ -27,365 \end{array}$
5. $\begin{array}{r} \$59.25 \\ -32.68 \end{array}$

Subtract.

1. 6,238
    − 2,873

2. 5,624
    − 1,586

3. 1,324
    − 786

4. 9,640
    − 958

5. 5,003
    − 1,678

6. 8,302
    − 3,249

7. 6,000
    − 2,354

8. 7,002
    − 683

9. 48,378
    − 26,795

10. 72,340
    − 16,875

11. $76.00
    − 24.25

12. $59.25
    − 4.98

13. 6,823 − 2,476

14. 7,210 − 3,463

15. 8,001 − 2,675

16. 3,628 − 789

17. 34,286 − 7,529

18. $27.30 − $3.59

19. Find the difference between 3,726 and 8,002.

20. Find the difference between 42,831 and 24,365.

21. Find the difference between $28.75 and $65.20.

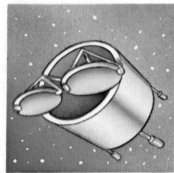

Solve.

22. A satellite was 6,023 km from Earth at its farthest point in orbit and 1,756 km at its closest point What is the difference in these distances?

23. Write a question about this data. Solve your own problem.
    Satellite A: 7,263 km from Earth
    Satellite B: 3,670 km from Earth

THINK

Patterns

Find the pattern in the answers.

$120 − 12 + 3 = n$

$1,230 − 123 + 4 = n$

$12,340 − 1,234 + 5 = n$

$123,450 − 12,345 + 6 = n$

Write and solve the equation that would come next.

MATH

Estimating Differences

Jeff wondered about how much more the boots cost than the hat. To find out, he **rounded** the prices and subtracted.

$$
\begin{array}{r}
\$27.95 \\
-\ 6.25 \\
\hline
\end{array}
\qquad
\begin{array}{l}
\text{nearest dollar} \\
\text{nearest dollar}
\end{array}
\qquad
\begin{array}{r}
\$28.00 \\
-\ 6.00 \\
\hline
\$22.00
\end{array}
$$

The boots were about $22 more than the hat.

Other Examples

nearest ten		nearest hundred		nearest dollar	
59 →	60	812 →	800	$7.89 →	$8.00
− 22	− 20	− 289	− 300	− 5.25	− 5.00
	40		500		$3.00

Warm Up

Estimate by rounding to the nearest ten.

1. $\begin{array}{r} 81 \\ -\ 39 \\ \hline \end{array}$
2. $\begin{array}{r} 69 \\ -\ 23 \\ \hline \end{array}$
3. $\begin{array}{r} 86 \\ -\ 29 \\ \hline \end{array}$
4. $\begin{array}{r} 73 \\ -\ 48 \\ \hline \end{array}$

Estimate by rounding to the nearest hundred.

5. $\begin{array}{r} 379 \\ -\ 198 \\ \hline \end{array}$
6. $\begin{array}{r} 607 \\ -\ 398 \\ \hline \end{array}$
7. $\begin{array}{r} 590 \\ -\ 221 \\ \hline \end{array}$
8. $\begin{array}{r} 918 \\ -\ 388 \\ \hline \end{array}$

Estimate by rounding to the nearest dollar.

9. $\begin{array}{r} \$7.95 \\ -\ 1.25 \\ \hline \end{array}$
10. $\begin{array}{r} \$6.15 \\ -\ 3.98 \\ \hline \end{array}$
11. $\begin{array}{r} \$12.89 \\ -\ 8.15 \\ \hline \end{array}$
12. $\begin{array}{r} \$10.17 \\ -\ 2.79 \\ \hline \end{array}$

Find the special differences.

1. 90
 − 40

2. 130
 − 40

3. 700
 − 500

4. 1,700
 − 900

5. $13.00
 − 7.00

Estimate by rounding to the nearest ten.

6. 78
 − 25

7. 39
 − 18

8. 81
 − 49

9. 92
 − 59

10. 67
 − 21

Estimate by rounding to the nearest hundred.

11. 695
 − 213

12. 720
 − 480

13. 396
 − 189

14. 615
 − 399

Estimate by rounding to the nearest dollar.

15. $8.95
 − 2.15

16. $6.08
 − 3.95

17. $10.95
 − 3.79

18. $13.89
 − 4.20

★ Estimate by rounding to the nearest thousand.

19. 7,825
 − 1,088

20. 9,123
 − 4,789

21. 8,090
 − 4,896

22. About how much more does the 18-piece cook set cost?

Cook Set
$21.95
18 piece

Cook Set
$18.98
16 piece

THINK

Logical Reasoning

Find the missing digits. They are all the same.

1 7 6
− ▓▓ ▓▓
▓▓ ▓▓

MATH

PROBLEM SOLVING
Using Data from a Catalog

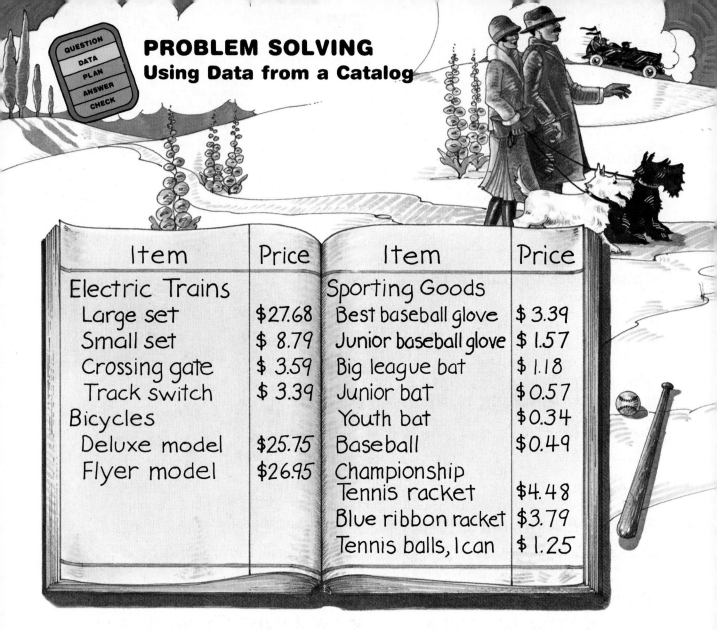

Item	Price	Item	Price
Electric Trains		Sporting Goods	
Large set	$27.68	Best baseball glove	$3.39
Small set	$8.79	Junior baseball glove	$1.57
Crossing gate	$3.59	Big league bat	$1.18
Track switch	$3.39	Junior bat	$0.57
Bicycles		Youth bat	$0.34
Deluxe model	$25.75	Baseball	$0.49
Flyer model	$26.95	Championship	
		Tennis racket	$4.48
		Blue ribbon racket	$3.79
		Tennis balls, I can	$1.25

Use the 1927 catalog price list above to help you solve the following problems.

1. How much more was the small train set than the crossing gate?

2. How much less was the small train set than the large train set?

3. How much would it cost to buy a crossing gate and a track switch?

4. How much would you get back from $10.00 if you bought the small train set?

5. How much would you get back from $5.00 if you bought the crossing gate?

6. How much more is the Best baseball glove than the Junior glove?

7. Suppose you bought a Junior glove, a Youth bat, and a baseball. How much would you spend?

8. How much more is the Big League bat than the Junior bat?

9. How much would it cost for a can of tennis balls and a Blue Ribbon racket?

10. If you bought both kinds of bicycles, how much would you spend?

11. Estimate the cost of a Best baseball glove and a Blue Ribbon racket.

12. You have $10.00. Estimate how much money you would get back if you bought a track switch.

13. **DATA HUNT** Choose an item from the catalog. Find the difference between today's price and the catalog price.

14. *Try This* You have a 10-dollar bill and a 5-dollar bill. You buy a crossing gate, a Best glove, and a Championship racket. How much money will you have left?

PROBLEM SOLVING
Guess and Check

QUESTION
DATA
PLAN
ANSWER
CHECK

SOME PROBLEMS REQUIRE MORE THAN JUST DECIDING WHETHER TO ADD OR SUBTRACT. TO HELP US SOLVE A PROBLEM SUCH AS THIS, WE CAN USE THE STRATEGY SHOWN BELOW.

Try This Jenny keeps her 12 pet rabbits in two pens, one large and one small. The large pen has 2 more rabbits than the small pen. How many rabbits are in the small pen?

GUESS AND CHECK

I'LL START BY GUESSING 4. THEN THE LARGE PEN WOULD HAVE 6.

GUESS

Small Pen 4   large Pen 4 + 2 = 6

THEN I'LL CHECK MY GUESS. IT'S TOO SMALL.

CHECK

4 + 6 = 10

I'LL GUESS AGAIN USING A LARGER NUMBER.

GUESS

Small pen 5   large pen 5 + 2 = 7

THIS CHECKS. THERE ARE 5 RABBITS IN THE SMALL PEN.

CHECK

5 + 7 = 12

It checks.

Solve.

1. Jack had 10 checkers. He made two stacks. One stack had 2 more checkers than the other. How many were in each stack?

2. Diane spent $13 for two books. One book cost $1 more than the other. How much did the higher priced book cost?

Add.

1. 38
   + 46

2. 914
   + 820

3. $9.86
   + 0.58

4. 3,924
   + 5,187

5. $17.54
   + 13.89

6. 62,753
   + 19,628

Estimate the sums. Round as indicated.

| nearest ten | nearest hundred | nearest dollar |

7. 79
   + 53

8. 267
   + 413

9. $6.95
   + 3.25

Add.

10. 27
     58
    + 39

11. $1.50
     2.34
    + 3.76

12. 326
     58
     39
    + 125

13. 623
     5,817
    + 6,985

14. $ 2.29
     25.63
    + 37.14

Subtract.

15. 72
   − 38

16. $6.25
   − 2.98

17. 604
   − 179

18. 3,004
   − 1,627

19. 62,375
   − 14,827

Estimate the differences. Round as indicated.

| nearest ten | nearest hundred | nearest dollar |

20. 26
   − 11

21. 813
   − 295

22. $12.13
   − 4.87

Solve.

23. How much taller is the Cairo Tower?
   Leaning Tower of Pisa   54 m
   Cairo Tower   225 m

24. How much for both?
   Train Set $19.56
   Ball glove $ 2.95

ANOTHER LOOK

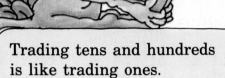

Trading tens and hundreds is like trading ones.

```
  1 1  ← 1 ten
  746
+ 587
1,333  ← 3 ones
```

13 ones = 1 ten and 3 ones

13 tens = **1** hundred and **3** tens
13 hundreds = **1** thousand and
3 hundreds

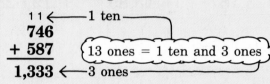

70 tens = 69 tens and 10 ones

```
 6 9 14
  704
- 278
  426
```

THINK
I need more ones.

THINK
```
  3
3 7
2 8
4 9
+ 1 7
1 3 1
```
7 + 8 = 15
15 + 9 = 24
24 + 7 = 31

Add.

1. 275 + 186	**2.** 359 + 175	**3.** 867 + 346
4. 407 + 621	**5.** 364 + 542	**6.** 286 + 107
7. 2,759 + 1,678	**8.** 4,563 + 9,875	**9.** 2,864 + 9,358

Subtract.

10. 342 - 127	**11.** 702 - 169	**12.** 802 - 175
13. 7,210 - 3,651	**14.** 9,026 - 3,554	**15.** 7,000 - 2,674

Add.

16. 36 29 + 15	**17.** 76 38 57 + 25	**18.** 462 375 468 + 103
19. 356 279 + 135	**20.** 9,214 3,652 + 1,837	**21.** 4,692 5,867 + 2,547

The Greatest Sum Game

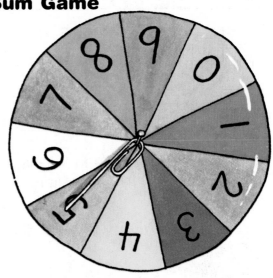

1. Make a spinner board like the one shown to the right.

2. Each player draws an addition grid.

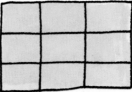

Rico's Grid   Beth's Grid

3. In turn, each player spins the spinner and writes the spinner number in any one of the spaces in the top two rows of his or her grid.

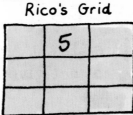

Rico's Grid   Beth's Grid

4. After 6 spinner numbers are written on the grid, the winner is the person who has the greatest sum. Who won this game?

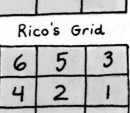

Rico's Grid   Beth's Grid

The Least Difference Game is very much like the Greatest Sum Game. Can you figure out how to play it?

Give the letter for the correct answer.

1. 4
    4
    + 3

    A 11   **B** 7
    C 10   **D** not given

2. 6
    2
    + 5

    A 12   **B** 11
    C 13   **D** not given

3. 1
    5
    + 3

    A 9   **B** 8
    C 7   **D** not given

4. 7
    2
    + 5

    A 16   **B** 14
    C 15   **D** not given

5. 8
    1
    + 3

    A 13   **B** 11
    C 12   **D** not given

6. 6
    4
    + 5

    A 16   **B** 13
    C 14   **D** not given

7. 5 hundreds
   4 tens
   6 ones

   A 465
   B 546
   C 654
   D not given

8. 6 tens
   0 ones
   7 hundreds

   A 760
   B 607
   C 706
   D not given

9. 3 thousands
   2 hundreds
   4 tens
   2 ones

   A 4,232
   B 2,342
   C 3,242
   D not given

Which statement is correct?

10. **A** 325 > 352
    B 352 < 325
    C 325 < 352
    D not given

11. **A** 1,781 > 1,779
    B 1,781 < 1,779
    C 1,779 > 1,781
    D not given

12. **A** 9,670 > 9,801
    B 9,670 < 9,801
    C 9,801 < 9,670
    D not given

13. Kim had 6 dollars. She earned 8 dollars. How much does Kim have now?

    A $13   **B** $15
    C $14   **D** not given

14. Gary had 17 marbles. He gave away 9 of the marbles. How many were left?

    A 8   **B** 6
    C 7   **D** not given

MULTIPLICATION FACTS 4

Alice Liddell lived in England. On July 4, 1862 Alice went on a picnic. That afternoon her friend Charles Dodgson told a story. It was about a 7-year-old girl named Alice. She sees a White Rabbit in a terrible hurry. Alice follows him. She falls into a rabbit hole. Alice Liddell begged Dodgson to write about Alice's adventures underground. He wrote *Alice's Adventures in Wonderland*. Dodgson's pen name was Lewis Carroll. Alice Liddell was 2 times the age of Alice in the story when the book was printed.

2 and 3 as Factors

The pet store is having a sale. How many fish are in the 5 bowls?

The bowls have the same number of fish. You **multiply** to find the total number.

5 Threes

$$5 \times 3 = 15$$

Factor   Factor   Product

$$\begin{array}{r} 3 \leftarrow \text{Factor} \\ \times\ 5 \leftarrow \text{Factor} \\ \hline 15 \leftarrow \text{Product} \end{array}$$

We read, **"Five times three equal fifteen."**

There are 15 fish in the bowls.

How many finches are on sale?

Each cage has the same number of birds. You multiply to find how many finches there are.

$$4 \times 2 = 8$$

There are 8 finches on sale.

4 Twos

Warm Up   Find the products.

1.

$$5 \times 2 = n$$

2. $\quad\begin{array}{r} 3 \\ \times\ 4 \\ \hline \end{array}$

82

Copy and complete the counting.

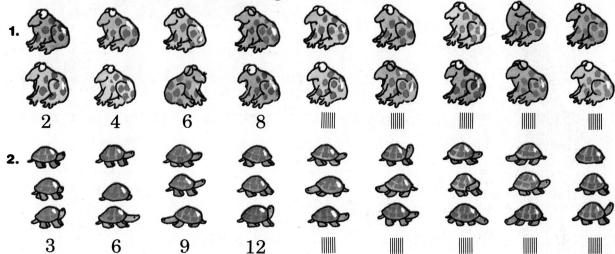

1.
2   4   6   8 |||| |||| |||| |||| ||||

2.
3   6   9   12 |||| |||| |||| |||| ||||

Find the products.

3. $\begin{array}{r} 3 \\ \times\,6 \\ \hline \end{array}$
4. $\begin{array}{r} 2 \\ \times\,5 \\ \hline \end{array}$
5. $\begin{array}{r} 3 \\ \times\,2 \\ \hline \end{array}$
6. $\begin{array}{r} 2 \\ \times\,8 \\ \hline \end{array}$
7. $\begin{array}{r} 2 \\ \times\,3 \\ \hline \end{array}$
8. $\begin{array}{r} 3 \\ \times\,6 \\ \hline \end{array}$
9. $\begin{array}{r} 3 \\ \times\,4 \\ \hline \end{array}$

10. $\begin{array}{r} 2 \\ \times\,6 \\ \hline \end{array}$
11. $\begin{array}{r} 3 \\ \times\,8 \\ \hline \end{array}$
12. $\begin{array}{r} 2 \\ \times\,7 \\ \hline \end{array}$
13. $\begin{array}{r} 2 \\ \times\,1 \\ \hline \end{array}$
14. $\begin{array}{r} 3 \\ \times\,9 \\ \hline \end{array}$
15. $\begin{array}{r} 3 \\ \times\,7 \\ \hline \end{array}$
16. $\begin{array}{r} 2 \\ \times\,4 \\ \hline \end{array}$

17. $\begin{array}{r} 3 \\ \times\,3 \\ \hline \end{array}$
18. $\begin{array}{r} 2 \\ \times\,2 \\ \hline \end{array}$
19. $\begin{array}{r} 2 \\ \times\,9 \\ \hline \end{array}$
20. $\begin{array}{r} 3 \\ \times\,1 \\ \hline \end{array}$
21. $\begin{array}{r} 3 \\ \times\,5 \\ \hline \end{array}$
22. $\begin{array}{r} 3 \\ \times\,8 \\ \hline \end{array}$
23. $\begin{array}{r} 2 \\ \times\,7 \\ \hline \end{array}$

24. $4 \times 2 = n$
25. $5 \times 3 = n$
26. $6 \times 2 = n$
27. $7 \times 3 = n$

28. $3 \times 3 = n$
29. $8 \times 2 = n$

30. $3 \times 2 = n$
31. $1 \times 3 = n$

32. Multiply 3 by 7.

33. Multiply 2 by 8.

34. Multiply 3 by 5.

35. Find the product of 6 and 2.

36. Find the product of 9 and 3.

THINK

Logical Reasoning

Each missing number is the same.

🐭 × 🐭 = 4

🐭 + 🐭 = 4

Can you find it?

→ MATH ←

4 and 5 as Factors

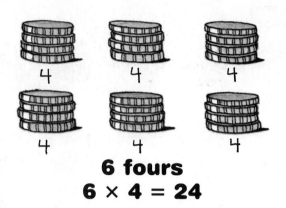

6 fours
$6 \times 4 = 24$

7 fives
$7 \times 5 = 35$

Doris has 6 silver dollars. Each dollar is worth 4 quarters. How many quarters can Doris get for her 6 silver dollars?

Since each dollar is worth the same number of quarters, you multiply.

Doris can get 24 quarters for her 6 dollars.

David has 7 nickels. Each nickel is worth 5 pennies. How many pennies can David get for his 7 nickels?

Since each nickel is worth the same number of pennies, you multiply.

David can get 35 pennies for his 7 nickels.

Warm Up   Copy and complete counting the coins.

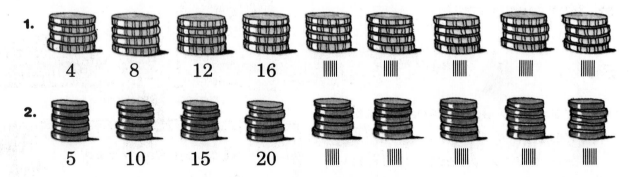

1. 4   8   12   16

2. 5   10   15   20

Find the products.

3. $8 \times 4 = n$ **4.** $5 \times 5 = n$ **5.** $9 \times 5 = n$ **6.** $6 \times 4 = n$

7. $\begin{array}{r} 5 \\ \times 4 \\ \hline \end{array}$
8. $\begin{array}{r} 4 \\ \times 4 \\ \hline \end{array}$
9. $\begin{array}{r} 4 \\ \times 7 \\ \hline \end{array}$
10. $\begin{array}{r} 5 \\ \times 8 \\ \hline \end{array}$
11. $\begin{array}{r} 4 \\ \times 5 \\ \hline \end{array}$
12. $\begin{array}{r} 5 \\ \times 6 \\ \hline \end{array}$
13. $\begin{array}{r} 5 \\ \times 3 \\ \hline \end{array}$

Find the products.

1. 4
    × 4

2. 5
    × 6

3. 5
    × 9

4. 4
    × 1

5. 5
    × 2

6. 5
    × 5

7. 4
    × 5

8. 4
    × 9

9. 4
    × 6

10. 5
    × 8

11. 4
    × 9

12. 5
    × 4

13. 4
    × 3

14. 4
    × 7

15. 5
    × 8

16. 5
    × 1

17. 4
    × 2

18. 5
    × 9

19. 4
    × 8

20. 5
    × 3

21. 4
    × 9

22. 5
    × 7

23. 5×5

24. 3×4

25. 2×5

26. 8×4

27. 7×4

28. 1×5

29. 8×5

30. 6×4

31. 4×4

32. 4×5

33. 5×4

34. 6×5

35. Multiply 4 by 6.

36. Multiply 5 by 8.

37. Multiply 5 by 7.

Solve.

38. Chico has 6 quarters. Each quarter is worth 5 nickels. How many nickels can Chico get for his 6 quarters?

39. Carla has 45 quarters. Each quarter is worth 5 nickels. How many nickels can Carla get for her 45 quarters?

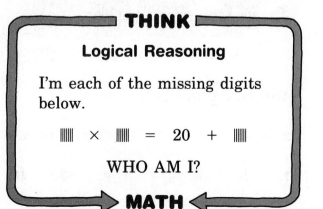

THINK

Logical Reasoning

I'm each of the missing digits below.

‖‖‖ × ‖‖‖ = 20 + ‖‖‖

WHO AM I?

MATH

Multiplication Properties

These special multiplication properties can help you find products.

THE ORDER PROPERTY

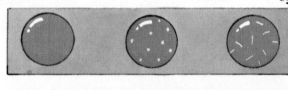

2 × 3 = 6   **3 × 2 = 6**

When the order of the factors is changed, the product is the same.

THE "1" PROPERTY   THE "0" PROPERTY

3 × 1 = 3   **3 × 0 = 0**

When one factor is 1, the product is the same as the other factor.

When one factor is 0, the product is 0.

Warm Up Find the products.

1. 7×3 2. 3×7 3. 9×4 4. 4×9

5. 6×5 6. 5×6 7. 8×2 8. 2×8

9. 0×6 10. 6×0 11. 1×7 12. 7×1

13. $\begin{array}{r} 3 \\ \times 9 \\ \hline \end{array}$
14. $\begin{array}{r} 9 \\ \times 3 \\ \hline \end{array}$
15. $\begin{array}{r} 5 \\ \times 8 \\ \hline \end{array}$
16. $\begin{array}{r} 8 \\ \times 5 \\ \hline \end{array}$
17. $\begin{array}{r} 0 \\ \times 9 \\ \hline \end{array}$
18. $\begin{array}{r} 9 \\ \times 0 \\ \hline \end{array}$

Find the products.

1. 7 × 4
   4 × 7

2. 8 × 5
   5 × 8

3. 8 × 2
   2 × 8

4. 9 × 3
   3 × 9

5. 6 × 5
   5 × 6

6. 6 × 2
   2 × 6

7. 6 × 3
   3 × 6

8. 5 × 4
   4 × 5

9. 9 × 2
   2 × 9

10. 7 × 3
    3 × 7

11. 8 × 4
    4 × 8

12. 3 × 5
    5 × 3

13.   4
    × 6

14.   6
    × 4

15.   3
    × 8

16.   8
    × 3

17.   5
    × 9

18.   9
    × 5

19.   0
    × 8

20.   1
    × 7

21.   8
    × 1

22.   9
    × 0

23.   9
    × 1

24.   1
    × 6

Solve.

25. There are 5 packages of muffins. There are 4 muffins in a package. How many muffins are there in all?

★ 26. Make up a story for this number sentence:

6 × 2 = 12

SKILLKEEPER

Add or subtract.

1.   76
     − 32

2.   275
     + 383

3.   5,935
    +   784
      6719

4. $5.65
     − 0.48
       5.17

5.   680
     − 275
       465

6.   600
     − 183

7.   53,645
    + 16,536

8.   700
     − 183

9. $6.25
     + 2.98

10.   4,153
     − 1,675

PROBLEM SOLVING
Using Data from a Recipe

Holiday Salad
Serves 6
4 apples
½ cup of raisins
6 small stalks of celery

9 walnuts
2 bananas

Chop and lightly toss the ingredients above. Use 1 cup yogurt with a squeeze of fresh lemon for dressing.

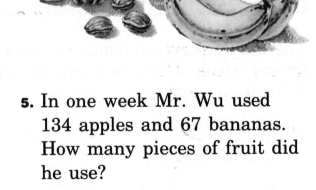

Mr. Wu is a chef. Here is one of his recipes that is a favorite. Solve the following problems. Use data from the recipe as needed.

1. One Friday Mr. Wu served 174 people for lunch and 256 for dinner. How many people did he serve that day?

2. That Friday Mr. Wu made 5 batches of his salad. How many apples did he use?

3. How many walnuts did Mr. Wu use when he made the 5 batches of salad?

4. One Saturday Mr. Wu served 187 people for lunch and 312 for dinner. How many more people did Mr. Wu serve for dinner than for lunch?

5. In one week Mr. Wu used 134 apples and 67 bananas. How many pieces of fruit did he use?

6. How many bananas would Mr. Wu use for 3 batches of salad?

7. *Try This* Mr. Wu had 11 pieces of fruit (apples and bananas) left. He had 3 more apples than bananas. How many apples did he have? Hint: Use guess and check.

PROBLEM SOLVING
Using Data from a Picture Graph

Record Sales

Monday	⊙ ⊙ ⊙ ⊙ ⊙
Tuesday	⊙ ⊙ ⊙
Wednesday	⊙ ⊙ ⊙ ⊙ ⊙ ⊙
Thursday	⊙ ⊙ ⊙
Friday	⊙ ⊙ ⊙ ⊙ ⊙
Saturday	⊙ ⊙ ⊙ ⊙ ⊙ ⊙ ⊙ ⊙

Each ⊙ stands for 4 records.

The graph shows a music store's record sales for one week. Use the graph to answer the following questions.

1. On what day were the most records sold?

2. On what day were the fewest records sold?

3. How many records were sold on Monday?

4. How many records were sold on Saturday?

5. How many more records were sold on Saturday than on Monday?

6. How many records were sold on Wednesday and Thursday altogether?

7. How many fewer records were sold on Tuesday than on Saturday?

8. *Try This* Another week 14 records were sold on Monday and Tuesday. There were 2 more records sold on Tuesday than on Monday. How many records were sold on Monday?

6 and 7 as Factors

Emily and John went to a summer camp for 8 weeks. They went swimming 6 days each week. How many days did they swim?

Since we want the total for equal amounts, we multiply.

$$\begin{array}{l} 5 \text{ sixes} = 30 \\ 3 \text{ sixes} = 18 \end{array}$$

8 × 6 = 48

Emily and John went swimming 48 days.

There are 7 days in a week. How many days did Emily and John stay at camp?

Since we want the total for equal amounts, we multiply.

$$\begin{array}{l} 4 \text{ sevens} = 28 \\ 4 \text{ sevens} = 28 \end{array}$$

8 × 7 = 56

Emily and John were at camp 56 days.

Warm Up Copy and complete the skip counting.

1. 6,   12,   18,   24,   ▓,   ▓,   ▓,   ▓,   ▓.

2. 7,   14,   21,   28,   ▓,   ▓,   ▓,   ▓,   ▓.

Find the products.

3. 5×6 4. 4×7 5. 3×6 6. 5×7

7. 2×6 8. 7×7 9. 8×6 10. 0×6

11. $\begin{array}{r} 6 \\ \times 1 \\ \hline \end{array}$ 12. $\begin{array}{r} 7 \\ \times 6 \\ \hline \end{array}$ 13. $\begin{array}{r} 7 \\ \times 3 \\ \hline \end{array}$ 14. $\begin{array}{r} 6 \\ \times 9 \\ \hline \end{array}$ 15. $\begin{array}{r} 6 \\ \times 4 \\ \hline \end{array}$ 16. $\begin{array}{r} 7 \\ \times 8 \\ \hline \end{array}$

Find the products.

1. 6
   × 5

2. 7
   × 7

3. 6
   × 8

4. 7
   × 9

5. 7
   × 8

6. 7
   × 5

7. 6
   × 6

8. 7
   × 6

9. 6
   × 7

10. 7
    × 1

11. 6
    × 9

12. 7
    × 4

13. 7
    × 0

14. 6
    × 4

15. 6
    × 6

16. 7
    × 7

17. 3
    × 7

18. 6
    × 5

19. 3
    × 6

20. 9
    × 7

21. 8
    × 6

22. 6 × 6

23. 7 × 7

24. 9 × 6

25. 9 × 7

26. 6 × 8

27. 7 × 9

28. 6 × 9

29. 7 × 8

30. Multiply 6 by 8.

31. Multiply 7 by 9.

Solve.

32. Tom went to camp for 6 weeks. How many days did he spend in camp?

33. Jan went to camp for 4 weeks. She had a craft class 3 days each week. Write a question about Jan and solve your own problem.

THINK

Logical Reasoning

Each missing digit is the same.

▥ × ▥ = 30 + ▥

Can you find it?

➡ **MATH** ⬅

8 and 9 as Factors

There were 8 teams in the tournament. Each team had 9 players. How many players were in the tournament?

Since we want the total for equal groups, we multiply.

There were 72 players in the tournament.

That's 7 nines → 63
and 1 more nine. → 9

8 × 9 = 72

Other Examples

That's 4 eights → 32
and 4 eights. → 32

8 × 8 = 64

That's the same product as 8 × 9.

9 × 8 = 72

That's one more 9 than 8 × 9.

9 × 9 = 81

Warm Up Copy and complete the skip counting.

1. 8,   16,   24,   32, |||||, |||||, |||||, |||||, |||||.

2. 9,   18,   27,   36, |||||, |||||, |||||, |||||, |||||.

Find the products.

3. 3 × 8   **4.** 9 × 9   **5.** 4 × 9   **6.** 7 × 8

7. 9
    × 5

8. 6
    × 8

9. 8
    × 2

10. 9
     × 1

11. 9
     × 7

12. 8
     × 4

Find the products.

1. 9 ×4	**2.** 7 ×8	**3.** 8 ×3	**4.** 9 ×6	**5.** 5 ×9	**6.** 8 ×8	**7.** 9 ×3
8. 8 ×9	**9.** 6 ×9	**10.** 9 ×1	**11.** 8 ×4	**12.** 8 ×6	**13.** 9 ×5	**14.** 9 ×8
15. 9 ×7	**16.** 8 ×5	**17.** 8 ×0	**18.** 9 ×9	**19.** 5 ×8	**20.** 6 ×3	**21.** 9 ×9
22. 2 ×8	**23.** 6 ×8	**24.** 9 ×2	**25.** 7 ×4	**26.** 8 ×2	**27.** 9 ×4	**28.** 8 ×7

29. 8 × 9   **30.** 7 × 8   **31.** 9 × 7   **32.** 5 × 8

33. 1 × 8   **34.** 3 × 9   **35.** 8 × 6   **36.** 0 × 9

37. 9 × 5   **38.** 8 × 4   **39.** 8 × 4   **40.** 7 × 9

41. Find the product of 9 and 9.   **42.** Find the product of 9 and 6.

Solve.

43. After the first round of the tournament, 4 teams were left. How many players were still in the tournament?

★ **44.** This problem has missing data. Make up some data. Then find the answer.

> Each team has 8 players. How many players are there in all?

Multiples

The **multiples** of 5 are the products when 5 is one of the factors.

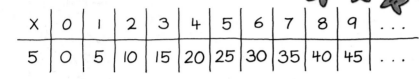

X	0	1	2	3	4	5	6	7	8	9	...
5	0	5	10	15	20	25	30	35	40	45	...

The multiples of 2 are the **even** numbers.
All other whole numbers are **odd** numbers.

Multiples of 2

X	0	1	2	3	4	5	6	7	8	9	...
2	0	2	4	6	8	10	12	14	16	18	...

The multiples of 9 have some interesting patterns.

0×9	1×9	2×9	3×9	4×9	5×9
0	9	18	27	36	45
		(1 + 8)	(2 + 7)	(3 + 6)	(4 + 5)

Give the remaining multiples of 9 through 9×9.

Warm Up Give the multiples.

Multiples of 4

X	0	1	2	3	4	5	6	7	8	9	...
4	0	4	8	12							...

Copy and complete each set of multiples.

1.

Multiples of 3											

X	0	1	2	3	4	5	6	7	8	9	. . .
3	0	3	6	9	▓	▓	▓	▓	▓	▓	. . .

2.

Multiples of 6											

X	0	1	2	3	4	5	6	7	8	9	. . .
6	0	6	12	18	▓	▓	▓	▓	▓	▓	. . .

3.

Multiples of 7											

X	0	1	2	3	4	5	6	7	8	9	. . .
7	0	7	14	21	▓	▓	▓	▓	▓	▓	. . .

4.

Multiples of 8											

X	0	1	2	3	4	5	6	7	8	9	. . .
8	0	8	16	24	▓	▓	▓	▓	▓	▓	. . .

Find the products.

5. $\begin{array}{r} 7 \\ \times 7 \\ \hline \end{array}$ **6.** $\begin{array}{r} 7 \\ \times 4 \\ \hline \end{array}$ **7.** $\begin{array}{r} 8 \\ \times 9 \\ \hline \end{array}$ **8.** $\begin{array}{r} 5 \\ \times 7 \\ \hline \end{array}$

9. $\begin{array}{r} 8 \\ \times 5 \\ \hline \end{array}$ **10.** $\begin{array}{r} 8 \\ \times 8 \\ \hline \end{array}$ **11.** $\begin{array}{r} 9 \\ \times 5 \\ \hline \end{array}$ **12.** $\begin{array}{r} 7 \\ \times 8 \\ \hline \end{array}$

THINK

Logical Reasoning

Of the numbers with 2 digits,
I'm the smallest with this fate.
I'm a multiple of 6 and
a multiple of 8.

WHO AM I?

➤ MATH ◀

PROBLEM SOLVING
Identifying Needed Data

The following problems have more data than you need. You will have to find the needed data to solve each problem.

1. The Douglas fir tree can grow as high as 76 m. Its trunk can have a width of between 89 cm and 243 cm. What is the difference in these widths?

2. Giant bamboos can grow as high as 36 m. Sometimes they can grow as fast as 7 m a week. At this rate how much would one grow in 3 weeks?

3. An elephant tree grew to a height of 914 cm. From side to side it was 9 m. The distance around it was about 3 times that. How many meters is it around the tree?

4. The loblolly pine tree grows to 30 m tall and 90 m across. Its needles usually come in bundles of 3. How many needles would be in 8 such bundles?

5. **DATA BANK** See page 384. How much taller is the Douglas fir tree than the yellow poplar tree?

6. *Try This* Jesse planted 15 apple and pear trees. He planted 7 more apple trees than pear trees. How many apple trees did he plant?

Practice the Facts

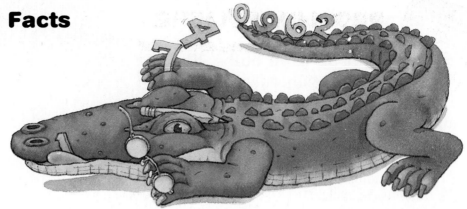

Multiply.

1. $\begin{array}{r} 8 \\ \times 6 \\ \hline \end{array}$	**2.** $\begin{array}{r} 4 \\ \times 7 \\ \hline \end{array}$	**3.** $\begin{array}{r} 3 \\ \times 5 \\ \hline \end{array}$	**4.** $\begin{array}{r} 0 \\ \times 5 \\ \hline \end{array}$	**5.** $\begin{array}{r} 3 \\ \times 6 \\ \hline \end{array}$	**6.** $\begin{array}{r} 7 \\ \times 8 \\ \hline \end{array}$	**7.** $\begin{array}{r} 9 \\ \times 2 \\ \hline \end{array}$
8. $\begin{array}{r} 1 \\ \times 3 \\ \hline \end{array}$	**9.** $\begin{array}{r} 6 \\ \times 7 \\ \hline \end{array}$	**10.** $\begin{array}{r} 5 \\ \times 5 \\ \hline \end{array}$	**11.** $\begin{array}{r} 3 \\ \times 8 \\ \hline \end{array}$	**12.** $\begin{array}{r} 9 \\ \times 4 \\ \hline \end{array}$	**13.** $\begin{array}{r} 7 \\ \times 3 \\ \hline \end{array}$	**14.** $\begin{array}{r} 6 \\ \times 1 \\ \hline \end{array}$
15. $\begin{array}{r} 7 \\ \times 9 \\ \hline \end{array}$	**16.** $\begin{array}{r} 4 \\ \times 8 \\ \hline \end{array}$	**17.** $\begin{array}{r} 9 \\ \times 0 \\ \hline \end{array}$	**18.** $\begin{array}{r} 2 \\ \times 7 \\ \hline \end{array}$	**19.** $\begin{array}{r} 4 \\ \times 3 \\ \hline \end{array}$	**20.** $\begin{array}{r} 8 \\ \times 8 \\ \hline \end{array}$	**21.** $\begin{array}{r} 3 \\ \times 2 \\ \hline \end{array}$

22. $7 \times 7 = n$ **23.** $9 \times 8 = n$ **24.** $6 \times 6 = n$ **25.** $4 \times 5 = n$

26. $5 \times 7 = n$ **27.** $4 \times 4 = n$ **28.** $1 \times 7 = n$ **29.** $9 \times 6 = n$

30. $0 \times 8 = n$ **31.** $8 \times 2 = n$ **32.** $3 \times 9 = n$ **33.** $8 \times 5 = n$

Guess each rule. Then give the missing numbers.

Maria said	Bob answered
3	15
0	0
4	20
34. 6	▓▓▓
35. ▓▓▓	40

Maria said	Bob answered
5	45
3	27
7	63
36. 8	▓▓▓
37. ▓▓▓	18

Maria said	Bob answered
4	28
2	14
9	63
38. 6	▓▓▓
39. ▓▓▓	21

Missing Factors

Sally bought 32 tulip bulbs. She wants to plant 4 in each row. How many rows of bulbs will she have?

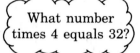

What number times 4 equals 32?

$\text{||||} \times 4 = 32$

If you don't know the answer, use **Guess and Check.**

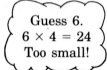

Guess 6.
$6 \times 4 = 24$
Too small!

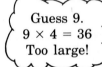

Guess 9.
$9 \times 4 = 36$
Too large!

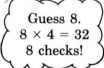

Guess 8.
$8 \times 4 = 32$
8 checks!

$\text{||||} \times 4 = 32$ $\text{||||} \times 4 = 32$ $8 \times 4 = 32$

Sally will have 8 rows of tulip bulbs.

Warm Up Find the missing factors.

How many 3s = 15?   How many 6s = 30?   How many 4s = 28?

1. $\text{||||} \times 3 = 15$ **2.** $\text{||||} \times 6 = 30$ **3.** $\text{||||} \times 4 = 28$

4. $\text{||||} \times 6 = 24$ **5.** $\text{||||} \times 5 = 30$ **6.** $\text{||||} \times 5 = 25$ **7.** $\text{||||} \times 3 = 18$

8. $8 \times \text{||||} = 40$ **9.** $6 \times \text{||||} = 36$ **10.** $4 \times \text{||||} = 20$ **11.** $3 \times \text{||||} = 12$

12. $\text{||||} \times 4 = 16$ **13.** $9 \times \text{||||} = 27$ **14.** $7 \times \text{||||} = 35$ **15.** $\text{||||} \times 6 = 0$

Find the missing factors.

What number times 2 equals 8?

1. |||| × 2 = 8

What number times 4 equals 12?

2. |||| × 4 = 12

What number times 2 equals 10?

3. |||| × 2 = 10

7 times what number equals 14?

4. 7 × |||| = 14

2 times what number equals 6?

5. 2 × |||| = 6

5 times what number equals 15?

6. 5 × |||| = 15

7. |||| × 7 = 28   **8.** 7 × |||| = 42   **9.** 5 × |||| = 35   **10.** |||| × 4 = 24

11. 6 × |||| = 48   **12.** |||| × 2 = 18   **13.** |||| × 8 = 32   **14.** 7 × |||| = 0

15. |||| × 6 = 30   **16.** 8 × |||| = 40   **17.** |||| × 5 = 20   **18.** 3 × |||| = 27

Solve.

19. Mark has 42 onion plants. He wants to plant 6 in each row. How many rows of onions will Mark have?

★ **20.** Carlos has 24 strawberry plants. How many ways could he plant them so he has the same number in each row?

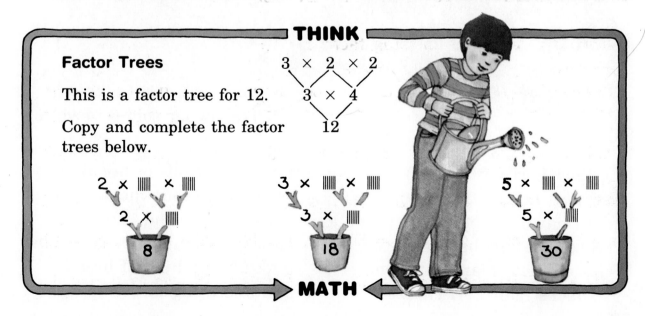

THINK

Factor Trees

This is a factor tree for 12.

Copy and complete the factor trees below.

$$3 \times 2 \times 2$$
$$3 \times 4$$
$$12$$

2 × |||| × ||||
2 × ||||
8

3 × |||| × ||||
3 × ||||
18

5 × |||| × ||||
5 × ||||
30

MATH

PROBLEM SOLVING
Make a List

QUESTION · DATA · PLAN · ANSWER · CHECK

THIS TYPE OF PROBLEM MAY REQUIRE MORE THAN JUST DECIDING TO ADD, SUBTRACT, OR MULTIPLY. A STRATEGY THAT WILL HELP YOU WITH THIS PROBLEM IS GIVEN BELOW.

Try This The bicycle shop had girls' bicycles and boys' bicycles. Both kinds come in three colors, red, blue, and white. The owner said, "Today I sold one of each kind of bicycle that I have." How many did he sell?

MAKE A LIST

IF I WANTED A BOY'S BICYCLE, I COULD GET IT IN 3 COLORS.

IF I WANTED A GIRL'S BICYCLE, I COULD GET IT IN 3 COLORS.

boy's -- red
boy's -- blue
boy's -- white

girl's -- red
girl's -- blue
girl's -- white

The owner sold 6 bicycles.

Solve.

1. When Lori got home from school, her mother said, "You can have an apple or a pear. Also, you can have milk or juice." How many different "snacks" can Lori choose?

2. Ed had 3 kinds of bread—rye, white, and wheat. He found cheese and turkey. How many sandwiches can he make? (One kind of bread and one thing on it.)

Find the products.

1. 4×5	**2.** 8×6	**3.** 7×6	**4.** 3×0	**5.** 5×7	**6.** 9×7	**7.** 4×7
8. 7×8	**9.** 3×2	**10.** 9×9	**11.** 4×4	**12.** 6×6	**13.** 5×6	**14.** 7×7
15. 8×8	**16.** 5×5	**17.** 9×6	**18.** 4×6	**19.** 8×9	**20.** 3×1	**21.** 9×3

22. Give the next 6 multiples of 8.

×	0	1	2	3	4	5	6	7	8	9
8	0	8	16	24																																				

Find the missing factors.

23. ||||| $\times 4 = 12$ **24.** $3 \times$ ||||| $= 18$ **25.** ||||| $\times 2 = 10$ **26.** $3 \times$ ||||| $= 6$

27. $4 \times$ ||||| $= 20$ **28.** ||||| $\times 6 = 30$ **29.** $8 \times$ ||||| $= 24$ **30.** ||||| $\times 5 = 15$

Solve.

31.

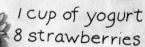

STRAWBERRY SMOOTHIE MIX
1 cup of yogurt
8 strawberries

How many strawberries would it take to make 6 smoothies?

32. Kevin has a plant that is 57 cm tall. Rob's plant is 48 cm tall. How much taller is Kevin's plant than Rob's?

1 2 3 4 5

Think 3 sevens → 21
and 3 sevens. → 21

$6 \times 7 = 42$

Think 6 fours → 24
and another 4. → 4

$7 \times 4 = 28$

Find the products.

1. 8×5 **2.** 5×9 **3.** 7×7

4. 6×5 **5.** 8×4 **6.** 7×9

7. 8×9 **8.** 7×6 **9.** 4×9

10. 4×6 **11.** 8×7 **12.** 9×9

$6 \times 2 = 12$
$6 \times 3 = 18$
$6 \times 4 = 24$
$6 \times 5 = 30$

$6 \times \text{▥} = 30$

Find the missing factors.

13. $5 \times \text{▥} = 20$ **14.** $\text{▥} \times 4 = 12$

15. $\text{▥} \times 5 = 10$ **16.** $9 \times \text{▥} = 27$

17. $\text{▥} \times 5 = 10$ **18.** $\text{▥} \times 6 = 18$

19. $2 \times \text{▥} = 6$ **20.** $5 \times \text{▥} = 35$

Logical Reasoning

Use the drawing to answer the questions.

1. How many ducks are in the shadow?

2. How many ducks are in the pond?

3. How many ducks are inside the fence?

4. How many ducks are inside the fence *and* in the shadow?

5. How many ducks are in the shadow but not in the pond?

6. How many ducks are not in the shadow and not in the pond?

7. How many ducks are in the pond, not in the shadow, and inside the fence?

8. How many ducks are in the pond, not inside the fence, and are in the shadow?

9. Tell where the colored duck is.

TECHNOLOGY

Flowcharts

Flowcharts show a step-by-step way of doing things. They are used to plan instructions for computers. Special shapes are used for the different steps.

(START)   or   (STOP)   [Instruction]   ◇ Question ◇

Sharpening a Pencil

(START)

↓

Put pencil in sharpener.

↓

Turn handle.

↓

Take pencil out of sharpener.

↓

(STOP)

Crossing the Street

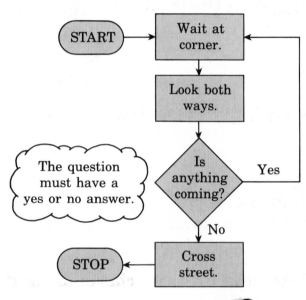

(START) → Wait at corner.

↓

Look both ways.

↓

The question must have a yes or no answer.

Is anything coming? — Yes →

↓ No

Cross street.

(STOP) ←

1. What is the second step in sharpening a pencil?

2. What do you do after you turn the handle?

3. What is the step after you wait at the corner?

4. If a car is coming, what do you do?

5. If there is nothing coming, what do you do?

Give the missing instructions.

1. Going to a Movie

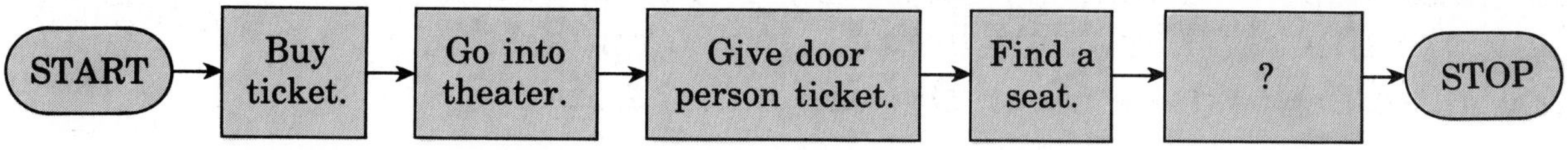

START → Buy ticket. → Go into theater. → Give door person ticket. → Find a seat. → ? → STOP

2. Watching a TV Show

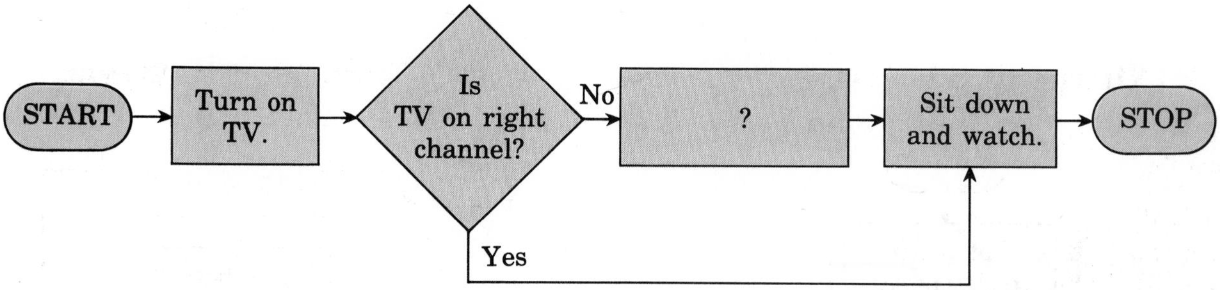

START → Turn on TV. → Is TV on right channel? → No → ? → Sit down and watch. → STOP

Yes

3. Calling on the Phone

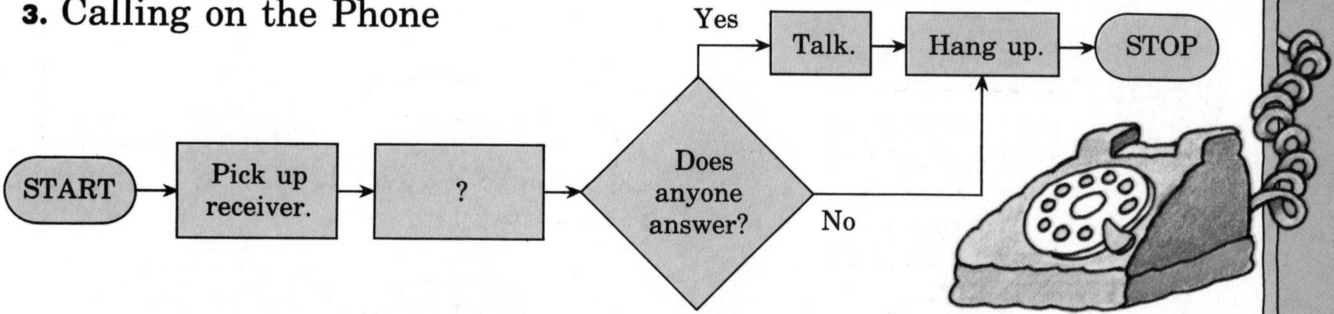

START → Pick up receiver. → ? → Does anyone answer? → Yes → Talk. → Hang up. → STOP

No

Make your own flowcharts using the following shapes.

4. Washing your Hands

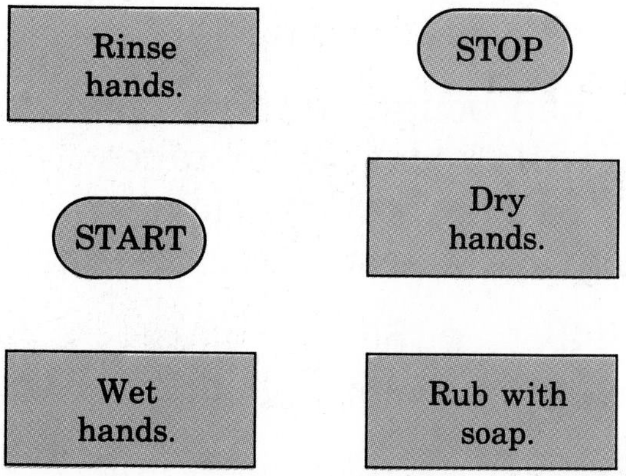

Rinse hands.

STOP

START

Dry hands.

Wet hands.

Rub with soap.

5. Planting a Tree

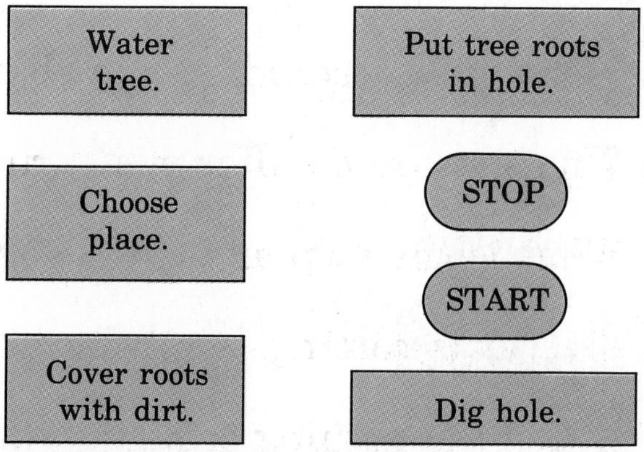

Water tree.

Put tree roots in hole.

Choose place.

STOP

START

Cover roots with dirt.

Dig hole.

Give the letter for the correct answer.

1. 53 rounded to the nearest ten

   A 60   B 50
   c 30   D not given

2. 87 rounded to the nearest ten

   A 70   B 80
   c 90   D not given

3. 351 rounded to the nearest ten

   A 360   B 340
   c 350   D not given

4. 246 rounded to the nearest ten

   A 240   B 250
   c 260   D not given

5. 2,375 rounded to the nearest hundred

   A 2,400   B 2,300
   c 2,000   D not given

6. 4,435 rounded to the nearest hundred

   A 4,500   B 4,400
   c 4,000   D not given

7. $\begin{array}{r} 26 \\ + 45 \end{array}$ A 71   B 73
   c 61   D not given

8. $\begin{array}{r} 63 \\ + 59 \end{array}$ A 112   B 113
   c 123   D not given

9. $\begin{array}{r} 256 \\ + 185 \end{array}$ A 341   B 331
   c 441   D not given

10. $\begin{array}{r} \$7.76 \\ + 1.35 \end{array}$ A $9.11   B $8.01
    c $8.11   D not given

11. $\begin{array}{r} 1,578 \\ + 7,456 \end{array}$ A 9,034   B 9,924
    c 7,034   D not given

12. $\begin{array}{r} 556 \\ 428 \\ + 119 \end{array}$ A 1,083   B 1,104
    c 1,103   D not given

13. Greg bought a game for $15, a ball for $8, and a book for $7. How much did he spend?

    A $30   B $32
    c $20   D not given

14. Carmen bought a radio for $38. She spent $9 for tapes and $12 on posters. How much did she spend?

    A $49   B $57
    c $59   D not given

Find the quotients.

1. $2\overline{)12}$ **2.** $3\overline{)24}$ **3.** $3\overline{)12}$ **4.** $2\overline{)14}$ **5.** $3\overline{)21}$ **6.** $2\overline{)6}$

7. $3\overline{)15}$ **8.** $2\overline{)10}$ **9.** $2\overline{)4}$ **10.** $3\overline{)18}$ **11.** $2\overline{)18}$ **12.** $3\overline{)9}$

13. $2\overline{)14}$ **14.** $3\overline{)21}$ **15.** $2\overline{)8}$ **16.** $3\overline{)6}$ **17.** $3\overline{)27}$ **18.** $2\overline{)16}$

19. $8 \div 2$ **20.** $21 \div 3$ **21.** $18 \div 2$ **22.** $12 \div 3$

23. $18 \div 3$ **24.** $6 \div 3$ **25.** $16 \div 2$ **26.** $6 \div 2$

27. $12 \div 2$ **28.** $4 \div 2$ **29.** $27 \div 3$ **30.** $15 \div 3$

31. $9 \div 3$ **32.** $10 \div 2$ **33.** $24 \div 3$ **34.** $14 \div 2$

Solve.

35. Romaine spent $16 for some tickets. The tickets cost $2 each. How many tickets did Romaine buy?

36. Nita had a 5-dollar bill and three 1-dollar bills. She spent all of her money for 2-dollar tickets. How many did she buy?

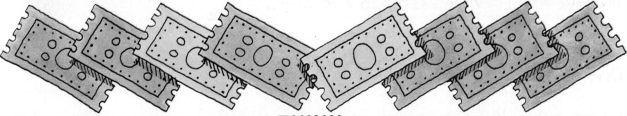

THINK

The Calculator Digits

You can build any of the calculator digits with 7 or fewer toothpicks. For example, 3 is a 5-toothpick digit.

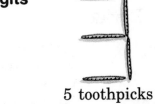

5 toothpicks

1. Which other digits take 5 toothpicks?
2. Which digit takes all 7 toothpicks?
3. Which digit takes fewest toothpicks?
4. Which digits take the same number of toothpicks as their number?

→ **MATH** ←

More Practice, page 398, Set C

Fact Families: Dividing by 4 and 5

4 × 5 = 20

If you know one multiplication fact, you know another multiplication fact and two division facts.

Fact Family

4 × 5 = 20
5 × 4 = 20
20 ÷ 5 = 4
20 ÷ 4 = 5

Warm Up   Find the products and quotients.

1. $4 \times 3 = n$	2. $5 \times 2 = n$	3. $3 \times 5 = n$	4. $2 \times 4 = n$
$3 \times 4 = n$	$2 \times 5 = n$	$5 \times 3 = n$	$4 \times 2 = n$
$12 \div 3 = n$	$10 \div 2 = n$	$15 \div 5 = n$	$8 \div 4 = n$
$12 \div 4 = n$	$10 \div 5 = n$	$15 \div 3 = n$	$8 \div 2 = n$

You can find quotients by thinking of missing factors.

THINK
? × 4 = 24

5. $24 \div 4 = n$

THINK
? × 5 = 35

6. $35 \div 5 = n$

THINK
? × 4 = 36

7. $36 \div 4 = n$

THINK
? × 5 = 40

8. $40 \div 5 = n$

THINK
? × 4 = 32

9. $32 \div 4 = n$

THINK
? × 5 = 45

10. $45 \div 5 = n$

110

Divide. Think about fact families or missing factors.

1. $12 \div 4$ **2.** $15 \div 5$ **3.** $14 \div 2$ **4.** $28 \div 4$

5. $20 \div 5$ **6.** $27 \div 3$ **7.** $40 \div 5$ **8.** $18 \div 2$

9. $16 \div 4$ **10.** $36 \div 4$ **11.** $21 \div 3$ **12.** $30 \div 5$

13. $4\overline{)8}$ **14.** $2\overline{)16}$ **15.** $5\overline{)45}$ **16.** $5\overline{)40}$ **17.** $3\overline{)15}$ **18.** $4\overline{)24}$

19. $5\overline{)10}$ **20.** $4\overline{)20}$ **21.** $3\overline{)18}$ **22.** $4\overline{)32}$ **23.** $5\overline{)35}$ **24.** $2\overline{)12}$

25. $5\overline{)20}$ **26.** $2\overline{)10}$ **27.** $4\overline{)36}$ **28.** $3\overline{)24}$ **29.** $4\overline{)28}$ **30.** $5\overline{)25}$

Write a multiplication and a division equation for each picture.

Example

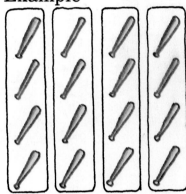

31.

32.

33.

34.

$$4 \times 4 = 16$$
$$16 \div 4 = 4$$

SKILLKEEPER

Find the products.

1. $\begin{array}{r} 3 \\ \times 9 \\ \hline \end{array}$ **2.** $\begin{array}{r} 5 \\ \times 6 \\ \hline \end{array}$ **3.** $\begin{array}{r} 4 \\ \times 8 \\ \hline \end{array}$ **4.** $\begin{array}{r} 2 \\ \times 7 \\ \hline \end{array}$ **5.** $\begin{array}{r} 8 \\ \times 6 \\ \hline \end{array}$ **6.** $\begin{array}{r} 7 \\ \times 7 \\ \hline \end{array}$

7. $\begin{array}{r} 9 \\ \times 8 \\ \hline \end{array}$ **8.** $\begin{array}{r} 0 \\ \times 9 \\ \hline \end{array}$ **9.** $\begin{array}{r} 7 \\ \times 8 \\ \hline \end{array}$ **10.** $\begin{array}{r} 9 \\ \times 9 \\ \hline \end{array}$ **11.** $\begin{array}{r} 5 \\ \times 5 \\ \hline \end{array}$ **12.** $\begin{array}{r} 6 \\ \times 7 \\ \hline \end{array}$

Division Properties

There are some special 0 and 1 properties for division.

Examples   Properties

$7 \times 1 = 7$
$7 \div 1 = 7$

Any number divided by 1 is that number.

$1 \times 6 = 6$
$6 \div 6 = 1$
Any number (not 0) divided by itself is 1.

$0 \times 4 = 0$
$0 \div 4 = 0$
Zero divided by any number (not 0) is 0.

$n \times 0 = 9$ $n \times 0 = 0$
$9 \div 0 = n$ $0 \div 0 = n$
Remember: We never divide by 0.

No number works.   Any number works.

Find the quotients.

1. $0 \div 8$	**2.** $9 \div 1$	**3.** $0 \div 2$	**4.** $4 \div 1$
5. $8 \div 8$	**6.** $28 \div 4$	**7.** $0 \div 6$	**8.** $30 \div 5$
9. $18 \div 3$	**10.** $3 \div 3$	**11.** $8 \div 1$	**12.** $5 \div 5$

13. $7\overline{)0}$ **14.** $4\overline{)24}$ **15.** $1\overline{)7}$ **16.** $5\overline{)45}$ **17.** $4\overline{)4}$ **18.** $5\overline{)0}$

19. $9\overline{)9}$ **20.** $3\overline{)0}$ **21.** $2\overline{)16}$ **22.** $1\overline{)3}$ **23.** $3\overline{)21}$ **24.** $1\overline{)5}$

25. $5\overline{)40}$ **26.** $1\overline{)6}$ **27.** $4\overline{)20}$ **28.** $4\overline{)0}$ **29.** $7\overline{)7}$ **30.** $5\overline{)35}$

PROBLEM SOLVING
Understanding the Operation

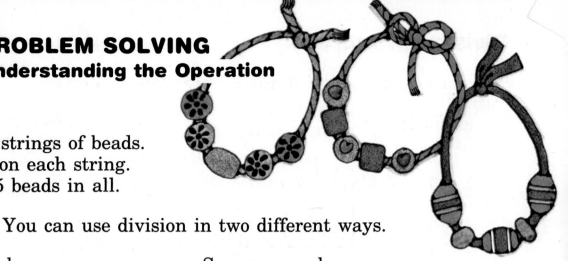

There are 3 strings of beads.
5 beads are on each string.
There are 15 beads in all.

You can use division in two different ways.

Suppose you know:
   15 beads, 5 for each string.

You can **divide** to find **how many strings.**

$$15 \div 5 = 3$$

There are 3 strings.

> Division can tell
> how many sets.

Suppose you know:
   15 beads, the same number on each of 3 strings.

You can **divide** to find **how many on each string.**

$$15 \div 3 = 5$$

There are 5 beads on each string.

> Division can tell
> how many in each set.

Solve.

1. There are 20 beads. Put the same number on each of 4 strings. How many beads are on each string?

2. Janis has 12 beads. She puts 3 beads on each string. How many strings does she have?

3. There are 16 berries. The berries are shared equally by 4 children. How many berries are there for each child?

4. Alex spent 15 dollars for tickets. Each ticket cost 5 dollars. How many tickets did he buy?

5. Phil bought 7 tickets. He spent 14 dollars. How much was each ticket?

6. *Try This* Lyn can buy an A ticket, a B ticket, or a C ticket. How many ways can Lyn buy 2 different tickets? Hint: Make a list.

113

PROBLEM SOLVING ⭐ Using the 5-Point Checklist

To solve a problem
- ☆ 1. Understand the Question
- ☆ 2. Find the needed Data
- ☆ 3. Plan what to do
- ☆ 4. Find the Answer
- ☆ 5. Check back

QUESTION
DATA
PLAN
ANSWER
CHECK

Made in Denver 1924

Liberty Dime

Large Cent—1851

Use the 5-Point Checklist to help you solve the following problem.

Jasmine has a 1924 penny made in Denver. Robin has an 1851 Large Cent. How many years apart are these dates?

1. Understand the QUESTION
   What is the difference in the two dates?

2. Find the needed DATA
   Denver penny: 1924   Large Cent: 1851

3. PLAN what to do
   Since we want the difference in two numbers, we subtract.

4. Find the ANSWER
   $1924 - 1851 = 73$ The dates are 73 years apart.

Indian Head Penny

5. CHECK back
   Check by adding 73 to 1851. 73 seems about right.

Solve. Use the 5-Point Checklist.

1. Tod has Denver pennies in his coin book. One page has 5 rows with 4 in each row. How many pennies is this?

2. Lisa has 18 Denver pennies. She will put them in 3 rows in her coin book. How many should she put in each row?

114

Solve.

1. Sal has a 1901 Indian head penny. He also has a Denver penny made 28 years later. What is the date of his Denver penny?

2. Glen has one page of Lincoln head pennies. It has 6 rows with 5 pennies in each row. How many pennies does he have?

3. Dotty has 20 coins to put in her book. She puts 4 coins in each row. How many rows does she have?

4. Leah has an 1851 Large Cent that is worth $7.95. She has an Indian head penny worth $2.75. How much are both coins worth?

5. Eva put 24 coins in rows of 4 in her book. How many rows does she have?

6. Lou put 12 coins in rows of 4 in his book. How many rows did he make?

7. Jill has 8 Indian head pennies and 12 Lincoln head pennies. She put them into 5 equal rows. How many did she put in each row?

8. Della sold 8 Large Cents for $6 each. She also sold a Liberty dime for $7. How much money did she get?

9. *Try This* Al has 15 pennies on one page. They are either Indian head or Denver pennies. There are 3 more Indian head pennies than Denver pennies. How many Denver pennies are on the page?

Dividing by 6 and 7

Lynn bought 42 cans of juice. They are packaged in boxes of 6. How many boxes of juice did Lynn buy?

$$42 \div 6 = 7$$

Lynn bought 7 boxes of juice.

Lynn plans to use one can of juice each day. How many weeks will the 42 cans last?

$$42 \div 7 = 6$$

The juice will last 6 weeks.

Warm Up Divide.

THINK
$? \times 6 = 30$

1. $30 \div 6 = n$

THINK
$? \times 7 = 28$

2. $28 \div 7 = n$

THINK
$? \times 6 = 48$

3. $48 \div 6 = n$

THINK
$? \times 7 = 63$

4. $63 \div 7 = n$

THINK
$? \times 6 = 18$

5. $18 \div 6 = n$

THINK
$? \times 6 = 54$

6. $54 \div 6 = n$

7. $6\overline{)30}$ **8.** $7\overline{)35}$ **9.** $7\overline{)28}$ **10.** $6\overline{)48}$ **11.** $7\overline{)56}$

12. $7\overline{)49}$ **13.** $6\overline{)54}$ **14.** $7\overline{)63}$ **15.** $6\overline{)36}$ **16.** $6\overline{)24}$

Find the quotients.

1. $18 \div 6$

2. $35 \div 5$

3. $14 \div 2$

4. $14 \div 7$

5. $42 \div 6$

6. $8 \div 1$

7. $24 \div 3$

8. $56 \div 7$

9. $54 \div 6$

10. $40 \div 5$

11. $12 \div 6$

12. $24 \div 4$

13. $7 \div 7$

14. $49 \div 7$

15. $42 \div 7$

16. $32 \div 4$

17. $21 \div 3$

18. $24 \div 6$

19. $6\overline{)54}$

20. $4\overline{)36}$

21. $7\overline{)63}$

22. $7\overline{)0}$

23. $5\overline{)30}$

24. $2\overline{)18}$

25. $7\overline{)35}$

26. $6\overline{)6}$

27. $6\overline{)36}$

28. $3\overline{)27}$

29. $6\overline{)48}$

30. $5\overline{)45}$

31. $7\overline{)21}$

32. $6\overline{)42}$

33. $4\overline{)28}$

34. $7\overline{)49}$

35. $7\overline{)56}$

36. $9\overline{)81}$

37. $7\overline{)42}$

38. $9\overline{)72}$

39. Divide 35 by 7.

40. Divide 45 by 9.

41. Divide 54 by 6.

42. Divide 30 by 6.

43. Divide 63 by 7.

44. Divide 56 by 7.

Solve.

45. Karl bought 48 cans of grape juice. They were packed in boxes of 6. How many boxes did he buy?

46. Write a question for this data. Solve your own problem. Justin bought 24 cans of orange juice and 18 cans of grapefruit juice. He uses one of these cans of juice each day.

THINK

Calculator

Rules: You can only press these keys: 6 + − X ÷ =

1. Make your display read 7.

2. Make your display read 13.

MATH

Dividing by 8 and 9

There were 72 students going to the picnic. There were 9 station wagons to take them. How many students should ride in each one?

Eight students should ride in each station wagon.

When all 72 students arrived, they divided equally into 8 baseball teams. How many were on each team?

There were 9 students on each team.

$$8 \times 9 = 72$$

$$72 \div 9 = 8$$

$$9 \times 8 = 72$$

$$72 \div 8 = 9$$

Warm Up Divide.

THINK
? × 8 = 32

1. $32 \div 8 = n$

THINK
? × 9 = 27

2. $27 \div 9 = n$

THINK
? × 8 = 40

3. $40 \div 8 = n$

THINK
? × 9 = 45

4. $45 \div 9 = n$

THINK
? × 8 = 56

5. $56 \div 8 = n$

THINK
? × 9 = 54

6. $54 \div 9 = n$

7. $9\overline{)72}$ **8.** $8\overline{)40}$ **9.** $9\overline{)54}$ **10.** $9\overline{)36}$ **11.** $8\overline{)16}$

12. $8\overline{)64}$ **13.** $9\overline{)81}$ **14.** $8\overline{)72}$ **15.** $9\overline{)63}$ **16.** $9\overline{)18}$

Find the quotients.

1. $40 \div 8$ 2. $35 \div 7$ 3. $45 \div 9$ 4. $48 \div 6$

5. $32 \div 4$ 6. $81 \div 9$ 7. $40 \div 5$ 8. $24 \div 8$

9. $36 \div 9$ 10. $72 \div 8$ 11. $49 \div 7$ 12. $20 \div 4$

13. $35 \div 5$ 14. $30 \div 6$ 15. $18 \div 9$ 16. $64 \div 8$

17. $8 \div 8$ 18. $63 \div 9$ 19. $24 \div 4$ 20. $56 \div 7$

21. $6\overline{)36}$ 22. $9\overline{)9}$ 23. $8\overline{)56}$ 24. $7\overline{)42}$ 25. $4\overline{)28}$

26. $8\overline{)48}$ 27. $5\overline{)25}$ 28. $6\overline{)54}$ 29. $9\overline{)27}$ 30. $8\overline{)32}$

31. $4\overline{)36}$ 32. $9\overline{)54}$ 33. $7\overline{)63}$ 34. $8\overline{)16}$ 35. $6\overline{)42}$

36. Divide 63 by 9.   37. Divide 49 by 7.   38. Divide 48 by 8.

39. Divide 32 by 8.   40. Divide 40 by 8.   41. Divide 54 by 9.

Solve.

42. There were 54 students and 9 picnic tables. The same number of students sat at each table. How many were at each table?

43. There were 48 students who left the picnic early. 8 rode in each station wagon. How many station wagons were needed?

★ 44. After the 48 students left, the rest divided into 4 equal teams for volleyball. How many were on each team?

THINK

Logical Reasoning

Find the mystery number.

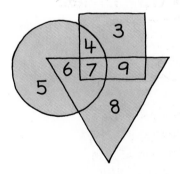

1. It is inside the circle.
2. It is inside the square.
3. It is not inside the triangle.

→ MATH ←

Practice the Facts

Find the quotients.

1. 30 ÷ 5   2. 42 ÷ 7   3. 24 ÷ 3   4. 36 ÷ 6

5. 54 ÷ 9   6. 16 ÷ 2   7. 72 ÷ 8   8. 28 ÷ 4

9. 21 ÷ 3   10. 40 ÷ 5   11. 10 ÷ 2   12. 56 ÷ 7

13. 24 ÷ 6   14. 32 ÷ 4   15. 28 ÷ 7   16. 63 ÷ 9

17. 2 ÷ 2   18. 48 ÷ 6   19. 15 ÷ 3   20. 25 ÷ 5

21. $4\overline{)24}$ 22. $6\overline{)18}$ 23. $3\overline{)27}$ 24. $6\overline{)54}$ 25. $5\overline{)45}$

26. $7\overline{)63}$ 27. $5\overline{)35}$ 28. $2\overline{)18}$ 29. $4\overline{)0}$ 30. $9\overline{)81}$

31. $8\overline{)48}$ 32. $1\overline{)3}$ 33. $4\overline{)36}$ 34. $5\overline{)20}$ 35. $2\overline{)14}$

36. Divide 35 by 7.   37. Divide 27 by 9.   38. Divide 72 by 9.

39. Divide 56 by 8.   40. Divide 63 by 9.   41. Divide 42 by 6.

Copy and complete each table.

Divide by 7	
42	6
42. 56					
43. 28					
44. 63					
45. 35					
46. 49					

Divide by 8	
32	4
47. 56					
48. 72					
49. 40					
50. 48					
51. 64					

Divide by 9	
45	5
52. 54					
53. 81					
54. 63					
55. 36					
56. 72					

Factors

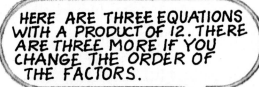

HERE ARE THREE EQUATIONS WITH A PRODUCT OF 12. THERE ARE THREE MORE IF YOU CHANGE THE ORDER OF THE FACTORS.

Factor		Factor		Product
1	×	12	=	12
2	×	6	=	12
3	×	4	=	12

THE FACTORS OF 12 ARE 1, 2, 3, 4, 6, AND 12.

Other Examples

$1 \times 6 = 6$
$2 \times 3 = 6$

The factors of 6 are 1, 2, 3, and 6.

$1 \times 4 = 4$
$2 \times 2 = 4$

The factors of 4 are 1, 2, and 4.

$1 \times 3 = 3$

The factors of 3 are 1 and 3.

Copy and complete the equations.
Then list all the factors of the product.

1. $1 \times \text{▦} = 8$
$2 \times \text{▦} = 8$

2. $1 \times \text{▦} = 2$

3. $1 \times \text{▦} = 9$
$3 \times \text{▦} = 9$

4. $1 \times \text{▦} = 5$

5. $1 \times \text{▦} = 10$
$2 \times \text{▦} = 10$

6. $1 \times \text{▦} = 7$

7. $1 \times \text{▦} = 15$
$3 \times \text{▦} = 15$

8. $1 \times \text{▦} = 16$
$2 \times \text{▦} = 16$
$4 \times \text{▦} = 16$

9. $1 \times \text{▦} = 18$
$2 \times \text{▦} = 18$
$3 \times \text{▦} = 18$

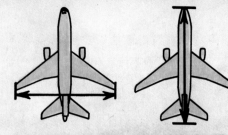

Aircraft	Wingspan*	Length*
DC-9	28	36
DC-10	47	56
L-1011	47	54
727	33	47
747	60	71
767	48	49

* Approximate number of meters

Use the data given in the table to solve these problems.

1. How much longer is the 747 than the DC-9?

2. Charles Lindbergh made the first solo flight across the Atlantic Ocean. It would take 7 of Lindbergh's planes end-to-end to be as long as a DC-10. How long was Lindbergh's plane?

1927

3. The DC-8 has a wingspan that is 17 m greater than the DC-9. What is the wingspan of the DC-8?

4. An early private plane had a length of 7 m. A 737 jet is just 4 times that long. How long is the 737?

5. If you add the length and the wingspan of the DC-9 and divide by 8, you'll have its approximate height. About how high is the DC-9?

★ 6. The Wright brothers built the first plane to achieve true flight. The wingspan of the DC-9 is just 4 times that of one of their gliders. What was the wingspan of the glider?

7. **Try This** The DC-8 is longer than the A300. The DC-8 is shorter than the Concorde. The A300 is longer than the 757. Which of the planes is longest?

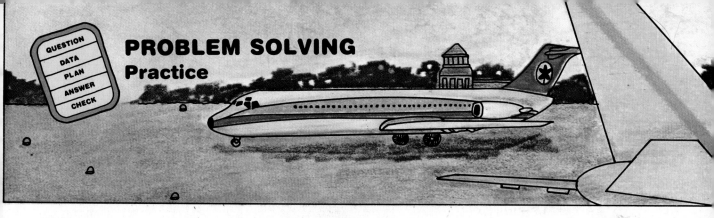

PROBLEM SOLVING
Practice

QUESTION
DATA
PLAN
ANSWER
CHECK

Solve.

1. A 747 carried 529 people from Los Angeles to Honolulu and 487 on the return trip. What was the total number of people?

2. The 747 can seat 550 people. The 767 can seat 289 people. How many more people can the 747 seat?

3. There were 63 crew members working on Friday. 7 of them were on each flight. How many flights was this?

4. A 747 plane has 550 seats. Only 67 seats are empty. How many seats are used?

5. There were 7 flight crews who reported for work on Monday. There were 8 people in each crew. How many people reported for work?

6. One section has 72 seats. Each row has 9 seats. How many rows are there?

7. There were 5 crews with 6 people each and 7 crews with 8 people each. How many people is this?

8. The late flight crews had 29 men and 27 women. There were 8 flights with the same number of crew members on each flight. How many were on each flight?

9. DATA BANK See page 387. How many more can an L-1011 seat than a DC-10?

10. Try This There were 13 crew members for two flights. The early flight had 3 more members than the late flight. How many crew members were on each flight?

PROBLEM SOLVING
Make a Table

QUESTION
DATA
PLAN
ANSWER
CHECK

Try This Hiro is riding his bicycle. He rides 2 miles every 10 minutes. At this rate, how far will he go in 60 minutes?

TO SOLVE A PROBLEM SUCH AS THIS, YOU MAY NEED TO DO MORE THAN JUST ADD, SUBTRACT, MULTIPLY, OR DIVIDE. A STRATEGY THAT MIGHT HELP YOU IS GIVEN BELOW.

MAKE A TABLE

FIRST, I'LL MAKE A TABLE AND WRITE WHAT I KNOW.

NOW I'LL FILL IN THE TABLE TO FIND THE ANSWER.

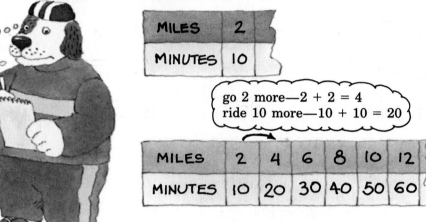

MILES	2
MINUTES	10

go 2 more—2 + 2 = 4
ride 10 more—10 + 10 = 20

MILES	2	4	6	8	10	12
MINUTES	10	20	30	40	50	60

When the number reaches 60 minutes, you will have the number of miles in your table.

Hiro will ride 12 miles in 60 minutes.

Solve.

1. A recipe calls for 3 eggs and 4 cups of flour. A baker used 24 eggs. How many cups of flour did he use? Copy and complete the table.

EGGS	3	6	9
FLOUR	4	8	12

2. Cups are $3 and saucers are $2. How much will you have to spend for saucers if you spend $27 for cups? Copy and complete the table.

CUPS	$3	$6	$9	$12
SAUCERS	$2	$4	$6	$8

124

Find the quotients.

1. 32 ÷ 4   **2.** 63 ÷ 9   **3.** 30 ÷ 5   **4.** 42 ÷ 7

5. 56 ÷ 8   **6.** 0 ÷ 2   **7.** 30 ÷ 6   **8.** 35 ÷ 5

9. 21 ÷ 3   **10.** 48 ÷ 6   **11.** 36 ÷ 4   **12.** 28 ÷ 7

13. 7)35   **14.** 3)27   **15.** 5)45   **16.** 6)18   **17.** 4)28

18. 9)45   **19.** 6)6   **20.** 8)64   **21.** 9)36   **22.** 2)16

23. 9)54   **24.** 6)36   **25.** 8)48   **26.** 9)72   **27.** 4)24

28. 7)49   **29.** 5)40   **30.** 1)7   **31.** 4)36   **32.** 7)28

33. 3)24   **34.** 8)32   **35.** 2)14   **36.** 6)42   **37.** 5)25

38. List all the factors of 15.   **39.** List all the factors of 17.

$$1 \times 5 = 15$$
$$3 \times 5 = 15$$

$$1 \times 17 = 17$$

Solve.

40. Linda has 48 Lincoln pennies to put in her book. Each row of the book holds 6 pennies. How many rows can she fill?

41. There were 8 planes leaving in the next hour. Each one had a crew of 7. How many crew members is this in all?

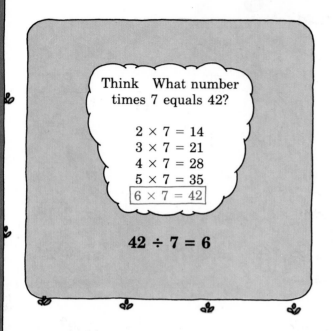

Think What number
times 7 equals 42?

$2 \times 7 = 14$
$3 \times 7 = 21$
$4 \times 7 = 28$
$5 \times 7 = 35$
$\boxed{6 \times 7 = 42}$

$42 \div 7 = 6$

Find the quotients.

1. $45 \div 5$ **2.** $35 \div 7$

3. $12 \div 2$ **4.** $24 \div 6$

5. $72 \div 9$ **6.** $8 \div 8$

7. $32 \div 8$ **8.** $27 \div 3$

9. $36 \div 4$ **10.** $21 \div 7$

11. $28 \div 4$ **12.** $81 \div 9$

13. $16 \div 8$ **14.** $63 \div 9$

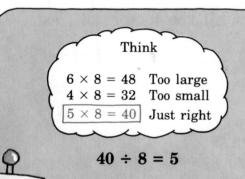

Think

$6 \times 8 = 48$ Too large
$4 \times 8 = 32$ Too small
$\boxed{5 \times 8 = 40}$ Just right

$40 \div 8 = 5$

15. $6\overline{)30}$ **16.** $2\overline{)14}$ **17.** $9\overline{)63}$

18. $9\overline{)81}$ **19.** $7\overline{)42}$ **20.** $5\overline{)40}$

21. $4\overline{)24}$ **22.** $6\overline{)0}$ **23.** $6\overline{)12}$

24. $8\overline{)40}$ **25.** $5\overline{)30}$ **26.** $1\overline{)7}$

27. $2\overline{)18}$ **28.** $6\overline{)18}$ **29.** $3\overline{)18}$

Prime Numbers

When a number has just two **different** factors, itself and 1, the number is a **PRIME NUMBER.**

7 has no other factors.
7 is prime.

$$7 \times 1 = 7$$

↑ Factor ↑ Factor

Other Examples

3 is prime.

$$3 \times 1 = 3$$

15 is not prime.

$$15 \times 1 = 15$$
$$5 \times 3 = 15$$

17 is prime.

$$17 \times 1 = 17$$

1. Is 9 prime?

$9 \times 1 = 9$
$3 \times 3 = 9$

2. Is 5 prime?

$5 \times 1 = 5$

3. Is 13 prime?

$13 \times 1 = 13$

4. Is 2 prime?

$2 \times 1 = 2$

5. Is 21 prime?

$21 \times 1 = 21$
$7 \times 3 = 21$

6. Is 25 prime?

$25 \times 1 = 25$
$5 \times 5 = 25$

7. Which of these four numbers are prime?

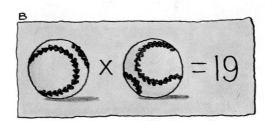

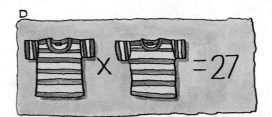

CUMULATIVE REVIEW

Give the letter for the correct answer.

1. $2 + 4$
   - **A** 5
   - **B** 6
   - **C** 8
   - **D** not given

2. $6 + 8$
   - **A** 14
   - **B** 13
   - **C** 12
   - **D** not given

3. $3 + 9$
   - **A** 11
   - **B** 13
   - **C** 12
   - **D** not given

4. $5 + 7$
   - **A** 13
   - **B** 12
   - **C** 15
   - **D** not given

5. $10 - 5$
   - **A** 5
   - **B** 4
   - **C** 6
   - **D** not given

6. $15 - 7$
   - **A** 9
   - **B** 7
   - **C** 8
   - **D** not given

7. $12 - 8$
   - **A** 2
   - **B** 4
   - **C** 3
   - **D** not given

8. $88 - 69$
   - **A** 29
   - **B** 21
   - **C** 19
   - **D** not given

9. $782 - 367$
   - **A** 315
   - **B** 425
   - **C** 415
   - **D** not given

10. $560 - 58$
    - **A** 502
    - **B** 518
    - **C** 512
    - **D** not given

11. $\$7.52 - 3.75$
    - **A** $3.77
    - **B** $4.23
    - **C** $4.87
    - **D** not given

12. $\$4.76 - 3.78$
    - **A** $1.08
    - **B** $1.98
    - **C** $1.02
    - **D** not given

13. A paint set costs $9.50. Ann has $5.75. How much more will she need to buy the paint set?
    - **A** $3.75
    - **B** $4.25
    - **C** $4.85
    - **D** not given

14. Curtis has 282 stamps. Todd has 321 stamps. How many more stamps does Todd have?
    - **A** 161
    - **B** 49
    - **C** 39
    - **D** not given

128

MEASUREMENT: Metric Units

6

The gym clock read 4:25. They had been playing for 1 hour. There were 5 seconds left in the fourth quarter. The score was 44 to 43. The other team was ahead. Tyler held the ball tightly. He had made baskets from this far away before. But it was not an easy angle. At his old school Tyler had been one of the best players. Making this basket would show the new coach how good he was. Tyler saw that a teammate near the basket was open. The coach was always talking about how important teamwork was. Four seconds left . . .

Telling Time

Alan was supposed to be home by 6 o'clock. He looked at his watch when he walked in the door. Did he make it?

Alan did make it. He was 10 minutes early!

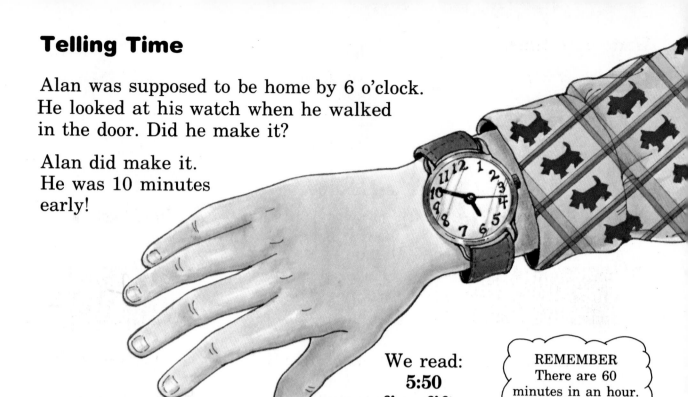

We read:
5:50
five fifty
10 minutes to 6

> REMEMBER
> There are 60
> minutes in an hour.

Other Examples

We read:
10:15
ten fifteen
15 minutes past 10
quarter past 10

We read:
two forty-five
15 minutes to 3
quarter to 3

We read:
3:30
three thirty
half past 3

Warm Up   Give each time.

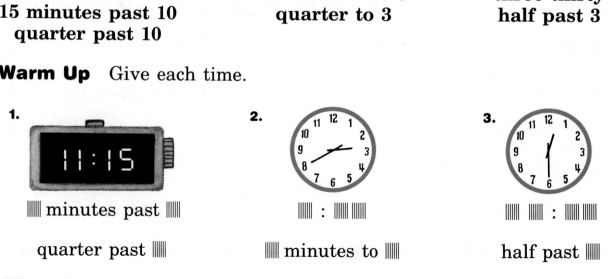

1.

||||| minutes past |||||

quarter past |||||

2.

||||| : ||||| |||||

||||| minutes to |||||

3.

||||| ||||| : ||||| |||||

half past |||||

130

Write each time.

1.

|||| minutes past |||||

quarter past |||||

2.

||||| : ||||| |||||

|||| minutes to |||||

3.

||||| ||||| : ||||| |||||

half past |||||

4.

|||| minutes past |||||

quarter past |||||

5.

|||| minutes to |||||

quarter to |||||

6.

|||| minutes to |||||

|||| minutes past |||||

7.

||||| : ||||| |||||

|||| minutes to |||||

★ **8.**

||||| ||||| : ||||| |||||

|||| minutes past |||||

★ **9.**

||||| : ||||| |||||

|||| minutes to |||||

Match.

10. 6:05   **A** 20 minutes to 3

11. 3:20   **B** quarter past 10

12. 10:15   **c** 5 minutes to 6

13. 2:40   **D** quarter to 10

14. 5:55   **E** 5 minutes past 6

15. 9:45   **F** 20 minutes past 3

THINK

Estimating Time

The minute hand has fallen off these clocks. Estimate the times.

MATH

131

a.m. and p.m.

The hour hand goes around twice each day, once for the a.m. hours and once for the p.m. hours.

The minute hand goes around once each hour.

The hours between midnight and noon are the a.m. hours.

The hours between noon and midnight are the p.m. hours.

MIDNIGHT　　8:05 a.m.　　NOON　　8:05 p.m.　　MIDNIGHT

Write each time as a.m. or p.m.

1. Lois got up early and ate breakfast at 7:00 ▓ .

2. Guy was out of school and roller-skating by 3:15 ▓ .

3. Carol had an early lunch at 11:30 ▓ .

4. On Saturday Dean likes to sleep until 8:00 ▓ .

5. One afternoon May rode her bicycle until 5:00 ▓ .

6. Kirk fished all day until 6:00 ▓ .

7. One night the late show wasn't over until 1:45 ▓ .

8. Kay's family has dinner at 6:30 ▓ .

9. Paco's school starts at 8:45 ▓ .

10. Peg's has afternoon recess at 2:10 ▓ .

PROBLEM SOLVING
Using Data from a Table

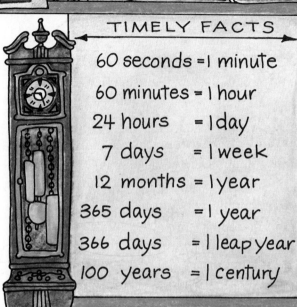

TIMELY FACTS

60 seconds	= 1 minute
60 minutes	= 1 hour
24 hours	= 1 day
7 days	= 1 week
12 months	= 1 year
365 days	= 1 year
366 days	= 1 leap year
100 years	= 1 century

Use the data in the table to solve the following problems.

1. Mike's school is open 180 days each year. How many days is his school closed in a leap year?

2. Helen sleeps 9 hours each night. How many hours is Helen awake each day?

3. School is divided into 6-week periods. How many days are in 6 weeks?

4. Summer vacation lasted for 63 days. How many weeks was this?

5. Cathy swam underwater for 27 seconds. How much less than 1 minute was this?

6. Gregory went to school for 180 days and summer school for 38 days. During a regular year, how many days was he not in school?

★ 7. Brian jogged for 37 minutes. Then for 26 minutes he walked to cool off. Did his jogging and walking take more or less than 1 hour?

8. *Try This* Mr. Hill gives piano lessons to 3 boys and 4 girls every day except Sunday. When he has taught 18 boys, how many girls has he taught? Hint: Complete the table.

boys	3	6	9	
girls	4	8	12	

More About Time

Dina gets out of school for lunch at 11:30 a.m. She has 45 minutes. What time should she be back to school?

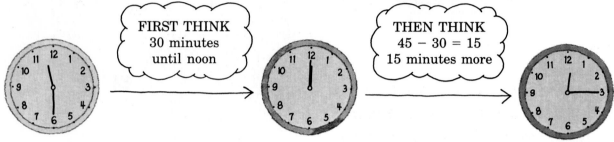

FIRST THINK
30 minutes
until noon

THEN THINK
45 − 30 = 15
15 minutes more

Dina should be back to school by 12:15 p.m.

Other Examples

5 hours later than 10:00 a.m.   40 minutes before 7:10 a.m.

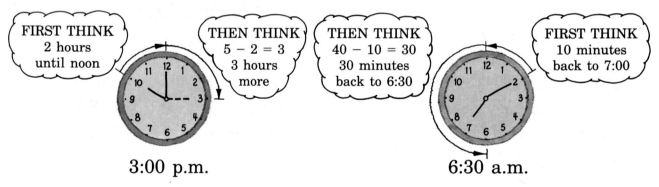

FIRST THINK
2 hours
until noon

THEN THINK
5 − 2 = 3
3 hours
more

THEN THINK
40 − 10 = 30
30 minutes
back to 6:30

FIRST THINK
10 minutes
back to 7:00

3:00 p.m.   6:30 a.m.

Give the times.

1. What time was it 5 hours before 2:00 p.m.?

2. What time will it be 25 minutes after 8:50 a.m.?

3. What time was it 45 minutes before 4:55 p.m.?

4. What time will it be 8 hours after 9:00 a.m.?

Solve.

1. Jane Ruel goes to work at 8:00 a.m. She is at the office for 8 hours. What time does she leave work?

2. Frank Winters owns a paint store. He opens at 9:00 a.m. and stays open for 9 hours. What time does he close?

3. School starts at 8:10 a.m. Amy needs 20 minutes to get there. What time should she leave for school?

4. Roger Woo needs 50 minutes to drive to work. He must be there at 8:30 a.m. What time should he leave for work?

5. Adam James is a guard. He starts work at 10:00 p.m. and works for 8 hours. What time does he get off?

6. Gail takes 45 minutes to get ready for school. What time should she get up if she wants to leave home at 7:30 a.m.?

7. Lena works 2 hours each day. She starts at 3:30 p.m. What time does she get off from work?

8. Ron gets paid by the hour for baby-sitting. One night he started at 7:30 p.m. and quit at 12:30 a.m. How many hours did he baby-sit?

★ 9. Ruth Fine starts work at 8:45 a.m. She works 7 hours and 30 minutes. What time does she get off from work?

Reading the Calendar

Use the calendar art to help you answer the following questions. The months are shown in order from top to bottom beginning with the first month, January.

1. What is the seventh month?

2. The first Wednesday in December is December 2. What is the date of the fourth Wednesday?

3. The Camera Club meets on the second Tuesday of each month. On what date will they meet in December?

4. The Stamp Club usually meets on the fourth Friday. In December, they met 5 days late. When did they meet?

5. How many days is it from the second Thursday to the third Monday?

6. Jo gave her birth date like this: 6/24/77. This means the 6th month, the 24th day of 1977. Write your birth date that way.

7. Write today's date like Jo would.

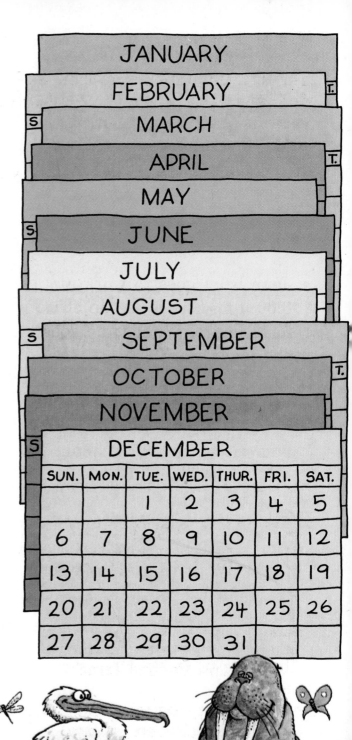

JANUARY
FEBRUARY
MARCH
APRIL
MAY
JUNE
JULY
AUGUST
SEPTEMBER
OCTOBER
NOVEMBER
DECEMBER

SUN.	MON.	TUE.	WED.	THUR.	FRI.	SAT.
		1	2	3	4	5
6	7	8	9	10	11	12
13	14	15	16	17	18	19
20	21	22	23	24	25	26
27	28	29	30	31		

Time Zones

The time-zone map shows times in different parts of the United States when it is 12:00 noon in the Central zone.

Use the map to answer the following questions.

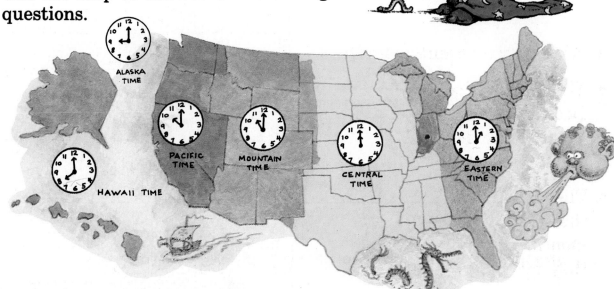

1. What is the Eastern Time?

2. What is the Mountain Time?

3. What is the Alaska Time?

4. How many hours' difference is there between Eastern Time and Pacific Time?

5. How many hours' difference is there between Central Time and Hawaii Time?

6. When it is 12:00 noon Pacific Time, what time is it in the Eastern Time zone?

7. When it is 12:00 midnight Eastern Time, what is the Hawaii Time?

★ 8. Suppose you leave Chicago (Central Time) at 9:00 a.m. on a nonstop flight to Hawaii. You arrive in Hawaii at 2:00 p.m. How long was your flight?

9. DATA HUNT Look up world time zones. Plan a phone call to London. Find out what time you should call so that it will be 10:00 a.m. in London.

Measuring with Centimeter Units

Sara is making a small planter box. She cut the board below for one of the end pieces. What is the length of the board to the nearest centimeter?

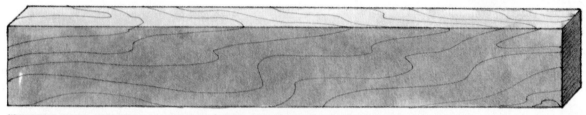

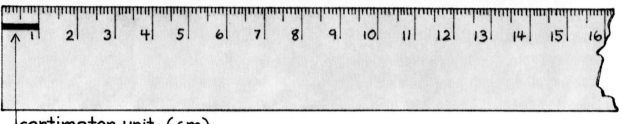

centimeter unit (cm)

The length of the board to the nearest centimeter is 15 cm.

Warm Up

Sara used different size nails for the planter box. Give the length to the nearest centimeter.

1.   2.   3.

Sara cut these sticks for signs. Give the length to the nearest centimeter.

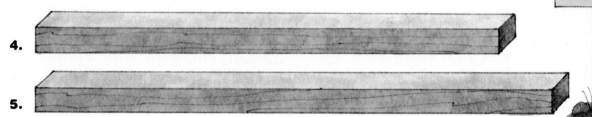

4.

5.

Sara kept a record of how corn, peppers, and beans grew for a three-week period. Write the height of each plant to the nearest centimeter.

first week second week third week

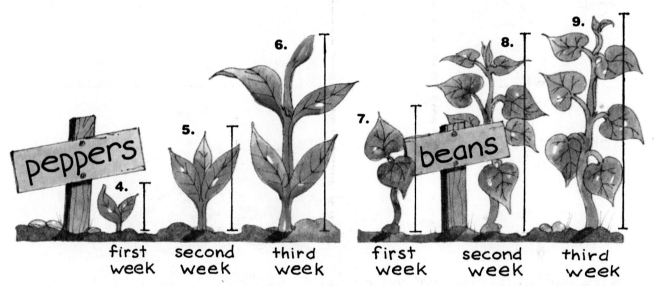

first week second week third week first week second week third week

10. Which plant was tallest the first week?

11. Which plant was tallest the second week?

12. Which plant grew the least in the three weeks?

Find a box in your classroom.

13. How tall is the box?

14. How long is the box?

15. How wide is the box?

THINK

Estimation

Suppose this is the unit. ▭
(Length 1)

Estimate each of these lengths.

1. ▭

2. ▭

Find a way to check your estimate.

MATH

139

Meters and Kilometers

The **meter** is a large metric unit used to measure length or distance.

1 meter (m) = 100 centimeters

Trudy found that a meter stick came up to the underside of her arm.

The **kilometer** is a still larger unit used to measure distance.

1 kilometer (km) = 1,000 meters

You might walk 1 km in about 10 minutes.

Warm Up Give the missing unit **m** or **km**.

1. The distance across town is 7 __?__.

2. The tree is 10 __?__ tall.

3. Jane ran in the 400 __?__ race.

4. The jet is flying 8 __?__ high.

5. Copy and complete the table to show how far you could walk in different amounts of time.

km	1	2	3	▓	▓	▓
minutes	10	20	30	▓	▓	60

6. If it takes you 20 minutes to walk to school, about how far is it?

7. Suppose you walk for an hour. About how far will you have walked?

Write the missing unit **cm**, **m**, or **km**.

1. The pool is 40 _?_ long.
2. The pencil is 14 _?_ long.
3. The bus traveled 80 _?_ in an hour.
4. The door is 2 _?_ high.
5. The plant is 5 _?_ high.
6. The lake is 5 _?_ long.

Solve.

7. Suppose you ride your bicycle 3 km in 10 minutes. Copy and complete the table to show how far you could ride in different amounts of time.

km	3	6	9	|||||	|||||	|||||
minutes	10	20	30	|||||	|||||	60

8. If it takes you 40 minutes to ride to the park, about how far is it?

9. About how far can you ride in an hour?

10. Suppose you can drive a car 15 km in 10 minutes. Copy and complete the table to show how far you can drive in different amounts of time.

km	15	30	45	|||||	|||||	|||||
minutes	10	20	30	|||||	|||||	60

11. If it takes 50 minutes to drive to the lake, about how far is the lake?

12. About how far can you drive in an hour?

SKILLKEEPER

Divide.

1. $4\overline{)36}$
2. $5\overline{)35}$
3. $7\overline{)56}$
4. $9\overline{)81}$
5. $8\overline{)72}$

6. $6\overline{)54}$
7. $3\overline{)27}$
8. $8\overline{)64}$
9. $5\overline{)20}$
10. $6\overline{)36}$

Perimeter

Casey drew a plan for a pen for his dog. He wanted to know how much fence he would need to go all the way around.

The distance around a figure is its **perimeter.**

To find the perimeter, we add the lengths of the sides.

$$\begin{array}{r} \overset{2}{19} \\ 14 \\ 19 \\ +\ 14 \\ \hline 66 \end{array}$$

The perimeter of the pen is 66 m.

Casey will need 66 m of fence.

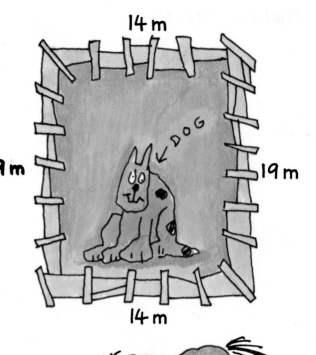

Warm Up   Find the perimeter.

1.

18 cm

34 cm   34 cm

18 cm

2.

32 m   40 m

29 m

3.

130 cm

62 cm   62 cm

130 cm

Find the perimeter.

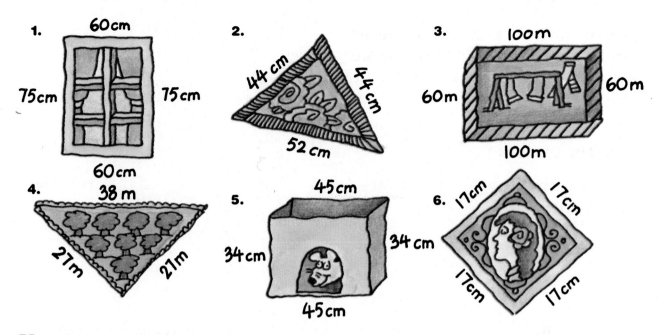

1. 60 cm · 75 cm · 75 cm · 60 cm

2. 44 cm · 44 cm · 52 cm

3. 100 m · 60 m · 60 m · 100 m

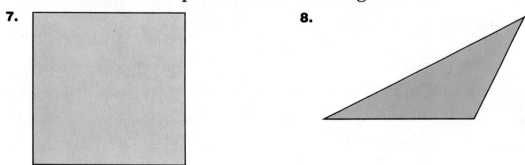

4. 38 m · 27 m · 21 m

5. 45 cm · 34 cm · 34 cm · 45 cm

6. 17 cm · 17 cm · 17 cm · 17 cm

Use your centimeter ruler to measure the sides. Then find the perimeter of each figure.

7.

8.

9. Find the perimeter of a picture or drawing in your classroom.

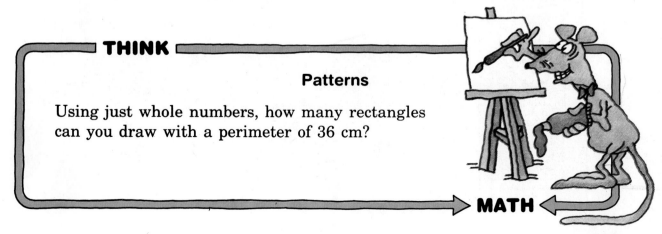

THINK

Patterns

Using just whole numbers, how many rectangles can you draw with a perimeter of 36 cm?

MATH

Area

Tony put tile on the wall behind his kitchen sink. You can think of one tile as the unit of measurement.

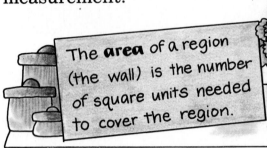

The **area** of a region (the wall) is the number of square units needed to cover the region.

There are 3 rows with 7 tiles in each row.

$$3 \times 7 = 21$$

The area of the space Tony tiled is 21 square units.

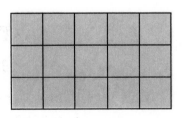

You can find the area of a rectangular region by multiplying the length by the width.

Area = length × width

Warm Up Find the area of each rectangular region.

1.

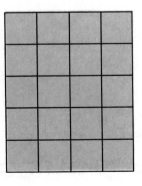

2.

3.

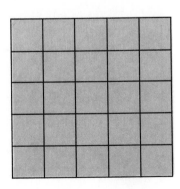

Use the grid squares as units. Give the area of each region.

1.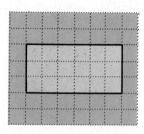

2.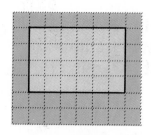

3.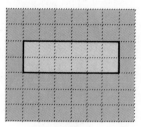

4.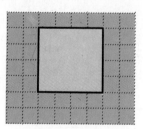

5.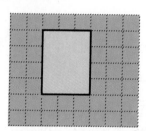

6.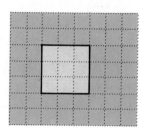

Give the area of each rectangle.
Remember: Area = length × width.

7.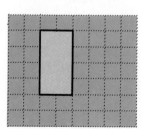

8.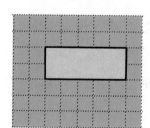

9.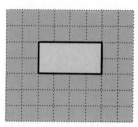

10.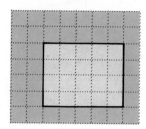

11.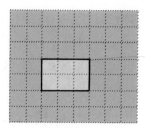

12.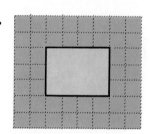

Use graph paper. Draw shapes with these areas.

13. 12 square units

14. 32 square units

15. 24 square units

16. 36 square units

THINK

Space Perception

How many rectangles of different shapes can you find that have an area of 24 square units?

MATH

Volume

Kyle bought a box of number cubes. There were 3 rows of cubes with 4 cubes in each row. There was just 1 layer of cubes.

How many cubes did Kyle get?

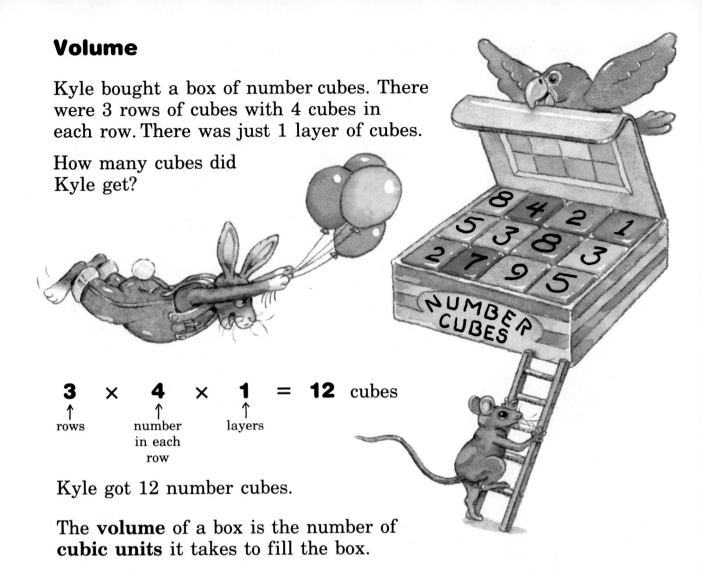

$$\underset{\substack{\uparrow \\ \text{rows}}}{\textbf{3}} \times \underset{\substack{\uparrow \\ \text{number} \\ \text{in each} \\ \text{row}}}{\textbf{4}} \times \underset{\substack{\uparrow \\ \text{layers}}}{\textbf{1}} = \textbf{12} \text{ cubes}$$

Kyle got 12 number cubes.

The **volume** of a box is the number of **cubic units** it takes to fill the box.

Warm Up Give the volume of each box in cubic units.

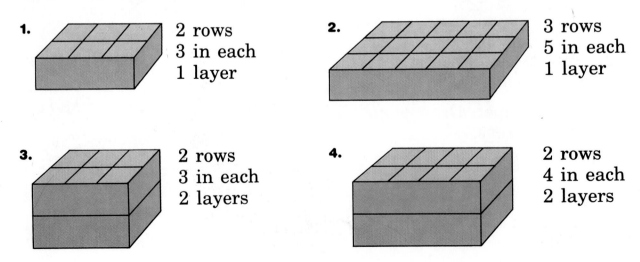

1. 2 rows
3 in each
1 layer

2. 3 rows
5 in each
1 layer

3. 2 rows
3 in each
2 layers

4. 2 rows
4 in each
2 layers

146

Write the volume of each box in cubic units.

1.

8 in each row
2 rows
1 layer

2.

3 in each row
2 rows
1 layer

3.

3 in each row
2 rows
2 layers

4.

3 in each row
1 row
2 layers

5.

4 in each row
2 rows
3 layers

6.

3 in each row
3 rows
3 layers

★ **7.** How many centimeter cubes will this box hold?

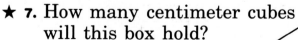
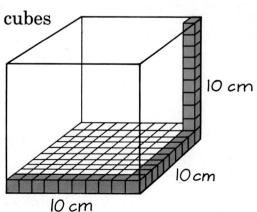

10 cm
10 cm
10 cm

10 rows
10 in each row
10 layers

Capacity

Lee saw this sign at a supermarket. He decided to learn as much as he could about the **liter.** He made the poster below.

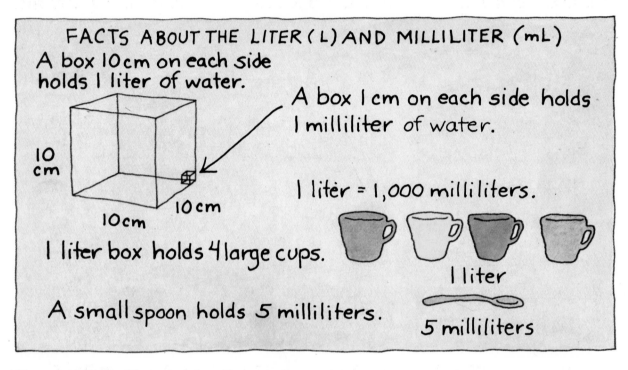

FACTS ABOUT THE LITER (L) AND MILLILITER (mL)

A box 10 cm on each side holds 1 liter of water.

A box 1 cm on each side holds 1 milliliter of water.

10 cm
10 cm
10 cm

1 liter = 1,000 milliliters.

1 liter box holds 4 large cups.

1 liter

A small spoon holds 5 milliliters.

5 milliliters

Warm Up   Choose the better answer.

1. A sink

A more than 1 liter

B less than 1 liter

2. One raindrop

A more than 1 milliliter

B less than 1 milliliter

3. A paper cup

A more than 1 liter

B less than 1 liter

148

Choose the better measure of capacity.

1.

A 4 L   B 4 mL

2.

A 1 L   B 1 mL

3.

A 200 L   B 200 mL

4.

A 25 L   B 25 mL

5.

A 175 L   B 175 mL

6.

A 15 L   B 15 mL

7.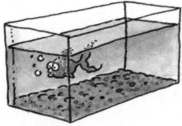

A 30 L   B 30 mL

8.

A 100 L   B 100 mL

9.

A 8 L   B 8 mL

SKILLKEEPER

Add or subtract.

1. 76 + 43	**2.** 56 − 13	**3.** 165 + 751	**4.** $7.15 − 0.32	**5.** 983 + 378
6. 26 10 + 45	**7.** 148 − 73	**8.** 627 + 445	**9.** 740 − 283	**10.** $58.26 − 32.67

Weight

Sandy read that 1 liter of water weighs 1 **kilogram** (kg). She checked this by putting a liter of water in a plastic bag and weighing it.

Sandy also found out that 1 milliliter of water weighs 1 **gram** (1 g).

1 kilogram = 1,000 grams

Other Examples

pencil

about 5 grams

large book

about 1 kilogram

Give the better measure of weight.

1.

A 1 g   **B** 1 kg

2.
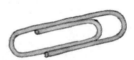
A 1 g   **B** 1 kg

3.

A 20 g   **B** 20 kg

4.

A 16 g   **B** 16 kg

5.

A 6 g   **B** 6 kg

6.

A 240 g   **B** 240 kg

7.

A 35 g   **B** 35 kg

8.
A 200 g   **B** 200 kg

9.
A 5 g   **B** 5 kg

Temperature

Becky's mother said, "You have to wear your sweater this morning. The temperature outside is 10 degrees."

Becky's mother was giving the temperature in degrees **Celsius** (°C). The thermometer shows different Celsius temperatures.

Choose the better measure of temperature.

1.

Hot cocoa

A 75°C   B 35°C

2.

Ice tea

A 20°C   B 2°C

3.

Warm bread

A 65°C   B 25°C

4.

Frozen yogurt

A 20°C   B ⁻5°C

5.

Warm bath

A 50°C   B 80°C

6.

Hot day

A 10°C   B 30°C

°C

Boiling point of water

Hot soup

Normal body temperature

Room temperature

Freezing point of water

Cold day

115
105
95
85
75
65
55
45
35
25
15
5
⁻5
⁻15

110
100
90
80
70
60
50
40
30
20
10
0
⁻10

PROBLEM SOLVING
Using Estimation

Use estimation to decide which answer is most reasonable.

1. In a year with 365 days, Al Gunn worked 248 days. How many days did he not work?

   A 17 days **B** 117 days **C** 217 days

2. Julio swam for 27 minutes. He jogged for 39 minutes. How long did he exercise?

   A 46 min **B** 66 min **C** 86 min

3. Vida planted a tree that was 87 cm tall. In 5 years the tree was 316 cm tall. How much had it grown in the 5 years?

   A 229 cm **B** 129 cm **C** 329 cm

4. Lori Chu drove 289 km, ate lunch, then drove 315 km. How far did she drive that day?

   A 404 km **B** 504 km **C** 604 km

5. Ana Ruiz had a rectangular fence built. Two sides were 98 m and two sides 105 m. How much fence was this?

   A 406 m **B** 203 m **C** 304 m

6. Ian has a square bulletin board. Each side is 96 cm. What is the perimeter of the bulletin board?

   A 192 cm **B** 288 cm **C** 384 cm

7. Trisha has 750 mL of juice. She used 397 mL. How much juice does Trisha have left?

   A 353 mL **B** 313 mL **C** 403 mL

8. *Try This* There are two roads, Crest and Pine, from Reed to Troy. There are three roads, Wolfe, Mills, and Birch, from Troy to Upland. How many ways can you get from Reed to Upland going through Troy?

PROBLEM SOLVING
Practice

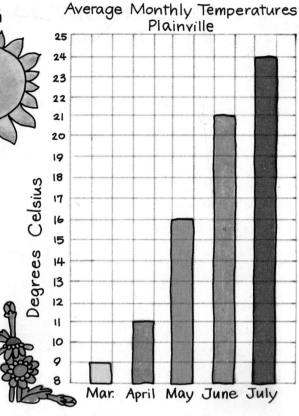

Average Monthly Temperatures Plainville

The bar graph shows average monthly temperatures in degrees Celsius. Use the graph for problems 1, 2, and 3.

1. How much higher was the average temperature in July than it was in April?

2. The average temperature in August was three times what it was in March. What was the average temperature in August?

3. The average temperature for January was 17°C less than it was in June. What was the average temperature in January?

4. Bev had a pet calf that weighed 287 kg in February. By July it weighed 423 kg. How much weight had Bev's calf gained?

5. During a 3-day storm, 15 cm of rain fell on Plainville. If it rained the same amount each day, how much rain fell on the first day?

6. The Whites used 567 liters of oil to heat their home in January. They used 485 liters in February. How many liters of oil did they use in two months?

7. **DATA HUNT** Find your weight in kilograms. Find the weight of a friend. How much more or less do you weigh than your friend?

8. *Try This* One year in Plainville, July had more rain than August. May had less rain than August. Also, May had more rain than June. Which month had the most rain?

PROBLEM SOLVING
Find a Pattern

YOU MAY NEED TO DO MORE THAN JUST ADD, SUBTRACT, MULTIPLY, OR DIVIDE TO SOLVE THIS PROBLEM. A STRATEGY THAT MAY HELP YOU IS GIVEN BELOW.

Try This Julia put 3 tiles in row one, 7 tiles in row two, 11 tiles in row three, 15 tiles in row four, and so on.

ROW 1
ROW 2
ROW 3
ROW 4

How many tiles will she put in row eight?

FIND A PATTERN

I'LL MAKE A TABLE AND LOOK FOR A PATTERN.

I SEE THE PATTERN. THERE ARE 4 MORE TILES IN EACH ROW. I'LL COMPLETE THE TABLE TO ROW 8.

ROW NUMBER	1	2	3	4
TILES	3	7	11	15

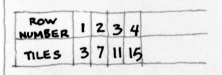

ROW NUMBER	1	2	3	4	5	6	7	8
TILES	3	7	11	15	19	23	27	31

Julia will put 31 tiles in row 8.

Solve.

1. Bruce did 3 push-ups every day the first week, 6 push-ups every day the second week, 9 the third, and so on. How many push-ups did he do each day the tenth week?

2. In a video game, the first goal is worth 1 point, the second 2 points, the third 4 points, the fourth 8 points, and so on. How many points is the eighth goal worth?

Write each time
as a.m. or p.m.

1. Marcia left for school each morning at _____.

2. She returned home in the afternoon at _____.

Use a centimeter ruler. Find the length to the nearest centimeter.

3.

4.

Write the missing unit—cm, m, or km.

5. Jerry's mother drove 57 _____ to the park.

6. Rosa's brother is 2 _____ tall.

7. Find the perimeter.

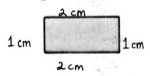

8. Find the area in square units.

9. Find the volume.

10. Choose the better estimate.

A 250 mL   **B** 250 L

11. Choose the better weight for a bag of potatoes.

A 5 g   **B** 5 kg

12. Choose the better temperature for boiling water.

A 10°C   **B** 100°C

Solve.

13. Amelia practices the clarinet 30 minutes each day. In 6 days how many hours will she practice?
Hint: 60 minutes = 1 hour

14. Mr. Fitch built a fence around his garden. Two sides were 53 m and two sides were 48 m. How much fence was this? Choose the best estimate.

A 100 m   **B** 200 m   **C** 150 m

ANOTHER LOOK

What is the time
45 minutes before 4:15 p.m.?

45 − 15 = 30	15 minutes
30 minutes	back to
more back	4:00
to 3:30	

Write each time.

1. What time was it 3 hours before 1 p.m.?

2. What time will it be 30 minutes after 7:50 a.m.?

3. What time was it 20 minutes before 3:05 p.m.?

Find the perimeter and area.

```
        8
7               7
        8
```

Perimeter
7 + 8 + 7 + 8 =   30 units

Area
7 × 8 =   56 square units

4. Find the perimeter and area.

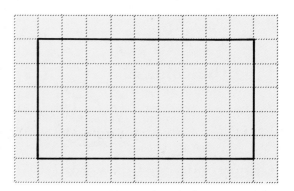

Find the volume.

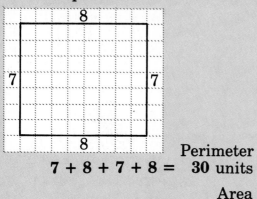

2 rows
3 in each
2 layers

2 × 3 × 2 = 12 cubes

Find the volume.

5.

3 rows
4 in each
1 layer

Space Perception

Each face of a cube is 1 square unit. You are going to paint as much of the cubes as you can without moving them. For each position tell how many square units you could paint.

1 SQUARE UNIT

1. Standing on one corner

2. Sitting on the floor against a wall

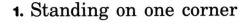

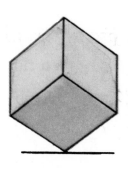

Hint: How many faces can you not see?

Hint: How many faces are against the wall or floor?

3. Sitting in a corner

4. Count carefully.

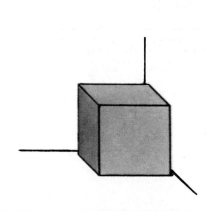

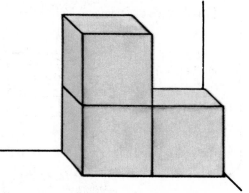

CUMULATIVE REVIEW

Give the letter for the correct answer.

Round to the nearest thousand.

1. 3,500
   A 3,000   B 4,000
   C 5,000   D not given

2. 6,489
   A 6,000   B 7,000
   C 6,500   D not given

Round to the nearest dollar.

3. $25.98
   A $25   B $26
   C $24   D not given

4. $16.35
   A $17   B $15
   C $16   D not given

What is the standard number?

5. thirteen thousand, five
   hundred twenty
   A 15,282   B 13,520
   C 13,250   D not given

6. twenty-seven thousand,
   forty-six
   A 27,426   B 28,536
   C 27,036   D not given

7. five hundred thirty thousand,
   four hundred fifty-nine
   A 53,459   B 530,459
   C 534,590   D not given

8. two hundred fifteen million,
   five hundred thirteen
   thousand
   A 215,513,000   B 215,513
   C 250,513,000   D not given

9.   3   A 12   B 24
   × 6   c 18   D not given

10.   4   A 4   B 40
    × 0   c 0   D not given

11.   7   A 48   B 56
    × 8   c 63   D not given

12.   6   A 54   B 72
    × 9   c 81   D not given

13. Matt planted 8 rows of corn.
    He planted 8 seeds in each
    row. How many seeds did
    Matt plant?
    A 6   B 48
    C 64   D not given

14. Mona's bicycle is 22 inches
    long. Randy's bicycle is
    26 inches long. How much
    longer is Randy's bicycle than
    Mona's?
    A 4 inches   B 3 inches
    C 2 inches   D not given

MULTIPLICATION: 1-Digit Factors

7

Ekwa's class was studying animals that may become extinct. They prepared special reports. Some children drew pictures. Others talked about plans to save the animals. They made a movie of their reports. Ekwa's mother taught them to use a video camera. They learned to move it very slowly. They used a special lens for close-ups. They taped their show two times. Between tapings they decided which parts to cut out. Their first taping was 2 times as long as the second. The second taping was 26 minutes long. They showed it on the school television. Other classes were invited to watch.

Special Products: Mental Math

Kristy and Gerald played a game. Kristy had to pay the rent on Hawaii Avenue 4 times. Gerald had to pay the rent on Alaska Avenue 4 times. How much rent did each person pay in all?

Since we want the totals for equal amounts, we multiply.

Kristy's rent

$(4 \times 3 \text{ tens} = 12 \text{ tens})$

4 × 30 = 120

Gerald's rent

$(4 \times 3 \text{ hundreds} = 12 \text{ hundreds})$

4 × 300 = 1,200

Kristy paid $120 rent and Gerald paid $1,200 rent.

Other Examples

6 × 10 = 60   **5 × 3,000 = 15,000**   **4 × 500 = 2,000**

$(20 \text{ hundreds} = 2 \text{ thousand})$

Warm Up   Give each product aloud.

1. 5×10
2. 4×20
3. 7×30

4. 1×80
5. 9×40
6. 3×50

7. 8×500
8. 3×900
9. 4×600

10. 7×400
11. 3×300
12. 5×500

13. $9 \times 1,000$
14. $7 \times 2,000$
15. $4 \times 8,000$

16. $2 \times 3,000$
17. $4 \times 4,000$
18. $3 \times 7,000$

Find the products. Write answers only.

1. 7×10
2. 6×30
3. 2×90
4. 3×80
5. 5×20
6. 4×50
7. 9×100
8. 6×200
9. 8×400
10. 5×300
11. 2×700
12. 3×200
13. $6 \times 1,000$
14. $2 \times 8,000$
15. $9 \times 6,000$
16. $3 \times 6,000$
17. $4 \times 9,000$
18. $8 \times 5,000$
19. 2×400
20. $8 \times 1,000$
21. 7×60

22. Multiply 7 and 1,000.
23. Multiply 2 and 8,000.

Solve.

24. The rent on Montana Avenue is $40. Claire paid the rent 7 times. How much rent did she pay in all?

25. Each time you pass HOME, you collect $300. How much do you get for passing HOME 3 times?

★ 26. You land on Lindsey Place. The rent is 10 times the sum of the numbers on the cubes. What is the rent?

THINK

Logical Reasoning

At what times during a day does a digital clock read the same forward and backward?

Example

MATH

Multiplying Three Numbers

Kent and Sandra work in a supply room. They want to know how many envelopes they have. There are 2 boxes of envelopes. Each box holds 4 packages and each package holds 100 envelopes.

Kent and Sandra got the same answer but they used different groupings when they multiplied.

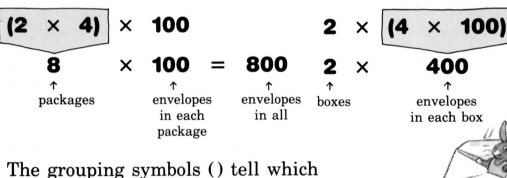

Kent's Way	Sandra's Way

$$(2 \times 4) \times 100 \qquad\qquad 2 \times (4 \times 100)$$

$$\underset{\substack{\uparrow \\ \text{packages}}}{8} \times \underset{\substack{\uparrow \\ \text{envelopes} \\ \text{in each} \\ \text{package}}}{100} = \underset{\substack{\uparrow \\ \text{envelopes} \\ \text{in all}}}{800} \qquad \underset{\substack{\uparrow \\ \text{boxes}}}{2} \times \underset{\substack{\uparrow \\ \text{envelopes} \\ \text{in each box}}}{400} = \underset{\substack{\uparrow \\ \text{envelopes} \\ \text{in all}}}{800}$$

The grouping symbols ( ) tell which multiplication to do first. When you multiply, you get the same product even if you change the groupings.

Find these products. Use the grouping shown.

1. $(3 \times 2) \times 100 \ = \square$

2. $3 \times (2 \times 100) \ = \square$

3. $(4 \times 1) \times 10 \ = \square$

4. $4 \times (1 \times 10) \ = \square$

5. $(3 \times 3) \times 1{,}000 = \square$

6. $3 \times (3 \times 1{,}000) = \square$

Find these products. Use any grouping you want.

7. $2 \times 3 \times 100 \ = \square$

8. $6 \times 1 \times 10 \ = \square$

9. $2 \times 4 \times 1{,}000 = \square$

10. $3 \times 3 \times 100 \ = \square$

11. $7 \times 1 \times 10 \ = \square$

12. $1 \times 8 \times 1{,}000 = \square$

More Practice, page 400, Set A

Practice the Facts

Find the products.

1. $\begin{array}{r}4\\ \times 3\\\hline\end{array}$	2. $\begin{array}{r}2\\ \times 2\\\hline\end{array}$	3. $\begin{array}{r}5\\ \times 2\\\hline\end{array}$	4. $\begin{array}{r}3\\ \times 6\\\hline\end{array}$	5. $\begin{array}{r}5\\ \times 3\\\hline\end{array}$	6. $\begin{array}{r}5\\ \times 5\\\hline\end{array}$	7. $\begin{array}{r}3\\ \times 8\\\hline\end{array}$
8. $\begin{array}{r}3\\ \times 2\\\hline\end{array}$	9. $\begin{array}{r}8\\ \times 4\\\hline\end{array}$	10. $\begin{array}{r}5\\ \times 6\\\hline\end{array}$	11. $\begin{array}{r}4\\ \times 4\\\hline\end{array}$	12. $\begin{array}{r}4\\ \times 6\\\hline\end{array}$	13. $\begin{array}{r}3\\ \times 7\\\hline\end{array}$	14. $\begin{array}{r}4\\ \times 2\\\hline\end{array}$
15. $\begin{array}{r}5\\ \times 4\\\hline\end{array}$	16. $\begin{array}{r}8\\ \times 3\\\hline\end{array}$	17. $\begin{array}{r}5\\ \times 1\\\hline\end{array}$	18. $\begin{array}{r}3\\ \times 4\\\hline\end{array}$	19. $\begin{array}{r}4\\ \times 1\\\hline\end{array}$	20. $\begin{array}{r}0\\ \times 5\\\hline\end{array}$	21. $\begin{array}{r}4\\ \times 7\\\hline\end{array}$
22. $\begin{array}{r}3\\ \times 5\\\hline\end{array}$	23. $\begin{array}{r}3\\ \times 9\\\hline\end{array}$	24. $\begin{array}{r}2\\ \times 1\\\hline\end{array}$	25. $\begin{array}{r}6\\ \times 5\\\hline\end{array}$	26. $\begin{array}{r}4\\ \times 5\\\hline\end{array}$	27. $\begin{array}{r}7\\ \times 3\\\hline\end{array}$	28. $\begin{array}{r}0\\ \times 4\\\hline\end{array}$
29. $\begin{array}{r}6\\ \times 9\\\hline\end{array}$	30. $\begin{array}{r}7\\ \times 7\\\hline\end{array}$	31. $\begin{array}{r}5\\ \times 9\\\hline\end{array}$	32. $\begin{array}{r}7\\ \times 8\\\hline\end{array}$	33. $\begin{array}{r}9\\ \times 7\\\hline\end{array}$	34. $\begin{array}{r}7\\ \times 6\\\hline\end{array}$	35. $\begin{array}{r}9\\ \times 8\\\hline\end{array}$
36. $\begin{array}{r}9\\ \times 4\\\hline\end{array}$	37. $\begin{array}{r}6\\ \times 6\\\hline\end{array}$	38. $\begin{array}{r}7\\ \times 5\\\hline\end{array}$	39. $\begin{array}{r}9\\ \times 9\\\hline\end{array}$	40. $\begin{array}{r}8\\ \times 6\\\hline\end{array}$	41. $\begin{array}{r}8\\ \times 8\\\hline\end{array}$	42. $\begin{array}{r}9\\ \times 6\\\hline\end{array}$
43. $\begin{array}{r}9\\ \times 5\\\hline\end{array}$	44. $\begin{array}{r}8\\ \times 9\\\hline\end{array}$	45. $\begin{array}{r}4\\ \times 9\\\hline\end{array}$	46. $\begin{array}{r}6\\ \times 7\\\hline\end{array}$	47. $\begin{array}{r}8\\ \times 7\\\hline\end{array}$	48. $\begin{array}{r}8\\ \times 5\\\hline\end{array}$	49. $\begin{array}{r}6\\ \times 8\\\hline\end{array}$
50. $\begin{array}{r}7\\ \times 7\\\hline\end{array}$	51. $\begin{array}{r}5\\ \times 8\\\hline\end{array}$	52. $\begin{array}{r}7\\ \times 9\\\hline\end{array}$	53. $\begin{array}{r}5\\ \times 7\\\hline\end{array}$	54. $\begin{array}{r}9\\ \times 4\\\hline\end{array}$	55. $\begin{array}{r}9\\ \times 9\\\hline\end{array}$	56. $\begin{array}{r}5\\ \times 9\\\hline\end{array}$

Multiplication and Addition

Alvaro and Dennis are playing a card game.

Rules: Multiply each number on the yellow ones' card and the red tens' card by the number on the times card. Add the products.

Alvaro's cards

What is Alvaro's score?

1. Multiply ones. ——→ **4 × 6 = 24**
2. Multiply tens. ——→ **4 × 30 = 120**
3. Add the products. ————————→ **144**

Alvaro's score is 144.

Give the total score for each turn below.

1. Find 3 × 7.
   Find 3 × 50.
   Then add.

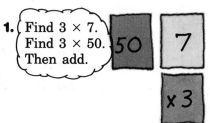

2. Find 6 × 3.
   Find 6 × 40.
   Then add.

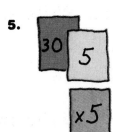

3.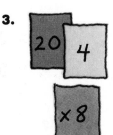

4.

5. 30 5 ×5

6. 70 8 ×4

The boys played a game using blue hundreds' cards. Give the total score for each turn.

7. 200 40 8 ×3

8.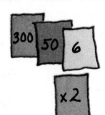

9.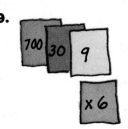

164

Multiply and Then Add: Mental Math

Portia bought 3 tickets for children and 1 for an adult for admission into the fair. How much did she pay for tickets?

Portia paid $9 for tickets.

$3 \times 2 = 6$

and 3 more make 9

Multiply and then add 2. Write answers only.

1. 6×2 2. 7×5 3. 4×9 4. 8×0

5. 2×3 6. 4×1 7. 6×6 8. 3×8

Multiply and then add 3. Write answers only.

9. 3×4 10. 4×8 11. 2×0 12. 5×1

13. 7×2 14. 9×9 15. 6×4 16. 8×3

Multiply and then add 4. Write answers only.

17. 2×5 18. 6×7 19. 3×2 20. 7×4

21. 8×1 22. 5×5 23. 4×0 24. 9×2

Multiply and then add 5. Write answers only.

25. 5×2 26. 4×7 27. 3×3 28. 5×0

29. 2×9 30. 8×6 31. 6×3 32. 7×3

Multiply and then add 6. Write answers only.

33. 9×3 34. 4×6 35. 6×8 36. 5×7

37. 2×9 38. 3×0 39. 7×7 40. 8×2

Multiply and then add 7. Write answers only.

41. 3×5 42. 6×9 43. 2×7 44. 9×4

45. 7×0 46. 4×4 47. 5×9 48. 8×4

Multiplying: Trading Ones

A trout swims 24 km/h (kilometers per hour). A flying fish can swim 3 times as fast as a trout. How many kilometers per hour can a flying fish swim?

Since we want the total for equal amounts, we multiply.

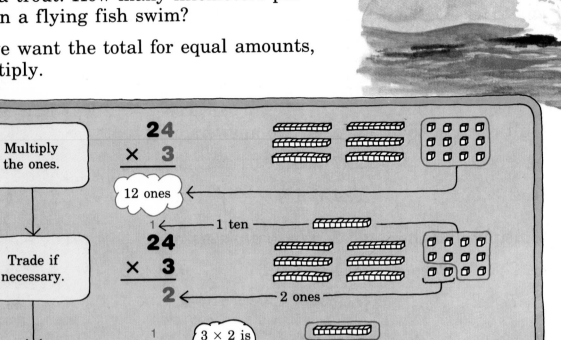

A flying fish can swim 72 km/h.

Other Examples

$$\begin{array}{r} 23 \\ \times\ 3 \\ \hline 69 \end{array}$$

NO TRADE NECESSARY

$$\begin{array}{r} ^{2} \\ 17 \\ \times\ 4 \\ \hline 68 \end{array}$$

$$\begin{array}{r} 20 \\ \times\ 4 \\ \hline 80 \end{array}$$

NO TRADE NECESSARY

$$\begin{array}{r} ^{3} \\ 15 \\ \times\ 6 \\ \hline 90 \end{array}$$

Warm Up Multiply.

1. $\begin{array}{r} 21 \\ \times\ 3 \\ \hline \end{array}$

2. $\begin{array}{r} 37 \\ \times\ 2 \\ \hline \end{array}$

3. $\begin{array}{r} 12 \\ \times\ 3 \\ \hline \end{array}$

4. $\begin{array}{r} 18 \\ \times\ 4 \\ \hline \end{array}$

5. $\begin{array}{r} 19 \\ \times\ 5 \\ \hline \end{array}$

6. $\begin{array}{r} 25 \\ \times\ 2 \\ \hline \end{array}$

Find the products.

1. $\begin{array}{r} 23 \\ \times\ 4 \\ \hline \end{array}$	**2.** $\begin{array}{r} 34 \\ \times\ 2 \\ \hline \end{array}$	**3.** $\begin{array}{r} 14 \\ \times\ 6 \\ \hline \end{array}$	**4.** $\begin{array}{r} 32 \\ \times\ 3 \\ \hline \end{array}$	**5.** $\begin{array}{r} 15 \\ \times\ 4 \\ \hline \end{array}$
6. $\begin{array}{r} 14 \\ \times\ 5 \\ \hline \end{array}$	**7.** $\begin{array}{r} 25 \\ \times\ 3 \\ \hline \end{array}$	**8.** $\begin{array}{r} 20 \\ \times\ 4 \\ \hline \end{array}$	**9.** $\begin{array}{r} 12 \\ \times\ 8 \\ \hline \end{array}$	**10.** $\begin{array}{r} 46 \\ \times\ 2 \\ \hline \end{array}$
11. $\begin{array}{r} 16 \\ \times\ 6 \\ \hline \end{array}$	**12.** $\begin{array}{r} 33 \\ \times\ 3 \\ \hline \end{array}$	**13.** $\begin{array}{r} 24 \\ \times\ 3 \\ \hline \end{array}$	**14.** $\begin{array}{r} 12 \\ \times\ 4 \\ \hline \end{array}$	**15.** $\begin{array}{r} 29 \\ \times\ 2 \\ \hline \end{array}$

16. 4×19 **17.** 2×33 **18.** 3×31

19. 5×18 **20.** 3×30 **21.** 2×27

22. Multiply 17 by 3.   **23.** Multiply 13 by 6.   **24.** Multiply 21 by 4.

25. Multiply 48 by 2.   **26.** Multiply 16 by 5.   **27.** Multiply 15 by 5.

28. A penguin swims 14 km/h. A dolphin swims 4 times as fast as a penguin. How many kilometers per hour can a dolphin swim?

29. Write a question for this story and then solve the problem.

Salmon can swim 36 km/h. Tuna can swim twice as fast as salmon.

30. A person can swim 133 meters per minute. At this rate, how many meters can a person swim in 5 minutes? In 1 hour (60 minutes)?

THINK

Logical Reasoning

The missing digits are all the same. There are 2 different answers. Find them.

MATH

Multiplying: Trading Ones and Tens

Jeffrey hopes to skate in the Winter Olympics someday. He trained 4 hours a day on each of the 31 days in March. How many hours did he train in March?

Since we want the total for equal amounts of time, we multiply.

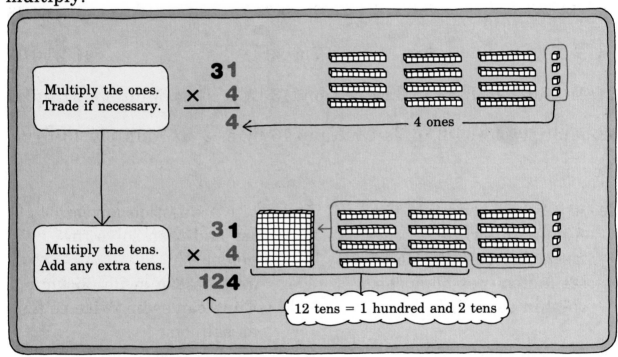

Multiply the ones. Trade if necessary.

$$\begin{array}{r} 3\mathbf{1} \\ \times\ 4 \\ \hline 4 \end{array}$$

← 4 ones

Multiply the tens. Add any extra tens.

$$\begin{array}{r} 3\mathbf{1} \\ \times\ 4 \\ \hline 124 \end{array}$$

12 tens = 1 hundred and 2 tens

Jeffrey trained for 124 hours in March.

Other Examples

$$\begin{array}{r} 52 \\ \times\ 3 \\ \hline 156 \end{array} \qquad \begin{array}{r} {\scriptstyle 1} \\ 43 \\ \times\ 6 \\ \hline 258 \end{array} \qquad \begin{array}{r} {\scriptstyle 2} \\ 35 \\ \times\ 5 \\ \hline 175 \end{array} \qquad \begin{array}{r} {\scriptstyle 2} \\ 75 \\ \times\ 4 \\ \hline 300 \end{array}$$

Warm Up Multiply.

1. $\begin{array}{r} 63 \\ \times\ 2 \end{array}$ 2. $\begin{array}{r} 31 \\ \times\ 8 \end{array}$ 3. $\begin{array}{r} 54 \\ \times\ 3 \end{array}$ 4. $\begin{array}{r} 29 \\ \times\ 4 \end{array}$ 5. $\begin{array}{r} 78 \\ \times\ 5 \end{array}$ 6. $\begin{array}{r} 34 \\ \times\ 9 \end{array}$

Find the products.

1.	62 × 3	2.	42 × 6	3.	43 × 5	4.	41 × 7	5.	23 × 4
6.	99 × 2	7.	53 × 9	8.	37 × 3	9.	78 × 8	10.	80 × 5
11.	67 × 6	12.	78 × 4	13.	47 × 2	14.	96 × 9	15.	75 × 7

16. 6×35 17. 8×16 18. 4×26

19. 7×16 20. 3×96 21. 2×84

22. Give the product of 7 and 58. 23. Give the product of 5 and 62.

24. Give the product of 8 and 67. 25. Give the product of 6 and 84.

Solve.

26. Jeffrey trained 28 days in April. He trained 3 hours on each of those days. How many hours did he train in April?

27. Each member of the 8-person skating team trained for 1,083 hours in a year. How many hours did the whole team train in a year?

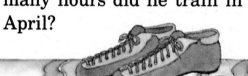

SKILLKEEPER

Write each time.

Multiplying Larger Numbers: One Trade

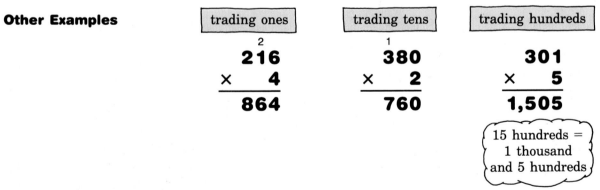

Washington State Ferryboats

Number of autos each ferryboat carries

Super ferryboats	162
Yakima	
Hyak	
Kaleetan	
Jumbo ferryboats	206
Walla Walla	
Spokane	

How many autos could the 3 super ferryboats carry if they were full?

Since we want the total for equal numbers of autos, we multiply.

Multiply the ones. Trade if necessary.	→	Multiply the tens. Add any extra tens. Trade if necessary.	→	Multiply the hundreds. Add any extra hundreds.

$$\begin{array}{r} 16\textbf{2} \\ \times\quad 3 \\ \hline 6 \end{array}$$

$$\begin{array}{r} \overset{1}{1}6\textbf{2} \\ \times\quad 3 \\ \hline \textbf{86} \end{array}$$
18 tens = 1 hundred and 8 tens

$$\begin{array}{r} \overset{1}{1}62 \\ \times\quad 3 \\ \hline \textbf{486} \end{array}$$

The 3 super ferryboats could carry 486 autos.

Other Examples

trading ones
$$\begin{array}{r} \overset{2}{2}16 \\ \times\quad 4 \\ \hline 864 \end{array}$$

trading tens
$$\begin{array}{r} \overset{1}{3}80 \\ \times\quad 2 \\ \hline 760 \end{array}$$

trading hundreds
$$\begin{array}{r} 301 \\ \times\quad 5 \\ \hline 1{,}505 \end{array}$$
15 hundreds = 1 thousand and 5 hundreds

Warm Up   Multiply.

1.	2.	3.	4.	5.
241 × 3	435 × 2	322 × 4	302 × 3	120 × 5

Find the products.

1.	227 × 3	**2.**	161 × 6	**3.**	421 × 4	**4.**	306 × 2	**5.**	171 × 5
6.	411 × 7	**7.**	219 × 4	**8.**	912 × 4	**9.**	232 × 3	**10.**	109 × 9
11.	294 × 2	**12.**	510 × 6	**13.**	71 × 8	**14.**	401 × 5	**15.**	283 × 3

16. 4 × 621   **17.** 5 × 181   **18.** 2 × 523

19. 3 × 129   **20.** 2 × 49   **21.** 6 × 812

22. Multiply 3 times 703.   **23.** Multiply 2 times 182.

24. Multiply 5 times 115.   **25.** Multiply 9 times 181.

Solve.

26. How many autos could the 2 jumbo ferryboats carry if they were full?

27. The Hiyu ferryboat is 45 m long. The Walla Walla is 3 times as long as the Hiyu. How long is the Walla Walla?

28. DATA BANK See page 385. Find the number of autos the ferryboat Columbia can carry. If there were 3 people in each auto how many people could go on the ferryboat?

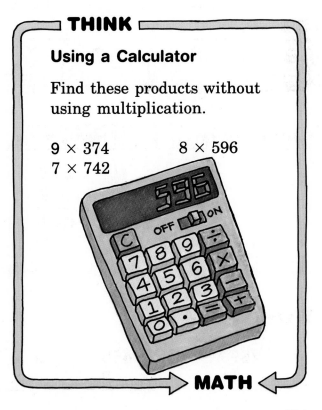

THINK

Using a Calculator

Find these products without using multiplication.

9 × 374   8 × 596
7 × 742

MATH

Multiplying Larger Numbers: Two or More Trades

Mr. Rowe's class wants to make 6 batches of modeling clay. How many milliliters of cornstarch do they need?

Since we want the total for 6 equal amounts, we multiply.

Recipe for Modeling Clay
250 mL Baking Soda
125 mL Cornstarch
165 mL Warm Water
This recipe makes one batch.

Multiply the ones. Trade if necessary. → Multiply the tens. Add any extra tens. Trade if necessary. → Multiply the hundreds. Add any extra hundreds.

$$
\begin{array}{r}
\overset{3}{125} \\
\times\ \ 6 \\
\hline
0
\end{array}
\qquad
\begin{array}{r}
\overset{1\ 3}{125} \\
\times\ \ 6 \\
\hline
50
\end{array}
\qquad
\begin{array}{r}
\overset{1\ 3}{125} \\
\times\ \ 6 \\
\hline
750
\end{array}
$$

30 ones = 3 tens and 0 ones

15 tens = 1 hundred and 5 tens

Mr. Rowe's class needs 750 mL of cornstarch.

Other Examples

$$
\begin{array}{r}
\overset{3}{318} \\
\times\ \ 4 \\
\hline
1{,}272
\end{array}
\qquad
\begin{array}{r}
\overset{1\ 2}{237} \\
\times\ \ 3 \\
\hline
711
\end{array}
\qquad
\begin{array}{r}
\overset{3}{871} \\
\times\ \ 5 \\
\hline
4{,}355
\end{array}
\qquad
\begin{array}{r}
\overset{1}{706} \\
\times\ \ 2 \\
\hline
1{,}412
\end{array}
\qquad
\begin{array}{r}
\overset{2\ 4}{625} \\
\times\ \ 8 \\
\hline
5{,}000
\end{array}
$$

Warm Up Multiply.

1. $\begin{array}{r} 237 \\ \times\ \ 4 \\ \hline \end{array}$
2. $\begin{array}{r} 453 \\ \times\ \ 3 \\ \hline \end{array}$
3. $\begin{array}{r} 807 \\ \times\ \ 2 \\ \hline \end{array}$
4. $\begin{array}{r} 744 \\ \times\ \ 7 \\ \hline \end{array}$
5. $\begin{array}{r} 735 \\ \times\ \ 6 \\ \hline \end{array}$

Find the products.

1. $\begin{array}{r} 342 \\ \times\ \ 5 \\ \hline \end{array}$	**2.** $\begin{array}{r} 468 \\ \times\ \ 2 \\ \hline \end{array}$	**3.** $\begin{array}{r} 591 \\ \times\ \ 4 \\ \hline \end{array}$	**4.** $\begin{array}{r} 412 \\ \times\ \ 8 \\ \hline \end{array}$	**5.** $\begin{array}{r} 154 \\ \times\ \ 6 \\ \hline \end{array}$
6. $\begin{array}{r} 807 \\ \times\ \ 3 \\ \hline \end{array}$	**7.** $\begin{array}{r} 59 \\ \times\ \ 9 \\ \hline \end{array}$	**8.** $\begin{array}{r} 360 \\ \times\ \ 3 \\ \hline \end{array}$	**9.** $\begin{array}{r} 903 \\ \times\ \ 5 \\ \hline \end{array}$	**10.** $\begin{array}{r} 623 \\ \times\ \ 9 \\ \hline \end{array}$
11. $\begin{array}{r} 79 \\ \times\ \ 4 \\ \hline \end{array}$	**12.** $\begin{array}{r} 649 \\ \times\ \ 2 \\ \hline \end{array}$	**13.** $\begin{array}{r} 764 \\ \times\ \ 5 \\ \hline \end{array}$	**14.** $\begin{array}{r} 650 \\ \times\ \ 7 \\ \hline \end{array}$	**15.** $\begin{array}{r} 135 \\ \times\ \ 8 \\ \hline \end{array}$

16. 3×276 **17.** 2×971 **18.** 4×704

19. 9×841 **20.** 8×825 **21.** 6×243

22. Find the product of 184 and 3. **23.** Find the product of 521 and 7.

24. Find the product of 230 and 5. **25.** Find the product of 375 and 2.

Solve.

26. Look at the recipe on page 172. How many milliliters of baking soda does Mr. Rowe's class need to make 6 batches of modeling clay?

27. Write a question for this data and solve the problem.
A box of cornstarch weighs 454 g. Leo bought 3 boxes.

28. DATA BANK See page 383. How many milliliters of cornstarch are needed to make 5 batches of finger paint?

THINK

Logical Reasoning

Find the missing digits for this problem.

$$\begin{array}{r} \text{▥ ▥ ▥} \\ \times \qquad \text{▥} \\ \hline 4\ 4\ 4 \end{array}$$

Example: $\begin{array}{r} 444 \\ \times\ \ \ \ 1 \\ \hline 444 \end{array}$

There are 3 more ways.

MATH

More Practice, page 402, Set A

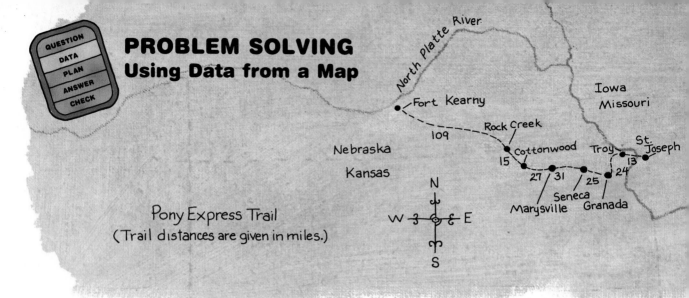

PROBLEM SOLVING
Using Data from a Map

This map shows some of the stations along the Pony Express Trail.

Find each distance.

1. Fort Kearny to Rock Creek

2. Rock Creek to Cottonwood

3. Granada to Troy

4. St. Joseph to Troy

5. Seneca to Rock Creek

6. Troy to Cottonwood

Find the total round-trip distance for problems 7–12.

7. between Rock Creek and Fort Kearny

8. between Marysville and Cottonwood

9. between Marysville and Seneca

10. between Cottonwood and Fort Kearny

11. between Rock Creek and Marysville

12. between Cottonwood and Seneca

Use the data from the map to solve the following problems.

13. A rider traveled between Cottonwood and Marysville 4 times a week. How many miles did he travel each week?

14. A rider traveled between Fort Kearny and Rock Creek 4 times in a month. How many miles did he travel each month?

Solve.

15. Pony Express riders were paid $125 a month. How much money did a rider earn in 6 months?

16. Each station needed 2 men to take care of the horses and supplies. How many stations could be cared for by 14 men?

17. There were 198 Pony Express stations. If each station had 3 horses, how many horses did the Pony Express have in all?

18. The Pony Express traveled from St. Joseph to Salt Lake City in 124 hours. It took 116 more hours to get to San Francisco. How many hours did it take to get from St. Joseph to San Francisco?

19. The first Pony Express mail that left San Francisco on April 3, 1860 carried a total of 85 letters. The charge for each letter was $5. How much money was collected for this first mail?

20. In good weather one rider traveled 10 miles each hour. At this rate how many miles did he travel in 8 hours?

21. *Try This* Strawberry station was east of Moss station. Lakeside was east of Strawberry station. Sportsman Hall station was west of Moss but east of Placerville station. Which of these stations was the farthest west?

Estimating Products: Mental Math

A black-footed penguin eats 475 g of fish in 1 day. **About** how much fish would a penguin eat in 1 week (7 days)?

Since you want an answer that is only **close** to the exact answer, you **estimate** by rounding and then multiplying in your head.

Think of the problem. $\longrightarrow$  7×475

Round and multiply. $\longrightarrow$ **$7 \times 500 = 3,500$**

A black-footed penguin eats **about** 3,500 g of fish in 1 week.

Other Examples

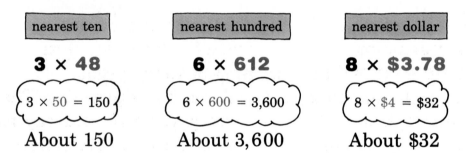

nearest ten	nearest hundred	nearest dollar
3 × 48	**6 × 612**	**8 × \$3.78**
$3 \times 50 = 150$	$6 \times 600 = 3,600$	$8 \times \$4 = \$32$
About 150	About 3,600	About \$32

Warm Up Estimate by rounding to the nearest ten.

1. 4×58 **2.** 3×65 **3.** 7×84

Estimate by rounding to the nearest hundred.

4. 3×205 **5.** 7×894 **6.** 2×913

Estimate by rounding to the nearest dollar.

7. $8 \times \$7.45$ **8.** $9 \times \$2.50$ **9.** $6 \times \$5.91$

Estimate the products. Write estimated answers only.
Estimate by rounding to the nearest ten.

1. 4 × 21   **2.** 3 × 38   **3.** 6 × 53   **4.** 7 × 25

5. 5 × 13   **6.** 2 × 79   **7.** 4 × 61   **8.** 9 × 36

Estimate by rounding to the nearest hundred.

9. 6 × 310   **10.** 8 × 185   **11.** 2 × 99   **12.** 9 × 506

13. 3 × 665   **14.** 4 × 783   **15.** 7 × 450   **16.** 8 × 275

Estimate by rounding to the nearest dollar.

17. 8 × $2.03   **18.** 3 × $5.88   **19.** 5 × $3.23   **20.** 2 × $9.13

21. 4 × $2.82   **22.** 7 × $5.18   **23.** 6 × $1.43   **24.** 3 × $1.50

Solve.

25. A rock-hopper penguin is 38 cm tall. An emperor penguin is 3 times as tall as a rock-hopper penguin. About how tall is an emperor penguin?

26. Tell what information is extra in this story, then answer the question.
A zoo has 9 penguins. The zoo pays $6.75 each day for penguin food. About how much do they pay in one week?

Multiplying Larger Numbers: All Trades

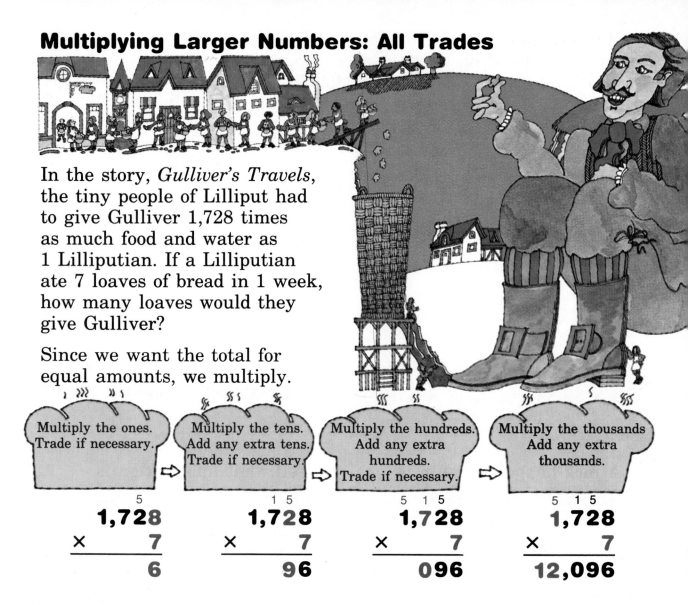

In the story, *Gulliver's Travels*, the tiny people of Lilliput had to give Gulliver 1,728 times as much food and water as 1 Lilliputian. If a Lilliputian ate 7 loaves of bread in 1 week, how many loaves would they give Gulliver?

Since we want the total for equal amounts, we multiply.

Multiply the ones. Trade if necessary.

Multiply the tens. Add any extra tens. Trade if necessary.

Multiply the hundreds. Add any extra hundreds. Trade if necessary.

Multiply the thousands Add any extra thousands.

$$
\begin{array}{r}
{\scriptstyle 5} \\
1,728 \\
\times \quad 7 \\
\hline
6
\end{array}
\qquad
\begin{array}{r}
{\scriptstyle 1\ 5} \\
1,728 \\
\times \quad 7 \\
\hline
96
\end{array}
\qquad
\begin{array}{r}
{\scriptstyle 5\ 1\ 5} \\
1,728 \\
\times \quad 7 \\
\hline
096
\end{array}
\qquad
\begin{array}{r}
{\scriptstyle 5\ 1\ 5} \\
1,728 \\
\times \quad 7 \\
\hline
12,096
\end{array}
$$

Gulliver would get 12,096 loaves of bread each week.

Other Examples

$$
\begin{array}{r}
{\scriptstyle 1\ \ 1\ 3} \\
3,428 \\
\times \quad 4 \\
\hline
13,712
\end{array}
\qquad
\begin{array}{r}
{\scriptstyle 3\ \ \ 3} \\
2,505 \\
\times \quad 6 \\
\hline
15,030
\end{array}
\qquad
\begin{array}{r}
{\scriptstyle 4\ 8} \\
1,049 \\
\times \quad 9 \\
\hline
9,441
\end{array}
\qquad
\begin{array}{r}
{\scriptstyle 1} \\
7,006 \\
\times \quad 3 \\
\hline
21,018
\end{array}
$$

Warm Up   Find the products.

1. $\begin{array}{r} 3,458 \\ \times \quad 2 \\ \hline \end{array}$
2. $\begin{array}{r} 5,389 \\ \times \quad 6 \\ \hline \end{array}$
3. $\begin{array}{r} 4,703 \\ \times \quad 4 \\ \hline \end{array}$
4. $\begin{array}{r} 5,072 \\ \times \quad 7 \\ \hline \end{array}$
5. $\begin{array}{r} 8,003 \\ \times \quad 5 \\ \hline \end{array}$

178

Find the products.

1.	3,172 × 3	**2.** 6,314 × 8	**3.** 6,956 × 4	**4.** 3,205 × 9	**5.** 7,095 × 2

1. 3,172 × 3
2. 6,314 × 8
3. 6,956 × 4
4. 3,205 × 9
5. 7,095 × 2

6. 4,009 × 7
7. 3,418 × 5
8. 868 × 6
9. 9,538 × 3
10. 9,087 × 9

11. 5,279 × 8
12. 208 × 4
13. 9,837 × 2
14. 3,990 × 6
15. 7,148 × 8

16. 5 × 7,926   **17.** 9 × 6,041   **18.** 3 × 4,086

19. 4 × 3,519   **20.** 7 × 1,386   **21.** 8 × 3,007

22. Find the product of 2,691 and 2.

23. Find the product of 1,274 and 6.

24. Find the product of 5,240 and 5.

25. Find the product of 3,807 and 9.

Solve.

26. If a person in Lilliput eats 4 fish each week, how many fish would Gulliver get? (Remember, Gulliver gets 1,728 times as much as a person in Lilliput.)

27. Write and then solve a problem for this data.
There are 5,862 soldiers in Lilliput's army. Each soldier eats 3 chickens in 1 month.

THINK

Greatest Product Game

1. Number a cube 1 through 6. Each player draws a grid.

2. Take turns tossing the cube. After each toss, write the number in one of the boxes. Do this 5 times.

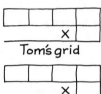

3. Find your product. The winner is the player with the greatest product.

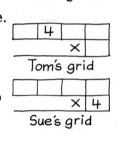

Who won?

→ **MATH** ←

Multiplying with Money

MENU

#1. Taco, beans, rice $2.35

#2. Burrito, beans, rice $2.79

#3. Enchilada, beans, rice $2.85

#4. Taco, Enchilada, beans, rice $3.25

The Wilson family went out to dinner. They wanted 5 orders of the number 4 dinner. How much did the Wilsons pay for the food?

Since we want the total for 5 dinners of the same price, we multiply.

Multiply as with whole numbers.

$$
\begin{array}{r}
\overset{1\ \ 2}{\$3.25} \\
\times \quad 5 \\
\hline
1625
\end{array}
$$

→

Show the product using dollars and cents.

$$
\begin{array}{r}
\overset{1\ \ 2}{\$3.25} \\
\times \quad 5 \\
\hline
\$16.25
\end{array}
$$

The Wilsons paid $16.25 for the food.

Other Examples

$$
\begin{array}{r}
\overset{5\ 2\ 5}{\$27.38} \\
\times \quad 7 \\
\hline
\$191.66
\end{array}
\qquad
\begin{array}{r}
\overset{\ \ \ 2}{\$30.04} \\
\times \quad 6 \\
\hline
\$180.24
\end{array}
\qquad
\begin{array}{r}
\overset{2\ 4}{\$6.25} \\
\times \quad 8 \\
\hline
\$50.00
\end{array}
\qquad
\begin{array}{r}
\overset{3}{\$0.79} \\
\times \quad 4 \\
\hline
\$3.16
\end{array}
$$

Warm Up Multiply. Write the answers with dollars and cents.

1. $34.27 × 7
2. $6.98 × 3
3. $20.05 × 4
4. $75.75 × 8
5. $0.35 × 6

Multiply. Write the amounts with dollars and cents.

1. $19.43
    ×   2

2. $13.59
    ×   5

3. $10.72
    ×   9

4. $0.87
    ×   4

5. $6.82
    ×   5

6. $83.70
    ×   6

7. $14.08
    ×   8

8. $0.93
    ×   7

9. $23.74
    ×   3

10. $57.62
     ×   2

11. $9.85
     ×   9

12. $0.23
     ×   8

13. $36.19
     ×   4

14. $70.04
     ×   5

15. $51.60
     ×   7

16. 6 × $41.26   17. 3 × $5.01   18. 5 × $0.75

19. 2 × $80.98   20. 9 × $34.66   21. 4 × $40.80

22. 8 at $49.60 each   23. 3 at $0.89 each

24. 7 at $8.95 each   25. 6 at $75.42 each

Solve.

26. How much would 6 orders of the number 2 dinner cost? Use the menu to find the cost of one dinner.

27. The cook buys tomatoes by the crate. Each crate costs $12.75. How much will 7 crates cost?

28. **DATA HUNT** Get a menu from a place where you like to eat. Pick something you would want to order. How much would it cost for 7 orders?

THINK

Using a Calculator

How many books did Dr. Thomas buy?

Books $17.45 each

Book Store
$ 17.45
×   IIII
Total $122.15

MATH

PROBLEM SOLVING
Using Data from an Order Form

Marion Miller owns the Costume Shop in San Francisco. She is ordering some costumes to sell in her store. She has filled out the order form to show how many of each item she wants.

COSTUME FACTORY
New York, New York

Name __The Costume Shop__
Address __1234 Market St.__
  __San Francisco, California__

Item	Catalog Number	Quantity	PRICE EACH		TOTAL PRICE	
			Dollars	Cents	Dollars	Cents
1. Clown wig	21-281	8	$ 7.	45	$ 59.	60
2. Clown suit	23-281	5	17.	98		
3. Rabbit suit	25-116	—	19.	98		
4. Superman suit	25-118	1	19.	98		
5. Wonder Woman suit	27-118	—	22.	49		
6. Pirate suit	25-114	3	21.	99		
7. Witch hat	27-356	6	5.	98		
8. Witch suit	23-545	6	18.	75		

TOTAL FOR ORDER [   ]

Use the order form to answer these questions.

1. How much do 5 clown suits cost?

2. What is the cost of 1 clown wig and 1 clown suit?

3. How much more does a Wonder Woman suit cost than a Superman suit?

Use the order form to answer these questions.

1. Marion is ordering 3 pirate suits. How much will they cost in all?

2. How much does it cost to order 1 witch hat and 1 witch suit?

3. How much will Marian pay for the witch suits she wants to order?

4. Which suits cost more than the Superman suit?

5. What is the difference in price between the rabbit suit and the Wonder Woman suit?

6. What is the total price for the witch hats Marian is ordering?

7. How many items in all is Marian ordering?

8. How much will it cost in all for the witch suits and the Superman suit Marian wants to order?

9. How much more will 3 pirate suits cost than 1 Superman suit?

10. How much will 6 complete witch outfits cost? (A witch outfit is hat and suit together.)

11. *Try This* A space suit and hat cost $30. The suit costs $8 more than the hat. How much is the space suit?

PROBLEM SOLVING
Work Backward

Try This Farmer Jones decided to stop raising hogs. He sold 17. He divided the rest equally among his 6 children. Each child got 8 hogs. How many hogs did Farmer Jones start with?

TO SOLVE THIS PROBLEM, YOU NEED TO DO MORE THAN JUST QUICKLY DECIDE TO ADD, SUBTRACT, MULTIPLY OR DIVIDE. A STRATEGY THAT MIGHT BE HELPFUL TO YOU IS GIVEN BELOW.

WORK BACKWARD

SINCE EACH OF THE 6 CHILDREN GOT 8 HOGS, I'LL MULTIPLY TO FIND THE NUMBER THAT WERE DIVIDED EQUALLY.

SINCE 17 WERE SOLD, I'LL "ADD BACK" THAT NUMBER TO SEE HOW MANY THERE WERE TO START.

$$8 \times 6 = 48$$
hogs children number divided equally

$$48 + 17 = 65$$
number shared number sold number at the start

Farmer Jones started with 65 hogs.

Solve.

1. Andrew bought 6 books. Each book cost $3. Then he spent $7 for a tape. How much money did Andrew start with if he had no money left?

2. Loni had some cards. She gave 6 friends 5 cards each. She gave another friend 7. Loni kept 9 cards. How many cards did she start with?

Multiply.

1. 3×50 2. 9×40 3. 7×400 4. $4 \times 8,000$

5. $2 \times 2 \times 100 = \square$ 6. $6 \times 1 \times 10 = \square$ 7. $2 \times 4 \times 1,000 = \square$

8.
$$\begin{array}{r} 63 \\ \times\ 9 \\ \hline \end{array}$$
9.
$$\begin{array}{r} 78 \\ \times\ 3 \\ \hline \end{array}$$
10.
$$\begin{array}{r} 34 \\ \times\ 5 \\ \hline \end{array}$$
11.
$$\begin{array}{r} 612 \\ \times\ 4 \\ \hline \end{array}$$
12.
$$\begin{array}{r} 105 \\ \times\ 7 \\ \hline \end{array}$$

13.
$$\begin{array}{r} 243 \\ \times\ 3 \\ \hline \end{array}$$
14.
$$\begin{array}{r} 116 \\ \times\ 6 \\ \hline \end{array}$$
15.
$$\begin{array}{r} 386 \\ \times\ 2 \\ \hline \end{array}$$
16.
$$\begin{array}{r} 637 \\ \times\ 5 \\ \hline \end{array}$$
17.
$$\begin{array}{r} 436 \\ \times\ 9 \\ \hline \end{array}$$

Estimate. Round as indicated.

18. nearest ten 19. nearest hundred 20. nearest dollar

4×83 7×315 $6 \times \$8.79$

Multiply.

21.
$$\begin{array}{r} 6,351 \\ \times\ 3 \\ \hline \end{array}$$
22.
$$\begin{array}{r} 4,036 \\ \times\ 8 \\ \hline \end{array}$$
23.
$$\begin{array}{r} 8,607 \\ \times\ 6 \\ \hline \end{array}$$
24.
$$\begin{array}{r} 7,050 \\ \times\ 4 \\ \hline \end{array}$$
25.
$$\begin{array}{r} 5,812 \\ \times\ 7 \\ \hline \end{array}$$

26.
$$\begin{array}{r} \$0.13 \\ \times\ 5 \\ \hline \end{array}$$
27.
$$\begin{array}{r} \$0.46 \\ \times\ 7 \\ \hline \end{array}$$
28.
$$\begin{array}{r} \$1.08 \\ \times\ 8 \\ \hline \end{array}$$
29.
$$\begin{array}{r} \$6.87 \\ \times\ 6 \\ \hline \end{array}$$
30.
$$\begin{array}{r} \$84.28 \\ \times\ 9 \\ \hline \end{array}$$

Solve.

31. How much do 5 witch hats cost?

32. How much more does the witch suit cost than the witch hat?

ITEM	PRICE EACH	
	DOLLARS	CENTS
1. WITCH HAT	5.	98
2. WITCH SUIT	18.	75

Trading Ones

$$\overset{1}{25} \times 3 = 75$$

Think
3 × 5 = 15
15 ones = 1 ten and 5 ones

Think
3 × 2 tens = 6 tens
and 1 more ten makes 7 tens

Trading Tens

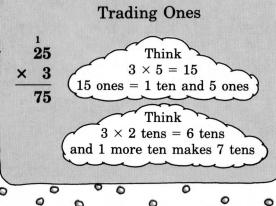

$$\overset{2}{68} \times 3 = 204$$

2 tens

24 ones = 2 tens and 4 ones

20 tens = 2 hundreds and 0 tens

Trading Hundreds

$$\overset{3\,3}{879} \times 4 = 3516$$

36 ones = 3 tens and 6 ones

31 tens = 3 hundreds and 1 ten

35 hundreds =
3 thousands and 5 hundreds

Multiply.

1.	17 × 4	**2.**	16 × 5	**3.**	26 × 3
4.	48 × 2	**5.**	13 × 6	**6.**	23 × 4
7.	19 × 3	**8.**	37 × 2	**9.**	17 × 5
10.	67 × 4	**11.**	73 × 6	**12.**	49 × 3
13.	78 × 2	**14.**	51 × 5	**15.**	65 × 8
16.	33 × 7	**17.**	83 × 3	**18.**	75 × 9
19.	576 × 2	**20.**	607 × 3	**21.**	765 × 4
22.	437 × 4	**23.**	852 × 5	**24.**	386 × 7
25.	650 × 8	**26.**	432 × 6	**27.**	906 × 4

Using a Calculator

The multiplication table below has some factors and products missing. Copy the table and use your calculator to find the missing numbers. To help you, the factors are shaded red and the products are shaded blue.

REMEMBER:

1. Missing products are found by multiplying.

2. Missing factors are found by dividing.

×	37	Hint 4,088 ÷ 73		19
	1,406			
Hint 3,293 ÷ 37	3,293			
67			5,226	Hint 67 × 19
73	4,088			

CUMULATIVE REVIEW

Give the letter for the correct answer.

Estimate by rounding to the nearest ten.

1. 62
   + 27
   A 10   B 80
   C 90   D not given

2. 86
   − 25
   A 40   B 60
   C 50   D not given

Estimate by rounding to the nearest hundred.

3. 412
   + 350
   A 700   B 900
   C 800   D not given

4. 675
   − 349
   A 300   B 400
   C 200   D not given

Estimate by rounding to the nearest dollar.

5. $7.28
   + 3.62
   A $11   B $10
   C $12   D not given

6. $5.50
   − 3.29
   A $2   B $3
   C $4   D not given

Which answer is correct?

7. $42 \div 6$
   A 9   B 8
   C 7   D not given

8. $36 \div 4$
   A 9   B 8
   C 7   D not given

9. $0 \div 7$
   A 0   B 7
   C 1   D not given

10. $81 \div 9$
    A 7   B 8
    C 9   D not given

11. $48 \div 8$
    A 5   B 6
    C 2   D not given

12. $4 \div 4$
    A 0   B 1
    C 2   D not given

13. Al planted 12 pumpkins. There were 6 pumpkins in each row. How many rows of pumpkins did Al plant?
    A 6   B 2
    C 3   D not given

14. Laura picked 16 apples. She divided them equally among 4 friends. How many apples did each friend get?
    A 3   B 5
    C 4   D not given

DIVISION: 1-Digit Divisors

Because Katie was blind, she always jogged with a friend. Katie needed some running shoes. Proper shoes would protect her body from the hard pounding when she ran. The shoe store had 64 different kinds of shoes. The clerk said her store had 4 times as many kinds of shoes as there were in the whole world in 1967. She pointed out the thick, flexible sole on the bottom of the shoe. She said there should be enough room for the toes, and the heel should not slip. Katie tried out several pairs of shoes. Then she made her choice.

Using Division Facts: Mental Math

Ms. Benson gives tennis lessons. She needs to buy 120 tennis balls. There are 3 balls in each can. How many cans does she need to order?

Since each can has the same number of balls, we divide.

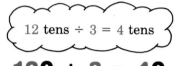

12 tens ÷ 3 = 4 tens

120 ÷ 3 = 40

Ms. Benson needs to order 40 cans of tennis balls.

Other Examples

80 ÷ 4 = 20   **90 ÷ 9 = 10**   **420 ÷ 6 = 70**   **300 ÷ 6 = 50**

Warm Up   Give the quotients aloud.

1. $80 \div 4$	**2.** $50 \div 5$	**3.** $80 \div 2$	**4.** $90 \div 3$
5. $60 \div 2$	**6.** $70 \div 7$	**7.** $40 \div 2$	**8.** $60 \div 6$
9. $120 \div 2$	**10.** $150 \div 3$	**11.** $180 \div 6$	**12.** $240 \div 8$
13. $490 \div 7$	**14.** $350 \div 5$	**15.** $320 \div 4$	**16.** $450 \div 9$
17. $200 \div 4$	**18.** $400 \div 5$	**19.** $300 \div 5$	**20.** $100 \div 5$
21. $180 \div 2$	**22.** $270 \div 3$	**23.** $160 \div 8$	**24.** $250 \div 5$

Find the quotients. Write answers only.

1. $40 \div 4$ 2. $60 \div 3$ 3. $80 \div 2$ 4. $90 \div 3$

5. $80 \div 4$ 6. $80 \div 8$ 7. $60 \div 2$ 8. $40 \div 2$

9. $80 \div 2$ 10. $70 \div 7$ 11. $50 \div 5$ 12. $60 \div 6$

13. $160 \div 4$ 14. $120 \div 3$ 15. $150 \div 5$ 16. $240 \div 6$

17. $210 \div 7$ 18. $320 \div 8$ 19. $270 \div 9$ 20. $160 \div 2$

21. $20 \div 2$ 22. $360 \div 6$ 23. $210 \div 3$ 24. $450 \div 9$

25. $360 \div 4$ 26. $560 \div 8$ 27. $60 \div 3$ 28. $720 \div 8$

29. $180 \div 9$ 30. $200 \div 4$ 31. $90 \div 3$ 32. $480 \div 6$

33. Divide 280 by 4.   34. Divide 240 by 3.   35. Divide 560 by 7.

Solve.

36. Mr. Cox gives golf lessons. He needs to buy 60 golf balls. There are 3 balls to a box. How many boxes of balls does he need to order?

37. Write a question for this story and then answer it. Ms. Benson ordered 300 ping-pong balls. There are 6 balls in each box.

38. In one day a factory makes 72,000 tennis balls. There are 3 tennis balls in each can and 24 cans in a case. How many cases of tennis balls does the factory make in one day?

Finding Quotients and Remainders

Victor has 25 dog biscuits. He wants to divide them equally among his 3 dogs. How many biscuits will he give to each dog? How many biscuits will be left?

Since the dogs are sharing equally, we divide.

$3 \times ?$ is close to 25?

$3 \times 7 = 21$ That is close.
$3 \times 8 = 24$ That is closer.
$3 \times 9 = 27$ That is too large.
      I'll try 8.

biscuits used

$$\begin{array}{r} 8 \ R1 \\ 3\overline{)25} \\ -24 \\ \hline 1 \end{array}$$

biscuits remaining

Victor gave 8 biscuits to each dog. He had 1 extra biscuit.

Other Examples

$$\begin{array}{r} 1 \ R3 \\ 5\overline{)8} \\ -5 \\ \hline 3 \end{array} \qquad \begin{array}{r} 0 \ R2 \\ 4\overline{)2} \\ -0 \\ \hline 2 \end{array} \qquad \begin{array}{r} 4 \ R5 \\ 6\overline{)29} \\ -24 \\ \hline 5 \end{array} \qquad \begin{array}{r} 5 \\ 8\overline{)40} \\ -40 \\ \hline 0 \end{array}$$

Warm Up Find the quotients and remainders.

1. $3\overline{)7}$　　2. $4\overline{)6}$　　3. $7\overline{)5}$　　4. $2\overline{)9}$　　5. $8\overline{)4}$

6. $5\overline{)18}$　　7. $6\overline{)26}$　　8. $9\overline{)40}$　　9. $4\overline{)15}$　　10. $7\overline{)47}$

11. $9\overline{)63}$　　12. $8\overline{)62}$　　13. $3\overline{)29}$　　14. $6\overline{)46}$　　15. $4\overline{)34}$

Find the quotients and remainders.

1. $5\overline{)31}$ **2.** $7\overline{)9}$ **3.** $4\overline{)35}$ **4.** $9\overline{)3}$ **5.** $2\overline{)17}$

6. $6\overline{)13}$ **7.** $8\overline{)26}$ **8.** $5\overline{)27}$ **9.** $7\overline{)45}$ **10.** $4\overline{)9}$

11. $8\overline{)37}$ **12.** $9\overline{)51}$ **13.** $3\overline{)8}$ **14.** $6\overline{)21}$ **15.** $5\overline{)49}$

16. $9\overline{)77}$ **17.** $6\overline{)5}$ **18.** $7\overline{)15}$ **19.** $3\overline{)23}$ **20.** $2\overline{)7}$

21. $4\overline{)27}$ **22.** $9\overline{)55}$ **23.** $3\overline{)7}$ **24.** $8\overline{)65}$ **25.** $7\overline{)39}$

26. $13 \div 2 = n$ **27.** $37 \div 4 = n$ **28.** $5 \div 3 = n$

29. $79 \div 9 = n$ **30.** $43 \div 5 = n$ **31.** $16 \div 6 = n$

32. What is 66 divided by 8?   **33.** What is 5 divided by 2?

34. What is 4 divided by 6?   **35.** What is 41 divided by 5?

Solve.

36. Josh has 29 cat treats. He divided them equally among his 4 cats. How many treats did he give to each cat? How many extra treats are left?

37. Write a story and question for this data. Then answer the question.

    goldfish in all—   56
    goldfish in each tank—   8

More Practice, page 403, Set B

THINK

Logical Reasoning

Find the missing divisors.

$$\begin{array}{r} 6\ \text{R2} \\ \underline{\ \ \ \ \ \ }\overline{)38} \\ -\ 36 \\ \hline 2 \end{array}$$

A.

$$\begin{array}{r} 7\ \text{R7} \\ \underline{\ \ \ \ \ \ }\overline{)63} \\ -\ 56 \\ \hline 7 \end{array}$$

B.

MATH

2-Digit Quotients

A chess game has 32 pieces. There are 2 players. How many pieces does each player get?

Since the pieces are shared equally, we divide.

Dividing Tens
- Divide
- Multiply
- Subtract
- Compare

$$
\begin{array}{r}
1 \\
2\overline{)32} \\
-2 \\
\hline
1
\end{array}
$$

- $2\overline{)3}^{\,1}$
- 1×2
- $3 - 2$
- $1 < 2$

Each player gets 1 ten.

Dividing Ones
- Bring down the ones next to the tens.

$$
\begin{array}{r}
1 \\
2\overline{)32} \\
-2\downarrow \\
\hline
12
\end{array}
$$

Trade the 1 ten for 10 ones.

10 ones and 2 ones equal 12 ones.

- Divide

$$
\begin{array}{r}
16 \\
2\overline{)32} \\
-2 \\
\hline
12 \\
-12 \\
\hline
0
\end{array}
$$

- $2\overline{)12}^{\,6}$

- Multiply
- Subtract
- Compare

- $6 \times 2 = 12$
- $12 - 12 = 0$
- $0 < 2$

Divide the ones. Each player gets 6 ones.

Each player gets 16 pieces.

Other Examples

$$
\begin{array}{r}
16\text{ R1} \\
4\overline{)65} \\
-4 \\
\hline
25 \\
-24 \\
\hline
1
\end{array}
\qquad
\begin{array}{r}
30 \\
3\overline{)90} \\
-9 \\
\hline
00 \\
-0 \\
\hline
0
\end{array}
\qquad
\begin{array}{r}
15\text{ R4} \\
6\overline{)94} \\
-6 \\
\hline
34 \\
-30 \\
\hline
4
\end{array}
\qquad
\begin{array}{r}
10\text{ R2} \\
7\overline{)72} \\
-7 \\
\hline
02 \\
-0 \\
\hline
2
\end{array}
$$

Warm Up Find the quotients and remainders.

1. $3\overline{)42}$ 2. $4\overline{)61}$ 3. $6\overline{)63}$ 4. $2\overline{)80}$ 5. $8\overline{)85}$

Find the quotients and remainders.

1. $4\overline{)52}$ **2.** $2\overline{)75}$ **3.** $5\overline{)57}$ **4.** $8\overline{)97}$ **5.** $3\overline{)59}$

6. $2\overline{)60}$ **7.** $4\overline{)19}$ **8.** $7\overline{)89}$ **9.** $6\overline{)80}$ **10.** $5\overline{)53}$

11. $3\overline{)67}$ **12.** $9\overline{)99}$ **13.** $8\overline{)81}$ **14.** $3\overline{)96}$ **15.** $5\overline{)39}$

16. $4\overline{)71}$ **17.** $7\overline{)37}$ **18.** $2\overline{)36}$ **19.** $5\overline{)83}$ **20.** $4\overline{)86}$

21. $94 \div 3 = n$ **22.** $71 \div 6 = n$ **23.** $42 \div 4 = n$

24. $80 \div 7 = n$ **25.** $57 \div 2 = n$ **26.** $64 \div 5 = n$

27. Divide 93 by 8. **28.** Divide 76 by 6.

29. Divide 76 by 4. **30.** Divide 96 by 9.

Solve.

31. Four children played a game with 48 cards. They divided the cards equally among them. How many cards did each player get?

32. DATA HUNT Find a card game and count the cards. If you divide the cards equally among 3 players, how many cards will each player get?

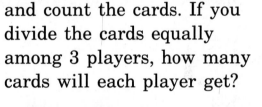

━━━━━ **SKILLKEEPER** ━━━━━

Multiply.

1. $\begin{array}{r} 20 \\ \times\ 4 \\ \hline \end{array}$ **2.** $\begin{array}{r} 12 \\ \times\ 8 \\ \hline \end{array}$ **3.** $\begin{array}{r} 46 \\ \times\ 2 \\ \hline \end{array}$ **4.** $\begin{array}{r} 33 \\ \times\ 3 \\ \hline \end{array}$ **5.** $\begin{array}{r} 31 \\ \times\ 9 \\ \hline \end{array}$

6. $\begin{array}{r} 75 \\ \times\ 7 \\ \hline \end{array}$ **7.** $\begin{array}{r} 60 \\ \times\ 5 \\ \hline \end{array}$ **8.** $\begin{array}{r} 302 \\ \times\ 3 \\ \hline \end{array}$ **9.** $\begin{array}{r} 410 \\ \times\ 6 \\ \hline \end{array}$ **10.** $\begin{array}{r} 649 \\ \times\ 2 \\ \hline \end{array}$

Checking Division

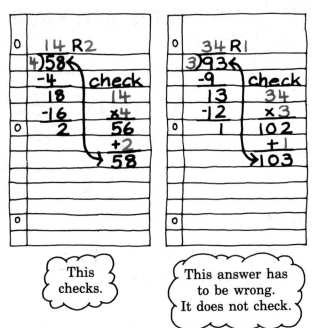

14 R2		34 R1	
4)58	check	3)93	check
-4	14	-9	34
18	×4	13	×3
-16	56	-12	102
2	+2	1	+1
	58		103

This checks.

This answer has to be wrong. It does not check.

Tracey checked two of her division problems using this method. She multiplied the quotient by the divisor and then added the remainder. If the total is the same as the number she divided, the problem checks.

Can you find Tracey's mistake?

Write the check for each problem and tell whether the problem is correct.

1. 2)35 — 17 R1

2. 6)75 — 10 R5

3. 3)62 — 20

4. 5)39 — 7 R4

5. 4)92 — 20 R2

Divide and then check your answers.

6. 3)52

7. 2)67

8. 4)23

9. 6)87

10. 5)72

11. 4)50

12. 6)58

13. 2)71

14. 3)78

15. 7)82

16. 3)20

17. 8)99

18. 3)92

19. 8)47

20. 2)98

21. $66 \div 4 = n$

22. $44 \div 3 = n$

23. $40 \div 7 = n$

24. $90 \div 6 = n$

25. $59 \div 5 = n$

26. $91 \div 8 = n$

27. Check this problem. Is it correct?   532 R5
    9)4673

PROBLEM SOLVING
Practice

QUESTION
DATA
PLAN
ANSWER
CHECK

Solve.

1. The library shelf is 76 cm long. Mrs. Abbot wants to put new books on the shelf. Each book is 4 cm thick. How many books can she fit on the shelf?

2. The library has 56 books about desert animals and 83 about jungle animals. How many fewer books are there about desert animals than about jungle animals?

3. The library has 87 books on water animals. Mrs. Abbot ordered 9 more. How many books will the library have on water animals?

4. George returned a library book that was 6 days overdue. He paid a 90¢ fine. What was the fine for each day?

5. Mrs. Abbot has $75 to buy new books for the library. Each book costs $9. How many books can she buy? How much money will be left?

6. There are 23 history books on each of 4 shelves and 18 history books on a fifth shelf. How many history books are there?

7. There are 56 old chairs and 24 new chairs in the library. Mrs. Abbot wants to put 6 chairs at each table. At how many tables can she put 6 chairs?

8. *Try This* Mrs. Abbot took all of the books out of a bookcase. She put 28 books on one table. Then she put the rest on another table in 7 stacks of 8. How many books were in the bookcase when she started? Hint: Work backward.

197

3-Digit Quotients

Ms. Collins paid $756 for 3 airplane tickets. The tickets were the same price. How much did she pay for each ticket?

Since each ticket costs the same, we divide.

Dividing Hundreds	Dividing Tens	Dividing Ones
• Divide	• Bring down	• Bring down
• Multiply	• Divide	• Divide
• Subtract	• Multiply	• Multiply
• Compare	• Subtract	• Subtract
	• Compare	• Compare

```
      2              25             252
  3)756          3)756          3)756
  - 6            - 6            - 6
    1              15             15
                 - 15           - 15
                   0              06          Check
                                - 6            252
                                  0          ×   3
                                               756
```

Ms. Collins paid $252 for each ticket.

Other Examples

```
   143 R3              181 R2              342 R1
 4)575               5)907               2)685
 - 4     Check       - 5     Check       - 6     Check
   17     143          40     181          08     342
 - 16   ×   4        - 40   ×   5        - 8    ×   2
   15     572          07     905          05     684
 - 12   +   3        -  5   +   2        - 4    +   1
    3     575           2     907           1     685
```

Warm Up Divide and check.

1. 3)417   2. 4)725   3. 6)705   4. 5)580   5. 4)448

Divide and check.

1. $2\overline{)356}$ 2. $4\overline{)635}$ 3. $3\overline{)456}$ 4. $6\overline{)675}$ 5. $7\overline{)807}$

6. $4\overline{)700}$ 7. $3\overline{)639}$ 8. $2\overline{)937}$ 9. $8\overline{)931}$ 10. $5\overline{)781}$

11. $4\overline{)924}$ 12. $8\overline{)894}$ 13. $2\overline{)246}$ 14. $3\overline{)805}$ 15. $6\overline{)935}$

16. $5\overline{)575}$ 17. $6\overline{)790}$ 18. $5\overline{)630}$ 19. $7\overline{)815}$ 20. $3\overline{)364}$

21. $663 \div 4 = n$ 22. $500 \div 3 = n$ 23. $939 \div 8 = n$

24. $573 \div 2 = n$ 25. $817 \div 6 = n$ 26. $333 \div 3 = n$

27. What is 836 divided by 2?

28. What is 777 divided by 6?

29. What is 591 divided by 4?

30. What is 609 divided by 5?

Solve.

31. The travel agent sold 5 airline tickets for $670. The tickets are all the same price. What is the price of each ticket?

★ 32. Mr. Kingston had $500. He bought 3 tickets that were all the same price and had $5 left. How much was each ticket?

33. Write a story and question for this equation.

$$\$465 \div 3 = \$155$$

More Practice, page 404, Set B

THINK

Using a Calculator

Start with 184.

Now guess how many times you can subtract 8 to reach 0.

Try it.

```
              184
1 time   −      8
              176
2 times  −      8
              168
```
Keep subtracting!

Was your guess too large, too small, or just right?

MATH

Deciding Where to Start

It takes 8 diamonds to
make each star in this quilt.
Sylvia has cut out 186 diamonds.
How many stars can she make
with these diamonds?

Since each star takes the same
number of diamonds, we divide.

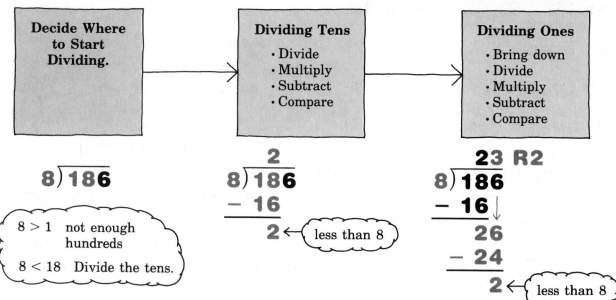

Decide Where to Start Dividing.	Dividing Tens	Dividing Ones
	• Divide • Multiply • Subtract • Compare	• Bring down • Divide • Multiply • Subtract • Compare

8)186

8 > 1   not enough hundreds
8 < 18   Divide the tens.

```
    2
8)186
 - 16
    2  ← less than 8
```

```
   23 R2
8)186
 - 16 ↓
    26
  - 24
     2  ← less than 8
```

Sylvia has enough diamonds to make
23 stars. She will have 2 extra diamonds.

Other Examples

```
   33 R3        71 R1         68          134 R3
4)135        8)569        3)204        5)673
 - 12         - 56         - 18         - 5
   15           09           24           17
 - 12          - 8          - 24         - 15
    3            1            0            23
                                         - 20
                                            3
```

Warm Up   Divide and check.

1. 3)167   2. 5)275   3. 4)125   4. 7)308   5. 6)825

200

Divide and check.

1. $2\overline{)156}$ 2. $3\overline{)185}$ 3. $6\overline{)409}$ 4. $8\overline{)340}$ 5. $7\overline{)234}$

6. $6\overline{)309}$ 7. $4\overline{)456}$ 8. $3\overline{)250}$ 9. $8\overline{)283}$ 10. $6\overline{)379}$

11. $5\overline{)893}$ 12. $8\overline{)489}$ 13. $2\overline{)109}$ 14. $9\overline{)378}$ 15. $7\overline{)300}$

16. $5\overline{)355}$ 17. $3\overline{)704}$ 18. $4\overline{)356}$ 19. $2\overline{)835}$ 20. $7\overline{)569}$

21. $430 \div 9$ 22. $170 \div 5$ 23. $200 \div 3$

24. $147 \div 2$ 25. $910 \div 8$ 26. $324 \div 4$

27. Divide 292 by 3.   28. Divide 209 by 5.

29. Divide 521 by 6.   30. Divide 168 by 8.

Solve.

31. Each square in the quilt takes 4 dark triangles. Sylvia has 104 triangles. How many squares can she make?

★ 32. Mr. Orr is making a quilt that takes 252 triangles. He needs the same number of red, green, and yellow triangles. How many of each color should he cut?

THINK

Greatest Quotient Game

1. Draw a division grid for each player.
2. Take turns tossing a number cube. After each toss, write the number in one of the boxes. Do this four times.

Mindy's grid

Diane's grid

3. Find your quotient and remainder. The winner is the player with the greatest quotient.

| 3 | 5 | 4 | 6 |

Mindy's grid

| 4 | 6 | 5 | 3 |

Diane's grid

Who won?

➡ **MATH** ⬅

Zero in the Quotient

The Great Pyramid in Egypt has a perimeter of 920 m around the base. The pyramid has a square base. What is the length of each side of the base?

Since we want to know the number of meters for each of the sides, we divide.

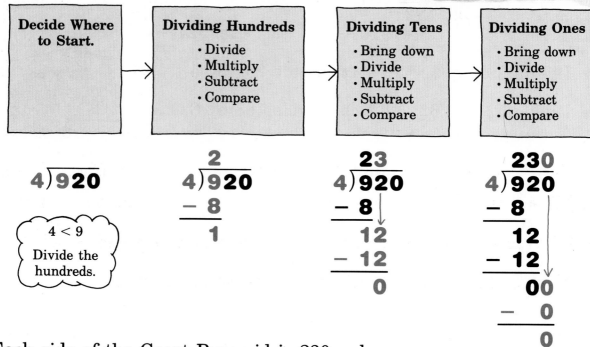

Decide Where to Start.	Dividing Hundreds	Dividing Tens	Dividing Ones
	• Divide • Multiply • Subtract • Compare	• Bring down • Divide • Multiply • Subtract • Compare	• Bring down • Divide • Multiply • Subtract • Compare

$$4\overline{)920}$$

4 < 9

Divide the hundreds.

$$\begin{array}{r} 2 \\ 4\overline{)920} \\ -\,8 \\ \hline 1 \end{array}$$

$$\begin{array}{r} 23 \\ 4\overline{)920} \\ -\,8\downarrow \\ \hline 12 \\ -\,12 \\ \hline 0 \end{array}$$

$$\begin{array}{r} 230 \\ 4\overline{)920} \\ -\,8 \\ \hline 12 \\ -\,12 \\ \hline 00 \\ -\;\,0 \\ \hline 0 \end{array}$$

Each side of the Great Pyramid is 230 m long.

Other Examples

$$\begin{array}{r} 10\ \text{R}5 \\ 6\overline{)65} \\ -\,6 \\ \hline 05 \\ -\,0 \\ \hline 5 \end{array}$$

$$\begin{array}{r} 406\ \text{R}1 \\ 2\overline{)813} \\ -\,8 \\ \hline 01 \\ -\,0 \\ \hline 13 \\ -\,12 \\ \hline 1 \end{array}$$

$$\begin{array}{r} 200\ \text{R}2 \\ 3\overline{)602} \\ -\,6 \\ \hline 00 \\ -\,0 \\ \hline 02 \\ -\,0 \\ \hline 2 \end{array}$$

$$\begin{array}{r} 40 \\ 8\overline{)320} \\ -\,32 \\ \hline 00 \\ -\,0 \\ \hline 0 \end{array}$$

Warm Up Divide.

1. $3\overline{)31}$ 2. $4\overline{)837}$ 3. $6\overline{)844}$ 4. $5\overline{)504}$ 5. $9\overline{)456}$

Divide.

1. $2\overline{)61}$ 2. $3\overline{)928}$ 3. $4\overline{)563}$ 4. $7\overline{)735}$ 5. $5\overline{)350}$

6. $3\overline{)632}$ 7. $6\overline{)485}$ 8. $7\overline{)73}$ 9. $5\overline{)543}$ 10. $8\overline{)806}$

11. $2\overline{)741}$ 12. $8\overline{)812}$ 13. $7\overline{)703}$ 14. $5\overline{)53}$ 15. $2\overline{)121}$

16. $650 \div 6 = n$ 17. $993 \div 9 = n$ 18. $902 \div 3 = n$
19. $321 \div 4 = n$ 20. $60 \div 6 = n$ 21. $801 \div 4 = n$

22. What is 212 divided by 3?   23. What is 83 divided by 4?

24. What is 418 divided by 2?   25. What is 846 divided by 7?

Solve.

26. The Third Pyramid has a perimeter of 436 m around its square base. How long is each side of the base?

27. **DATA BANK** See page 384. What is the length of each side of the base for the North Stone Pyramid?

SKILLKEEPER

Divide.

1. $9\overline{)27}$ 2. $5\overline{)25}$ 3. $7\overline{)63}$ 4. $6\overline{)42}$ 5. $4\overline{)32}$

6. $9\overline{)81}$ 7. $7\overline{)28}$ 8. $6\overline{)24}$ 9. $8\overline{)40}$ 10. $3\overline{)27}$

Dividing with Money

Ira bought a subscription to a science magazine for children. It cost $6.00 for 8 magazines. How much did each magazine cost?

Since we want the cost of each magazine, we divide.

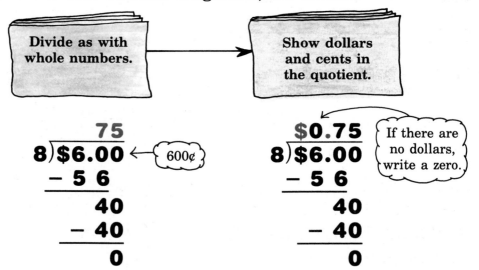

| Divide as with whole numbers. | → | Show dollars and cents in the quotient. |

```
    75
8)$6.00  ← 600¢
  -5 6
    40
   -40
     0
```

```
   $0.75        If there are
8)$6.00         no dollars,
  -5 6          write a zero.
    40
   -40
     0
```

Each magazine cost 75 cents.

Other Examples

```
   $0.91
5)$4.55
  -4 5
    05
   - 5
     0
```

```
   $1.04
8)$8.32
  -8
   0 3
  - 0
    32
   -32
     0
```

```
   $0.05        If there are
9)$0.45         no dimes,
  -45           write a zero.
    0
```

Warm Up Divide. Show dollars and cents.

1. 2)$7.30   2. 4)$8.20   3. 6)$1.50   4. 3)$0.48   5. 5)$0.20

Divide. Show dollars and cents.

1. $5 \overline{)\$9.15}$
2. $6 \overline{)\$7.86}$
3. $7 \overline{)\$3.50}$
4. $4 \overline{)\$0.84}$
5. $2 \overline{)\$0.10}$

6. $7 \overline{)\$7.00}$
7. $8 \overline{)\$4.24}$
8. $3 \overline{)\$0.90}$
9. $6 \overline{)\$8.94}$
10. $4 \overline{)\$0.24}$

11. $3 \overline{)\$2.55}$
12. $7 \overline{)\$7.91}$
13. $3 \overline{)\$0.15}$
14. $2 \overline{)\$6.08}$
15. $8 \overline{)\$0.96}$

16. $4 \overline{)\$8.76}$
17. $2 \overline{)\$0.56}$
18. $8 \overline{)\$9.60}$
19. $6 \overline{)\$0.36}$
20. $5 \overline{)\$4.00}$

21. $\$1.40 \div 2 = n$
22. $\$9.00 \div 3 = n$
23. $\$0.32 \div 8 = n$

24. $\$0.80 \div 4 = n$
25. $\$5.46 \div 3 = n$

26. $\$0.78 \div 6 = n$
27. Divide $3.68 by 4.

28. Divide $0.63 by 7.

Solve.

29. Jamie bought a subscription that cost $9.60. There were 6 magazines. How much did each magazine cost?

30. The daily rate for a newspaper is $1.80 each week. This rate includes a paper for each day of the week except Sunday. What is the cost for each day?

31. The subscription price for the Sunday newspaper for one year is $28.60. If there are 52 Sundays in the year, what is the price for each paper?

More Practice, page 406, Set A

THINK

Logical Reasoning

Find the missing subscription price for 8 magazines.

MAGAZINES
8 for ?

$$
\begin{array}{r}
\$1.23 \\
8 \overline{)\text{\rule{2cm}{0.4pt}}} \\
-\ 8 \\
\hline
18 \\
-\ 16 \\
\hline
24 \\
-\ 24 \\
\hline
0
\end{array}
$$

MATH

Finding Averages

Tico, Josh, and Mary Lou went fishing. They put all their fish together and shared them equally. The number of fish each got is the average number of fish caught by each child. What is the average?

Since we want to find the average of 3 numbers, we add the numbers and divide the sum by 3.

Find the sum of all of the numbers. → Divide by the number of addends. → The quotient is the average of the numbers.

$$\begin{array}{r} 13 \\ 12 \\ + 17 \\ \hline 42 \end{array}$$

fish caught by Tico, Josh, and Mary Lou

$$\begin{array}{r} 14 \\ 3\overline{)42} \\ -3 \\ \hline 12 \\ -12 \\ \hline 0 \end{array}$$

14
The average number of fish caught by each child was 14.

Other Example

Distance

21 miles   17 miles   13 miles   13 miles

The average distance is 16 miles.

$$\begin{array}{r} 21 \\ 17 \\ 13 \\ + 13 \\ \hline 64 \end{array}$$

$$\begin{array}{r} 16 \\ 4\overline{)64} \\ -4 \\ \hline 24 \\ -24 \\ \hline 0 \end{array}$$

Find the averages of these numbers.

1. 16, 15, 22, 31

2. 14, 18, 19

3. 23, 19, 20, 22

4. 39, 47, 85

5. 16, 9, 15, 7, 13

6. 125, 138, 115, 126

More Practice, page 406, Set B

PROBLEM SOLVING
Using Data from a Table

The third, fourth, and fifth grade classes had an aluminum can drive to earn money for soccer equipment.

ALUMINUM CAN DRIVE

	First Week	Second Week	Third Week	Fourth Week
MS. TEO Grade 3	73	56	68	87
Mr. JOHNSON Grade 3	59	48	76	81
MRS. RIVERA Grade 4	102	87	53	62
MS. HANSON Grade 4	82	85	89	84
MR. MONROE Grade 5	78	66	67	105
MRS. WHITE Grade 5	66	72	83	75

Use the data in the table to answer these questions.

1. How many cans did Ms. Teo's class collect during the four weeks?

2. What is the average number of cans collected each week by Ms. Teo's class?

3. How many cans did Mrs. Rivera's class collect during the four weeks?

4. What is the average number of cans collected each week by Mrs. Rivera's class?

5. Which fifth grade class collected the most cans?

6. How many cans were collected by all classes during the second week?

7. What is the average number of cans collected by each class during the second week?

8. What is the average number of cans collected each week by Mr. Johnson's class?

9. *Try This* If 17 children brought in 5 cans each, and the rest of the children brought in 49 cans, what would be the total number of cans?

207

Estimating Quotients: Mental Math

In 4 hours a hot-air balloon traveled 116 km. If the balloon traveled the same distance each hour, about how many kilometers did it travel each hour?

Since you want an answer that is only **close** to the exact answer, **estimate** by rounding and dividing in your head.

Think of the problem. $\longrightarrow$ $116 \div 4$

Round and divide. $\longrightarrow$ **$120 \div 4 = 30$**

The hot-air balloon traveled about 30 km each hour.

Other Examples

nearest ten	nearest ten	nearest dollar

$87 \div 3$

$90 \div 3 = 30$

About 30

$475 \div 8$

$480 \div 8 = 60$

About 60

$\$41.98 \div 6$

$\$42 \div 6 = \$7$

About $7

Warm Up Estimate by rounding to the nearest ten.

1. $32 \div 3$
2. $78 \div 4$
3. $41 \div 2$
4. $57 \div 3$

5. $119 \div 3$
6. $238 \div 6$
7. $153 \div 5$
8. $346 \div 7$

Estimate by rounding to the nearest dollar.

9. $\$7.98 \div 2$
10. $\$6.25 \div 3$
11. $\$23.95 \div 6$
12. $\$19.85 \div 4$

Estimate the quotients. Write estimated answers only.
Estimate by rounding to the nearest ten.

1. $91 \div 3$ 2. $75 \div 4$ 3. $58 \div 2$ 4. $49 \div 5$

5. $252 \div 5$ 6. $423 \div 7$ 7. $357 \div 9$ 8. $182 \div 3$

9. $4\overline{)83}$ 10. $7\overline{)74}$ 11. $3\overline{)92}$ 12. $2\overline{)58}$

13. $5\overline{)451}$ 14. $6\overline{)535}$ 15. $7\overline{)142}$ 16. $3\overline{)213}$

Estimate by rounding to the nearest dollar.

17. $\$5.95 \div 2$ 18. $\$3.89 \div 2$ 19. $\$8.25 \div 4$ 20. $\$8.98 \div 3$

21. $\$32.19 \div 4$ 22. $\$12.10 \div 3$ 23. $\$47.95 \div 8$ 24. $\$24.95 \div 5$

25. $3\overline{)\$9.15}$ 26. $4\overline{)\$7.95}$ 27. $6\overline{)\$6.25}$ 28. $2\overline{)\$4.05}$

29. $5\overline{)\$24.98}$ 30. $9\overline{)\$45.25}$ 31. $3\overline{)\$11.75}$ 32. $5\overline{)\$9.98}$

Solve.

33. A hot-air balloon traveled 86 km in 3 hours. If the balloon traveled the same distance each hour, about how many kilometers did it travel each hour?

34. It cost $34.95 for 5 people to take a ride in a hot-air balloon. About how many dollars did the ride cost for each person?

THINK

Estimation

Estimate by rounding to the nearest ten. Which of these answers are about 600?

A $3 \times 22 = n$ B $47 + 12 = n$ C $995 - 411 = n$

D $190 \div 3 = n$ E $6 \times 9 = n$ F $378 + 213 = n$

→ MATH ←

PROBLEM SOLVING
Understanding the Answer

Sometimes division does not give you the answer you want. You have to understand how to use the remainder.

There are 82 campers who want to be on rowing teams. Each team has 7 people. How many teams can they make?

$$\begin{array}{r} 11\ R5 \\ 7\overline{)82} \\ -\ 7 \\ \hline 12 \\ -\ 7 \\ \hline 5 \end{array}$$

11 teams can be made.

> The 5 remaining campers are not enough for another team.

Vans took 130 campers to visit the local caves. Each van held 9 campers. How many vans were needed?

$$\begin{array}{r} 14\ R4 \\ 9\overline{)130} \\ -\ 9 \\ \hline 40 \\ -\ 36 \\ \hline 4 \end{array}$$

15 vans were needed.

> There were 14 full vans, but a fifteenth van was needed for the 4 remaining campers.

Lindy had $20 to spend. She bought T-shirts that cost $6 each. How much money did Lindy have after she bought the T-shirts?

$$\begin{array}{r} 3\ R2 \\ 6\overline{)20} \\ -\ 18 \\ \hline 2 \end{array}$$

Lindy had $2 left.

> She bought 3 T-shirts, but the question asks how much she has left. It does not ask how many T-shirts she bought.

Warm Up   Answer these problems carefully.

1. Each cabin holds 8 campers. How many cabins are needed for 235 campers?

2. Camp pictures cost $4 each. How many pictures can Lou buy with $15?

Answer each problem carefully.

1. A roll of film costs $3. Joyce had $11. She used the money to buy film. How much money was left?

2. The cook needs 250 glasses of juice for breakfast. A can of juice fills 7 glasses. How many cans should the cook open?

3. The campers needed 2 sheets for each bed. How many beds could they make if they used 471 sheets?

4. Some campers went to a cave. Each tour group had 5 campers. How many tour groups were needed for 87 campers?

5. The cook had 38 eggs. He used 4 eggs for each cake. He made as many cakes as he could. How many eggs were left?

6. About 129 campers went to a swim class every day. There were 9 campers in each class. How many classes were there?

7. The cook bought 432 rolls. Each package held 8 rolls. How many packages did the cook buy?

★ 8. There are 6 campers on a volleyball team. It takes 2 teams to play a game. How many games can be played at the same time with 54 campers?

9. *Try This* The cook asked for 1 boy and 1 girl to help him. 3 boys, Ned, Tim, and Ray, and 3 girls, Liz, Jeri, and Pat, wanted to help. How many ways could the cook choose?

PROBLEM SOLVING
Use Logical Reasoning

SOME PROBLEMS REQUIRE MORE THAN DECIDING WHETHER TO ADD, SUBTRACT, MULTIPLY, OR DIVIDE. TO SOLVE A PROBLEM LIKE THIS, YOU MIGHT USE THE STRATEGY GIVEN BELOW.

Try This The Seals club had 9 members who won ribbons at the swim meet. 7 of them won one blue ribbon. 6 of them won one red ribbon. How many of the Seals won both a blue and a red ribbon?

USE LOGICAL REASONING

7 BLUE RIBBONS WERE WON. 6 RED RIBBONS WERE WON. SO, 13 RIBBONS WERE WON IN ALL.

ONLY 9 OF THE SEALS WON RIBBONS.

THERE ARE 4 MORE RIBBONS THAN SEALS.

The Seals won 13 ribbons.

9 of the Seals won ribbons.

4 of the Seals must have won both a red and a blue ribbon.

Solve.

1. There are 24 children in Dan's class. 15 of them are in the music club and 18 of them are in the art club. Everyone is in one of the clubs. How many are in both clubs?

2. Everyone in the room is in one of the clubs. There are 10 in the room. There are 8 in the science club and 6 in the math club. How many are in both clubs?

212

Find the quotients and remainders.

1. $3\overline{)28}$ 2. $5\overline{)42}$ 3. $6\overline{)51}$ 4. $8\overline{)77}$ 5. $9\overline{)75}$

6. $7\overline{)86}$ 7. $4\overline{)91}$ 8. $2\overline{)54}$ 9. $5\overline{)66}$ 10. $8\overline{)93}$

11. $3\overline{)845}$ 12. $8\overline{)934}$ 13. $4\overline{)709}$ 14. $3\overline{)937}$ 15. $6\overline{)692}$

16. $3\overline{)280}$ 17. $2\overline{)623}$ 18. $3\overline{)818}$ 19. $5\overline{)592}$ 20. $6\overline{)715}$

21. $2\overline{)81}$ 22. $5\overline{)531}$ 23. $8\overline{)967}$ 24. $8\overline{)\$6.00}$ 25. $2\overline{)\$7.50}$

Find the averages of these numbers.

26. 89, 42, 16   27. 22, 16, 10, 12   28. 116, 147, 109, 124

Estimate by rounding to the nearest ten or dollar.

29. $92 \div 3$ 30. $158 \div 4$ 31. $356 \div 4$ 32. $\$3.95 \div 2$

Solve.

33. The cook made corn bread. Each pan of corn bread served 8 campers. How many pans of corn bread were needed to serve 208 campers?

34. There are 12 shelves of science books in the library. Each shelf holds 28 books. How many science books are there in the library?

ANOTHER LOOK

Find the right quotient.

$$3\overline{)26}$$

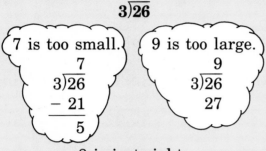

7 is too small.
$$\begin{array}{r} 7 \\ 3\overline{)26} \\ -21 \\ \hline 5 \end{array}$$

9 is too large.
$$\begin{array}{r} 9 \\ 3\overline{)26} \\ 27 \end{array}$$

8 is just right.
$$\begin{array}{r} 8 \\ 3\overline{)26} \\ -24 \\ \hline 2 \end{array}$$

Find the quotients and remainders.

1. $2\overline{)15}$ 2. $3\overline{)26}$ 3. $4\overline{)31}$

4. $5\overline{)36}$ 5. $6\overline{)53}$ 6. $7\overline{)48}$

7. $8\overline{)51}$ 8. $9\overline{)57}$ 9. $4\overline{)26}$

10. $2\overline{)59}$ 11. $3\overline{)85}$ 12. $4\overline{)70}$

Decide where to start.

Put an X to show where to start.

$$\overset{X}{3\overline{)784}}$$ (3 < 7 so divide hundreds.)

$$\overset{X}{5\overline{)362}}$$ (5 > 3 so divide tens.)

$$\overset{X}{7\overline{)483}}$$ (7 > 4 so divide tens.)

$$\overset{X}{4\overline{)539}}$$ (4 < 5 so divide hundreds.)

Put an X to show where to start.

13. $4\overline{)632}$ 14. $7\overline{)551}$

15. $8\overline{)813}$ 16. $6\overline{)235}$

Find the quotients and remainders.

17. $4\overline{)273}$ 18. $3\overline{)418}$

19. $2\overline{)934}$ 20. $6\overline{)325}$

Square Numbers

You can use colored chips to show odd numbers. Put the chips in the pattern shown below.

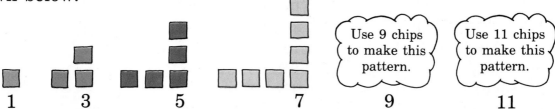

1   3   5   7   9   11

Use 9 chips to make this pattern.

Use 11 chips to make this pattern.

Now add the first two odd numbers. Show this with chips.

$$1 + 3 = 4$$

This new pattern is a square. Numbers with this pattern are **square numbers.** So 4 is a square number. There are two chips on each side. You used the first two odd numbers. So 4 is the square number for 2.

Now add the third odd number. There are three chips on each side. You used the first three odd numbers. Notice that 9 makes a square pattern. So 9 is the square number for 3.

$$1 + 3 + 5 = 9$$

What will the square numbers be for the first four odd numbers? the first five? the first six?

Using Computer Programs

A **program** is a set of instructions for the computer. The **line number** tells the computer the order in which you want it to follow instructions. The programs below use special words such as PRINT, END, and RUN. They also use special symbols for multiplication (∗) and division (/). Other symbols are quotation marks (" ") and semicolons (;).

PROGRAM	RUN

```
10  PRINT "12 * 3"
20  PRINT 12 * 3
30  END
RUN
```

Press RETURN or ENTER.

```
12 * 3
36
```

```
10  PRINT 96/3
20  PRINT "96/3"
30  PRINT "96/3 = ";
40  PRINT 96/3
50  END
RUN
```

```
32
96/3
96/3 = 32
```

1. What did the quotation marks cause the computer to do to line 10 of the first program?

2. What did the semicolon cause the computer to do to line 40 of the second program?

When we want the computer to erase the last program, we use the command NEW. Write the RUN for each of these programs.

1. NEW
   10 PRINT 27 * 4
   20 END

2. NEW
   10 PRINT "27 * 4"
   20 END

3. NEW
   10 PRINT "27 * 4 = "
   20 PRINT 27 * 4
   30 END

4. NEW
   10 PRINT "27 * 4 = ";
   20 PRINT 27 * 4
   30 END

5. NEW
   10 PRINT "91/7"
   20 PRINT 91/7
   30 PRINT "91/7 = "
   40 PRINT 91/7
   50 END

6. NEW
   10 PRINT "83 + 79"
   20 PRINT 83 + 79
   30 PRINT "83 + 79 = ";
   40 PRINT 83 + 79
   50 END

7. NEW
   10 PRINT "152 - 86 = "
   20 PRINT 152 - 86
   30 END

8. NEW
   10 PRINT "38 * 6 = ";
   20 PRINT 38 * 6
   30 END

★Write a program for each RUN.

9. 8 + 4

10. 12

11. 8 + 4
    12

12. 8 + 4 = 12

13. 7 * 9
    63

14. 7 * 9 = 63

CUMULATIVE REVIEW

Choose the letter for the correct answer.

1. $\begin{array}{r} 2 \\ \times 5 \end{array}$ **A** 7 **B** 8 **C** 10 **D** not given

2. $\begin{array}{r} 9 \\ \times 3 \end{array}$ **A** 18 **B** 27 **C** 24 **D** not given

3. $\begin{array}{r} 5 \\ \times 6 \end{array}$ **A** 40 **B** 20 **C** 36 **D** not given

4. $\begin{array}{r} 9 \\ \times 1 \end{array}$ **A** 0 **B** 1 **C** 9 **D** not given

Give the missing factor.

5. $8 \times \text{||||} = 56$
    A 9
    B 7
    C 8
    D not given

6. $\text{||||} \times 3 = 18$
    A 5
    B 6
    C 4
    D not given

7. $\text{||||} \times 8 = 32$
    A 4
    B 3
    C 5
    D not given

Give each time.

8. 2:55
    A 5 minutes to 1
    B 5 minutes to 2
    C 5 minutes to 3
    D not given

9. 1:45
    A quarter to 12
    B quarter to 1
    C quarter to 2
    D not given

10.
    A 6:35
    B 6:25
    C 5:30
    D not given

11.
    A 12:38
    B 8:00
    C 12:22
    D not given

12.
    A 20 minutes past 10
    B 20 minutes past 9
    C 40 minutes past 9
    D not given

13. Mia's classroom has 7 rows of desks. 4 desks are in each row. How many desks are in Mia's classroom?
    A 32 **B** 24
    C 28 **D** not given

14. William fills his dog's water dish 2 times a day. How many times does William fill the water dish in 7 days?
    A 9 **B** 14
    C 10 **D** not given

FRACTIONS

9

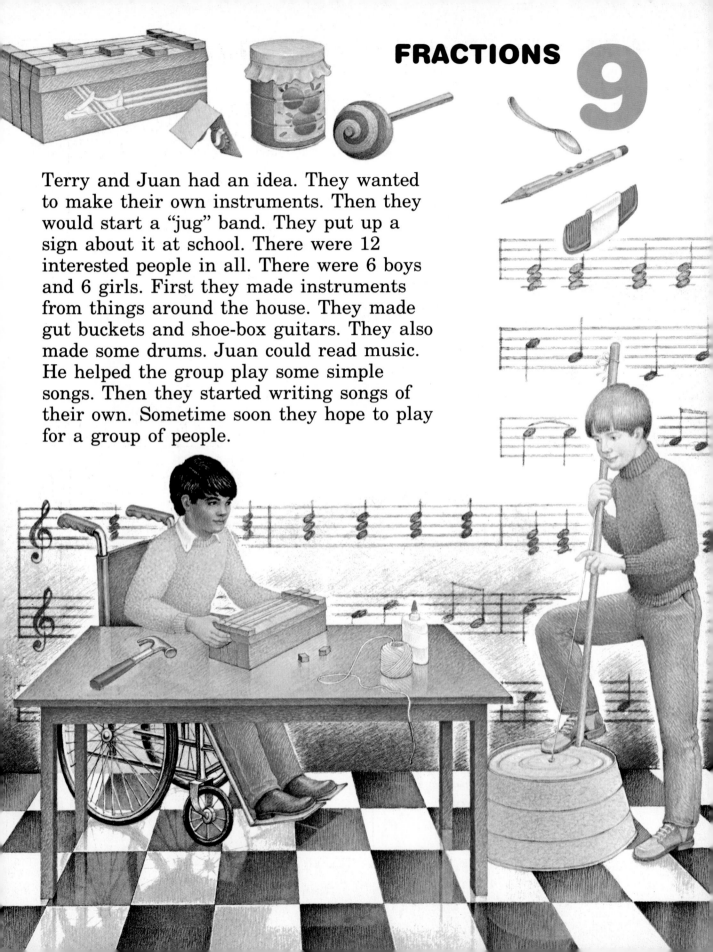

Terry and Juan had an idea. They wanted to make their own instruments. Then they would start a "jug" band. They put up a sign about it at school. There were 12 interested people in all. There were 6 boys and 6 girls. First they made instruments from things around the house. They made gut buckets and shoe-box guitars. They also made some drums. Juan could read music. He helped the group play some simple songs. Then they started writing songs of their own. Sometime soon they hope to play for a group of people.

Fractions and Regions

The field is divided into 3 equal parts. What part is planted?

Since **2** of the **3** equal parts are planted, we use a fraction to answer the question.

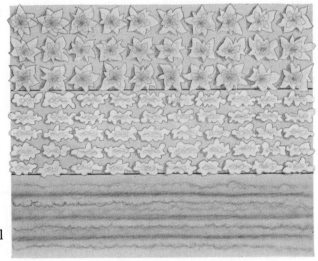

Numerator ⟶ $\mathbf{2}$
Number of parts planted

$\mathbf{3}$ ⟵ **Denominator**
Number of equal parts in all

We read the fraction as "**two thirds.**" $\frac{2}{3}$ of the field is planted.

Other Examples

$\frac{1}{2}$ is shaded.

$\frac{3}{8}$ is shaded.

$\frac{5}{5}$ is shaded.

One half is shaded.   Three eighths is shaded.   Five fifths is shaded.

Warm Up Write a fraction to tell what part is shaded. Read the fraction aloud.

1.

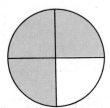

2.

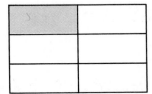

3.

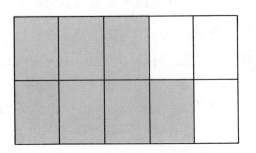

4.

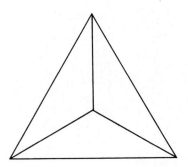

Write a fraction to tell what part is shaded.

1.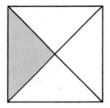

2.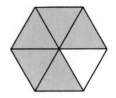

3.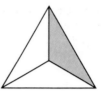

4.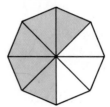

5.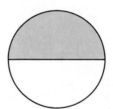

6.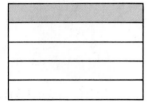

7.

8.

9.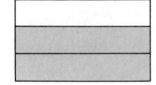

10.

11.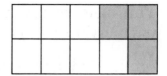

12.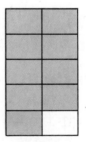

13. What fraction of this garden has been planted?

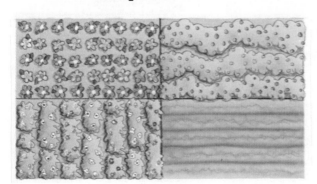

221

Fractions and Sets

The bulletin board is covered with papers from reading class. What fraction of the set of papers are yellow?

5 of the **8** papers are yellow.

$\frac{5}{8}$ of the papers are yellow.

Other Examples

What fraction of the papers are yellow?

$\frac{2}{5}$ of the papers are yellow.

What fraction of the books are red?

$\frac{3}{4}$ of the books are red.

What fraction of the set are pencils?

$\frac{1}{6}$ of the set are pencils.

Warm Up

1. What fraction of the papers are green?

2. What fraction of the books are blue?

3. What fraction of the set are pencils?

Write the fraction for each ▥.

1.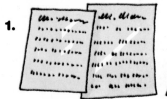

▥ of the papers are yellow.

2.

▥ of the papers are green.

3.

▥ of the books are blue.

4.

▥ of the books are open.

5.

▥ of the pencils are yellow.

6.

▥ of the set are pencils.

7.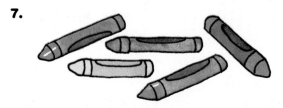

▥ of the crayons are green.

8.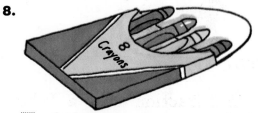

▥ of the crayons are missing.

THINK

Logical Reasoning

Give the fraction for each ▥.

▥ of the beach balls have **some** blue.

▥ of the beach balls have **no** blue.

▥ of the beach balls have **all** blue.

MATH

Equivalent Fractions

You can write two fractions for the part of this set that is brown.

4 of the **10** socks are brown.

$\frac{4}{10}$ of the socks are brown.

2 of the **5** pairs are brown.

$\frac{2}{5}$ of the socks are brown.

> Different fractions that name the same amount are **equivalent fractions.**

We write $\dfrac{4}{10} = \dfrac{2}{5}$

Other Examples

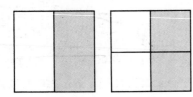

$\dfrac{1}{2} \overset{\times 2}{\underset{\times 2}{}} = \dfrac{2}{4}$

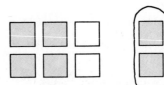

$\dfrac{4}{6} \quad = \quad \dfrac{2}{3}$

Warm Up Copy and complete.

1.

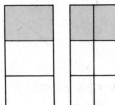

$\dfrac{1}{3} = \dfrac{}{}$

2.

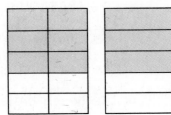

$\dfrac{6}{8} = \dfrac{}{}$

3.

$\dfrac{6}{10} = \dfrac{}{}$

Copy and complete.

1.

$$\frac{1}{2} = \frac{\text{▥}}{\text{▥}}$$

2.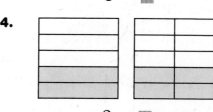

$$\frac{2}{3} = \frac{\text{▥}}{\text{▥}}$$

3.

$$\frac{2}{6} = \frac{\text{▥}}{\text{▥}}$$

4.

$$\frac{2}{5} = \frac{\text{▥}}{\text{▥}}$$

5.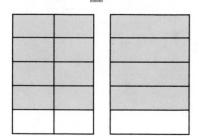

$$\frac{8}{10} = \frac{\text{▥}}{\text{▥}}$$

6. Write a pair of equivalent fractions for this set.

═══ **THINK** ═══

Shape Perception

From a sheet of notebook paper, cut a square about 8 in. on each side. Then:

1. Fold it once.

Fold

2. Fold it again.

Fold

3. Hold the corner with four tips and fold along the diagonal.

Fold

4. Now unfold it and color it to answer this question. How can exactly half of a square window be painted so that the unpainted part remains a perfect square?

→ **MATH** ←

More About Equivalent Fractions

The same amount of each pizza is left.

We can use multiplication to find equivalent fractions.

This pizza was cut into fourths.

This pizza was cut into eighths.

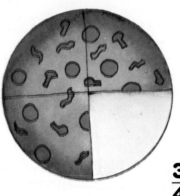

$$\frac{3}{4} = \frac{6}{8}$$

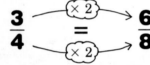

$$\frac{3}{4} = \frac{6}{8}$$

To find an equivalent fraction, multiply both the numerator and denominator by the same number.

Other Examples

$$\frac{1}{2} \overset{\times 2}{\underset{\times 2}{=}} \frac{2}{4} \qquad \frac{1}{2} \overset{\times 3}{\underset{\times 3}{=}} \frac{3}{6} \qquad \frac{1}{2} \overset{\times 4}{\underset{\times 4}{=}} \frac{4}{8} \qquad \frac{1}{2} \overset{\times 5}{\underset{\times 5}{=}} \frac{5}{10}$$

Warm Up   Find equivalent fractions.

1. $\frac{1}{3} \overset{\times 2}{\underset{\times 2}{=}}$ ▥

2. $\frac{1}{3} \overset{\times 3}{\underset{\times 3}{=}}$ ▥

3. $\frac{1}{3} \overset{\times 4}{\underset{\times 4}{=}}$ ▥

4. $\frac{2}{5} \overset{\times 2}{\underset{\times 2}{=}}$ ▥

5. $\frac{2}{5} \overset{\times 3}{\underset{\times 3}{=}}$ ▥

6. $\frac{2}{5} \overset{\times 4}{\underset{\times 4}{=}}$ ▥

Find equivalent fractions.

1. $\dfrac{1}{4} \begin{smallmatrix}(\times 2)\\ = \\ (\times 2)\end{smallmatrix}$ ▦

2. $\dfrac{1}{4} \begin{smallmatrix}(\times 3)\\ = \\ (\times 3)\end{smallmatrix}$ ▦

3. $\dfrac{1}{4} \begin{smallmatrix}(\times 4)\\ = \\ (\times 4)\end{smallmatrix}$ ▦

4. $\dfrac{4}{5} \begin{smallmatrix}(\times 2)\\ = \\ (\times 2)\end{smallmatrix}$ ▦

5. $\dfrac{4}{5} \begin{smallmatrix}(\times 3)\\ = \\ (\times 3)\end{smallmatrix}$ ▦

6. $\dfrac{4}{5} \begin{smallmatrix}(\times 4)\\ = \\ (\times 4)\end{smallmatrix}$ ▦

7. $\dfrac{2}{3} \begin{smallmatrix}(\times 2)\\ = \\ (\times 2)\end{smallmatrix}$ ▦

8. $\dfrac{2}{3} \begin{smallmatrix}(\times 3)\\ = \\ (\times 3)\end{smallmatrix}$ ▦

9. $\dfrac{2}{3} \begin{smallmatrix}(\times 4)\\ = \\ (\times 4)\end{smallmatrix}$ ▦

Multiply the numerator and denominator by
2, 3, and 4 to find a set of equivalent fractions.

Example $\qquad \dfrac{1}{5} = \dfrac{2}{10} = \dfrac{3}{15} = \dfrac{4}{20}$

10. $\dfrac{3}{4} = \dfrac{▦}{▦} = \dfrac{▦}{▦} = \dfrac{▦}{▦}$

11. $\dfrac{5}{8} = \dfrac{▦}{▦} = \dfrac{▦}{▦} = \dfrac{▦}{▦}$

12. $\dfrac{2}{3} = \dfrac{▦}{▦} = \dfrac{▦}{▦} = \dfrac{▦}{▦}$

13. $\dfrac{3}{5} = \dfrac{▦}{▦} = \dfrac{▦}{▦} = \dfrac{▦}{▦}$

14. $\dfrac{7}{10} = \dfrac{▦}{▦} = \dfrac{▦}{▦} = \dfrac{▦}{▦}$

15. $\dfrac{1}{8} = \dfrac{▦}{▦} = \dfrac{▦}{▦} = \dfrac{▦}{▦}$

SKILLKEEPER

Find the quotients and remainders.

1. $4\overline{)6}$ 　　2. $4\overline{)15}$ 　　3. $5\overline{)31}$ 　　4. $6\overline{)13}$ 　　5. $2\overline{)12}$

6. $7\overline{)21}$ 　　7. $5\overline{)56}$ 　　8. $3\overline{)99}$ 　　9. $2\overline{)40}$ 　　10. $5\overline{)82}$

Lowest Terms Fractions

The store had only 24 tennis balls left. Letta bought 15 of them. What fraction of the tennis balls did Letta buy?

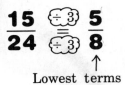

Letta bought $\frac{15}{24}$ of the tennis balls.

Letta bought 5 of the 8 cans. She bought $\frac{5}{8}$ of the tennis balls.

$$\frac{15}{24} \overset{\div 3}{\underset{\div 3}{=}} \frac{5}{8}$$

↑ Lowest terms

You can use division to "reduce" a fraction to an equivalent fraction in **lowest terms**.

To reduce a fraction, divide both the numerator and the denominator by a whole number greater than 1.

A fraction is in **lowest terms** when it cannot be reduced.

Other Examples

$$\frac{6}{12} \overset{\div 2}{\underset{\div 2}{=}} \frac{3}{6} \overset{\div 3}{\underset{\div 3}{=}} \frac{1}{2}$$
↑ Lowest terms

$$\frac{8}{12} \overset{\div 4}{\underset{\div 4}{=}} \frac{2}{3}$$
↑ Lowest terms

$$\frac{6}{10} \overset{\div 2}{\underset{\div 2}{=}} \frac{3}{5}$$
↑ Lowest terms

Warm Up Reduce each fraction to lowest terms.

1. $\frac{6}{8} \overset{\div 2}{\underset{\div 2}{=}} \blacksquare$

2. $\frac{6}{15} \overset{\div 3}{\underset{\div 3}{=}} \blacksquare$

3. $\frac{12}{16} \overset{\div 4}{\underset{\div 4}{=}} \blacksquare$

4. $\frac{4}{6}$

5. $\frac{2}{10}$

6. $\frac{10}{16}$

7. $\frac{9}{12}$

8. $\frac{3}{9}$

9. $\frac{8}{20}$

10. $\frac{4}{16}$

Is the fraction in lowest terms? Answer yes or no.

1. $\frac{6}{8}$ 2. $\frac{1}{2}$ 3. $\frac{10}{12}$ 4. $\frac{10}{15}$ 5. $\frac{3}{8}$ 6. $\frac{5}{6}$

7. $\frac{2}{4}$ 8. $\frac{7}{10}$ 9. $\frac{4}{6}$ 10. $\frac{6}{10}$ 11. $\frac{1}{4}$ 12. $\frac{8}{12}$

If possible, reduce to lowest terms.

13. $\frac{3}{9}$ 14. $\frac{2}{10}$ 15. $\frac{10}{16}$ 16. $\frac{3}{30}$ 17. $\frac{9}{10}$ 18. $\frac{8}{20}$

19. $\frac{4}{16}$ 20. $\frac{20}{32}$ 21. $\frac{15}{24}$ 22. $\frac{8}{12}$ 23. $\frac{4}{8}$ 24. $\frac{2}{16}$

25. $\frac{5}{40}$ 26. $\frac{5}{8}$ 27. $\frac{15}{20}$ 28. $\frac{10}{15}$ 29. $\frac{18}{24}$ 30. $\frac{5}{25}$

Write each fraction in lowest terms.

31. Jay played tennis for $\frac{12}{60}$ of an hour.

32. On a weekend, Pam spends $\frac{3}{24}$ of a full day playing tennis.

33. Bill used $\frac{4}{12}$ of his new tennis balls.

╔═ **THINK** ═

Shape Perception

The rubber band divides the yellow part of the geoboard into halves.

Can you find 4 other ways to place the rubber band so that it divides the yellow part into halves?

Show your ways on dot paper.

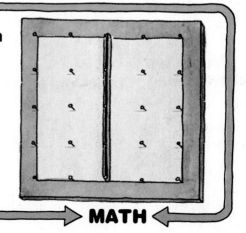

MATH

Comparing Fractions

Emma lives $\frac{9}{10}$ of a mile from school. Ian lives $\frac{7}{10}$ of a mile from school. Who lives farther from school?

When the denominators are the same, the fraction with the greater numerator is greater.

$$9 > 7 \quad \text{so} \quad \frac{9}{10} > \frac{7}{10}$$

Emma lives farther from school than Ian.

When the denominators are different, find equivalent fractions that have the same denominator.

Example: Compare $\frac{1}{2}$ and $\frac{3}{8}$.

Look at the denominators.	Write equivalent fractions with the same denominators.	Compare the numerators.	The fractions compare the same way the numerators compare.
$\frac{1}{2}$ $\frac{3}{8}$	$\frac{1}{2} = \frac{4}{8}$ $\frac{3}{8} = \frac{3}{8}$	$4 > 3$	$\frac{4}{8} > \frac{3}{8}$ so $\frac{1}{2} > \frac{3}{8}$ or $\frac{3}{8} < \frac{1}{2}$

Warm Up Write $>$, $<$, or $=$, for each . The equivalent-fraction table on page 231 may help you.

1. $\frac{1}{2} = \frac{3}{6}$
$\frac{1}{3} = \frac{2}{6}$
$\frac{1}{2}$ ⬤ $\frac{1}{3}$

2. $\frac{1}{5} = \frac{4}{20}$
$\frac{1}{4} = \frac{5}{20}$
$\frac{1}{5}$ ⬤ $\frac{1}{4}$

3. $\frac{1}{2} = \frac{4}{8}$
$\frac{5}{8} = \frac{5}{8}$
$\frac{1}{2}$ ⬤ $\frac{5}{8}$

4. $\frac{1}{2}$ ⬤ $\frac{1}{4}$

5. $\frac{2}{5}$ ⬤ $\frac{1}{2}$

6. $\frac{8}{10}$ ⬤ $\frac{4}{5}$

Write $>$, $<$, or $=$, for each ◕ .

1. $\frac{3}{10} = \frac{3}{10}$
   $\frac{2}{5} = \frac{4}{10}$ $\frac{3}{10}$ ◕ $\frac{2}{5}$

2. $\frac{2}{3} = \frac{10}{15}$
   $\frac{3}{5} = \frac{9}{15}$ $\frac{2}{3}$ ◕ $\frac{3}{5}$

3. $\frac{1}{4} = \frac{3}{12}$
   $\frac{1}{3} = \frac{4}{12}$ $\frac{1}{4}$ ◕ $\frac{1}{3}$

4. $\frac{1}{8} = \frac{1}{8}$
   $\frac{1}{2} = \frac{4}{8}$ $\frac{1}{8}$ ◕ $\frac{1}{2}$

5. $\frac{1}{4} = \frac{5}{20}$
   $\frac{3}{10} = \frac{6}{20}$ $\frac{1}{4}$ ◕ $\frac{3}{10}$

6. $\frac{2}{5} = \frac{4}{10}$
   $\frac{1}{2} = \frac{5}{10}$ $\frac{2}{5}$ ◕ $\frac{1}{2}$

7. $\frac{1}{8}$ ◕ $\frac{1}{10}$

8. $\frac{2}{3}$ ◕ $\frac{3}{4}$

9. $\frac{1}{2}$ ◕ $\frac{1}{8}$

10. $\frac{5}{8}$ ◕ $\frac{3}{4}$

11. $\frac{1}{5}$ ◕ $\frac{1}{3}$

12. $\frac{1}{2}$ ◕ $\frac{2}{3}$

EQUIVALENT-FRACTION TABLE
$\frac{1}{2} = \frac{2}{4} = \frac{3}{6} = \frac{4}{8} = \frac{5}{10} = \frac{6}{12}$
$\frac{1}{3} = \frac{2}{6} = \frac{3}{9} = \frac{4}{12} = \frac{5}{15} = \frac{6}{18}$
$\frac{2}{3} = \frac{4}{6} = \frac{6}{9} = \frac{8}{12} = \frac{10}{15} = \frac{12}{18}$
$\frac{1}{4} = \frac{2}{8} = \frac{3}{12} = \frac{4}{16} = \frac{5}{20} = \frac{6}{21}$
$\frac{3}{4} = \frac{6}{8} = \frac{9}{12} = \frac{12}{16} = \frac{15}{20} = \frac{18}{24}$
$\frac{1}{5} = \frac{2}{10} = \frac{3}{15} = \frac{4}{20} = \frac{5}{25} = \frac{6}{30}$
$\frac{2}{5} = \frac{4}{10} = \frac{6}{15} = \frac{8}{20} = \frac{10}{25} = \frac{12}{30}$
$\frac{1}{8} = \frac{2}{16} = \frac{3}{24} = \frac{4}{32} = \frac{5}{40} = \frac{6}{48}$
$\frac{5}{8} = \frac{10}{16} = \frac{15}{24} = \frac{20}{32} = \frac{25}{40} = \frac{30}{48}$
$\frac{1}{10} = \frac{2}{20} = \frac{3}{30} = \frac{4}{40} = \frac{5}{50} = \frac{6}{60}$
$\frac{3}{10} = \frac{6}{20} = \frac{9}{30} = \frac{12}{40} = \frac{15}{50} = \frac{18}{60}$

Solve.

13. Roberto walked $\frac{1}{2}$ of a mile to the store. Erika rode her sister's bicycle $\frac{3}{10}$ of a mile to the store. Who traveled farther?

More Practice, page 407, Set C

THINK

Estimation

Choose the fraction that best tells how full each container is.

1.
   $\frac{3}{4}$ $\frac{1}{2}$ $\frac{1}{3}$

2.
   $\frac{7}{8}$ $\frac{2}{3}$ $\frac{1}{3}$

3.
   $\frac{3}{4}$ $\frac{1}{2}$ $\frac{2}{5}$

4.
   $\frac{3}{5}$ $\frac{1}{2}$ $\frac{1}{4}$

MATH

Fractions of a Number

Ellen gathered 8 shells at the beach. $\frac{1}{2}$ of the shells are yellow. How many of Ellen's shells are yellow?

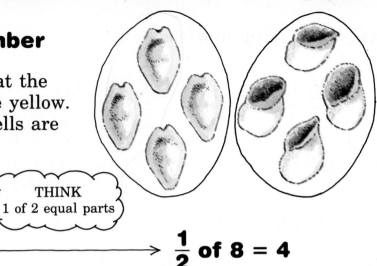

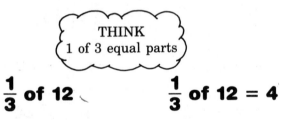

THINK
1 of 2 equal parts

$\frac{1}{2}$ of 8 $\longrightarrow$ $\frac{1}{2}$ of 8 = 4

To find $\frac{1}{2}$ of a number, **divide by 2.**

4 of Ellen's shells are yellow.

Other Examples

THINK
1 of 3 equal parts

$\frac{1}{3}$ of 12 $\frac{1}{3}$ of 12 = 4

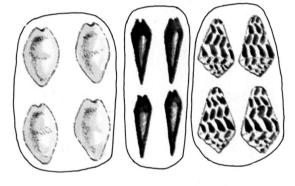

To find $\frac{1}{3}$ of a number, **divide by 3.**

THINK
1 of 4 equal parts

$\frac{1}{4}$ of 8 $\frac{1}{4}$ of 8 = 2

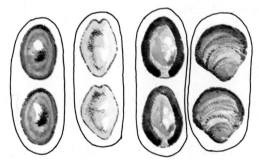

To find $\frac{1}{4}$ of a number, **divide by 4.**

Warm Up   Find the missing number.

1.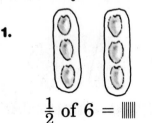

$\frac{1}{2}$ of 6 = ▯

2.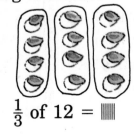

$\frac{1}{3}$ of 12 = ▯

3.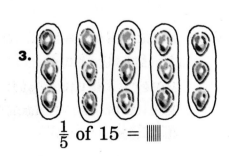

$\frac{1}{5}$ of 15 = ▯

Find the missing number.

1.
$\frac{1}{2}$ of 4

2.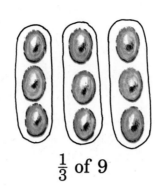
$\frac{1}{3}$ of 9

3.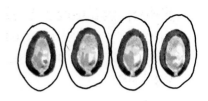
$\frac{1}{4}$ of 4

4.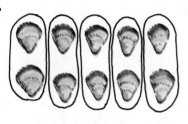
$\frac{1}{5}$ of 10

5.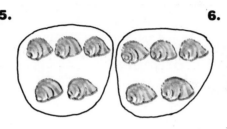
$\frac{1}{2}$ of 10

6.
$\frac{1}{3}$ of 15

7. $\frac{1}{2}$ of 12   **8.** $\frac{1}{3}$ of 6   **9.** $\frac{1}{4}$ of 20   **10.** $\frac{1}{5}$ of 30

11. $\frac{1}{4}$ of 16   **12.** $\frac{1}{2}$ of 18   **13.** $\frac{1}{3}$ of 18   **14.** $\frac{1}{8}$ of 24

15. $\frac{1}{3}$ of 24   **16.** $\frac{1}{2}$ of 16   **17.** $\frac{1}{5}$ of 20   **18.** $\frac{1}{2}$ of 14

Solve.

19. Ben collected 15 shells. $\frac{1}{3}$ of Ben's shells are white. How many of Ben's shells are white?

★ 20. Ross collected 12 large and 15 small shells. He gave away $\frac{1}{3}$ of his shells and kept the rest. How many shells did Ross keep?

THINK

Fraction Puzzle

A store has 18 toy cars. $\frac{1}{2}$ of them are yellow. $\frac{1}{3}$ of them are blue. The others are red. How many are red?

MATH

More About Fractions of a Number

Miranda brought 12 pieces of
fruit to the party. $\frac{1}{3}$ of the pieces
were oranges. $\frac{2}{3}$ of the pieces
were apples. How many oranges
and how many apples did
Miranda bring to the party?

$\frac{1}{3}$ of 12 → (1 of 3 equal parts / Divide by 3.) → $\frac{1}{3}$ of 12 = 4

Miranda brought 4 oranges.

$\frac{2}{3}$ of 12 → (2 of 3 equal parts / Divide by 3. / Multiply by 2.) → $\frac{2}{3}$ of 12 = 8

Miranda brought 8 apples.

Other Examples

$\frac{3}{4}$ of 8 → (3 of 4 equal parts / Divide by 4. / Multiply by 3.) → $\frac{3}{4}$ of 8 = 6

$\frac{4}{5}$ of 15 → (4 of 5 equal parts / Divide by 5. / Multiply by 4.) → $\frac{4}{5}$ of 15 = 12

Warm Up   Find the missing number.

1. $\frac{2}{3}$ of 9 = ▓▓▓

2. $\frac{3}{4}$ of 12 = ▓▓▓

3. $\frac{2}{5}$ of 10 = ▓▓▓

234

Find the missing numbers.

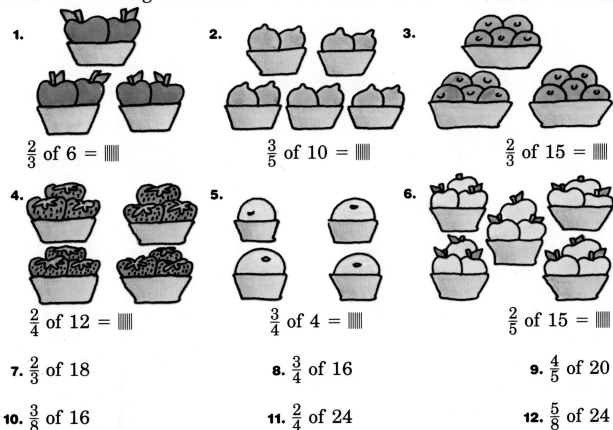

1. $\frac{2}{3}$ of 6 = ▥

2. $\frac{3}{5}$ of 10 = ▥

3. $\frac{2}{3}$ of 15 = ▥

4. $\frac{2}{4}$ of 12 = ▥

5. $\frac{3}{4}$ of 4 = ▥

6. $\frac{2}{5}$ of 15 = ▥

7. $\frac{2}{3}$ of 18

8. $\frac{3}{4}$ of 16

9. $\frac{4}{5}$ of 20

10. $\frac{3}{8}$ of 16

11. $\frac{2}{4}$ of 24

12. $\frac{5}{8}$ of 24

13. $\frac{2}{3}$ of 21

14. $\frac{3}{4}$ of 20

15. $\frac{2}{5}$ of 25

Solve.

16. Felix brought 15 cans of juice to the party. $\frac{2}{5}$ of the cans were grape juice. How many cans of grape juice did Felix bring to the party?

★ 17. Daryl brought 36 sandwich rolls. $\frac{1}{4}$ of them were for hot dogs. The rest were for hamburgers. How many hamburger rolls did Daryl bring?

THINK

Logical Reasoning

The party bus left at 6:50 a.m. The trip takes 35 minutes. Because of rain the trip took an extra 7 minutes. What time did the bus arrive?

MATH

More Practice, page 408, Set B

PROBLEM SOLVING
Using Data from a Circle Graph

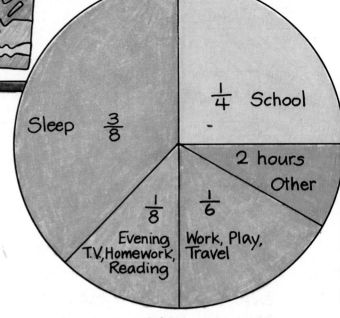

Sleep $\frac{3}{8}$ · $\frac{1}{4}$ School · 2 hours Other · $\frac{1}{8}$ Evening T.V., Homework, Reading · $\frac{1}{6}$ Work, Play, Travel

24 hours
How Jaime spends his day

The full circle stands for 24 hours (1 day). The parts of the circle show the fraction of the day used for different things. Use the circle graph to solve the problems below.

1. Jaime is in school $\frac{1}{4}$ of the 24 hours. How many hours does Jaime spend in school?

2. How much time does Jaime have in the evening?

3. One evening Jaime took 35 minutes to eat and 45 minutes for homework. How much time did he take for these two things?

4. Jaime takes $\frac{1}{5}$ of an hour to take a bath. An hour has 60 minutes. How many minutes does it take Jaime to bathe?

5. How much time does Jaime take for work, play, and travel?

6. One Saturday, Jaime took 7 trips on his bicycle to deliver groceries. Each trip took about 25 minutes. How long did the 7 trips take?

7. **Try This** Ruben started painting at 12:00 noon. Jaime joined him later. Ruben quit at 4:00. Jaime worked until 6:00. Jaime worked 5 hours. How long did they work together? Hint: Use logical reasoning.

PROBLEM SOLVING
Practice

Many people collect stamps as a hobby. Different stamps, new or old and local or foreign, may have interest and value to the stamp collector.

Solve.

1. Michele started her stamp collection with a package of 24 stamps. $\frac{1}{3}$ of them were from France. How many of Michele's stamps were from France?

2. Rich bought a package of 36 stamps. $\frac{1}{4}$ of his stamps were from England. How many of Rich's stamps were from England?

3. Michele paid $2.98 for her stamps. Rich paid $4.25. How much more did Rich pay than Michele?

4. Kathy has a book of stamps. $\frac{1}{5}$ of them are from Mexico and $\frac{1}{4}$ of them are from Canada. Are there more from Mexico or Canada?

5. Susan has 6 full pages of stamps in her book. Each page has 24 stamps. How many stamps does Susan have on these 6 pages?

6. Candy had 84 stamps. She sold $\frac{1}{3}$ of them. How many stamps did Candy sell?

7. Connie has a collection of 96 stamps. $\frac{1}{2}$ of them are from Europe. How many stamps does Connie have from Europe?

8. *Try This* Ted put 12 stamps on one page of his stamp book and 15 on another. He put the rest on 3 pages of 8 each. How many stamps are in the package? Hint: Work backward.

Mixed Numbers

There were 9 people who wanted the breakfast special. How many grapefruit does the restaurant need for them?

$\frac{9}{2}$ (nine halves) is the same amount as $4\frac{1}{2}$ (four and one half).

$$\frac{9}{2} = 4\frac{1}{2}$$

fraction greater than 1   mixed number (whole number and fraction)

You can use division to write a mixed number for a fraction greater than 1.

When the numerator is greater than the denominator, the fraction is greater than 1.

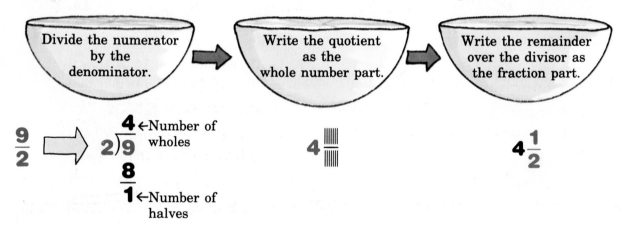

Divide the numerator by the denominator. → Write the quotient as the whole number part. → Write the remainder over the divisor as the fraction part.

$\frac{9}{2}$ ⇒ $2\overline{)9}$ **4** ←Number of wholes   **8**   **1** ←Number of halves

$4\ \vphantom{|}$ $4\frac{1}{2}$

Other Example

$\frac{18}{3}$ ⇒ $3\overline{)18}$ **6** ← Number of wholes   **18**   **0** ← Number of thirds   ⇒ $\frac{18}{3} = 6$

Warm Up   Write a mixed number for each fraction.

1. $\frac{7}{2}$ 2. $\frac{20}{4}$ 3. $\frac{27}{4}$ 4. $\frac{25}{3}$ 5. $\frac{12}{3}$ 6. $\frac{23}{5}$

Write as a whole number.

1. $\frac{15}{3}$
2. $\frac{16}{2}$
3. $\frac{40}{5}$
4. $\frac{24}{3}$
5. $\frac{14}{2}$
6. $\frac{36}{4}$

7. $\frac{16}{8}$
8. $\frac{3}{3}$
9. $\frac{18}{2}$
10. $\frac{5}{5}$
11. $\frac{42}{6}$
12. $\frac{21}{3}$

Write as a mixed number.

13. $\frac{11}{2}$
14. $\frac{37}{5}$
15. $\frac{11}{3}$
16. $\frac{19}{2}$
17. $\frac{23}{6}$
18. $\frac{35}{4}$

19. $\frac{22}{3}$
20. $\frac{71}{8}$
21. $\frac{9}{4}$
22. $\frac{29}{3}$
23. $\frac{17}{2}$
24. $\frac{51}{8}$

Write as a whole number or mixed number.
Reduce all fraction parts to lowest terms.

25. $\frac{10}{4}$
26. $\frac{14}{6}$
27. $\frac{35}{5}$
28. $\frac{19}{3}$
29. $\frac{38}{8}$
30. $\frac{14}{4}$

31. $\frac{10}{8}$
32. $\frac{34}{6}$
33. $\frac{21}{5}$
34. $\frac{28}{4}$
35. $\frac{18}{8}$
36. $\frac{56}{6}$

Solve.

37. A restaurant worker cuts pies into eighths. How many pies will be used if 45 pieces are served?

38. Another restaurant worker cuts pies into sixths. How many pies will be used if 45 pieces are served?

THINK

Shape Perception

Which two triangles are the same?

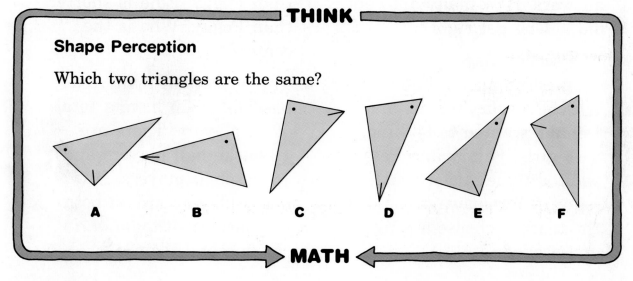

A   B   C   D   E   F

MATH

PROBLEM SOLVING
Using the Strategies

Use one or more of the strategies listed to solve each problem below.

1. Jolene took a math test. There were 20 problems on the test. Jolene got 10 more right answers than wrong answers. How many answers did Jolene get right?

2. The school play was about a king and a queen. Four boys, Nick, Preston, Robbie, and Donald, wanted to be king. Two girls, Hilary and Tess, wanted to be queen. How many different ways could the teacher choose a king and a queen?

3. The tallest girl on the team is the center. Peggy is taller than Linell. Ginny is shorter than Linell. Nancy is taller than Peggy. Edie is shorter than Peggy. Who is the center?

4. The basketball team and baseball team have a total of 24 players. There are 12 basketball players and 18 baseball players. How many players are on both the basketball team *and* the baseball team?

Write a fraction to tell what part is shaded.

1.   **2.** 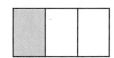   **3.**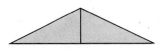

Write a fraction for the ▥.   Find equivalent fractions.

4. ▥ of the cards are red.

5. $\frac{2}{5} \underset{\times 2}{\overset{\times 2}{=}}$ ▥   **6.** $\frac{1}{2} \underset{\times 2}{\overset{\times 2}{=}}$ ▥

Reduce to lowest terms.

7. $\frac{6}{8}$ **8.** $\frac{12}{20}$ **9.** $\frac{10}{15}$ **10.** $\frac{6}{15}$ **11.** $\frac{10}{16}$

Give the correct sign, $>$, $<$, or $=$, for each ● .

12. $\frac{1}{3}$ ● $\frac{1}{2}$ **13.** $\frac{5}{8}$ ● $\frac{3}{4}$ **14.** $\frac{3}{4}$ ● $\frac{2}{3}$ **15.** $\frac{3}{6}$ ● $\frac{1}{2}$ **16.** $\frac{3}{8}$ ● $\frac{1}{4}$

Find the missing number.

17. $\frac{1}{2}$ of 14   **18.** $\frac{1}{3}$ of 12   **19.** $\frac{3}{4}$ of 20   **20.** $\frac{2}{5}$ of 15

Write as a whole number or a mixed number.

21. $\frac{15}{2}$ **22.** $\frac{24}{3}$ **23.** $\frac{27}{4}$ **24.** $\frac{10}{5}$ **25.** $\frac{31}{8}$

Solve.

26. Virginia bought a package of 48 stamps. $\frac{1}{6}$ of her stamps are from Germany. How many of Virginia's stamps are from Germany?

27. Roger has 7 full pages of stamps in his book. Each page has 20 stamps. How many stamps does Roger have on these 7 pages?

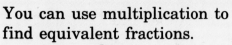

You can use multiplication to find equivalent fractions.

$$\frac{2}{3} = \frac{4}{6} = \frac{6}{9} = \frac{8}{12}$$

(2 × 2) (3 × 2) (4 × 2)
(2 × 3) (3 × 3) (4 × 3)
(2 × 4) (3 × 4) (4 × 4)

$$\frac{4}{5} = \frac{8}{10} = \frac{12}{15} = \frac{16}{20}$$

(2 × 5) (3 × 5) (4 × 5)

(20 ÷ 4)
$\frac{1}{4}$ of 20 = 5
1 of 4 equal parts

(20 ÷ 5)
$\frac{1}{5}$ of 20 = 4
1 of 5 equal parts

You can use division to reduce fractions.

(8 ÷ 2) (4 ÷ 2)
$$\frac{8}{20} = \frac{4}{10} = \frac{2}{5}$$
(20 ÷ 2) (10 ÷ 2)

(8 ÷ 4)
$$\frac{8}{20} = \frac{2}{5}$$
(20 ÷ 4)

Multiply the numerator and denominator by 2, 3, and 4 to find a set of equivalent fractions.

1. $\frac{3}{4} = \quad = \quad = \quad$

2. $\frac{3}{8} = \quad = \quad = \quad$

3. $\frac{2}{5} = \quad = \quad = \quad$

Find the missing number.

4. $\frac{1}{2}$ of 10 =
5. $\frac{1}{2}$ of 16 =
6. $\frac{1}{3}$ of 21 =
7. $\frac{1}{5}$ of 25 =
8. $\frac{1}{4}$ of 24 =
9. $\frac{1}{3}$ of 24 =
10. $\frac{1}{8}$ of 40 =
11. $\frac{1}{4}$ of 36 =

Reduce to lowest terms.

12. $\frac{2}{10}$ 13. $\frac{4}{32}$ 14. $\frac{3}{15}$

15. $\frac{9}{12}$ 16. $\frac{10}{16}$ 17. $\frac{4}{6}$

18. $\frac{4}{12}$ 19. $\frac{12}{16}$ 20. $\frac{8}{12}$

Shape Perception

This figure is $\frac{1}{4}$ of a square.

Four of them can be put together to make a square.

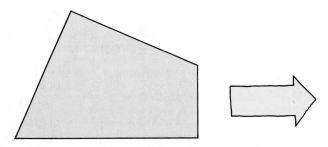

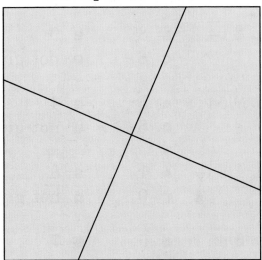

Each figure below is exactly $\frac{1}{4}$ of a square. Choose one and make four copies. Put them together to form a square.

1.

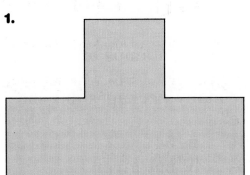

2.

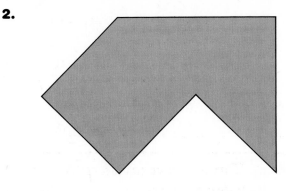

3.

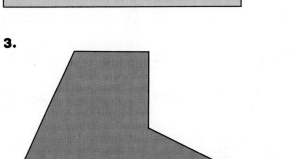

4.

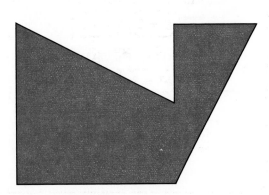

Give the letter for the correct answer.

1. 4)24
  A 7   **B** 6
  C 5   **D** not given

2. 8)64
  A 8   **B** 9
  C 6   **D** not given

3. 9)54
  A 5   **B** 4
  C 6   **D** not given

4. 1)8
  A 1   **B** 8
  C 0   **D** not given

5. 5)45
  A 5   **B** 7
  C 9   **D** not given

6. 7)7
  A 0   **B** 1
  C 7   **D** not given

7. 6)48
  A 5   **B** 7
  C 6   **D** not given

8. 22
    × 4
  A 88
  B 28
  C 26
  D not given

9. 36
    × 2
  A 62
  B 38
  C 72
  D not given

10. 64
     × 9
  A 546
  B 576
  C 572
  D not given

11. 213
     × 6
  A 1,278
  B 1,268
  C 1,276
  D not given

12. 207
     × 7
  A 1,449
  B 1,517
  C 1,409
  D not given

13. Gina put 3 stamps on each package. She used 18 stamps. How many packages did she have?
  A 15   **B** 54
  C 6   **D** not given

14. Travis made 10 baskets in the game. Each basket was worth 2 points. How many points did Travis make in the game?
  A 12   **B** 20
  C 5   **D** not given

ADDITION AND SUBTRACTION OF FRACTIONS

10

Diana remembered her trip to the art museum. The man in the painting by Rembrandt had looked so real. He seemed to be staring right at her. Picasso was her favorite painter. Sometimes people in Picasso's paintings looked like puzzle pieces. The pieces had seemed to fit together as she looked at them. There had been an interesting painting by Frank Stella. It took up $\frac{1}{3}$ of a wall. Stella had carefully measured and painted geometric shapes. Diana had spent a long time looking at it. After her trip, she decided to make her own painting.

Adding Fractions: Like Denominators

Ivy, Donald, and Vicki all live on the same road. The map shows how far apart they live. How far is it from Ivy's house to Vicki's house along the road?

Since we want the total distance, we add.

Look at the denominators.		Add the numerators.		Write the sum over the denominator.
$\frac{3}{10} + \frac{4}{10}$		$3 + 4 = 7$		$\frac{3}{10} + \frac{4}{10} = \frac{7}{10}$

Ivy lives $\frac{7}{10}$ mile from Vicki.

Other Examples

$$\frac{2}{10} + \frac{1}{10} = \frac{3}{10} \qquad \frac{3}{8} + \frac{1}{8} = \frac{4}{8} = \frac{1}{2}$$

$$\begin{array}{r} \frac{2}{5} \\ + \frac{1}{5} \\ \hline \frac{3}{5} \end{array} \qquad \begin{array}{r} \frac{5}{10} \\ + \frac{3}{10} \\ \hline \frac{8}{10} = \frac{4}{5} \end{array}$$

Warm Up Find the sums.

1. $\frac{1}{8} + \frac{4}{8}$ 2. $\frac{2}{10} + \frac{5}{10}$ 3. $\frac{4}{10} + \frac{1}{10}$ 4. $\frac{2}{8} + \frac{4}{8}$

5. $\begin{array}{r} \frac{1}{6} \\ + \frac{4}{6} \\ \hline \end{array}$ 6. $\begin{array}{r} \frac{1}{4} \\ + \frac{1}{4} \\ \hline \end{array}$ 7. $\begin{array}{r} \frac{2}{5} \\ + \frac{1}{5} \\ \hline \end{array}$ 8. $\begin{array}{r} \frac{1}{8} \\ + \frac{3}{8} \\ \hline \end{array}$ 9. $\begin{array}{r} \frac{1}{10} \\ + \frac{5}{10} \\ \hline \end{array}$ 10. $\begin{array}{r} \frac{1}{6} \\ + \frac{1}{6} \\ \hline \end{array}$

Find the sums.

1. $\frac{1}{3} + \frac{1}{3}$

2. $\frac{4}{8} + \frac{3}{8}$

3. $\frac{1}{6} + \frac{1}{6}$

4. $\frac{2}{6} + \frac{2}{6}$

5. $\frac{3}{6} + \frac{2}{6}$

6. $\frac{8}{10} + \frac{1}{10}$

7. $\frac{2}{6} + \frac{1}{6}$

8. $\frac{1}{5} + \frac{1}{5}$

9. $\frac{2}{10} + \frac{2}{10}$

10. $\frac{1}{8} + \frac{1}{8}$

11. $\frac{4}{10} + \frac{4}{10}$

12. $\frac{2}{4} + \frac{1}{4}$

13. $\frac{2}{8}$ $+ \frac{3}{8}$

14. $\frac{3}{10}$ $+ \frac{4}{10}$

15. $\frac{1}{5}$ $+ \frac{2}{5}$

16. $\frac{1}{4}$ $+ \frac{1}{4}$

17. $\frac{3}{8}$ $+ \frac{3}{8}$

18. $\frac{2}{10}$ $+ \frac{1}{10}$

19. $\frac{1}{6}$ $+ \frac{1}{6}$

20. $\frac{6}{10}$ $+ \frac{1}{10}$

21. $\frac{3}{10}$ $+ \frac{2}{10}$

22. $\frac{2}{4}$ $+ \frac{1}{4}$

23. $\frac{1}{10}$ $+ \frac{1}{10}$

24. $\frac{3}{6}$ $+ \frac{2}{6}$

25. $\frac{4}{10}$ $+ \frac{4}{10}$

26. $\frac{2}{8}$ $+ \frac{2}{8}$

27. $\frac{1}{6}$ $+ \frac{2}{6}$

Solve.

28. Barb lives between Peter and Gil. She lives $\frac{2}{10}$ mile from Peter and $\frac{3}{10}$ mile from Gil. How far does Peter live from Gil?

29. Use the map on page 246. Ivy lives between Les and Donald. She lives $\frac{3}{10}$ mile from Les. How far does Les live from Donald?

Use the map on page 246.

SKILLKEEPER

Write > or < for each ▥ .

1. 730 ▥ 726

2. 657 ▥ 654

3. 892 ▥ 982

4. 3,674 ▥ 4,035

5. 5,290 ▥ 5,277

6. 8,654 ▥ 8,564

Subtracting Fractions: Like Denominators

A recipe for muffins calls for $\frac{7}{8}$ cup of bran and $\frac{5}{8}$ cup of whole-wheat flour. How much more bran is used than whole-wheat flour?

Since we are comparing, we subtract.

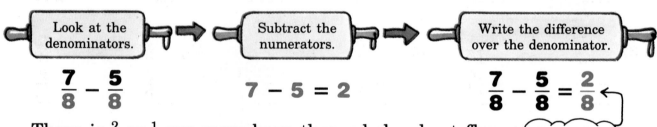

Look at the denominators.	Subtract the numerators.	Write the difference over the denominator.
$\frac{7}{8} - \frac{5}{8}$	$7 - 5 = 2$	$\frac{7}{8} - \frac{5}{8} = \frac{2}{8}$

There is $\frac{2}{8}$ or $\frac{1}{4}$ cup more bran than whole-wheat flour.

Remember $\frac{2}{8} = \frac{1}{4}$

Other Examples

$$\frac{4}{5} - \frac{3}{5} = \frac{1}{5} \qquad \frac{7}{8} - \frac{3}{8} = \frac{4}{8} = \frac{1}{2}$$

$$\begin{array}{r} \frac{5}{6} \\ - \frac{4}{6} \\ \hline \frac{1}{6} \end{array} \qquad \begin{array}{r} \frac{2}{3} \\ - \frac{2}{3} \\ \hline \frac{0}{3} = 0 \end{array}$$

Warm Up Find the differences.

1. $\frac{3}{4} - \frac{2}{4}$ 2. $\frac{7}{8} - \frac{2}{8}$ 3. $\frac{4}{6} - \frac{1}{6}$ 4. $\frac{7}{10} - \frac{2}{10}$

5. $\begin{array}{r} \frac{7}{10} \\ - \frac{4}{10} \\ \hline \end{array}$ 6. $\begin{array}{r} \frac{7}{8} \\ - \frac{1}{8} \\ \hline \end{array}$ 7. $\begin{array}{r} \frac{3}{4} \\ - \frac{1}{4} \\ \hline \end{array}$ 8. $\begin{array}{r} \frac{5}{6} \\ - \frac{2}{6} \\ \hline \end{array}$ 9. $\begin{array}{r} \frac{3}{5} \\ - \frac{1}{5} \\ \hline \end{array}$ 10. $\begin{array}{r} \frac{7}{8} \\ - \frac{7}{8} \\ \hline \end{array}$

Find the differences.

1. $\frac{5}{8} - \frac{2}{8}$

2. $\frac{5}{6} - \frac{1}{6}$

3. $\frac{2}{5} - \frac{1}{5}$

4. $\frac{11}{10} - \frac{7}{10}$

5. $\frac{2}{4} - \frac{1}{4}$

6. $\frac{2}{8} - \frac{1}{8}$

7. $\frac{7}{6} - \frac{5}{6}$

8. $\frac{15}{10} - \frac{8}{10}$

9. $\frac{3}{5}$ $- \frac{1}{5}$

10. $\frac{7}{8}$ $- \frac{4}{8}$

11. $\frac{7}{10}$ $- \frac{2}{10}$

12. $\frac{5}{6}$ $- \frac{2}{6}$

13. $\frac{2}{3}$ $- \frac{1}{3}$

14. $\frac{2}{8}$ $- \frac{1}{8}$

15. $\frac{6}{6}$ $- \frac{4}{6}$

16. $\frac{4}{4}$ $- \frac{2}{4}$

17. $\frac{13}{8}$ $- \frac{6}{8}$

18. $\frac{12}{10}$ $- \frac{5}{10}$

19. $\frac{5}{5}$ $- \frac{3}{5}$

20. $\frac{6}{4}$ $- \frac{2}{4}$

21. $\frac{5}{8}$ $- \frac{3}{8}$

22. $\frac{7}{10}$ $- \frac{4}{10}$

23. $\frac{5}{6}$ $- \frac{4}{6}$

24. $\frac{3}{4}$ $- \frac{1}{4}$

25. $\frac{5}{8}$ $- \frac{5}{8}$

26. $\frac{3}{10}$ $- \frac{2}{10}$

Solve.

27. The muffin recipe calls for $\frac{3}{4}$ cup milk and $\frac{1}{4}$ cup honey. How much more milk is used than honey?

★ 28. The muffin recipe calls for 2 tablespoons of oil, the same as $\frac{1}{8}$ cup. How much more bran is used than oil?

29. Write a question about this data. Solve your own problem.

Flo has a muffin recipe that calls for $\frac{5}{8}$ cup of enriched flour and $\frac{3}{8}$ cup of bran.

THINK

Guess and Check

The sum of two fractions is $\frac{7}{8}$. Their difference is $\frac{1}{8}$. They have the same denominator. What are the two fractions?

MATH

Adding and Subtracting: Mixed Numbers

Maria has a rain gauge. The gauge measures amounts of rainfall. On Monday it rained $\frac{7}{8}$ of an inch. On Tuesday it rained another $\frac{6}{8}$ of an inch. How much did it rain in the two days?

Since we want the total amount, we should add.

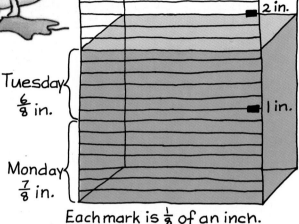

Tuesday $\frac{6}{8}$ in.

Monday $\frac{7}{8}$ in.

2 in.

1 in.

Each mark is $\frac{1}{8}$ of an inch.

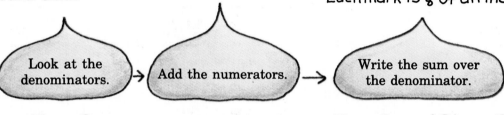

Look at the denominators.	Add the numerators.	Write the sum over the denominator.
$\frac{7}{8} + \frac{6}{8}$	$7 + 6 = 13$	$\frac{7}{8} + \frac{6}{8} = \frac{13}{8} = 1\frac{5}{8}$

It rained $\frac{13}{8}$ or $1\frac{5}{8}$ inches in the two days.

Other Examples

$$\frac{7}{10} + \frac{6}{10} = \frac{13}{10} = 1\frac{3}{10}$$

$$\begin{array}{r} 2\frac{1}{4} \\ + 3\frac{2}{4} \\ \hline 5\frac{3}{4} \end{array}$$

$$\begin{array}{r} 6\frac{7}{8} \\ - 2\frac{4}{8} \\ \hline 4\frac{3}{8} \end{array}$$

$$\begin{array}{r} 7\frac{9}{10} \\ - 5\frac{4}{10} \\ \hline 2\frac{5}{10} = 2\frac{1}{2} \end{array}$$

$$\begin{array}{r} 3\frac{1}{2} \\ + 1\frac{1}{2} \\ \hline 4\frac{2}{2} = 5 \end{array}$$

Warm Up Find the sums and differences.

1. $\frac{7}{8} + \frac{2}{8}$ 2. $\frac{3}{4} + \frac{3}{4}$ 3. $\frac{5}{6} + \frac{3}{6}$ 4. $\frac{7}{10} + \frac{8}{10}$

5. $\begin{array}{r} 4\frac{3}{8} \\ + 2\frac{4}{8} \\ \hline \end{array}$
6. $\begin{array}{r} 5\frac{5}{6} \\ - 1\frac{4}{6} \\ \hline \end{array}$
7. $\begin{array}{r} 7\frac{6}{10} \\ - 3\frac{5}{10} \\ \hline \end{array}$
8. $\begin{array}{r} 6\frac{1}{2} \\ + 5\frac{1}{2} \\ \hline \end{array}$
9. $\begin{array}{r} 9\frac{7}{10} \\ - 3\frac{4}{10} \\ \hline \end{array}$
10. $\begin{array}{r} 6\frac{2}{3} \\ - 4\frac{2}{3} \\ \hline \end{array}$

Find the sums and differences.

1. $\frac{6}{10} + \frac{5}{10}$ 2. $\frac{2}{3} + \frac{2}{3}$ 3. $\frac{4}{8} + \frac{7}{8}$ 4. $\frac{3}{4} + \frac{3}{4}$

5. $\frac{5}{6} + \frac{3}{6}$ 6. $\frac{1}{8} + \frac{7}{8}$ 7. $\frac{9}{10} + \frac{9}{10}$ 8. $\frac{1}{2} + \frac{1}{2}$

9. $\begin{array}{r} 7\frac{7}{8} \\ -\ 4\frac{2}{8} \\ \hline \end{array}$
   10. $\begin{array}{r} 3\frac{1}{4} \\ +\ 6\frac{1}{4} \\ \hline \end{array}$
   11. $\begin{array}{r} 8\frac{5}{6} \\ -\ 2\frac{4}{6} \\ \hline \end{array}$
   12. $\begin{array}{r} 9\frac{3}{4} \\ -\ 3\frac{2}{4} \\ \hline \end{array}$
   13. $\begin{array}{r} 3\frac{1}{2} \\ +\ 2\frac{1}{2} \\ \hline \end{array}$
   14. $\begin{array}{r} 6\frac{8}{10} \\ -\ 1\frac{5}{10} \\ \hline \end{array}$

15. $\begin{array}{r} 7\frac{5}{10} \\ +\ 1\frac{2}{10} \\ \hline \end{array}$
   16. $\begin{array}{r} 12\frac{3}{4} \\ -\ 4\frac{1}{4} \\ \hline \end{array}$
   17. $\begin{array}{r} 6\frac{2}{4} \\ +\ 1\frac{1}{4} \\ \hline \end{array}$
   18. $\begin{array}{r} 15\frac{5}{6} \\ -\ 9\frac{2}{6} \\ \hline \end{array}$
   19. $\begin{array}{r} 14\frac{6}{8} \\ -\ 7\frac{4}{8} \\ \hline \end{array}$
   20. $\begin{array}{r} 6\frac{5}{8} \\ +\ 1\frac{2}{8} \\ \hline \end{array}$

21. $\begin{array}{r} 12\frac{5}{10} \\ -\ 8\frac{1}{10} \\ \hline \end{array}$
   22. $\begin{array}{r} 6\frac{1}{4} \\ +\ 7\frac{2}{4} \\ \hline \end{array}$
   23. $\begin{array}{r} 10\frac{7}{8} \\ -\ 3\frac{5}{8} \\ \hline \end{array}$
   24. $\begin{array}{r} 8\frac{3}{8} \\ +\ 9\frac{1}{8} \\ \hline \end{array}$
   25. $\begin{array}{r} 11\frac{1}{2} \\ -\ 6\frac{1}{2} \\ \hline \end{array}$
   26. $\begin{array}{r} 17\frac{5}{8} \\ -\ 8\frac{1}{8} \\ \hline \end{array}$

Solve.

27. On Saturday it rained $\frac{3}{8}$ inch. On Sunday it rained $\frac{7}{8}$ inch. How much did it rain in the 2 days?

28. **DATA BANK** See page 384. If there is moderate rain for 1 hour and then light rain for 1 hour, about how much rain is this in the 2 hours?

SKILLKEEPER

Find equivalent fractions.

1. $\frac{1}{4}\genfrac{}{}{0pt}{}{\times 2}{\times 2} = \frac{}{}$ 2. $\frac{1}{4}\genfrac{}{}{0pt}{}{\times 3}{\times 3} = \frac{}{}$ 3. $\frac{4}{5}\genfrac{}{}{0pt}{}{\times 2}{\times 2} = \frac{}{}$

4. $\frac{4}{5}\genfrac{}{}{0pt}{}{\times 3}{\times 3} = \frac{}{}$ 5. $\frac{2}{3}\genfrac{}{}{0pt}{}{\times 2}{\times 2} = \frac{}{}$ 6. $\frac{2}{3}\genfrac{}{}{0pt}{}{\times 4}{\times 4} = \frac{}{}$

Reduce the fractions to the lowest terms.

7. $\frac{2}{10}$ 8. $\frac{4}{16}$ 9. $\frac{9}{12}$ 10. $\frac{8}{20}$ 11. $\frac{6}{15}$

PROBLEM SOLVING
Practice

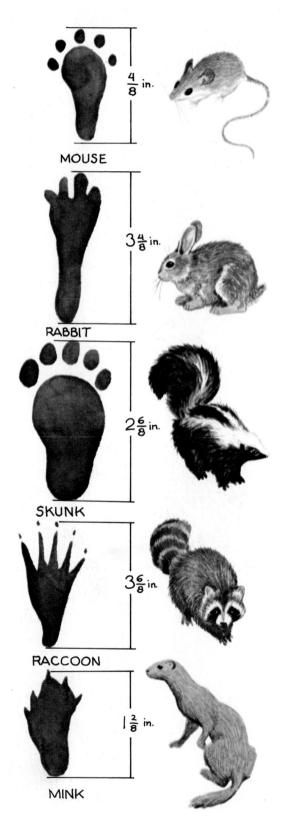

$\frac{4}{8}$ in.

MOUSE

$3\frac{4}{8}$ in.

RABBIT

$2\frac{6}{8}$ in.

SKUNK

$3\frac{6}{8}$ in.

RACCOON

$1\frac{2}{8}$ in.

MINK

The pictures show the tracks of the hind feet of different animals. The lengths given are average for adults. All fractional parts are given in eighths. Use the pictures to help you solve the following problems.

1. How much longer is the raccoon track than the mink track?

2. How much shorter is the quail track than the skunk track?

3. The skunk takes steps that are about 18 inches long. How many inches would it travel in 6 steps?

4. The front print of the weasel is $\frac{2}{8}$ inch long. How long are the front and hind prints end to end?

5. How much longer is the black bear print than the rabbit print?

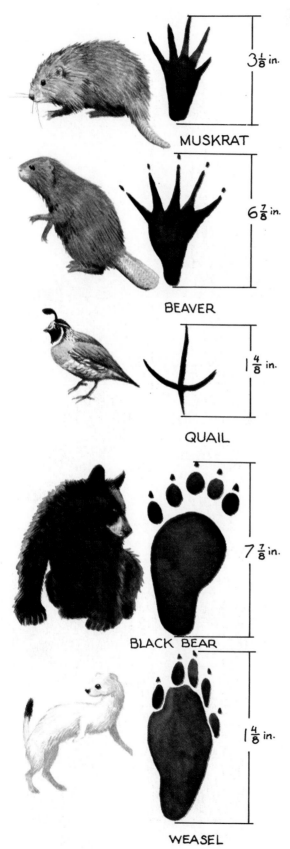

MUSKRAT

3 1/8 in.

BEAVER

6 7/8 in.

QUAIL

1 4/8 in.

BLACK BEAR

7 7/8 in.

WEASEL

1 4/8 in.

6. The muskrat takes steps that are 8 inches long. How many steps would it have to take to go 216 inches?

7. How much longer is the raccoon track than the mouse track?

8. The front footprint of the muskrat is $\frac{7}{8}$ inch long. How long are the front and hind prints end to end?

9. The beaver takes steps that are 18 inches long. How many inches will the beaver travel in 9 steps?

10. How much shorter is the beaver print than the black bear print?

11. The front footprint of the beaver is 3 inches long. How long are the front and hind prints end to end?

12. The rabbit may take steps about 7 inches long. How many steps will it take to travel 245 inches?

13. *Try This* There were 8 quail and rabbits in the meadow. There were 20 feet. How many of each were in the meadow?

253

Adding Fractions: Unlike Denominators

Owen is building a house. The plans call for a floor to have plywood that is $\frac{5}{8}$ inch thick and a layer of concrete that is $\frac{3}{4}$ inch thick. How thick is the floor?

Since we want to know the total thickness, we add.

| Look at the denominators | Find equivalent fractions with the same denominator. | Add the fractions. |

$$\begin{array}{r} \frac{3}{4} \\ +\ \frac{5}{8} \\ \hline \end{array} \text{ unlike}$$

$$\begin{array}{r} \frac{3 \,(\times 2)}{4 \,(\times 2)} = \frac{6}{8} \\ +\ \frac{5}{8} = \frac{5}{8} \\ \hline \end{array}$$

$$\begin{array}{r} \frac{6}{8} \\ +\ \frac{5}{8} \\ \hline \frac{11}{8} = 1\frac{3}{8} \end{array}$$

The floor is $1\frac{3}{8}$ inches thick.

Other Examples

$$\begin{array}{r} \frac{1 \,(\times 2)}{2 \,(\times 2)} = \frac{2}{4} \\ +\ \frac{1}{4} = +\ \frac{1}{4} \\ \hline \frac{3}{4} \end{array}$$

$$\begin{array}{r} \frac{5}{9} = \frac{5}{9} \\ +\ \frac{2 \,(\times 3)}{3 \,(\times 3)} = +\ \frac{6}{9} \\ \hline \frac{11}{9} = 1\frac{2}{9} \end{array}$$

$$\begin{array}{r} \frac{1}{6} = \frac{1}{6} \\ +\ \frac{1 \,(\times 2)}{3 \,(\times 2)} = +\ \frac{2}{6} \\ \hline \frac{3}{6} = \frac{1}{2} \end{array}$$

Warm Up Find the sums.

1. $\begin{array}{r} \frac{1}{8} \\ +\ \frac{1}{4} \\ \hline \end{array}$

2. $\begin{array}{r} \frac{2}{3} \\ +\ \frac{1}{6} \\ \hline \end{array}$

3. $\begin{array}{r} \frac{3}{5} \\ +\ \frac{1}{10} \\ \hline \end{array}$

4. $\begin{array}{r} \frac{1}{2} \\ +\ \frac{1}{6} \\ \hline \end{array}$

5. $\begin{array}{r} \frac{3}{8} \\ +\ \frac{1}{2} \\ \hline \end{array}$

6. $\begin{array}{r} \frac{1}{9} \\ +\ \frac{2}{3} \\ \hline \end{array}$

Find the sums.

1. $\dfrac{1}{4}\overset{\times 2}{\underset{\times 2}{=}}\dfrac{}{}$

$+\dfrac{3}{8}=\dfrac{}{}$

2. $\dfrac{1}{6}=\dfrac{}{}$

$+\dfrac{1}{3}\overset{\times 2}{\underset{\times 2}{=}}\dfrac{}{}$

3. $\dfrac{3}{10}=\dfrac{}{}$

$+\dfrac{1}{5}\overset{\times 2}{\underset{\times 2}{=}}\dfrac{}{}$

4. $\dfrac{5}{6}=\dfrac{}{}$

$+\dfrac{1}{2}\overset{\times 3}{\underset{\times 3}{=}}\dfrac{}{}$

5. $\dfrac{3}{4}\overset{\times 2}{\underset{\times 2}{=}}\dfrac{}{}$

$+\dfrac{1}{8}=\dfrac{}{}$

6. $\dfrac{3}{4}=\dfrac{}{}$

$+\dfrac{1}{2}\overset{\times 2}{\underset{\times 2}{=}}\dfrac{}{}$

7. $\dfrac{5}{8}$
$+\dfrac{1}{4}$

8. $\dfrac{1}{2}$
$+\dfrac{7}{8}$

9. $\dfrac{5}{6}$
$+\dfrac{1}{3}$

10. $\dfrac{1}{2}$
$+\dfrac{7}{10}$

11. $\dfrac{4}{10}$
$+\dfrac{1}{5}$

12. $\dfrac{3}{8}$
$+\dfrac{3}{4}$

13. $\dfrac{1}{4}$
$+\dfrac{1}{2}$

14. $\dfrac{7}{10}$
$+\dfrac{1}{5}$

15. $\dfrac{2}{5}$
$+\dfrac{1}{10}$

16. $\dfrac{3}{10}$
$+\dfrac{3}{5}$

Solve.

17. A house plan calls for floors with $\dfrac{3}{4}$ inch plywood and $\dfrac{7}{8}$ inch concrete. How thick is the floor?

18. A builder put tile that was $\dfrac{1}{8}$ inch thick on top of $\dfrac{3}{4}$ inch plywood. How thick is this?

19. This problem does not have enough data. Make up the missing data and solve.
A builder put hardwood flooring on top of $\dfrac{1}{2}$ inch plywood. How thick were these floors?

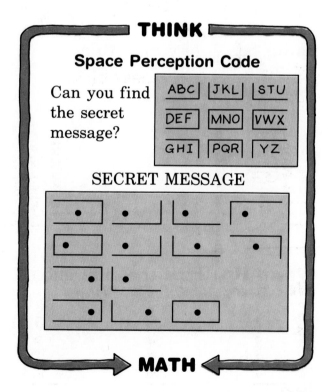

THINK

Space Perception Code

Can you find the secret message?

ABC	JKL	STU
DEF	MNO	VWX
GHI	PQR	YZ

SECRET MESSAGE

MATH

More Practice, page 410, Set A

Subtracting Fractions: Unlike Denominators

Anita lives $\frac{9}{10}$ mile from school. After she walks $\frac{1}{2}$ mile, how far does she still have to go?

Since we want to compare, we subtract.

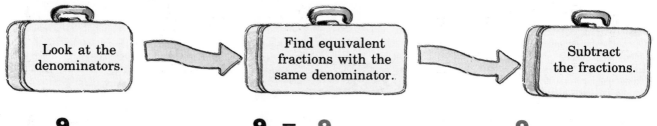

| Look at the denominators. | | Find equivalent fractions with the same denominator. | | Subtract the fractions. |

$$\begin{array}{r} \frac{9}{10} \\ -\frac{1}{2} \end{array} \quad \text{unlike}$$

$$\begin{array}{r} \frac{9}{10} = \frac{9}{10} \\ -\frac{1}{2} \stackrel{\times 5}{=} \frac{5}{10} \end{array}$$

$$\begin{array}{r} \frac{9}{10} \\ -\frac{5}{10} \\ \hline \frac{4}{10} = \frac{2}{5} \end{array}$$

Anita has $\frac{4}{10}$ or $\frac{2}{5}$ mile to go.

Other Examples

$$\begin{array}{r} \frac{1}{2} \stackrel{\times 2}{=} \frac{2}{4} \\ -\frac{1}{4} = -\frac{1}{4} \\ \hline \frac{1}{4} \end{array}$$

$$\begin{array}{r} \frac{2}{3} \stackrel{\times 3}{=} \frac{6}{9} \\ -\frac{1}{9} = -\frac{1}{9} \\ \hline \frac{5}{9} \end{array}$$

$$\begin{array}{r} \frac{2}{3} \stackrel{\times 2}{=} \frac{4}{6} \\ -\frac{1}{6} = -\frac{1}{6} \\ \hline \frac{3}{6} = \frac{1}{2} \end{array}$$

Warm Up   Find the differences.

1. $\frac{7}{8}$
$-\frac{1}{4}$

2. $\frac{2}{3}$
$-\frac{1}{6}$

3. $\frac{3}{5}$
$-\frac{1}{10}$

4. $\frac{1}{2}$
$-\frac{1}{6}$

5. $\frac{5}{8}$
$-\frac{1}{2}$

6. $\frac{1}{2}$
$-\frac{1}{4}$

Find the differences.

1. $\dfrac{3}{8} = \dfrac{\text{▓}}{\text{▓}}$
   $-\dfrac{1}{4} \overset{\times 2}{\underset{\times 2}{=}} \dfrac{\text{▓}}{\text{▓}}$

2. $1\dfrac{1}{3} \overset{\times 2}{\underset{\times 2}{=}} \dfrac{\text{▓}}{\text{▓}}$
   $-\dfrac{1}{6} = \dfrac{\text{▓}}{\text{▓}}$

3. $\dfrac{3}{10} = \dfrac{\text{▓}}{\text{▓}}$
   $-\dfrac{1}{5} \overset{\times 2}{\underset{\times 2}{=}} \dfrac{\text{▓}}{\text{▓}}$

4. $\dfrac{5}{6} = \dfrac{\text{▓}}{\text{▓}}$
   $-\dfrac{1}{2} \overset{\times 3}{\underset{\times 3}{=}} \dfrac{\text{▓}}{\text{▓}}$

5. $\dfrac{2}{3} \overset{\times 2}{\underset{\times 2}{=}} \dfrac{\text{▓}}{\text{▓}}$
   $-\dfrac{1}{6} = \dfrac{\text{▓}}{\text{▓}}$

6. $\dfrac{3}{4} \overset{\times 2}{\underset{\times 2}{=}} \dfrac{\text{▓}}{\text{▓}}$
   $-\dfrac{1}{8} = \dfrac{\text{▓}}{\text{▓}}$

7. $\dfrac{5}{8}$
   $-\dfrac{1}{4}$

8. $\dfrac{7}{8}$
   $-\dfrac{1}{2}$

9. $\dfrac{5}{6}$
   $-\dfrac{1}{3}$

10. $\dfrac{7}{10}$
    $-\dfrac{1}{2}$

11. $\dfrac{1}{2}$
    $-\dfrac{1}{4}$

12. $\dfrac{3}{4}$
    $-\dfrac{3}{8}$

13. $\dfrac{2}{3}$
    $-\dfrac{1}{9}$

14. $\dfrac{7}{10}$
    $-\dfrac{1}{5}$

15. $\dfrac{2}{5}$
    $-\dfrac{1}{10}$

16. $\dfrac{3}{5}$
    $-\dfrac{3}{10}$

Solve.

17. Jess lives $\frac{3}{4}$ mile from school. How far does he have to go after he has walked $\frac{1}{2}$ mile?

★ 18. Noell lives 1 mile from school. How far does she have to go when she has walked $\frac{3}{10}$ mile?

THINK

Patterns

Give the next three fractions or whole numbers.

1. $\frac{1}{10}$, $\frac{4}{10}$, $\frac{7}{10}$, 1, ▓, ▓, ▓,

2. $\frac{0}{6}$, $\frac{2}{6}$, $\frac{4}{6}$, 1, $\frac{8}{6}$, $\frac{10}{6}$, 2, $\frac{14}{6}$, ▓, ▓, ▓,

3. 0, $\frac{4}{8}$, 1, $\frac{12}{8}$, 2, ▓, ▓, ▓,

MATH

PROBLEM SOLVING
Using Data from a Circle Graph

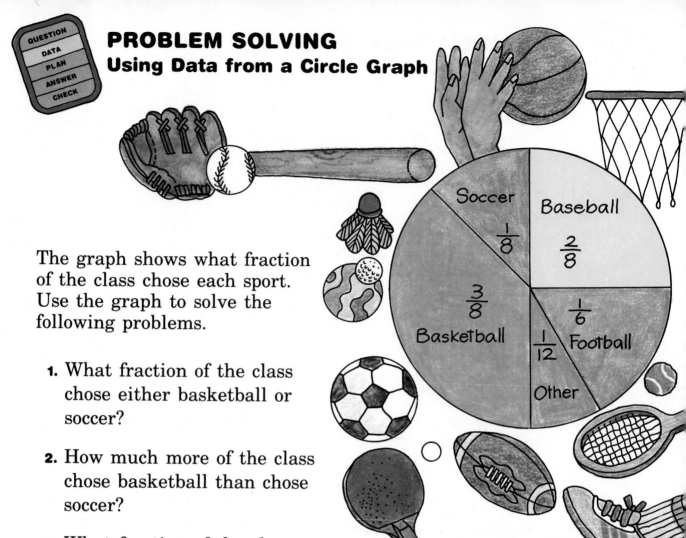

Favorite Sport
Room 38

The graph shows what fraction of the class chose each sport. Use the graph to solve the following problems.

1. What fraction of the class chose either basketball or soccer?

2. How much more of the class chose basketball than chose soccer?

3. What fraction of the class chose either soccer or baseball?

4. How much more of the class chose basketball than baseball?

5. What fraction of the class chose either basketball or baseball?

6. There were 24 children in the class. How many of them chose football?

★ 7. Of the 24 children in the class, how many of them chose basketball?

★ 8. How many more of the children chose baseball than football?

9. *Try This* Tickets are $2 and $3. Nancy sold 7 for $18. How many of each did she sell?

258

PROBLEM SOLVING
Practice

QUESTION
DATA
PLAN
ANSWER
CHECK

The May family drove
to the beach for a picnic.

Solve.

1. Mr. May drove $22\frac{5}{10}$ miles to the beach. When he drove home, he took a shortcut that was only $19\frac{3}{10}$ miles. How far did he drive in all?

2. The trip going took $\frac{3}{4}$ hour. Going home took $\frac{2}{4}$ hour. How much less time was the trip home?

3. There are 6 people in the May family. If $\frac{1}{2}$ of them went swimming, how many people went swimming?

4. If $\frac{1}{3}$ of the May family looked for shells, how many people looked for shells?

5. The May family decided to cook 8 hamburgers at the picnic. The children ate $\frac{1}{2}$ of them. How many hamburgers did the children eat?

6. Simon ate $\frac{2}{4}$ of a melon. Laura then ate $\frac{1}{4}$ of the melon. What part of a melon did the two children eat?

★ 7. Simon swam for $\frac{1}{2}$ hour. Laura swam only for $\frac{1}{4}$ hour. How much longer did Simon swim than Laura?

8. *Try This* The May family took wheat bread and rye bread to the picnic. They had ham, cheese, peanut butter, and turkey for sandwiches. How many different kinds of sandwiches could they make if they put just one thing on one kind of bread?

259

PROBLEM SOLVING
Using the Strategies

Use one or more of the strategies listed to solve each problem below.

PROBLEM-SOLVING STRATEGIES

CHOOSE THE OPERATIONS
DRAW A PICTURE
GUESS AND CHECK
MAKE A LIST
MAKE A TABLE
FIND A PATTERN
WORK BACKWARD
USE LOGICAL REASONING

1. Pretend a pet shop sold 3 fish on the first day of the month, 6 fish on the second day, 9 fish on the third day and so on. On what day of the month were 42 fish sold?

2. There are 13 people who work at the pet shop on weekends. 9 of them work on Saturday and 8 work on Sunday. How many work on both Saturday and Sunday?

3. Brenda bought her canary at the pet shop the twelfth day of the month, a Thursday. On what day of the week was the first day of the month?

4. Each time the pet shop orders 8 boxes of birdseed, 3 bird feeders are also ordered. How many bird feeders are ordered at the same time that 48 boxes of birdseed are ordered? Complete the table.

BIRDSEED	8	16	24
BIRDFEEDERS	3	6	9

Find the sums and differences.

1. $\begin{array}{r} \frac{2}{5} \\ + \frac{1}{5} \\ \hline \end{array}$

2. $\begin{array}{r} \frac{4}{8} \\ + \frac{2}{8} \\ \hline \end{array}$

3. $\begin{array}{r} \frac{1}{10} \\ + \frac{4}{10} \\ \hline \end{array}$

4. $\begin{array}{r} \frac{3}{4} \\ - \frac{2}{4} \\ \hline \end{array}$

5. $\begin{array}{r} \frac{5}{6} \\ - \frac{2}{6} \\ \hline \end{array}$

6. $\begin{array}{r} \frac{7}{8} \\ - \frac{1}{8} \\ \hline \end{array}$

7. $\begin{array}{r} 6\frac{1}{6} \\ + 2\frac{4}{6} \\ \hline \end{array}$

8. $\begin{array}{r} 3\frac{1}{3} \\ + 4\frac{1}{3} \\ \hline \end{array}$

9. $\begin{array}{r} 5\frac{4}{5} \\ - 2\frac{1}{5} \\ \hline \end{array}$

10. $\begin{array}{r} 8\frac{7}{10} \\ - 1\frac{6}{10} \\ \hline \end{array}$

11. $\begin{array}{r} \frac{7}{10} \\ + \frac{1}{5} \\ \hline \end{array}$

12. $\begin{array}{r} \frac{1}{6} \\ + \frac{2}{3} \\ \hline \end{array}$

13. $\begin{array}{r} \frac{3}{8} \\ + \frac{1}{2} \\ \hline \end{array}$

14. $\begin{array}{r} \frac{1}{4} \\ + \frac{1}{8} \\ \hline \end{array}$

15. $\begin{array}{r} \frac{1}{2} \\ + \frac{1}{4} \\ \hline \end{array}$

16. $\begin{array}{r} \frac{5}{6} \\ - \frac{1}{3} \\ \hline \end{array}$

17. $\begin{array}{r} \frac{9}{10} \\ - \frac{1}{5} \\ \hline \end{array}$

18. $\begin{array}{r} \frac{3}{8} \\ - \frac{1}{4} \\ \hline \end{array}$

19. $\begin{array}{r} \frac{7}{10} \\ - \frac{1}{5} \\ \hline \end{array}$

20. $\begin{array}{r} \frac{5}{8} \\ - \frac{1}{2} \\ \hline \end{array}$

Solve.

21. A beaver footprint is $6\frac{7}{8}$ inches. A muskrat footprint is $3\frac{1}{8}$ inches. How much longer is the beaver print than the muskrat print?

22. Judi and Paul shared an apple. Judi ate $\frac{1}{2}$ of the apple and Paul ate $\frac{1}{2}$ of the apple. How much apple did they eat altogether?

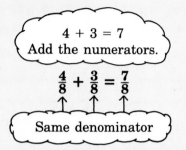

$$4 + 3 = 7$$
Add the numerators.

$$\frac{4}{8} + \frac{3}{8} = \frac{7}{8}$$

Same denominator

Find the sums and differences.

1. $\frac{5}{10} + \frac{4}{10}$ **2.** $\frac{3}{8} + \frac{1}{8}$

3. $\frac{1}{6} + \frac{2}{6}$ **4.** $\frac{1}{4} + \frac{1}{4}$

5. $\begin{array}{r} \frac{3}{5} \\ + \frac{1}{5} \\ \hline \end{array}$ **6.** $\begin{array}{r} \frac{7}{10} \\ + \frac{1}{10} \\ \hline \end{array}$ **7.** $\begin{array}{r} \frac{2}{8} \\ + \frac{1}{8} \\ \hline \end{array}$

$$9 - 6 = 3$$
Subtract the numerators.

$$\frac{9}{10} - \frac{6}{10} = \frac{3}{10}$$

Same denominator

8. $\frac{7}{10} - \frac{2}{10}$ **9.** $\frac{5}{6} - \frac{4}{6}$

10. $\frac{3}{8} - \frac{1}{8}$ **11.** $\frac{3}{4} - \frac{2}{4}$

12. $\begin{array}{r} \frac{5}{8} \\ - \frac{1}{8} \\ \hline \end{array}$ **13.** $\begin{array}{r} \frac{7}{10} \\ - \frac{6}{10} \\ \hline \end{array}$ **14.** $\begin{array}{r} \frac{4}{6} \\ - \frac{1}{6} \\ \hline \end{array}$

Change to a mixed number.

$$\frac{7}{8} + \frac{5}{8} = \frac{12}{8} = 1\frac{4}{8} = 1\frac{1}{2}$$

Change to lowest terms.

15. $\frac{5}{8} + \frac{4}{8}$ **16.** $\frac{7}{10} + \frac{6}{10}$

17. $\frac{5}{6} + \frac{4}{6}$ **18.** $\frac{3}{8} + \frac{7}{8}$

19. $\begin{array}{r} 6\frac{5}{8} \\ - 4\frac{2}{8} \\ \hline \end{array}$ **20.** $\begin{array}{r} 7\frac{6}{10} \\ - 3\frac{1}{10} \\ \hline \end{array}$ **21.** $\begin{array}{r} 2\frac{5}{6} \\ + 3\frac{2}{6} \\ \hline \end{array}$

Probability and Prediction

There are 12 marbles in the box. 3 of the marbles are red and 9 are blue. If you pick up a marble without looking, would you be more likely to get a blue marble or a red marble?

You have 3 chances in 12 of getting a red marble. The **probability** of getting a red marble is $\frac{3}{12}$.

You have 9 chances in 12 of getting a blue marble. The **probability** of getting a blue marble is $\frac{9}{12}$.

1. If you pick up a marble without looking, would you be more likely to get a green or an orange marble?

2. What is the probability of getting a green marble?

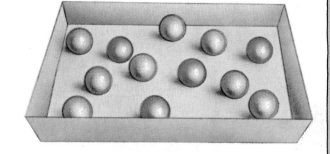

3. What is the probability of getting an orange marble?

4. Get a box and 12 marbles. Be sure there are 8 marbles of a dark color and 4 marbles of a light color. Take out a marble without looking. Check the color. Put it back. Do this 48 times. Keep a record of the marbles you take out. Check to see if you take out a light-colored marble about $\frac{4}{12}$ or $\frac{1}{3}$ of the time.

Give the letter for the correct answer.

Measure each length to the nearest centimeter.

1. |————————|
- **A** 3 cm **B** 5 cm
- **C** 4 cm **D** not given

2. |————————————|
- **A** 4 cm **B** 5 cm
- **C** 6 cm **D** not given

3. Give the perimeter.

2 cm — 2 cm
- **A** 2 cm **B** 4 cm
- **C** 8 cm **D** not given

4. Give the area.

- **A** 10 square units
- **B** 6 square units
- **C** 3 square units
- **D** not given

5. Give the volume.

- **A** 4 cubic units
- **B** 12 cubic units
- **C** 8 cubic units
- **D** not given

Choose the best measure.

6.

- **A** 1 mL **B** 10 mL
- **C** 1 L **D** not given

7.
- **A** 1 kg **B** 1 g
- **C** 10 kg **D** not given

8.

← Boiling Water

- **A** ⁻10°C **B** 10°C
- **C** 100°C **D** not given

Divide.

9. $6\overline{)52}$
- **A** 9 R2 **B** 8 R4
- **C** 8 R6 **D** not given

10. $5\overline{)44}$
- **A** 9 R1 **B** 9 R4
- **C** 8 R2 **D** not given

11. $3\overline{)215}$
- **A** 71 R2 **B** 61 R2
- **C** 71 R3 **D** not given

12. $5\overline{)457}$
- **A** 91 R5 **B** 9 R7
- **C** 91 R2 **D** not given

13. An apple pie serves 8 people. How many pies are needed to serve 21 people?

- **A** 2 **B** 3
- **C** 13 **D** not given

14. Jorgé needs 4 eggs to make a cake. How many cakes can he make with 15 eggs?

- **A** 3 **B** 5
- **C** 4 **D** not given

GEOMETRY AND GRAPHING 11

Alyssa saw a movie about Egypt. She liked the pyramids. They were built thousands of years ago. The Great Pyramid is at the city of Giza. It was built for a king named Khufu. Over 2 million blocks of stone were used to build it. Near it sits the Great Sphinx. It was carved of solid rock. Alyssa also liked the tall obelisks. There were hieroglyphics (picture writing) on them. They had been cut from a single piece of stone. Then they were dragged to the Nile River. They were floated on barges to different cities in Egypt.

Space Figures

Objects from the world around you suggest **space figures**.

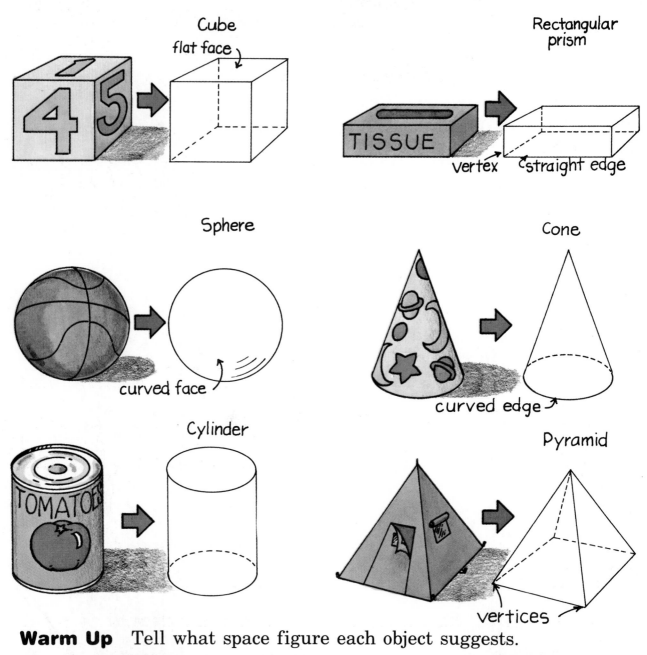

Cube
flat face

Rectangular prism
vertex   straight edge

Sphere
curved face

Cone
curved edge

Cylinder

Pyramid
vertices

Warm Up Tell what space figure each object suggests.

1.

2.

3.

Tell what space figure each object suggests.

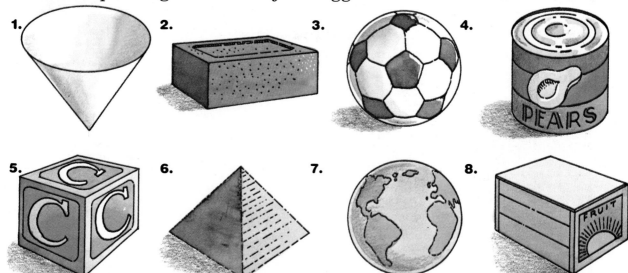

1.

2.

3.

4.

5.

6.

7.

8.

Copy and complete the table.

Name	Number of Flat Faces	Number of Vertices	Number of Straight Edges	Number of Curved Edges	Number of Curved Faces
Cube	6			0	0
Rectangular Prism					0
Sphere	0	0	0	0	
Cone	1	1			
Cylinder			0		
Pyramid				0	

THINK

Shape Perception

How many faces does
the icosahedron have?

How many faces does
the dodecahedron have?

icosahedron   dodecahedron

MATH

Plane Figures

Objects from the world around you suggest
plane figures. Plane figures lie on a flat
surface.

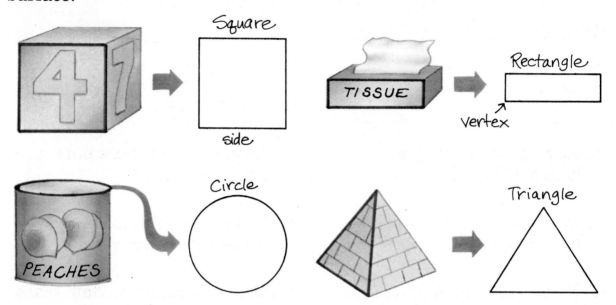

Square
side

Rectangle
vertex

Circle

Triangle

Some other plane figures are shown below.

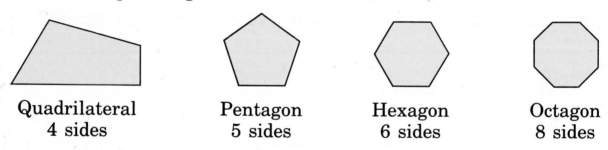

Quadrilateral
4 sides

Pentagon
5 sides

Hexagon
6 sides

Octagon
8 sides

Polygons are plane figures that have
all straight sides. Each pair of
sides meet at a vertex.

Warm Up Which of the figures below are polygons?
Name the polygon.

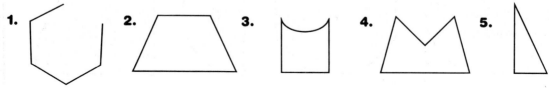

1. **2.** **3.** **4.** **5.**

Name the plane figure suggested by each object.

1. 2. 3. 4.

Name each of these polygons.

5. 6. 7. 8.

9. How many sides does a hexagon have?

10. How many vertices does a pentagon have?

11. How many vertices does a hexagon have?

12. Draw a quadrilateral. How many sides does it have?

13. How many sides does a pentagon have?

14. Draw an octagon. How many vertices does it have?

═ THINK ═

Logical Reasoning

Which figure does not belong?

A.

1   2   3   4

B.

1   2   3   4

➤ MATH ◄

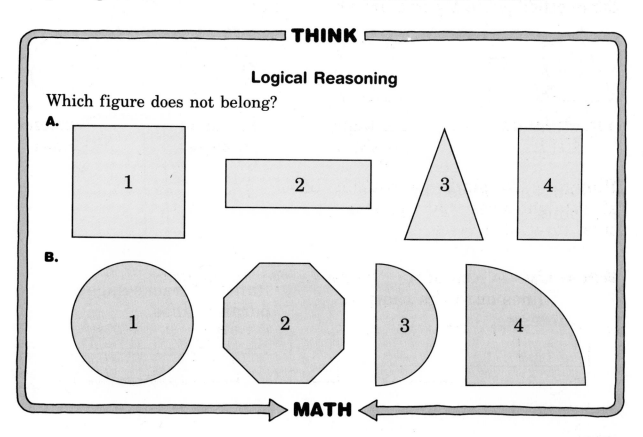

Points, Lines, and Segments

A long, straight road in the desert suggests the idea of a **line**.

A line is endless in both directions. A distant car on the road suggests the idea of a **point** on the line.

Points are named with capital letters. A distant crossroad suggests the idea of **intersecting** lines.

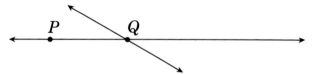

The two lines intersect at a point Q. A line is named by any two points on the line.

We write: $\overleftrightarrow{PQ}$ or $\overleftrightarrow{QP}$

The part of the road from the car to the intersection suggests a **segment**.

Segments are named by their endpoints.

We write: $\overline{PQ}$ or $\overline{QP}$

Parallel lines are lines that never intersect.

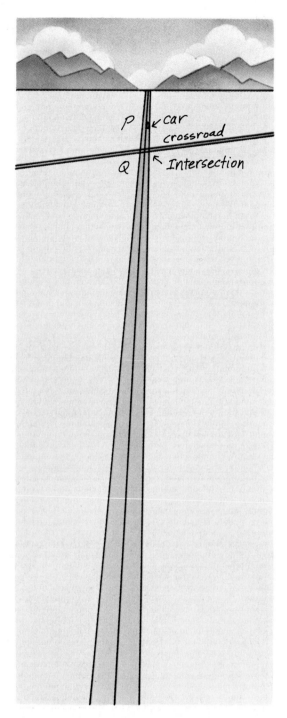

Railroad tracks suggest parallel lines.

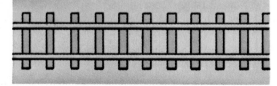

Write the name for each figure.

Example

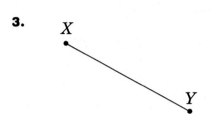

Answer $\overline{MN}$

1.

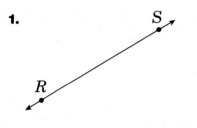

2.

A
•

3.

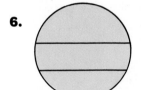

4.

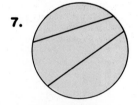

5.

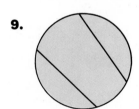

Pretend you are looking through a telescope at some far-off lines. Tell whether they are parallel or intersecting lines.

6.

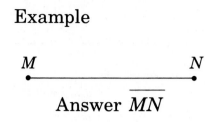

7.

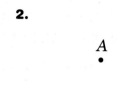

8.

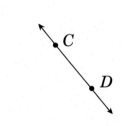

9.

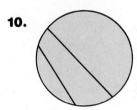

10.

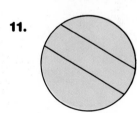

11.

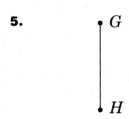

Draw and label a figure for each name.

12. $\overleftrightarrow{RS}$ **13.** T **14.** $\overline{YZ}$ **15.** $\overleftrightarrow{BA}$

THINK

Geometry Puzzle

Name the different segments in the figure below. How many are there?

Remember: $\overline{AB}$ and $\overline{BA}$ are the same segment.

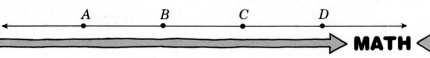

MATH

Rays and Angles

A rocket fired on a straight path into space suggests the idea of a **ray**.

A ray is part of a line. Ray AB has endpoint A and continues through B without end.

We write: $\overrightarrow{AB}$ $\overrightarrow{DC}$

An **angle** is two rays with the same endpoint.

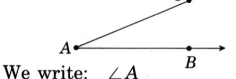

We write: $\angle A$

Polygons have angles at each of their vertices.

An angle at a "square corner" is a **right angle**.

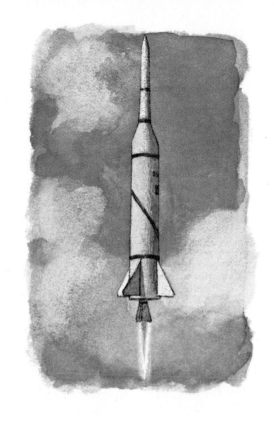

Name each ray.

1.

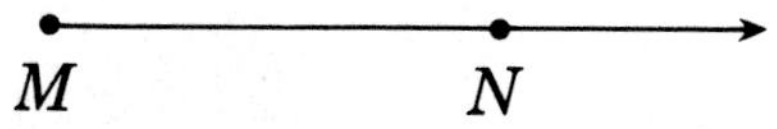

M   N

2.

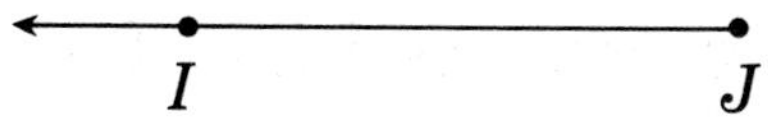

I   J

Name each angle.

3.

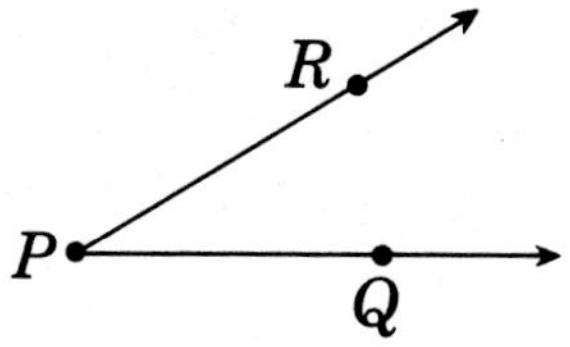

4.

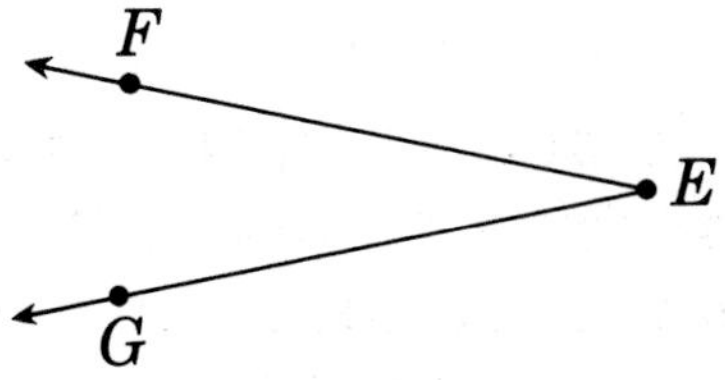

Tell whether the angle shown is a right angle. Write yes or no.

5.

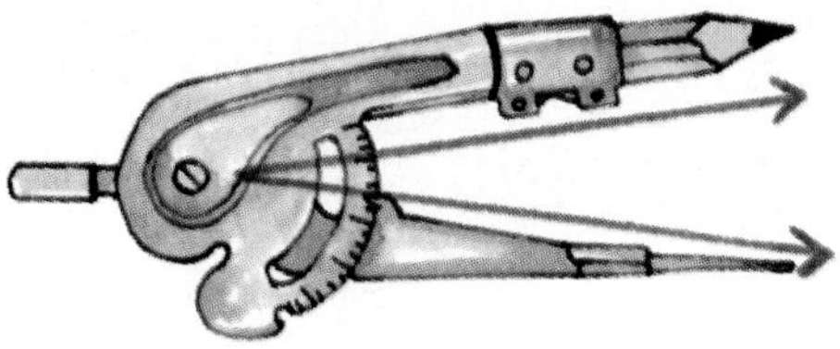

6.

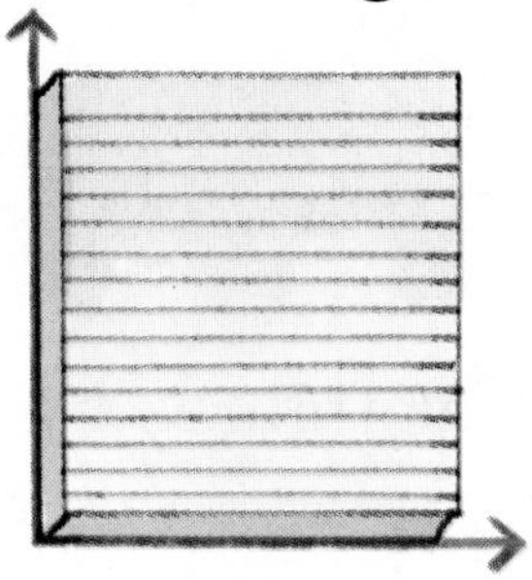

7.

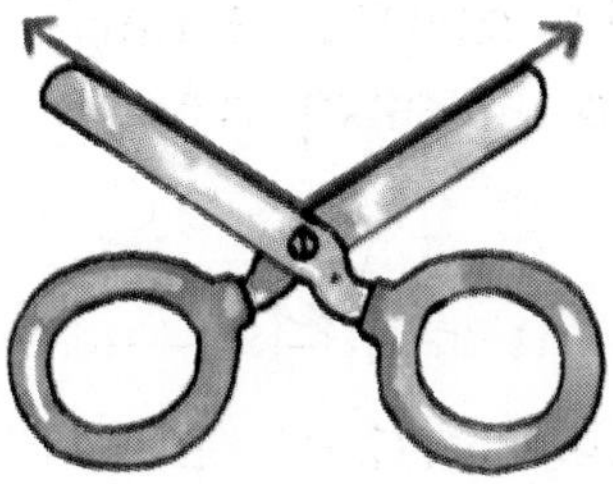

8.

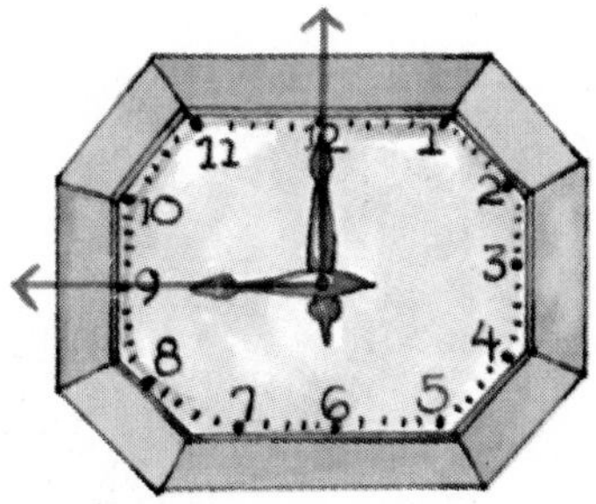

9.

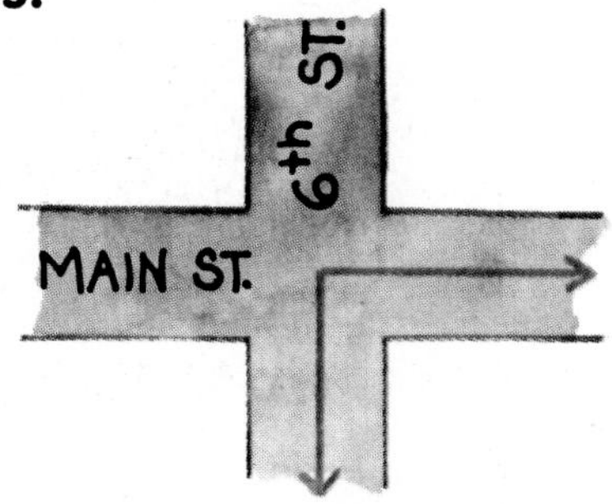

10.

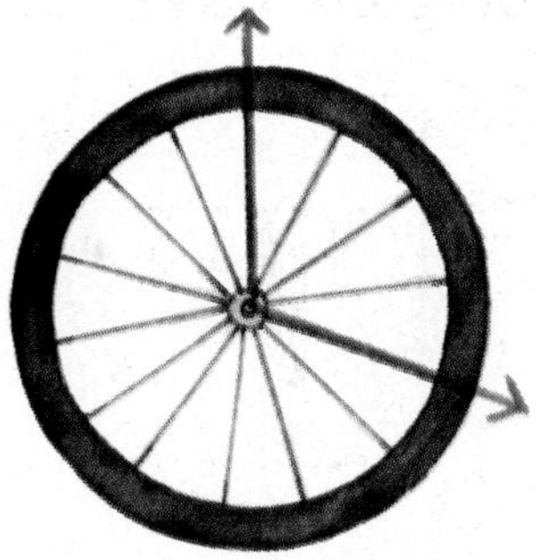

How many right angles does each polygon have?

11.

12.

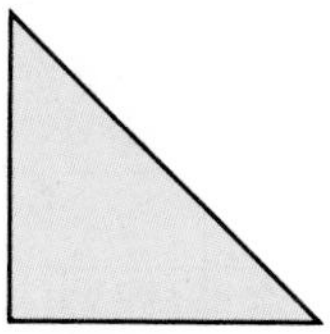

13.

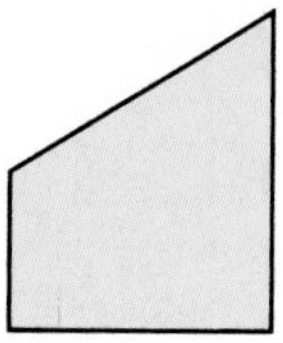

14.

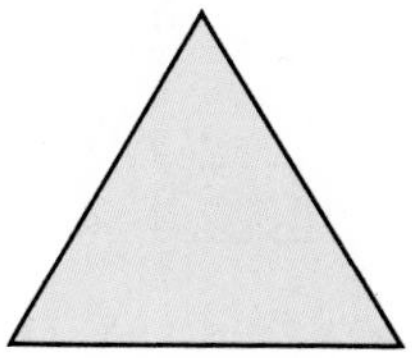

273

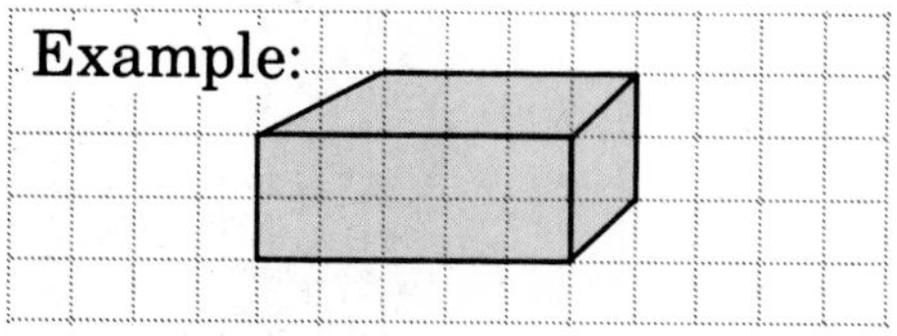

Congruent Figures

Fred is making copies of a geometric figure. The copy machine turns out figures that are the same size and shape. The figures are all congruent to each other.

You can also make congruent figures by tracing.

picture

tracing

Warm Up If you need help, make a tracing to decide whether the figures on the two papers are congruent to each other.

1.

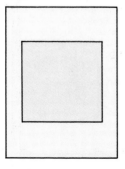 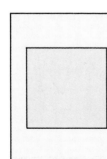

2.

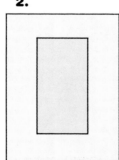 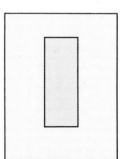

If you need help, make a tracing to decide whether the two figures are congruent. You may need to turn or flip your tracing to see if it fits.

1.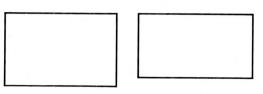

2.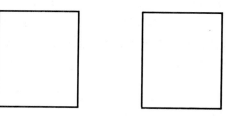

3.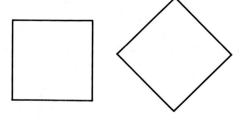

4.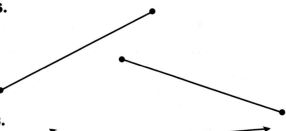

5.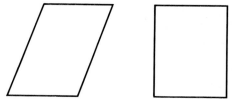

6.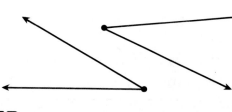

7.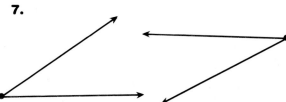

8.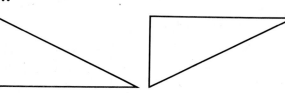

SKILLKEEPER

Find the sums and differences.

1. $\frac{3}{10}$
$+ \frac{6}{10}$

2. $\frac{5}{8}$
$- \frac{2}{8}$

3. $\frac{1}{3}$
$+ \frac{1}{3}$

4. $\frac{5}{6}$
$- \frac{4}{6}$

5. $\frac{2}{5}$
$+ \frac{2}{5}$

6. $\frac{5}{8}$
$+ \frac{4}{8}$

7. $5\frac{3}{4}$
$- 2\frac{2}{4}$

8. $\frac{2}{3}$
$+ \frac{2}{3}$

9. $7\frac{6}{10}$
$- 2\frac{4}{10}$

10. $\frac{5}{6}$
$+ \frac{3}{6}$

Similar Figures

Some copy machines will make larger or smaller copies of an original. Norma is making smaller copies of a geometric figure. The smaller figures are the same shape as the original.

Figures that have the same shape are **similar** to each other. Each small figure is similar to the original.

Warm Up   You can use different size graph paper to help you decide if two figures are similar. Write similar or not similar for each pair of figures.

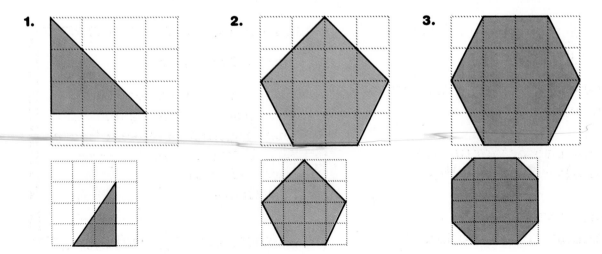

1.

2.

3.

Which figure in each row is similar to the first?

1.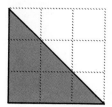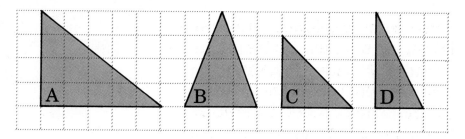

2.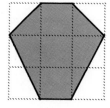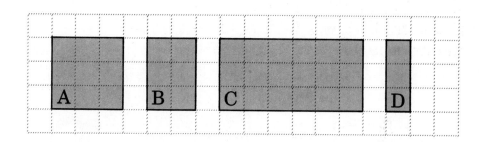

3.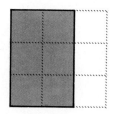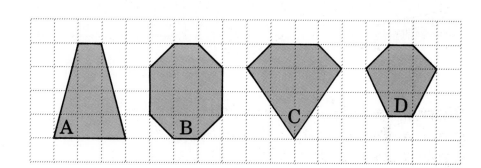

★ Write T (true) or F (false) for each statement.

4. Any two squares are similar to each other.

5. Any two octagons are similar to each other.

6. Any two circles are similar to each other.

THINK

Shape Perception

Trace the figure below. Cut out 4 copies of the figure. Put them together to make a figure that is larger than, but similar to this figure.

MATH

Symmetric Figures

A figure has a **line of symmetry** if it can be folded so that the two parts fit exactly (are congruent). The fold is the line of symmetry. A figure that has a line of symmetry is a **symmetric figure**.

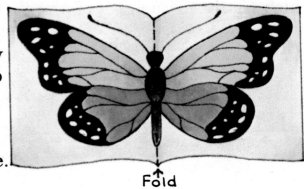

Fold

Here is a way you can make a symmetric figure.

Fold a piece of paper.

Make a cut that starts and ends on the fold.

Unfold the piece you cut out.

Warm Up Tell what the symmetric figure will be when cut out and unfolded.

1.
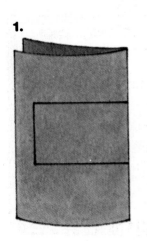

2.
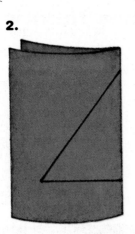

3.
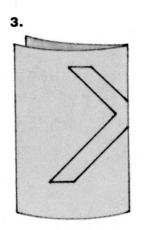

4.
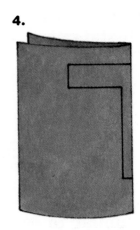

278

Which of these drawings of objects from nature come "close" to being symmetrical? Write yes or no.

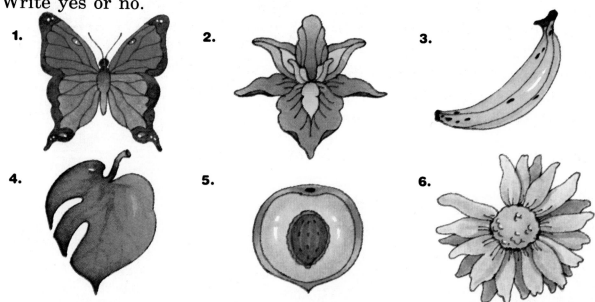

1.

2.

3.

4.

5.

6.

Does the dashed line appear to be a line of symmetry?

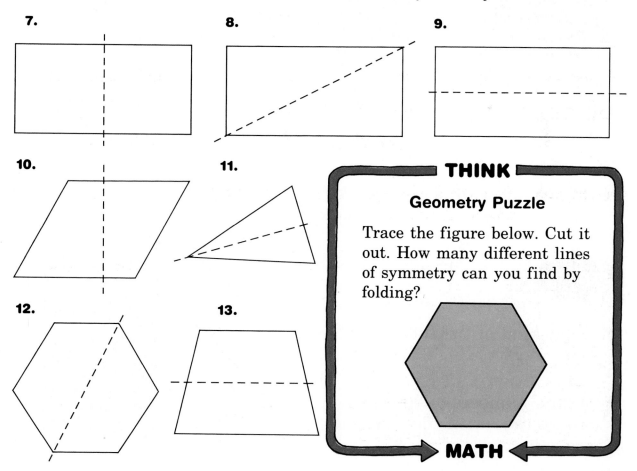

7.

8.

9.

10.

11.

12.

13.

THINK

Geometry Puzzle

Trace the figure below. Cut it out. How many different lines of symmetry can you find by folding?

MATH

Tallies and Bar Graphs

The children in Room 35 sold tickets for the school play. These are the tickets they sold.

Rita made a **tally chart** to show the kinds of tickets. She put one mark for each ticket. Rita shows 5 tickets as ||||| so the marks are easy to count.

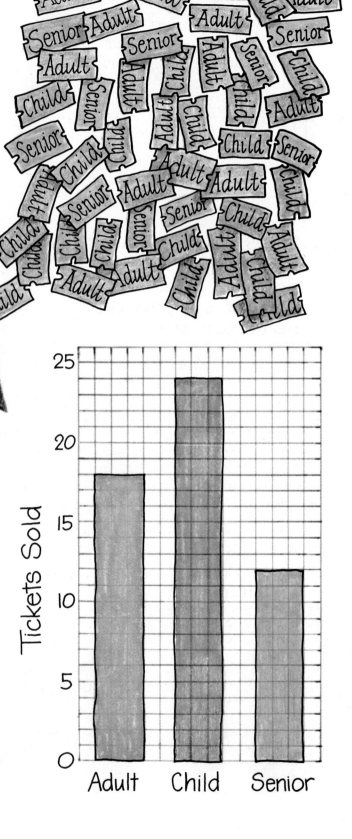

Tickets Sold — Rm 35

Adult |||| |||| |||| |||

Child |||| |||| |||| |||| ||||

Senior |||| |||| ||

Ted made a **bar graph** to show the tickets sold.

Warm Up

1. How many adult tickets were sold?

2. How many senior tickets were sold?

3. What kind of ticket sold the most?

4. Do the numbers in the tally chart agree with those on the graph?

Solve.

1. This tally chart shows the tickets sold by the children in Room 30. Make a bar graph to show their ticket sales.

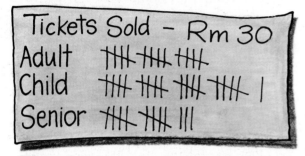

Tickets Sold – Rm 30
Adult   卌 卌 卌
Child   卌 卌 卌 卌 |
Senior   卌 卌 |||

2. The children in Room 32 also sold tickets. These are the tickets they sold. Make a tally chart to show the tickets they sold.

Adult | ult | ult | ult | ult | ult | ult | ult | ult | ult | ult | ult | ult | ult |

Child | ild | ild | ild | ild | ild | ild | ild | ild | ild | ild | ild | ild | ild | ild | ild | ild |

Senior | ior | ior | ior | ior | ior | ior | ior | ior | ior |

3. The children in Room 38 won the prize for most tickets sold. These are the tickets they sold. Make a tally chart and graph to show their sales.

Adult | ult | ult | ult | ult | ult | ult | ult | ult | ult | ult | ult | ult | ult | ult | ult | ult | ult | ult | ult |

Child | ild | ild | ild | ild | ild | ild | ild | ild | ild | ild | ild | ild | ild | ild | ild | ild | ild | ild | ild | ild | ild | ild | ild |

Senior | ior | ior | ior | ior | ior | ior | ior | ior | ior | ior | ior | ior | ior | ior | ior | ior | ior |

Picture Graphs

Tom Brown owns a TV store. The **picture graph** below shows how many TVs he sold in each of the first 6 months of the year. Each picture means 10 TVs sold. So Tom sold **5 × 10**, or **50**, TVs in January.

BROWN'S TV SALES

January	🖵 🖵 🖵 🖵 🖵
February	🖵 🖵 🖵 🖵
March	🖵 🖵 🖵 🖵 🖵 🖵 🖵 🖵 🖵
April	🖵 🖵 🖵 🖵 🖵 🖵 🖵
May	🖵 🖵 🖵 🖵 🖵 🖵
June	🖵 🖵 🖵 🖵

Each 🖵 means 10 TVs sold.

Warm Up

1. How many TVs did Tom Brown sell in February?

2. In what month were 60 TVs sold?

3. In what month were the most TVs sold? How many were sold?

4. Estimate how many TVs were sold in April.

5. Estimate the number of TVs sold in June.

Use the radio graph to answer
questions 1–5.

1. How many radios were sold
   in March?

2. In what two months were the
   same number of radios sold?

3. Estimate the number of
   radios sold in June.

4. In what month were the
   fewest radios sold? Estimate
   how many were sold.

5. About how many radios were
   sold in May?

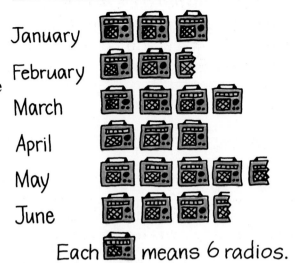

BROWN'S RADIO SALES

January
February
March
April
May
June

Each [radio] means 6 radios.

Use the stereo graph to answer
questions 6–8.

6. How many stereos were sold
   in January?

7. In what two months were
   about the same number of
   stereos sold?

8. Estimate the number of
   stereos sold in June.

★ 9. Make your own picture graph
   for this data.
     TVs sold:
     July—12, August—18,
     and September—15. Let
     each picture mean 3 TVs.

BROWN'S STEREO SALES

January
February
March
April
May
June

Each [stereo] means 4 stereos.

Number Pairs on a Graph

Graph the point for the number pair (3,2)

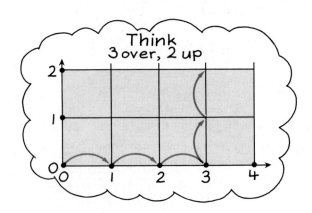

Think
3 over, 2 up

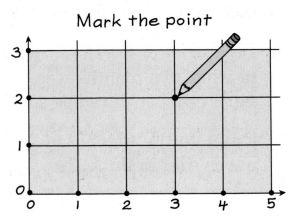

Mark the point

The triangle to the right was made by graphing and connecting these points in order:
(3,5) → (1,1) → (5,1) → (3,5)

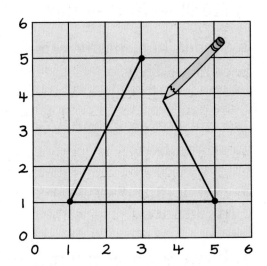

Warm Up Use graph paper to graph the points below. Number your graph 0 through 6 as shown in the example. Label each point with its letter.

1. A(1,2) B(4,2) C(4,5)
2. Connect the points in this order.
   A → B → C → A
3. What kind of a figure did you draw?

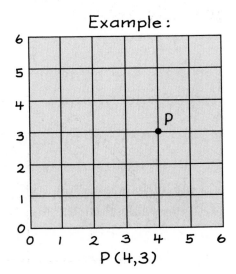

Example:

P (4,3)

284

Use graph paper to draw the following figures. Use the numbers 0 through 6 for each exercise.

1. Square: $(1,1) \rightarrow (5,1) \rightarrow (5,5) \rightarrow (1,5) \rightarrow (1,1)$

2. Rectangle: $(1,2) \rightarrow (5,2) \rightarrow (5,4) \rightarrow (1,4) \rightarrow (1,2)$

3. Right Triangle: $(2,1) \rightarrow (5,1) \rightarrow (5,6) \rightarrow (2,1)$

For each of the figures below you will need to use the numbers 0 through 10. Graph the points and connect them in order.

4. $(2,2) \rightarrow (0,2) \rightarrow (1,3) \rightarrow (2,3) \rightarrow (8,8) \rightarrow$
$(10,9) \rightarrow (9,7) \rightarrow (3,2) \rightarrow (3,1) \rightarrow (2,0) \rightarrow$
$(2,2)$

5. $(4,0) \rightarrow (5,3) \rightarrow (7,1) \rightarrow (8,1) \rightarrow (8,2) \rightarrow$
$(9,1) \rightarrow (10,2) \rightarrow (9,4) \rightarrow (5,8) \rightarrow (5,10) \rightarrow$
$(4,8) \rightarrow (3,10) \rightarrow (0,4) \rightarrow (4,0)$

6. $(1,4) \rightarrow (3,7) \rightarrow (3,9) \rightarrow (2,7) \rightarrow (3,4) \rightarrow$
$(4,5) \rightarrow (3,6) \rightarrow (5,6) \rightarrow (6,4) \rightarrow (7,6) \rightarrow$
$(7,2) \rightarrow (6,1) \rightarrow (6,2) \rightarrow (9,5) \rightarrow (8,6) \rightarrow$
$(8,5) \rightarrow (9,4) \rightarrow (10,4)$

7. Write a set of number pairs that would give this figure.

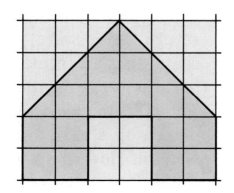

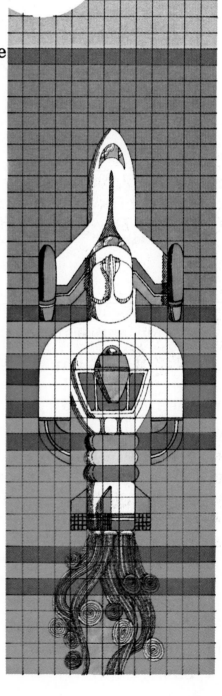

PROBLEM SOLVING
Using the Strategies

Use one or more of the strategies listed to solve each problem.

PROBLEM-SOLVING STRATEGIES

CHOOSE THE OPERATIONS

DRAW A PICTURE

GUESS AND CHECK

MAKE A LIST

MAKE A TABLE

FIND A PATTERN

WORK BACKWARD

USE LOGICAL REASONING

1. The bus left the downtown station and traveled 2 hours before stopping. The rest stop lasted 20 minutes. The bus then traveled an hour and a half before arriving in Middletown at 4:30 p.m. What time did the bus leave for Middletown?

2. There were 20 people left on the bus when it got to Middletown. There were 2 more men than women. How many men were on the bus?

3. On the trip, the bus passed through 5 towns. Bern was before Aden. Aden was before Dale. Eaton was after Dale. Center was between Bern and Aden. Which town did the bus leave last?

4. When the bus loaded to return, there were 3 empty seats—one in front, one in back, and one in the middle. The bus stopped at Bern and picked up a man and a woman. How many ways could they sit down?

Tell what space figure each object suggests

1.

2.

Name each polygon.

3.

4.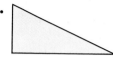

Are the lines parallel?

5.

6.

Are the angles right angles?

7.

8.

9. Which figure is congruent to the first?

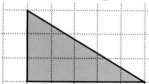 **A**  **B** 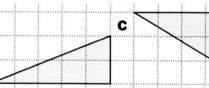 **C**

10. Which figure is similar to the first?

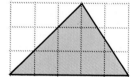 **A** 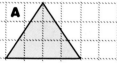 **B** **C**

11. Which shape has a line of symmetry?

A  **B** 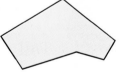 **C**

12. How many TVs were sold in June?

May
June
July

Each ▭ means 9 TVs.

13. If you connect the points, what figure will be made?

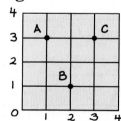

Space Figures

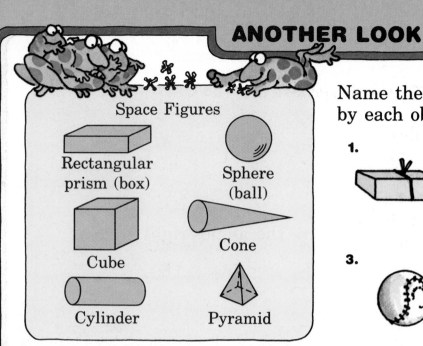

Rectangular prism (box)

Sphere (ball)

Cube

Cone

Cylinder

Pyramid

Plane Figures

Square

Rectangle

Circle

Triangle

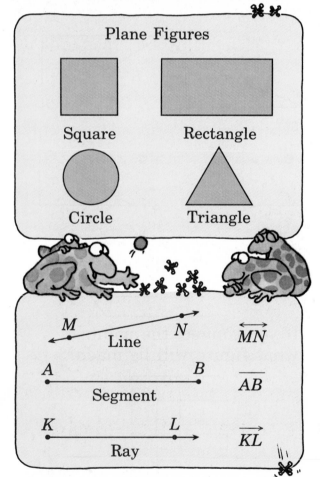

M — N
Line $\overleftrightarrow{MN}$

A — B
Segment $\overline{AB}$

K — L
Ray $\overrightarrow{KL}$

Name the space figure suggested by each object.

1.

2.

3.

4.

Name the plane figure suggested by each object.

5.

6.

7.

8.

Tell whether each object suggests a line, segment, or ray.

9.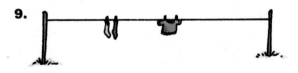

10.

Space Perception

This triangle, with all sides equal, has been carefully cut from a piece of green tagboard. It has an F (front) on one side and B (back) on the other. It can be put back into its hole six different ways.

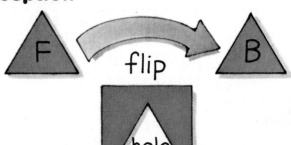

   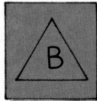  

Look at the figures below. First guess how many ways each figure can be put back into its hole. Draw each figure on graph paper. Cut it out and check your guess.

1.

 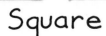

Square

2.
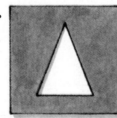

Isosceles triangle

3.

Rectangle

Computer Drawings

Logo is a special computer language. You can use it to draw pictures on a computer screen. A small triangle △, called a *turtle,* can move around to draw pictures. But you must tell the turtle what to do. The pictures show you how to make the turtle move and draw.

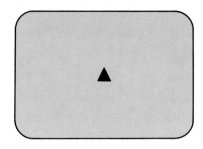

The turtle

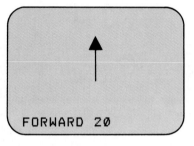

Move forward
20 units.

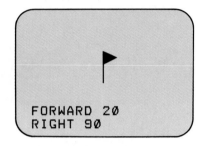

Turn right
90 degrees.

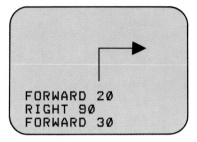

Move forward
30 units.

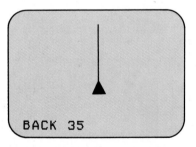

Move back 35 units.

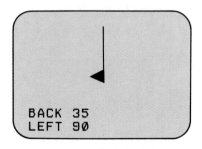

Turn left 90 degrees.

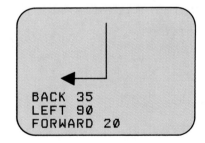

Move forward 20 units.

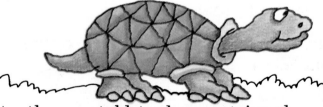

The turtle was told to draw a triangle that is 30 units long on each side.

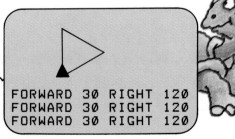

Give the missing word for each picture.

1.
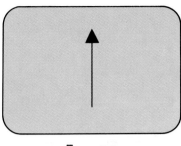
_?__ 40

2.
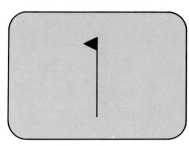
FORWARD 50
_?__ 90

3.
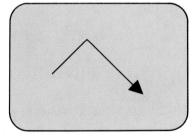
_?__ 30

4.
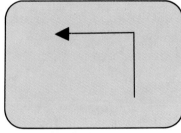
FORWARD 40
_?__ 90
FORWARD 40

5.
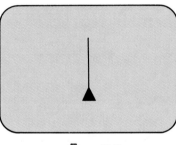
RIGHT 45 FORWARD 30
RIGHT 90 _?__ 40

6.
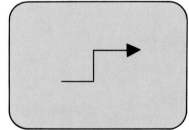
RIGHT 90 FORWARD 20
_?__ 90 FORWARD 20
RIGHT 90 FORWARD 20

7. Write commands to make the turtle draw this rectangle.

20 units
40 units

★ **8.** Write commands to make the turtle draw this shape.

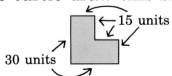
← 15 units
30 units

CUMULATIVE REVIEW

Give the letter for the correct answer.

1. $\begin{array}{r} 14 \\ \times\ 3 \\ \hline \end{array}$
    A 32
    B 42
    C 17
    D not given

2. $\begin{array}{r} 65 \\ \times\ 5 \\ \hline \end{array}$
    A 325
    B 305
    C 70
    D not given

3. $\begin{array}{r} 236 \\ \times\ 4 \\ \hline \end{array}$
    A 824
    B 944
    C 844
    D not given

4. $\begin{array}{r} 115 \\ \times\ 4 \\ \hline \end{array}$
    A 449
    B 440
    C 460
    D not given

5. $\begin{array}{r} 735 \\ \times\ 6 \\ \hline \end{array}$
    A 4,410
    B 441
    C 4,280
    D not given

6. $\begin{array}{r} \$0.23 \\ \times\ 6 \\ \hline \end{array}$
    A $10.38
    B $1.28
    C $1.38
    D not given

7. $\begin{array}{r} \$10.05 \\ \times\ 4 \\ \hline \end{array}$
    A $40.20
    B $4.20
    C $14.20
    D not given

What fraction is shaded?

8. A $\frac{1}{3}$ B $\frac{2}{3}$
    C $\frac{3}{4}$ D not given

9. A $\frac{2}{3}$ B $\frac{3}{6}$
    C $\frac{2}{6}$ D not given

Which statement is correct?

10. A $\frac{1}{2} = \frac{2}{8}$ B $\frac{1}{2} = \frac{2}{6}$
    C $\frac{1}{2} = \frac{2}{4}$ D not given

11. A $\frac{1}{3} < \frac{1}{2}$ B $\frac{1}{3} > \frac{1}{2}$
    C $\frac{1}{2} < \frac{1}{3}$ D not given

12. Reduce $\frac{12}{20}$ to the lowest terms.

    A $\frac{3}{5}$ B $1\frac{2}{5}$
    C $\frac{6}{10}$ D not given

13. Hans gave 2 apples to each of his 12 friends. How many apples did Hans give away?
    A 10   B 24
    C 6   D not given

14. One tomato costs $0.35. How much do 3 tomatoes cost?
    A $10.05   B $0.95
    C $1.05   D not given

Patrick sometimes meets his mother at the college. She is a student studying computer programming. First she learned to write directions. The directions are called a program. She writes the program in a certain language. Writing it is fun. It is like answering a puzzle. Next she tests her program. She tries it on the computer. She catches mistakes. This is "debugging." It means taking the "bugs" out. Her last lesson took 12 hours to write. Debugging it took 3 times as long. Patrick is interested in his mother's courses. She tells him about what she is learning. Patrick wants to do that kind of work someday, too.

Special Products: Mental Math

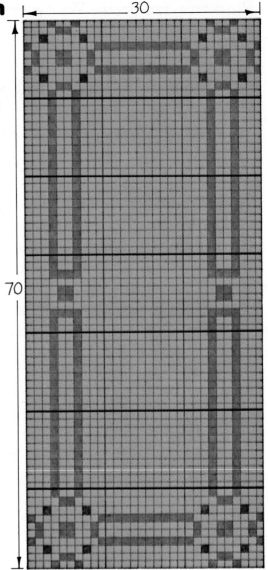

Janice and Roy covered the top of a table with tile. There are 70 rows with 30 pieces of tile in each row. How many pieces of tile did they use?

Since we want the total for equal rows, we multiply.

> THINK
> 7 tens × 3 tens = 21 hundreds

$$70 \times 30 = 2,100$$

> 21 hundreds =
> 2 thousand, 1 hundred

Janice and Roy used 2,100 pieces of tile.

Other Examples

$10 \times 60 = 600$ $20 \times 40 = 800$ $50 \times 40 = 2,000$

Warm Up   Find the products mentally.

1. 10×10	2. 10×40	3. 10×80	4. 10×30
5. 60×10	6. 40×10	7. 70×10	8. 90×10
9. 70×20	10. 50×50	11. 90×80	12. 80×50
13. 20×10	14. 80×10	15. 40×20	16. 40×30
17. 50×30	18. 30×60	19. 20×90	20. 80×70

294

Find the products. Write answers only.

1. 10×10 **2.** 10×30

3. 40×10 **4.** 10×60

5. 40×20 **6.** 20×20

7. 90×50 **8.** 50×60 **9.** 60×40 **10.** 80×30

11. 20×60 **12.** 90×20 **13.** 70×30 **14.** 80×40

15. 90×10 **16.** 20×70 **17.** 40×80 **18.** 60×80

★ **19.** $3 \times 10 \times 40$ ★ **20.** $10 \times 2 \times 20$ ★ **21.** $8 \times 10 \times 10$

★ **22.** $5 \times 10 \times 50$ ★ **23.** $10 \times 4 \times 20$ ★ **24.** $4 \times 10 \times 80$

Solve.

25. There are 40 rows with 60 pieces of tile in each row. How many pieces of tile are there?

26. A floor is a rectangle that is 30 meters wide and 50 meters long. What is the area of the floor in square meters?

THINK

▦ **Using a Calculator**

Guess the number of zeros in each product. Then multiply on the calculator to check your guess.

200×500	$800 \times 4,000$
$40 \times 5,000$	$4,000 \times 50$
$7,000 \times 40$	$90,000 \times 20$
500×800	$500 \times 6,000$

MATH

Multiplying by Multiples of Ten

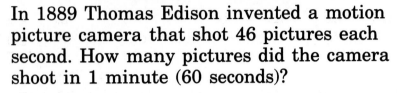

In 1889 Thomas Edison invented a motion picture camera that shot 46 pictures each second. How many pictures did the camera shoot in 1 minute (60 seconds)?

Since there are the same number of pictures each second, we multiply.

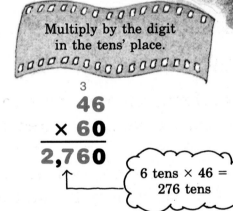

Multiply by the digit in the ones' place.

$$\begin{array}{r} 46 \\ \times\ 60 \\ \hline 0 \end{array}$$

$0 \times 46 = 0$

Multiply by the digit in the tens' place.

$$\begin{array}{r} 3 \\ 46 \\ \times\ 60 \\ \hline 2,760 \end{array}$$

6 tens × 46 = 276 tens

Edison's motion picture camera shot 2,760 pictures in 1 minute.

Other Examples

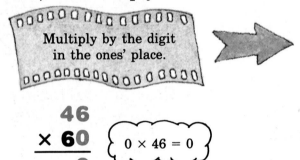

$$\begin{array}{r} 64 \\ \times\ 10 \\ \hline 640 \end{array}$$

1 ten × 4 = 4 tens

$$\begin{array}{r} 3 \\ 46 \\ \times\ 50 \\ \hline 2,300 \end{array}$$

5 tens × 6 = 30 tens

$$\begin{array}{r} 4 \\ 75 \\ \times\ 80 \\ \hline 6,000 \end{array}$$

$$\begin{array}{r} 40 \\ \times\ 30 \\ \hline 1,200 \end{array}$$

Warm Up Multiply.

1. $\begin{array}{r} 12 \\ \times\ 30 \\ \hline \end{array}$
2. $\begin{array}{r} 31 \\ \times\ 40 \\ \hline \end{array}$
3. $\begin{array}{r} 98 \\ \times\ 10 \\ \hline \end{array}$
4. $\begin{array}{r} 45 \\ \times\ 20 \\ \hline \end{array}$
5. $\begin{array}{r} 63 \\ \times\ 50 \\ \hline \end{array}$
6. $\begin{array}{r} 24 \\ \times\ 90 \\ \hline \end{array}$

7. $\begin{array}{r} 13 \\ \times\ 70 \\ \hline \end{array}$
8. $\begin{array}{r} 32 \\ \times\ 80 \\ \hline \end{array}$
9. $\begin{array}{r} 28 \\ \times\ 50 \\ \hline \end{array}$
10. $\begin{array}{r} 76 \\ \times\ 30 \\ \hline \end{array}$
11. $\begin{array}{r} 25 \\ \times\ 40 \\ \hline \end{array}$
12. $\begin{array}{r} 82 \\ \times\ 60 \\ \hline \end{array}$

Find the products.

1. 37 × 10	**2.** 23 × 30	**3.** 81 × 20	**4.** 63 × 40	**5.** 70 × 60	**6.** 36 × 40
7. 12 × 90	**8.** 42 × 70	**9.** 89 × 30	**10.** 25 × 80	**11.** 44 × 40	**12.** 13 × 50
13. 54 × 50	**14.** 70 × 20	**15.** 29 × 70	**16.** 86 × 10	**17.** 38 × 90	**18.** 41 × 60

19. 60×35 **20.** 20×32 **21.** 70×74

22. Multiply 79 by 50.

23. Multiply 51 by 90.

Solve.

24. Movie companies use cameras that shoot 24 pictures each second. How many pictures could be shot in 1 minute? (60 seconds = 1 minute)

25. Write a question for this story. Then answer the question.

A slow-motion camera shoots 54 pictures each second. The camera ran for 20 seconds.

26. DATA HUNT Find the number of pictures a home movie camera shoots in 1 second. How many pictures would it shoot in 1 minute?

More Practice, page 410, Set C

THINK

Estimation

Estimate to find which of these answers is about 500.

A $1{,}783 - 1{,}291 = \square$

B $82 \times 4 = \square$

C $156 \div 3 = \square$

D $235 + 275 = \square$

E $10 \times 48 = \square$

F $6{,}268 - 5{,}117 = \square$

→ **MATH** ←

Multiplication and Addition

Gretchen works at a greenhouse. She planted 2 rows of pink flowers and 10 rows of blue flowers. There are 24 flowers in each row. Here is how Gretchen figures out how many flowers she planted.

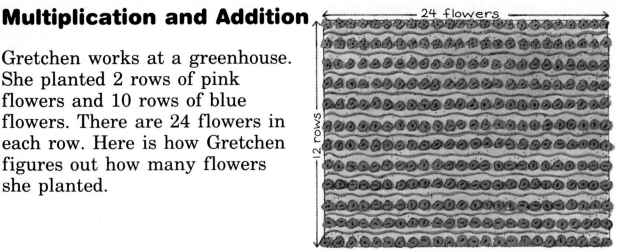

24 flowers

12 rows

Multiply to find the number of pink flowers.

$$\begin{array}{r} 24 \\ \times\ 2 \\ \hline 48 \end{array}$$ pink flowers

Multiply to find the number of blue flowers.

$$\begin{array}{r} 24 \\ \times\ 10 \\ \hline 240 \end{array}$$ blue flowers

Add to find the total number of flowers.

$$\begin{array}{r} 48 \\ +\ 240 \\ \hline 288 \end{array}$$ pink flowers blue flowers flowers

Gretchen planted 288 flowers.

How many flowers did each person plant?

1. Jon's flowers
   25 flowers in each row
   5 rows of red
   10 rows of blue

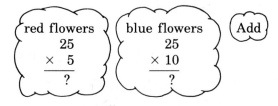

red flowers
$$\begin{array}{r} 25 \\ \times\ 5 \\ \hline ? \end{array}$$

blue flowers
$$\begin{array}{r} 25 \\ \times\ 10 \\ \hline ? \end{array}$$

Add

2. Bonnie's flowers
   18 flowers in each row
   4 rows of yellow
   10 rows of orange

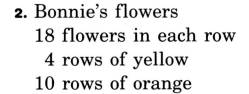

yellow flowers
$$\begin{array}{r} 18 \\ \times\ 4 \\ \hline ? \end{array}$$

orange flowers
$$\begin{array}{r} 18 \\ \times\ 10 \\ \hline ? \end{array}$$

Add

3. Hal's flowers
   36 flowers in each row
   3 rows of red
   10 rows of blue

★ **5.** Sylvi's flowers
   18 flowers in each row
   12 rows

4. Dana's flowers
   32 flowers in each row
   8 rows of yellow
   20 rows of orange

★ **6.** Corey's flowers
   24 flowers in each row
   16 rows

PROBLEM SOLVING
Practice

Solve.

1. Manuel planted 30 rows of flowers. There are 10 flowers in each row. How many flowers did Manuel plant?

2. Jody planted 134 pansies and 67 daisies. How many flowers did she plant?

3. Jessica sold 40 bags of tulip bulbs. There were 25 bulbs in each bag. How many bulbs did she sell?

4. Norman planted 345 flowers. 180 of them were red. The rest were yellow. How many yellow flowers did he plant?

5. Beth put 315 small plants in boxes to sell. Each box holds 9 plants. How many boxes did she use?

6. Darcy has 185 bulbs to plant. If she plants 99 bulbs today, how many more will she have to plant?

7. Rex bought 75 plants. Martha bought 25 more plants than Rex. How many plants did Martha buy?

8. Takeo planted 5 rows of daisies. He also planted 10 rows of pansies. There are 12 flowers in each row. How many flowers did he plant?

9. **Try This** Aaron planted 2 bulbs the first day, 4 bulbs the second day, 6 bulbs the third day, and so on. One day he planted 22 bulbs. How many did he plant the next day?

Multiplying with 2-Digit Factors

A small tugboat is 23 m long. An aircraft carrier is 13 times as long as the tugboat. How long is an aircraft carrier?

Since we want the total for equal lengths, we multiply.

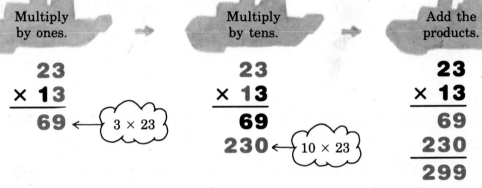

Multiply by ones.	Multiply by tens.	Add the products.
23	23	23
× 13	× 13	× 13
69 ← 3 × 23	69	69
	230 ← 10 × 23	230
		299

The aircraft carrier is 299 m long.

Other Examples

14	32	20
× 12	× 23	× 42
28 ← 2 × 14	96 ← 3 × 32	40 ← 2 × 20
140 ← 10 × 14	640 ← 20 × 32	800 ← 40 × 20
168	736	840

Warm Up   Multiply.

1. 22
   × 13

2. 12
   × 24

3. 22
   × 31

4. 11
   × 43

5. 70
   × 11

6. 14
   × 31

7. 33
   × 12

8. 34
   × 22

9. 22
   × 14

10. 20
   × 33

11. 24
   × 12

12. 30
   × 22

Find the products.

1. 32
   × 12

2. 21
   × 23

3. 12
   × 14

4. 40
   × 22

5. 24
   × 20

6. 30
   × 18

7. 12
   × 34

8. 78
   × 11

9. 43
   × 21

10. 33
    × 13

11. 11
    × 59

12. 12
    × 21

13. 10
    × 43

14. 32
    × 30

15. 22
    × 42

16. 30
    × 22

17. 31
    × 13

18. 14
    × 41

19. 24 × 21

20. 33 × 15

21. 44 × 19

22. 67 × 11

23. 40 × 21

24. 12 × 43

25. Multiply 14 times 21.

26. Multiply 34 times 22.

27. Multiply 41 times 12.

28. Multiply 32 times 23.

Solve.

29. A small tugboat is 23 m long. A passenger liner is 12 times longer. What is the length of the passenger liner?

30. Write a story to match the following equation.

$$11 \times 23 = 253$$

More Multiplying with 2-Digit Factors

A basketball court is 26 m long and 14 m wide. What is the area of a basketball court in square meters?

Since we want the area of a rectangle, we multiply the length by the width.

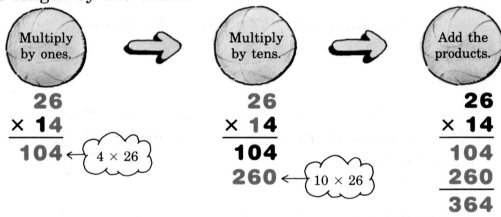

Multiply by ones.

$$\begin{array}{r} 26 \\ \times\ 14 \\ \hline 104 \end{array}$$ ← 4×26

Multiply by tens.

$$\begin{array}{r} 26 \\ \times\ 14 \\ \hline 104 \\ 260 \end{array}$$ ← 10×26

Add the products.

$$\begin{array}{r} 26 \\ \times\ 14 \\ \hline 104 \\ 260 \\ \hline 364 \end{array}$$

The area of the basketball court is 364 square meters.

Other Examples

$$\begin{array}{r} 34 \\ \times\ 24 \\ \hline 136 \\ 680 \\ \hline 816 \end{array}$$
136 ← 4×34
680 ← 20×34

$$\begin{array}{r} 42 \\ \times\ 32 \\ \hline 84 \\ 1260 \\ \hline 1{,}344 \end{array}$$
84 ← 2×42
1260 ← 30×42

$$\begin{array}{r} 54 \\ \times\ 65 \\ \hline 270 \\ 3240 \\ \hline 3{,}510 \end{array}$$
270 ← 5×54
3240 ← 60×54

$$\begin{array}{r} 25 \\ \times\ 48 \\ \hline 200 \\ 1000 \\ \hline 1{,}200 \end{array}$$
200 ← 8×25
1000 ← 40×25

Warm Up Multiply.

1. $\begin{array}{r} 53 \\ \times\ 15 \\ \hline \end{array}$
2. $\begin{array}{r} 52 \\ \times\ 26 \\ \hline \end{array}$
3. $\begin{array}{r} 33 \\ \times\ 34 \\ \hline \end{array}$
4. $\begin{array}{r} 53 \\ \times\ 41 \\ \hline \end{array}$
5. $\begin{array}{r} 42 \\ \times\ 62 \\ \hline \end{array}$
6. $\begin{array}{r} 25 \\ \times\ 84 \\ \hline \end{array}$

Find the products.

1. 16×53	**2.** 64×36	**3.** 34×14	**4.** 10×39	**5.** 25×52	**6.** 37×43
7. 76×19	**8.** 52×70	**9.** 94×45	**10.** 86×86	**11.** 30×40	**12.** 46×51
13. 60×68	**14.** 44×77	**15.** 92×93	**16.** 87×50	**17.** 73×27	**18.** 63×15

19. 23×66 **20.** 64×35 **21.** 95×28

22. 72×23 **23.** 88×77 **24.** 46×46

25. Find the product of 18 and 42.   **26.** Find the product of 37 and 55.

27. Find the product of 42 and 75.   **28.** Find the product of 63 and 53.

Solve.

29. The ice rink is a rectangle 64 m long and 33 m wide. What is the area of the ice rink?

30. What would the area of the ice rink in problem 29 be if it were only 58 m long?

31. The infield for softball is a square that is 18 m on each side. What is the area of the infield?

THINK

🖩 **Using a Calculator**

What number times itself gives 1,024?

|||||| $\times$ |||||| $= 1,024$

same   number

Use guess and check to find the number.

MATH

More Practice, page 411, Set B

Estimating Products: Mental Math

A hummingbird's heart beats 29 times faster than a camel's. About how many times does a hummingbird's heart beat in 1 minute?

HEARTBEATS IN 1 MINUTE			
CAMEL	31	HORSE	44
CHEETAH	75	PIG	72
GIRAFFE	66		

Since you want an answer that is only **close** to the exact answer, you **estimate** by rounding and multiplying in your head.

Think of the problem. → 29×31

Round and multiply. → **30 × 30 = 900**

A hummingbird's heart beats **about** 900 times in 1 minute.

Other Examples

13 × 37

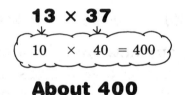

$10 \times 40 = 400$

About 400

33 × $6.75

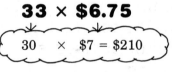

$30 \times \$7 = \$210$

About $210

Estimate the products. Round 2-digit numbers to the nearest ten and money to the nearest dollar.

1. 12×29
2. 38×21
3. 61×49
4. 52×19
5. 18×19
6. 11×47
7. 32×61
8. 48×78
9. $12 \times \$1.15$
10. $24 \times \$1.65$
11. $68 \times \$4.10$
12. $19 \times \$4.95$
13. 11×72
14. 19×39
15. 28×21
16. 48×12

17. **DATA BANK** See page 386. A canary's heart beats about 22 times faster than an elephant's. About how many times does a canary's heart beat in 1 minute?

PROBLEM SOLVING
Using Data from an Advertisement

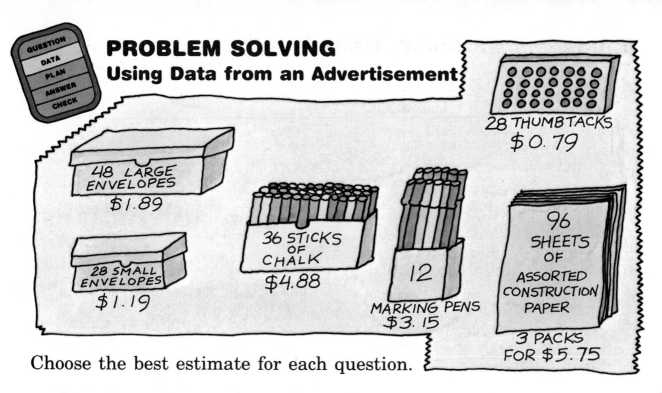

28 THUMBTACKS $0.79

48 LARGE ENVELOPES $1.89

28 SMALL ENVELOPES $1.19

36 STICKS OF CHALK $4.88

12 MARKING PENS $3.15

96 SHEETS OF ASSORTED CONSTRUCTION PAPER 3 PACKS FOR $5.75

Choose the best estimate for each question.

1. About how many large envelopes are in 3 boxes?

   A 90   **B** 150   **C** 60

2. About how many dollars would it cost to buy 18 boxes of small envelopes?

   A $20   **B** $40   **C** $30

3. About how many more dollars does a box of chalk cost than a pack of marking pens?

   A $1   **B** $8   **C** $2

4. About how many dollars does 1 pack of paper cost?

   A $6   **B** $2   **C** $18

5. About how many sheets of paper are in 50 packs?

   A 50   **B** 500   **C** 5,000

6. About how many dollars does it cost to buy 1 pack of thumbtacks and 1 pack of marking pens?

   A $4   **B** $5   **C** $40

7. About how many dollars does it cost to buy 5 boxes of chalk and 3 packs of paper?

   A $25   **B** $31   **C** $43

8. *Try This* Each time 5 boxes of clips are sold, 3 cards of tacks are sold. How many cards of tacks are sold when 40 boxes of clips are sold? Complete the table.

Clips	5	10	15	20	25
Tacks	3	6	9	12	15

305

Multiplying with 2- and 3-Digit Factors

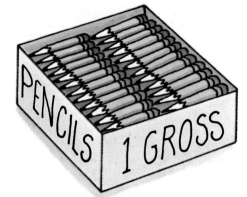

Ms. Tom ordered pencils for a school. She ordered 24 gross. There are 144 pencils in a gross. How many pencils did she order?

Since there are the same number in each gross, we multiply.

1 gross is 12 dozen.
12 × 12 = 144

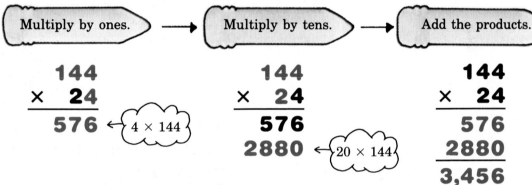

Multiply by ones.	Multiply by tens.	Add the products.

$$\begin{array}{r} 144 \\ \times\ 24 \\ \hline 576 \end{array}$$ ← 4 × 144

$$\begin{array}{r} 144 \\ \times\ 24 \\ \hline 576 \\ 2880 \end{array}$$ ← 20 × 144

$$\begin{array}{r} 144 \\ \times\ 24 \\ \hline 576 \\ 2880 \\ \hline 3,456 \end{array}$$

Ms. Tom ordered 3,456 pencils.

Other Examples

$$\begin{array}{r} 286 \\ \times\ 23 \\ \hline 858 \\ 5720 \\ \hline 6,578 \end{array}$$
$$\begin{array}{r} 305 \\ \times\ 82 \\ \hline 610 \\ 24400 \\ \hline 25,010 \end{array}$$
$$\begin{array}{r} 840 \\ \times\ 37 \\ \hline 5880 \\ 25200 \\ \hline 31,080 \end{array}$$
$$\begin{array}{r} 400 \\ \times\ 55 \\ \hline 2000 \\ 20000 \\ \hline 22,000 \end{array}$$

Warm Up   Multiply.

1. $\begin{array}{r} 416 \\ \times\ 24 \\ \hline \end{array}$
2. $\begin{array}{r} 584 \\ \times\ 15 \\ \hline \end{array}$
3. $\begin{array}{r} 597 \\ \times\ 13 \\ \hline \end{array}$
4. $\begin{array}{r} 398 \\ \times\ 21 \\ \hline \end{array}$
5. $\begin{array}{r} 437 \\ \times\ 34 \\ \hline \end{array}$

6. $\begin{array}{r} 638 \\ \times\ 52 \\ \hline \end{array}$
7. $\begin{array}{r} 309 \\ \times\ 27 \\ \hline \end{array}$
8. $\begin{array}{r} 430 \\ \times\ 18 \\ \hline \end{array}$
9. $\begin{array}{r} 600 \\ \times\ 38 \\ \hline \end{array}$
10. $\begin{array}{r} 125 \\ \times\ 44 \\ \hline \end{array}$

Find the products.

1.	276 × 31	2.	198 × 47	3.	168 × 53	4.	296 × 10	5.	63 × 59
6.	39 × 44	7.	400 × 63	8.	504 × 17	9.	835 × 28	10.	136 × 32
11.	800 × 75	12.	770 × 36	13.	78 × 83	14.	456 × 21	15.	605 × 53

16. 22×408

17. 50×935

18. 66×555

19. 38×760

20. 93×900

21. 42×806

22. Multiply 303 by 27.

23. Multiply 132 by 56.

24. Multiply 490 by 48.

25. Multiply 600 by 87.

Solve.

26. Ms. Tom ordered 15 boxes of erasers. Each box holds 1 gross. How many erasers did she order?

27. A ream has 500 sheets of paper. How many sheets are in 32 reams?

THINK

Patterns

Andy found this shortcut for multiplying factors with a difference of 2.
Example: 29×31

Think of the number between the 2 factors.
29, 30, 31

Multiply that number by itself.
$30 \times 30 = 900$

Subtract 1.
$900 - 1 = 899$

29×31 should be 899.
Check by multiplying.

Try Andy's method to find these products.

$8 \times 10 = \square$ $19 \times 21 = \square$ $49 \times 51 = \square$

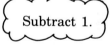 MATH

More Practice, page 411, Set C

Multiplying Money

FOURTH GRADE CAR WASH
FRIDAY AND SATURDAY
$3.75
each car

A fourth grade class held a car wash to make money for a class field trip. They washed 21 cars on Friday. How much money did they collect on Friday?

Since we want the total for equal amounts, we multiply.

Multiply as with whole numbers.

$$
\begin{array}{r}
\$3.75 \\
\times \quad 21 \\
\hline
375 \\
7500 \\
\hline
7875
\end{array}
$$

Show the product using dollars and cents.

$$
\begin{array}{r}
\$3.75 \\
\times \quad 21 \\
\hline
375 \\
7500 \\
\hline
\$78.75
\end{array}
$$

Use estimation to check
$20 \times \$4 = \$80$

$78.75 is close to $80. It checks.

The class collected $78.75 on Friday.

Other Examples

$$
\begin{array}{r}
\$7.65 \\
\times \quad 11 \\
\hline
765 \\
7650 \\
\hline
\$84.15
\end{array}
$$

$10 \times \$8$ is about $80

$$
\begin{array}{r}
\$4.25 \\
\times \quad 28 \\
\hline
3400 \\
8500 \\
\hline
\$119.00
\end{array}
$$

$30 \times \$4$ is about $120

$$
\begin{array}{r}
\$0.95 \\
\times \quad 41 \\
\hline
95 \\
3800 \\
\hline
\$38.95
\end{array}
$$

$40 \times \$1$ is about $40

Warm Up Find the amounts. Write the answers with dollars and cents. Use estimation to check.

1. $4.85
   × 21

2. $2.05
   × 29

3. $0.86
   × 12

4. $7.80
   × 52

5. $6.32
   × 14

Find the amounts.
Write the answers with dollars and cents.

1. $3.24 × 18	**2.** $9.38 × 38	**3.** $3.75 × 22	**4.** $0.75 × 44	**5.** $1.24 × 32
6. $2.78 × 12	**7.** $6.05 × 49	**8.** $1.99 × 20	**9.** $7.10 × 29	**10.** $6.09 × 11
11. $0.85 × 23	**12.** $4.95 × 51	**13.** $0.98 × 79	**14.** $8.07 × 58	**15.** $7.81 × 33

16. 11 × $3.80　　　**17.** 17 × $2.35　　　**18.** 20 × $0.85

Solve.

19. The class washed 52 cars on Saturday. How much money did they collect on Saturday?

20. Write a story to match this equation.

$$39 \times \$2.25 = \$87.75$$

SKILLKEEPER

Multiply.

1. 22 × 4	**2.** 19 × 5	**3.** 20 × 4	**4.** 33 × 3	**5.** 62 × 3
6. 75 × 7	**7.** 17 × 5	**8.** 706 × 3	**9.** 465 × 2	**10.** 234 × 6

More Practice, page 412, Set A

PROBLEM SOLVING
Using Data from a Floor Plan

Mr. Jackson is a building contractor. He builds schools. This is the floor plan for a new building at Hagginwood School.

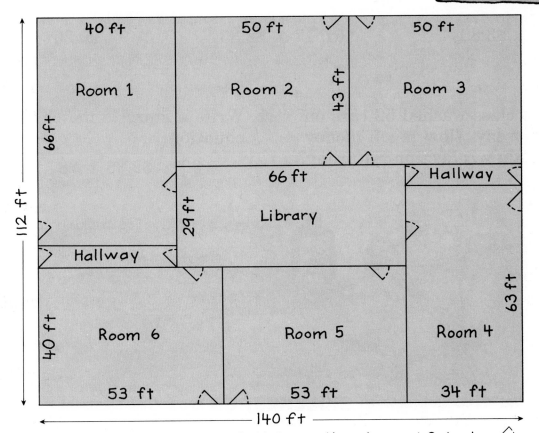

Floor plan for new building at Hagginwood School

Mr. Jackson used data from the floor plan to find the area of Room 4. Room 4 is 63 ft long and 34 ft wide. Since he wanted the area of a rectangle, Mr. Jackson used the formula of length times width. The area of Room 4 is 2,142 square feet.

310

Use data from the floor plan to answer these questions.

1. How many classrooms will the new building have?

2. What is the total number of rooms in the floor plan?

3. How long is the wall between Room 2 and Room 3?

4. How long is the wall between Room 6 and Room 5?

5. What is the area of Room 1 in square feet?

6. What is the area of the library in square feet?

7. There is 2,160 square feet of carpet for Room 3. Is there enough carpet to cover the floor?

8. There is 2,106 square feet of red carpet. Is there enough carpet to cover the floor in Room 6?

9. How many square feet of carpet will it take to cover the floor in Room 5?

10. What is the difference between the library's length and width?

11. What is the perimeter of the building?

12. *Try This* Mr. Jackson placed 32 chairs in the library and divided the rest equally among the 6 classrooms. Each classroom got 25 chairs. How many chairs did Mr. Jackson start with?

APPLIED PROBLEM SOLVING

A friend calls one evening and invites you to a picnic early the next morning. You are to be at her house at 8:00 a.m. with your lunch. What time will you need to wake up?

Some Things to Consider

- Your mother and father will not be able to help you get ready.
- You need to pack your lunch.
- You need to fix your breakfast.
- You need to get yourself ready—wash, brush your teeth, dress, and so on.

- You need 15 minutes to walk to your friend's house.
- You want to allow plenty of time so you are not late.

Some Questions to Answer

1. How long will it take to fix your lunch?
2. How long does it take you to fix and eat your breakfast?
3. How much time do you take to get yourself ready?
4. How much extra time do you plan to allow?
5. How much time do you need to get yourself awake?

What is Your Decision?

What time do you want to wake up?

Multiply.

1. 20 × 40   **2.** 60 × 10   **3.** 90 × 80   **4.** 50 × 70

5.　27
　　× 30

6.　57
　　× 40

7.　39
　　× 70

8.　82
　　× 10

9.　74
　　× 50

10.　21
　　× 32

11.　47
　　× 11

12.　30
　　× 23

13.　78
　　× 34

14.　63
　　× 28

Estimate the products. Round to the nearest ten, hundred, or dollar.

15. 78 × 51   **16.** 22 × 780   **17.** 13 × $4.75

Multiply.

18.　387
　　× 26

19.　152
　　× 65

20.　$9.63
　　× 39

21.　$2.38
　　× 44

22.　$6.38
　　× 25

Solve.

23. How much do 24 boxes of pencils cost?

24. What is the total area of this house in square feet?

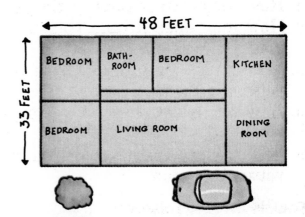

313

ANOTHER LOOK

Multiplying by Tens

$$\begin{array}{r} 31 \\ \times\ 20 \\ \hline 620 \end{array}$$

0 × 31 = 0

2 tens × 1 = 2 tens

2 tens × 3 tens = 6 hundreds

Multiply by Ones and Then Tens

$$\begin{array}{r} 31 \\ \times\ 23 \\ \hline 93 \\ 620 \\ \hline 713 \end{array}$$

3 × 31

20 × 31

Add

Trading with Each Step

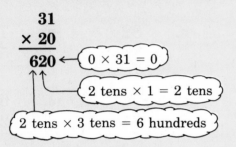

$$\begin{array}{r} \overset{3\,2}{\underset{}{4\,3}} \\ 365 \\ \times\ 57 \\ \hline 2555 \\ 18250 \\ \hline 20{,}805 \end{array}$$

Remember to cross out the traded tens and hundreds.

1. $\begin{array}{r} 52 \\ \times\ 10 \\ \hline \end{array}$ **2.** $\begin{array}{r} 28 \\ \times\ 30 \\ \hline \end{array}$ **3.** $\begin{array}{r} 16 \\ \times\ 20 \\ \hline \end{array}$

4. $\begin{array}{r} 65 \\ \times\ 50 \\ \hline \end{array}$ **5.** $\begin{array}{r} 81 \\ \times\ 40 \\ \hline \end{array}$ **6.** $\begin{array}{r} 33 \\ \times\ 90 \\ \hline \end{array}$

7. $\begin{array}{r} 34 \\ \times\ 70 \\ \hline \end{array}$ **8.** $\begin{array}{r} 27 \\ \times\ 60 \\ \hline \end{array}$ **9.** $\begin{array}{r} 14 \\ \times\ 80 \\ \hline \end{array}$

10. $\begin{array}{r} 14 \\ \times\ 21 \\ \hline \end{array}$ **11.** $\begin{array}{r} 56 \\ \times\ 11 \\ \hline \end{array}$ **12.** $\begin{array}{r} 32 \\ \times\ 13 \\ \hline \end{array}$

13. $\begin{array}{r} 24 \\ \times\ 22 \\ \hline \end{array}$ **14.** $\begin{array}{r} 13 \\ \times\ 31 \\ \hline \end{array}$ **15.** $\begin{array}{r} 20 \\ \times\ 32 \\ \hline \end{array}$

16. $\begin{array}{r} 22 \\ \times\ 23 \\ \hline \end{array}$ **17.** $\begin{array}{r} 21 \\ \times\ 43 \\ \hline \end{array}$ **18.** $\begin{array}{r} 12 \\ \times\ 33 \\ \hline \end{array}$

19. $\begin{array}{r} 424 \\ \times\ 46 \\ \hline \end{array}$ **20.** $\begin{array}{r} 657 \\ \times\ 35 \\ \hline \end{array}$

21. $\begin{array}{r} 338 \\ \times\ 26 \\ \hline \end{array}$ **22.** $\begin{array}{r} 245 \\ \times\ 19 \\ \hline \end{array}$

23. $\begin{array}{r} 617 \\ \times\ 43 \\ \hline \end{array}$ **24.** $\begin{array}{r} 363 \\ \times\ 58 \\ \hline \end{array}$

Networks

Streets in a neighborhood can be thought of as a **network** of streets. A newspaper carrier tried to plan her delivery routes in each neighborhood so that she traveled on every street in the network only one time.

Look at the route for Neighborhood A. Follow the numbers next to the arrows to see how this route is traveled.

Copy the street networks below. Draw arrows and numbers on each network to show a route that can be traveled by the newspaper carrier. One of the networks cannot be traveled unless a street is traveled 2 times. Which network is that?

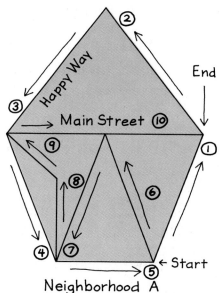

Neighborhood A

1.

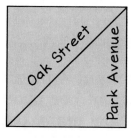

Neighborhood B

2.

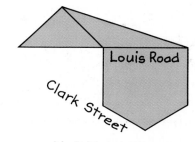

Neighborhood C

3.

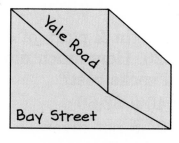

Neighborhood D

4.

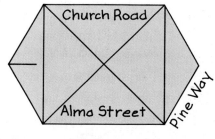

Neighborhood E

CUMULATIVE REVIEW

Give the letter for the correct answer.

1. $7\overline{)88}$
   - **A** 12 R7
   - **B** 12 R4
   - **C** 12 R8
   - **D** not given

2. $3\overline{)58}$
   - **A** 19 R2
   - **B** 12 R2
   - **C** 19 R1
   - **D** not given

3. $5\overline{)66}$
   - **A** 11 R1
   - **B** 13 R1
   - **C** 11 R3
   - **D** not given

4. $3\overline{)\$0.75}$
   - **A** $0.25
   - **B** $2.50
   - **C** $0.52
   - **D** not given

5. $4\overline{)509}$
   - **A** 126 R5
   - **B** 102 R1
   - **C** 127 R1
   - **D** not given

6. $3\overline{)280}$
   - **A** 93 R1
   - **B** 73 R1
   - **C** 9 R3
   - **D** not given

7. $2\overline{)\$7.50}$
   - **A** $3.75
   - **B** $3.25
   - **C** $3.15
   - **D** not given

Name each figure.

8.
   - **A** cylinder
   - **B** sphere
   - **C** circle
   - **D** not given

9.
   - **A** square
   - **B** cube
   - **C** rectangular prism
   - **D** not given

10.
   - **A** rectangle
   - **B** triangle
   - **C** quadrilateral
   - **D** not given

11.
   - **A** hexagon
   - **B** octagon
   - **C** pentagon
   - **D** not given

12.
   $C \quad D$
   - **A** CD
   - **B** $\overline{CD}$
   - **C** $\overleftrightarrow{CD}$
   - **D** not given

13. Holly can put 4 pictures on each page of her photo album. How many pages will she need for 53 pictures?
   - **A** 13
   - **B** 12
   - **C** 14
   - **D** not given

14. Jake bought 2 pairs of socks for $5.20. How much did each pair of socks cost?
   - **A** $10.40
   - **B** $2.60
   - **C** $2.10
   - **D** not given

Natalie stood next to her Uncle Charles. They were with a group of news reporters. The speech by Governor Smith was just over. They headed back to the news room. Charles entered his story into the computer. Natalie watched the screen. Charles told Natalie about newspaper deadlines. They are very important. He had 125 minutes to finish this story. This was 5 times as long as for yesterday's story. Charles finished his story. He let Natalie push the "send" button. This sent the story to the city editor. Last minute changes were made there. Then the story was ready to be printed.

Using Division Facts

Carmen has 150 pennies. Each penny wrapper holds 50 pennies. How many wrappers can she fill?

Since we separate the coins equally into wrappers, we divide.

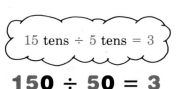

$$15 \text{ tens} \div 5 \text{ tens} = 3$$

150 ÷ 50 = 3   **OR**

$$5 \text{ tens)}\overline{15 \text{ tens}} = 3$$

$$50)\overline{150} = 3$$

Carmen can fill 3 penny wrappers.

Other Examples

$$2 \text{ tens)}\overline{8 \text{ tens}} = 4$$

$$\begin{array}{r} 4 \\ 20)\overline{80} \\ \underline{80} \\ 0 \end{array}$$

$$6 \text{ tens)}\overline{48 \text{ tens}} = 8$$

$$\begin{array}{r} 8 \\ 60)\overline{480} \\ \underline{480} \\ 0 \end{array}$$

$$8 \text{ tens)}\overline{40 \text{ tens}} = 5$$

$$\begin{array}{r} 5 \\ 80)\overline{400} \\ \underline{400} \\ 0 \end{array}$$

Warm Up Divide. Give the quotients aloud.

1. $20)\overline{60}$
2. $40)\overline{80}$
3. $30)\overline{60}$
4. $70)\overline{70}$
5. $10)\overline{60}$

6. $50)\overline{50}$
7. $20)\overline{80}$
8. $30)\overline{90}$
9. $20)\overline{40}$
10. $90)\overline{90}$

11. $20)\overline{140}$
12. $70)\overline{210}$
13. $50)\overline{200}$
14. $10)\overline{80}$
15. $60)\overline{120}$

16. $30)\overline{180}$
17. $40)\overline{320}$
18. $60)\overline{300}$
19. $80)\overline{240}$
20. $30)\overline{270}$

21. $10)\overline{60}$
22. $40)\overline{360}$
23. $30)\overline{150}$
24. $50)\overline{350}$
25. $90)\overline{360}$

Divide.

1. $10\overline{)70}$ **2.** $90\overline{)90}$ **3.** $30\overline{)90}$ **4.** $20\overline{)40}$ **5.** $40\overline{)80}$

6. $30\overline{)60}$ **7.** $10\overline{)40}$ **8.** $60\overline{)60}$ **9.** $20\overline{)60}$ **10.** $10\overline{)10}$

11. $30\overline{)120}$ **12.** $20\overline{)120}$ **13.** $20\overline{)160}$ **14.** $40\overline{)240}$ **15.** $60\overline{)360}$

16. $80\overline{)160}$ **17.** $20\overline{)100}$ **18.** $50\overline{)400}$ **19.** $70\overline{)210}$ **20.** $90\overline{)540}$

21. $20\overline{)180}$ **22.** $30\overline{)240}$ **23.** $80\overline{)640}$ **24.** $20\overline{)80}$ **25.** $50\overline{)100}$

26. $40\overline{)280}$ **27.** $10\overline{)30}$ **28.** $50\overline{)450}$ **29.** $60\overline{)240}$ **30.** $80\overline{)80}$

31. $70\overline{)490}$ **32.** $40\overline{)280}$ **33.** $30\overline{)90}$ **34.** $70\overline{)140}$ **35.** $90\overline{)360}$

36. $270 \div 90 = n$ **37.** $60 \div 30 = n$ **38.** $540 \div 60 = n$

39. $210 \div 30 = n$ **40.** $150 \div 50 = n$ **41.** $420 \div 70 = n$

42. How many 30s are in 270?

43. How many 80s are in 240?

44. How many 90s are in 630?

45. How many 50s are in 300?

Solve.

46. Joshua has 160 nickels. Each nickel wrapper holds 40 nickels. How many nickel wrappers can he fill?

47. **DATA HUNT** Find the number of dimes that a dime wrapper holds. How many wrappers could you fill if you had 150 dimes?

THINK

Using a Calculator

Guess the number of zeros in each quotient. Then divide with the calculator to check your guess.

A $270 \div 30$ **E** $8{,}000 \div 20$
B $600 \div 20$ **F** $900 \div 300$
C $2{,}400 \div 40$ **G** $18{,}000 \div 900$
D $3{,}000 \div 50$ **H** $40{,}000 \div 80$

MATH

Dividing by Multiples of Ten

Eric Heiden won 5 gold medals in speed skating at the 1980 Winter Olympics. Give Eric's time for the 5,000-meter race in minutes and seconds. (There are 60 seconds in 1 minute.)

Since there are the same number of seconds in each minute, we divide.

Eric Heiden's Race Time in Seconds*

500-meter race	38 seconds
1,000-meter race	75 seconds
1,500-meter race	116 seconds
5,000-meter race	422 seconds
10,000-meter race	868 seconds

*Race times to the nearest second

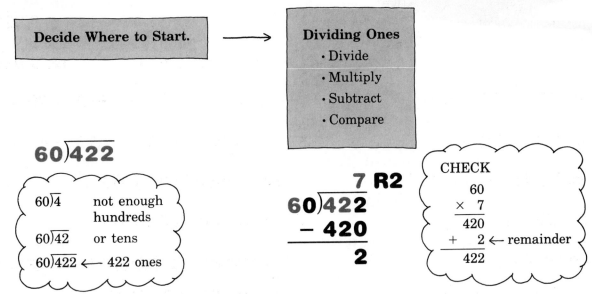

Decide Where to Start.	$\longrightarrow$	Dividing Ones • Divide • Multiply • Subtract • Compare

$$60\overline{)422}$$

$60\overline{)4}$ not enough hundreds

$60\overline{)42}$ or tens

$60\overline{)422}$ ← 422 ones

$$
\begin{array}{r}
7\ \mathbf{R2} \\
60\overline{)422} \\
-420 \\
\hline
2
\end{array}
$$

CHECK
$$
\begin{array}{r}
60 \\
\times\ 7 \\
\hline
420 \\
+\ \ 2 \leftarrow \text{remainder} \\
\hline
422
\end{array}
$$

Eric Heiden skated the 5,000-meter race in 7 minutes and 2 seconds.

Other Examples

$$
\begin{array}{r}
6\ \mathbf{R18} \\
40\overline{)258} \\
-240 \\
\hline
18
\end{array}
\qquad
\begin{array}{r}
2\ \mathbf{R12} \\
30\overline{)72} \\
-60 \\
\hline
12
\end{array}
\qquad
\begin{array}{r}
8\ \mathbf{R40} \\
70\overline{)600} \\
-560 \\
\hline
40
\end{array}
$$

Warm Up   Divide. Check your answers.

1. $10\overline{)65}$ 2. $20\overline{)89}$ 3. $40\overline{)96}$ 4. $70\overline{)290}$ 5. $50\overline{)275}$

6. $20\overline{)105}$ 7. $60\overline{)200}$ 8. $80\overline{)356}$ 9. $30\overline{)105}$ 10. $90\overline{)618}$

Divide and check.

1. $40\overline{)83}$ **2.** $20\overline{)54}$ **3.** $10\overline{)93}$

4. $30\overline{)159}$ **5.** $50\overline{)313}$ **6.** $60\overline{)195}$

7. $80\overline{)500}$ **8.** $20\overline{)67}$ **9.** $30\overline{)285}$

10. $50\overline{)491}$ **11.** $70\overline{)400}$ **12.** $90\overline{)193}$

13. $151 \div 20 = n$ **14.** $92 \div 60 = n$ **15.** $638 \div 70 = n$

16. $222 \div 30 = n$ **17.** $500 \div 90 = n$ **18.** $311 \div 40 = n$

19. Divide 73 by 40.   **20.** Divide 258 by 60.

21. Divide 612 by 90.   **22.** Divide 305 by 40.

Solve.

23. Give Eric's time for the 1,500-meter race in minutes and seconds.

24. Write and answer a question for this story.
   Michael Woods skated the 5,000-meter race in 431 seconds.

25. **DATA BANK** See page 386. Give Leah Mueller's time for the 1,000-meter race in minutes and seconds.

THINK

Guess and Check

Look at the cups below. You want each cup to have the same amount of water. Finish the directions so that this will happen.

cup 1   cup 2   cup 3

Pour ____ mL from cup 1 to cup 2 and ____ mL from cup 3 to cup 2.

→ MATH ←

1-Digit Quotients

Brad's soccer team has $66 to buy soccer balls. How many balls can they buy? How much money will they have left?

Since each of the balls costs the same amount, we divide.

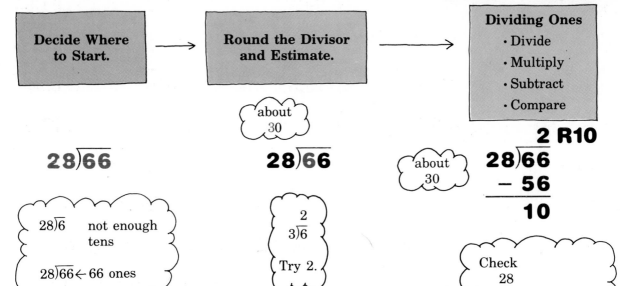

| Decide Where to Start. | $\rightarrow$ | Round the Divisor and Estimate. | $\rightarrow$ | Dividing Ones • Divide • Multiply • Subtract • Compare |

$$28\overline{)66}$$

$28\overline{)6}$ not enough tens

$28\overline{)66} \leftarrow$ 66 ones

about 30

$$28\overline{)66}$$

$\dfrac{2}{3\overline{)6}}$

Try 2.

about 30

$$\begin{array}{r} 2\ \text{R10} \\ 28\overline{)66} \\ -\ 56 \\ \hline 10 \end{array}$$

Check
$\begin{array}{r} 28 \\ \times\ 2 \\ \hline 56 \\ +\ 10 \leftarrow \text{remainder} \\ \hline 66 \end{array}$

Brad's team can buy 2 soccer balls. They will have $10 left.

Other Examples

40

$$\begin{array}{r} 1\ \text{R35} \\ 43\overline{)78} \\ -\ 43 \\ \hline 35 \end{array}$$

20

$$\begin{array}{r} 2\ \text{R11} \\ 15\overline{)41} \\ -\ 30 \\ \hline 11 \end{array}$$

$$\begin{array}{r} 0\ \text{R59} \\ 67\overline{)59} \\ -\ \ 0 \\ \hline 59 \end{array}$$

$$\begin{array}{r} 2 \\ 33\overline{)66} \\ -\ 66 \\ \hline 0 \end{array}$$

Warm Up   Divide and check.

1. $12\overline{)49}$ 2. $23\overline{)75}$ 3. $76\overline{)92}$ 4. $48\overline{)35}$ 5. $34\overline{)68}$

6. $41\overline{)85}$ 7. $58\overline{)73}$ 8. $44\overline{)38}$ 9. $23\overline{)69}$ 10. $19\overline{)67}$

Divide and check.

1. $32\overline{)53}$ 2. $18\overline{)42}$ 3. $29\overline{)92}$ 4. $43\overline{)92}$ 5. $54\overline{)83}$

6. $68\overline{)65}$ 7. $24\overline{)59}$ 8. $37\overline{)58}$ 9. $13\overline{)26}$ 10. $21\overline{)35}$

11. $29\overline{)75}$ 12. $35\overline{)80}$ 13. $19\overline{)83}$ 14. $53\overline{)55}$ 15. $68\overline{)75}$

16. $87\overline{)78}$ 17. $42\overline{)45}$ 18. $53\overline{)92}$ 19. $14\overline{)30}$ 20. $27\overline{)62}$

21. $82 \div 17 = n$ 22. $72 \div 39 = n$ 23. $32 \div 31 = n$

24. $75 \div 55 = n$ 25. $62 \div 53 = n$ 26. $44 \div 28 = n$

27. What is 89 divided by 11?   28. What is 92 divided by 23?

29. What is 83 divided by 34?   30. What is 65 divided by 38?

Solve.

31. Soccer bags are $17. The team has $80. How many bags can they buy? How much money will be left?

32. Make up and solve a division story problem for the data below. Have $75. Need soccer shoes at $15 each.

SKILLKEEPER

Multiply.

1. $\begin{array}{r} 22 \\ \times 13 \\ \hline \end{array}$
2. $\begin{array}{r} 11 \\ \times 43 \\ \hline \end{array}$
3. $\begin{array}{r} 24 \\ \times 12 \\ \hline \end{array}$
4. $\begin{array}{r} 12 \\ \times 30 \\ \hline \end{array}$
5. $\begin{array}{r} 70 \\ \times 11 \\ \hline \end{array}$

6. $\begin{array}{r} 31 \\ \times 13 \\ \hline \end{array}$
7. $\begin{array}{r} 42 \\ \times 32 \\ \hline \end{array}$
8. $\begin{array}{r} 17 \\ \times 42 \\ \hline \end{array}$
9. $\begin{array}{r} 286 \\ \times 23 \\ \hline \end{array}$
10. $\begin{array}{r} 305 \\ \times 82 \\ \hline \end{array}$

Changing Estimates

Sometimes you have to change your estimated quotient.

Erin made 50 dinner rolls. She puts 16 rolls into each bag. How many bags can she fill?

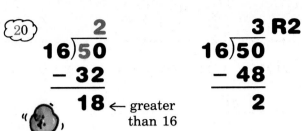

$$\begin{array}{r} (20) \quad 2 \\ 16\overline{)50} \\ -32 \\ \hline 18 \end{array} \leftarrow \text{greater than 16}$$

$$\begin{array}{r} 3\ \text{R2} \\ 16\overline{)50} \\ -48 \\ \hline 2 \end{array}$$

Erin had to change her estimate from 2 to 3.

Erin can fill 3 bags. There will be 2 remaining rolls.

How many dozen rolls did Erin make?

$$\begin{array}{r} (10) \quad 5 \\ 12\overline{)50} \\ -60 \\ \hline \end{array} \leftarrow \text{too large}$$

$$\begin{array}{r} 4\ \text{R2} \\ 12\overline{)50} \\ -48 \\ \hline 2 \end{array}$$

Erin had to change her estimate from 5 to 4.

Erin made 4 dozen and 2 rolls.

Warm Up

Decide which estimates must be changed and then change them. Finish the division.

1. $(20)\ 4$ $\quad 17\overline{)88}$

2. $(30)\ 2$ $\quad 28\overline{)86}$

3. $(40)\ 1$ $\quad 39\overline{)54}$

4. $(20)\ 4$ $\quad 16\overline{)97}$

5. $(30)\ 2$ $\quad 34\overline{)65}$

6. $(40)\ 2$ $\quad 42\overline{)85}$

7. $(10)\ 4$ $\quad 13\overline{)42}$

8. $(10)\ 5$ $\quad 14\overline{)52}$

Divide. Change your estimate if necessary.

9. $27\overline{)55}$

10. $35\overline{)82}$

11. $13\overline{)40}$

12. $15\overline{)79}$

Divide. Change your estimates if necessary.

1. $13\overline{)35}$ 2. $12\overline{)49}$ 3. $19\overline{)42}$ 4. $18\overline{)72}$ 5. $23\overline{)45}$

6. $31\overline{)91}$ 7. $27\overline{)58}$ 8. $14\overline{)83}$ 9. $35\overline{)80}$ 10. $42\overline{)81}$

11. $21\overline{)95}$ 12. $24\overline{)95}$ 13. $16\overline{)98}$ 14. $15\overline{)60}$ 15. $28\overline{)65}$

16. $36\overline{)75}$ 17. $32\overline{)70}$ 18. $17\overline{)71}$ 19. $25\overline{)75}$ 20. $34\overline{)62}$

21. $56 \div 18 = n$ 22. $80 \div 26 = n$ 23. $66 \div 15 = n$

24. $78 \div 39 = n$ 25. $59 \div 42 = n$ 26. $93 \div 45 = n$

27. How many 12s are in 46?   28. How many 16s are in 94?

29. How many 29s are in 75?   30. How many 23s are in 60?

Solve.

31. Evan made 60 bran muffins. How many dozen muffins did he make?

32. Evan put the 60 muffins into bags. Each bag will hold 15 muffins. How many bags did he fill?

33. A bakery makes 1,750 rolls each day. How many days will it take them to make 7,000 rolls?

⌐ **THINK** ⌐

Logical Reasoning

Pretend you cut in half a string 76 cm long. Then you cut each piece in half. What would be the length of each piece of string?

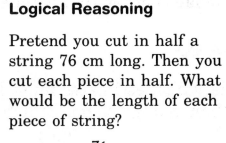

76 cm.

cut → $\frac{1}{2}$

cut $\frac{1}{2}$ again

➡ **MATH** ⟵

325

More 1-Digit Quotients

Mr. Burton used 279 units of electricity in his house in October (31 days). At this rate, how many units of electricity would he use each day in October?

Since we want the number of units each day, we divide.

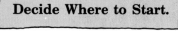

| Decide Where to Start. | → | **Dividing Ones** • Divide • Multiply • Subtract • Compare |

$$31\overline{)279}$$

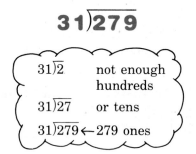

$31\overline{)2}$ not enough hundreds

$31\overline{)27}$ or tens

$31\overline{)279}$ ← 279 ones

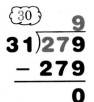

$$
\begin{array}{r}
30 \quad\quad 9 \\
31\overline{)279} \\
-279 \\
\hline
0
\end{array}
$$

CHECK
$$
\begin{array}{r}
31 \\
\times \ 9 \\
\hline
279
\end{array}
$$

Mr. Burton would use 9 units of electricity each day.

Other Examples

$$
\begin{array}{r}
6 \text{ R37} \\
48\overline{)325} \\
-288 \\
\hline
37
\end{array}
\quad
\begin{array}{r}
8 \text{ R1} \\
23\overline{)185} \\
-184 \\
\hline
1
\end{array}
\quad
\begin{array}{r}
\$0.06 \\
36\overline{)\$2.16} \\
-2\ 16 \\
\hline
0
\end{array}
$$

Warm Up   Divide and check.

1. $51\overline{)376}$ 2. $78\overline{)342}$ 3. $43\overline{)285}$ 4. $61\overline{)370}$ 5. $26\overline{)\$2.08}$

6. $18\overline{)141}$ 7. $13\overline{)100}$ 8. $93\overline{)500}$ 9. $48\overline{)399}$ 10. $35\overline{)\$2.45}$

Divide and check.

1. $28\overline{)250}$ 2. $63\overline{)260}$ 3. $51\overline{)185}$ 4. $92\overline{)652}$ 5. $35\overline{)\$2.45}$

6. $44\overline{)245}$ 7. $37\overline{)58}$ 8. $72\overline{)377}$ 9. $19\overline{)153}$ 10. $25\overline{)\$2.00}$

11. $78\overline{)311}$ 12. $57\overline{)425}$ 13. $41\overline{)372}$ 14. $21\overline{)85}$ 15. $67\overline{)\$6.03}$

16. $75\overline{)600}$ 17. $22\overline{)195}$ 18. $16\overline{)38}$ 19. $89\overline{)346}$ 20. $43\overline{)\$3.01}$

21. $395 \div 53 = n$ 22. $388 \div 72 = n$ 23. $478 \div 48 = n$

24. $100 \div 26 = n$ 25. $300 \div 39 = n$ 26. $222 \div 34 = n$

27. Divide 496 by 66.   28. Divide 309 by 72.

29. Divide 120 by 15.   30. Divide 834 by 88.

Solve.

31. A toy store used 120 units of electricity in 1 day (24 hours). At this rate, how many units were used each hour?

32. A 24-hour service station paid $336 for electricity for 1 week. At this rate, what number of dollars were paid for electricity each hour?

33. Write and then solve a division story problem for the data below.

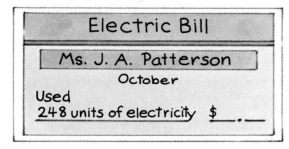

Electric Bill

Ms. J. A. Patterson

October

Used
248 units of electricity $_____._____

PROBLEM SOLVING
Using Data from a Line Graph

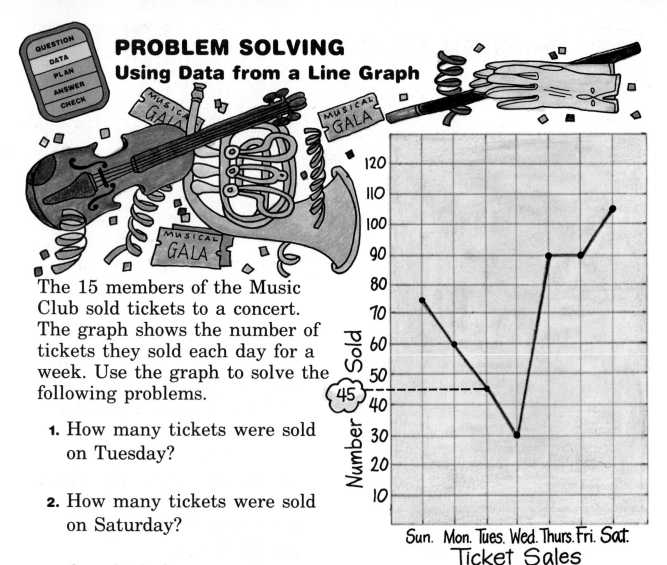

Ticket Sales

The 15 members of the Music Club sold tickets to a concert. The graph shows the number of tickets they sold each day for a week. Use the graph to solve the following problems.

1. How many tickets were sold on Tuesday?

2. How many tickets were sold on Saturday?

3. On which day were the fewest tickets sold?

4. How many more tickets were sold on Saturday than on Sunday?

5. How many tickets were sold on the first three days?

6. The tickets cost $3.75 each. How much money was collected on Wednesday?

7. If each member sold the same number of tickets on Saturday, how many tickets did each member sell?

8. *Try This* Lindy sold tickets for 8 days in a row. She sold the most tickets on the second day. The last day that she sold tickets was Wednesday. On which day of the week did Lindy sell the most tickets?

PROBLEM SOLVING
Practice

QUESTION
DATA
PLAN
ANSWER
CHECK

Solve.

1. There are 72 instruments in the orchestra. 26 are violins. How many of the instruments are not violins?

2. James practices the violin the same number of hours every day. He practiced 93 hours in March (31 days). How many hours does he practice a day?

3. There are 27 different sizes of clarinets. The longest is 274 cm and the shortest is 35 cm. What is the difference in these two sizes?

4. In the week before the concert the Music Club sold 495 tickets. On the day of the concert they sold 35 tickets in the afternoon and 108 tickets at night. How many tickets were sold?

5. The orchestra practiced 225 minutes in one week. Each practice session was 45 minutes long. How many sessions did they have?

6. The orchestra spent $304 to buy 38 new music stands. Each stand cost the same amount. What was the cost of each stand?

7. Ms. Adams bought 12 tickets. How much change did she get from $50 if the tickets cost $3.75 each?

8. There were 430 people at the Saturday night concert. 295 of them sat in chairs. The rest sat on benches. Each bench holds 15 people. How many benches were needed?

9. *Try This* There were 25 people in the front row. There were 3 more children than adults. How many children sat in the front row?

More Dividing by Tens

The Aristocrat Restaurant is planning to use 770 eggs to serve breakfast. Each egg flat holds 30 eggs. How many flats of eggs should the manager order?

Since we want to separate the eggs into equal amounts, we divide.

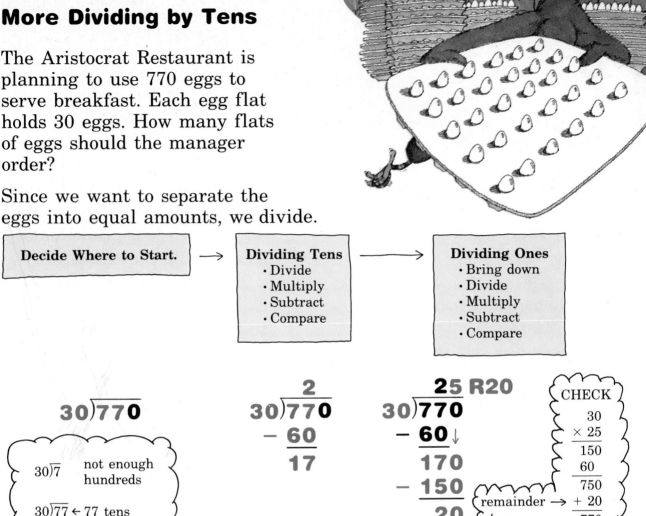

Decide Where to Start.	→	Dividing Tens · Divide · Multiply · Subtract · Compare	→	Dividing Ones · Bring down · Divide · Multiply · Subtract · Compare

$$30\overline{)770}$$

$30\overline{)7}$ not enough hundreds

$30\overline{)77}$ ← 77 tens

$$\begin{array}{r} 2 \\ 30\overline{)770} \\ -\ 60 \\ \hline 17 \end{array}$$

$$\begin{array}{r} 25 \text{ R20} \\ 30\overline{)770} \\ -\ 60\downarrow \\ \hline 170 \\ -\ 150 \\ \hline 20 \end{array}$$

CHECK

$$\begin{array}{r} 30 \\ \times\ 25 \\ \hline 150 \\ 60 \\ \hline 750 \\ \text{remainder} \rightarrow +\ 20 \\ \hline 770 \end{array}$$

Ms. Aris needs 25 full flats and 20 extra eggs, so she should order 26 flats of eggs.

Other Examples

$$\begin{array}{r} 23 \text{ R12} \\ 40\overline{)932} \\ -\ 80 \\ \hline 132 \\ -\ 120 \\ \hline 12 \end{array}$$

$$\begin{array}{r} 16 \text{ R35} \\ 50\overline{)835} \\ -\ 50 \\ \hline 335 \\ -\ 300 \\ \hline 35 \end{array}$$

$$\begin{array}{r} \$0.30 \\ 20\overline{)\$6.00} \\ -\ 6\ 0 \\ \hline 00 \\ -\ 0 \\ \hline 0 \end{array}$$

Warm Up   Divide and check.

1. $40\overline{)445}$ 2. $10\overline{)356}$ 3. $40\overline{)800}$ 4. $30\overline{)683}$ 5. $20\overline{)\$7.40}$

Divide and check.

1. $20\overline{)235}$ **2.** $30\overline{)386}$ **3.** $30\overline{)615}$ **4.** $40\overline{)495}$ **5.** $60\overline{)\$6.00}$

6. $10\overline{)234}$ **7.** $20\overline{)400}$ **8.** $30\overline{)742}$ **9.** $20\overline{)285}$ **10.** $30\overline{)\$9.60}$

11. $20\overline{)935}$ **12.** $10\overline{)678}$ **13.** $60\overline{)255}$ **14.** $50\overline{)750}$ **15.** $80\overline{)\$9.60}$

16. $794 \div 10 = n$ **17.** $999 \div 30 = n$ **18.** $350 \div 20 = n$

19. $587 \div 40 = n$ **20.** $419 \div 30 = n$ **21.** $835 \div 20 = n$

22. What is 800 divided by 40?   **23.** What is 105 divided by 10?

24. What is 333 divided by 20?   **25.** What is 938 divided by 90?

Solve.

26. Ms. Aris needs 950 eggs for Sunday brunch. How many flats of eggs will she need to order?

27. Make up and solve a story problem that would be solved with this number sentence.
$470 \div 30 = 15 \text{ R}20$

SKILLKEEPER

Add or subtract.

1. $\begin{array}{r} 25 \\ + 48 \\ \hline \end{array}$ **2.** $\begin{array}{r} 85 \\ + 51 \\ \hline \end{array}$ **3.** $\begin{array}{r} 67 \\ - 16 \\ \hline \end{array}$ **4.** $\begin{array}{r} 97 \\ - 65 \\ \hline \end{array}$ **5.** $\begin{array}{r} 326 \\ + 145 \\ \hline \end{array}$

6. $\begin{array}{r} 382 \\ + 135 \\ \hline \end{array}$ **7.** $\begin{array}{r} 83 \\ - 28 \\ \hline \end{array}$ **8.** $\begin{array}{r} 147 \\ - 74 \\ \hline \end{array}$ **9.** $\begin{array}{r} 135 \\ - 97 \\ \hline \end{array}$ **10.** $\begin{array}{r} 123 \\ - 66 \\ \hline \end{array}$

2-Digit Quotients

The aquarium park bought 700 kg of mackerel to feed the dolphins. Each case of food has 25 kg of mackerel. How many cases did the park buy?

Since we want the total number of equal cases, we divide.

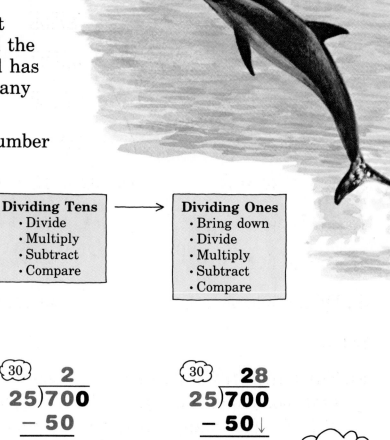

Decide Where to Start.	→	Dividing Tens	→	Dividing Ones
		• Divide		• Bring down
		• Multiply		• Divide
		• Subtract		• Multiply
		• Compare		• Subtract
				• Compare

• not enough hundreds, 25 > 7
• divide the tens, 25 < 70

$$25\overline{)700}$$

(30)

$$\begin{array}{r} 2 \\ 25\overline{)700} \\ -50 \\ \hline 20 \end{array}$$

(30)

$$\begin{array}{r} 28 \\ 25\overline{)700} \\ -50\downarrow \\ \hline 200 \\ -200 \\ \hline 0 \end{array}$$
← 30$\overline{)200}$

The aquarium park bought 28 cases of mackerel.

Other Examples

$$\begin{array}{r} 19\ \textbf{R23} \\ 38\overline{)745} \\ -38 \\ \hline 365 \\ -342 \\ \hline 23 \end{array}$$

$$\begin{array}{r} 20\ \textbf{R15} \\ 43\overline{)875} \\ -86 \\ \hline 15 \\ -0 \\ \hline 15 \end{array}$$

$$\begin{array}{r} \$0.58 \\ 16\overline{)\$9.28} \\ -80 \\ \hline 1\,28 \\ -1\,28 \\ \hline 0 \end{array}$$

Warm Up Divide and check.

1. 21$\overline{)345}$ **2.** 47$\overline{)564}$ **3.** 39$\overline{)790}$ **4.** 57$\overline{)900}$ **5.** 35$\overline{)\$7.35}$

Divide and check.

1. $18\overline{)205}$ **2.** $32\overline{)684}$ **3.** $43\overline{)868}$ **4.** $27\overline{)604}$ **5.** $56\overline{)\$6.72}$

6. $21\overline{)900}$ **7.** $12\overline{)257}$ **8.** $66\overline{)635}$ **9.** $83\overline{)867}$ **10.** $44\overline{)\$8.36}$

11. $29\overline{)590}$ **12.** $31\overline{)600}$ **13.** $15\overline{)750}$ **14.** $43\overline{)294}$ **15.** $17\overline{)\$3.57}$

16. $26\overline{)793}$ **17.** $13\overline{)125}$ **18.** $25\overline{)800}$ **19.** $88\overline{)935}$ **20.** $13\overline{)\$8.32}$

21. $483 \div 24 = n$ **22.** $732 \div 12 = n$ **23.** $567 \div 19 = n$

24. $805 \div 44 = n$ **25.** $356 \div 28 = n$ **26.** $660 \div 33 = n$

27. Divide 314 by 19.   **28.** Divide 783 by 34.

29. Divide 500 by 28.   **30.** Divide 610 by 32.

Solve.

31. The park bought 900 kg of seal food. Each box has 12 kg of food. How many boxes did the park buy?

32. The dolphins ate 525 kg of food in 3 weeks. At this rate, how many kilograms of food did they eat each day?

 33. The park spent $2,852 on food for the whales during January (31 days). At this rate, how much did the park spend for food each day?

PROBLEM SOLVING
Using Data from an Advertisement

Use the information on the packages to solve the following problems.

1. How many plates are in a package of paper plates?

2. What is the price of 1 paper plate?

3. How many ounces does the package of hamburger buns weigh?

4. How much does the box of trash bags cost in dollars and cents?

5. How many ounces does each hamburger bun weigh?

6. What is the price of each napkin?

7. How many ounces of juice will the 51 foam cups hold?

8. How many packages of paper plates can be bought with $10.00?

Smith's Foam Cups
51 cups
6 oz.
$2.55

Cheese-O
CHEESE SLICES
72 slices   11 oz.
$6.48

Wonder NAPKINS
10 in. × 10 in.
120¢   60

HANDY Trash Bags
2 ply
15 BAGS FOR 30 gal. Trash Cans
390¢

9. If you bought 5 boxes of plastic tableware, how many pieces would you have?

10. What would be the price of one trash bag?

11. How much does it cost to buy 3 packages of hamburger buns?

12. What is the price of 1 slice of cheese?

13. If you need 125 sandwich bags, how many boxes should you buy?

14. If you buy 4 packages of hamburger buns and use 39 of them, how many buns will be left?

15. If you use $5.00 to buy 1 package of napkins and 1 package of cups, how much change will you get?

16. *Try This* Meg, Tad, Evie, Dan, and Kari are in line at the market. Kari is between Meg and Tad. Dan is between Tad and Kari. Tad is ahead of Evie. Meg is first in line. Who is last?

APPLIED PROBLEM SOLVING

QUESTION
DATA
PLAN
ANSWER
CHECK

You are helping to plan a class party at a park. It is your job to bring the drinks. There are 30 people in your class. The drinks come in 1-liter bottles. How many bottles should you buy?

Some Things to Consider

- The party is outdoors in June. It may be hot.
- Games are planned that will require running.
- The party will last 4 hours.

- There is no water at the park.
- Each person will drink from 2 to 5 glasses.
- A liter will fill about 5 glasses.

Some Questions to Answer

1. How many glasses of drink will you need if each person drinks 2 glasses?
2. How many glasses of drink will you need if each person drinks 5 glasses?
3. How many liters would you buy if you wanted to fill 100 glasses?

What Is Your Decision?

How many bottles of drink will you buy for the party?

Divide.

1. $40\overline{)80}$ 2. $10\overline{)10}$ 3. $20\overline{)60}$ 4. $50\overline{)450}$ 5. $30\overline{)240}$

6. $20\overline{)27}$ 7. $30\overline{)68}$ 8. $50\overline{)67}$ 9. $20\overline{)76}$ 10. $40\overline{)91}$

11. $43\overline{)58}$ 12. $22\overline{)75}$ 13. $37\overline{)85}$ 14. $32\overline{)98}$ 15. $12\overline{)40}$

16. $12\overline{)49}$ 17. $25\overline{)75}$ 18. $41\overline{)85}$ 19. $15\overline{)65}$ 20. $35\overline{)80}$

21. $32\overline{)245}$ 22. $47\overline{)490}$ 23. $63\overline{)250}$ 24. $21\overline{)\$1.68}$ 25. $18\overline{)\$1.08}$

26. $20\overline{)678}$ 27. $30\overline{)390}$ 28. $40\overline{)495}$ 29. $20\overline{)\$5.00}$ 30. $70\overline{)\$9.10}$

31. $42\overline{)504}$ 32. $37\overline{)462}$ 33. $26\overline{)500}$ 34. $32\overline{)\$6.08}$ 35. $19\overline{)\$3.61}$

Solve.

36. There were 520 people at the Sunday night concert. 325 of them sat in chairs. The rest sat on benches. How many people sat on benches?

37. What is the price of each envelope?

ANOTHER LOOK

Use division facts.

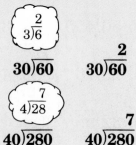

$$3\overline{)6} = 2$$

$$30\overline{)60} \qquad 30\overline{)60} = 2$$

$$4\overline{)28} = 7$$

$$40\overline{)280} \qquad 40\overline{)280} = 7$$

Put an X to show where to start.

$$\overset{X}{40\overline{)85}} \qquad \overset{\ \ X}{40\overline{)235}}$$

not enough tens,
40 > 8

start with ones,
40 < 85

not enough hundreds,
40 > 2

not enough tens,
40 > 23

start with ones,
40 < 235

Change estimates.

$$2\overline{)6} = 3$$

Try a smaller number.

$$\begin{array}{r} 3 \\ 24\overline{)67} \\ -\ 72 \leftarrow \text{too large} \end{array} \qquad \begin{array}{r} 2\ R19 \\ 24\overline{)67} \\ -\ 48 \\ \hline 19 \end{array}$$

$$3\overline{)8} = 2$$

Try a larger number.

$$\begin{array}{r} 2 \\ 26\overline{)89} \\ -\ 52 \\ \hline 37 \leftarrow \text{greater} \\ \text{than 26} \end{array} \qquad \begin{array}{r} 3\ R11 \\ 26\overline{)89} \\ -\ 78 \\ \hline 11 \end{array}$$

Find the quotients.

1. $2\overline{)8}$ **2.** $3\overline{)9}$ **3.** $4\overline{)36}$

$20\overline{)80}$ $30\overline{)90}$ $40\overline{)360}$

4. $2\overline{)14}$ **5.** $5\overline{)35}$ **6.** $8\overline{)32}$

$20\overline{)140}$ $50\overline{)350}$ $80\overline{)320}$

Put an X to show where to start.

7. $30\overline{)75}$ **8.** $10\overline{)43}$ **9.** $20\overline{)96}$

10. $40\overline{)324}$ **11.** $60\overline{)552}$ **12.** $30\overline{)267}$

13. $38\overline{)268}$ **14.** $31\overline{)182}$ **15.** $17\overline{)123}$

Divide.

16. $40\overline{)83}$ **17.** $30\overline{)75}$ **18.** $20\overline{)55}$

19. $50\overline{)308}$ **20.** $80\overline{)751}$ **21.** $60\overline{)378}$

22. $43\overline{)81}$ **23.** $22\overline{)80}$ **24.** $13\overline{)67}$

25. $27\overline{)85}$ **26.** $16\overline{)72}$ **27.** $35\overline{)78}$

Logical Reasoning

Colored arrows can be used to show relationships. The 10 letters below represent 10 people. The colored arrows show some of the ways these people are related to each other.

➡ points to a person's father.
➡ points to a person's mother.

The 10 people include a grandfather and grandmother, their 3 children, and 5 grandchildren.

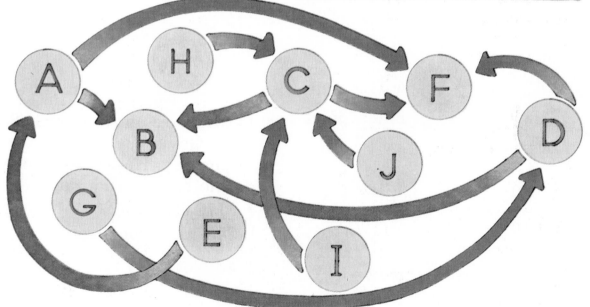

1. What letter represents the grandmother?
2. What letter represents the grandfather?
3. How are C and D related?

Give the letter for the correct answer.

1. $\frac{3}{6}$ **A** $\frac{5}{6}$ **B** $\frac{5}{12}$
$+\frac{2}{6}$ **C** 5   **D** not given

2. $\frac{1}{10}$ **A** 4   **B** $\frac{4}{10}$
$+\frac{3}{10}$ **C** $\frac{4}{20}$ **D** not given

3. $\frac{6}{10}$ **A** $\frac{3}{10}$ **B** $\frac{9}{10}$
$-\frac{3}{10}$ **C** $\frac{3}{0}$ **D** not given

4. $\frac{5}{8}$ **A** $\frac{9}{8}$ **B** $\frac{1}{0}$
$-\frac{4}{8}$ **C** $\frac{1}{8}$ **D** not given

5. $3\frac{2}{4}$ **A** $1\frac{1}{4}$ **B** $5\frac{3}{4}$
$+2\frac{1}{4}$ **C** $5\frac{3}{8}$ **D** not given

6. $7\frac{7}{10}$ **A** $4\frac{4}{10}$ **B** $3\frac{4}{20}$
$-4\frac{3}{10}$ **C** $3\frac{4}{10}$ **D** not given

7. 26   **A** 520   **B** 52
$\times 20$ **C** 420   **D** not given

8. 23   **A** 26   **B** 276
$\times 12$ **C** 69   **D** not given

9. 65   **A** 585
$\times 27$ **B** 1,655
C 1,755
D not given

10. $0.54   **A** $1.00
$\times 20$ **B** $1.08
C $10.08
D not given

11. $0.78   **A** $32.76
$\times 42$ **B** $32.66
C $2.96
D not given

12. $6.85   **A** $234.05
$\times 33$ **B** $226.05
C $42.00
D not given

13. Records are on sale for $6.88 each. Gavin sold 25 records in one day. How much money did he take in that day?
A $172.00 **B** $17.20
C $48.10   **D** not given

14. Eli's foot is $7\frac{2}{4}$ in. long. Kara's foot is $6\frac{1}{4}$ in. long. How much longer is Eli's foot than Kara's foot?
A $13\frac{3}{4}$ in. **B** $1\frac{3}{4}$ in.
C $1\frac{1}{4}$ in.   **D** not given

DECIMALS

Jenny Chen is on a gymnastics team. She trains about 15 hours a week. Jenny does best on the balance beam. It is only about 10.2 cm wide. She begins new tricks on a line on the floor. Then she works out on a low beam. Finally she is ready for the high beam. It is about 1.19 m high. Jenny works very hard. Sometimes she becomes very tired. Then she wonders if it is worth all the work. Other times it is very rewarding. Once Jenny's team was judged first place champions. Jenny felt like she was on top of the world.

Tenths

The glass holds two tenths of a liter. For two tenths, you can write a fraction or a **decimal.**

Fraction	Decimal
$\dfrac{2}{10}$	0.2
	↑
	Decimal point

We read, "**two tenths.**"

two tenths

1 LITER

The bucket holds one and three tenths liters. For one and three tenths you can write a mixed number or a decimal.

Mixed number	Decimal
$1\dfrac{3}{10}$	1.3
	↑
	Decimal point

We read, "**one and three tenths.**"

Warm Up   Write a decimal for each amount.

1.

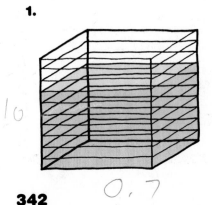

10

0.7

2.

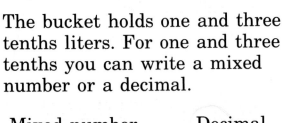

1.5

Write a decimal for each amount. You can
see only the front of each box.

Example

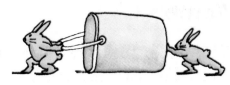

1.

answer 2.4

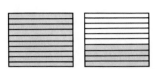

2.

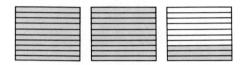

3.

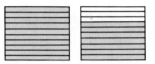

4.

5.

6.

THINK

Patterns

Give the next 3 decimals.

1. 2.2, 2.3, 2.4, __?__, __?__, __?__

2. 2.6, 2.7, 2.8, __?__, __?__, __?__

3. 9.7, 9.8, 9.9, __?__, __?__, __?__

7.

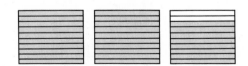

4. 24.6, 24.7, 24.8, __?__, __?__, __?__

MATH

Hundredths

Eric bought 2 full sheets of stamps and 36 out of 100 from another sheet.

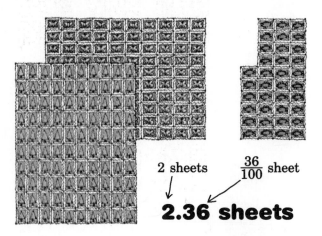

2 sheets $\frac{36}{100}$ sheet

2.36 sheets

We read "**two and thirty-six hundredths.**"

Eric bought 2.36 sheets of stamps.

Other Examples

The decimals tell how much is shaded.

1.3 or 1.30

$\frac{3}{10} = \frac{30}{100}$

0 ones . 2 tenths 3 hundredths

1 ones . 0 tenths 8 hundredths

One and three tenths or one and thirty hundredths

twenty-three hundredths

one and eight hundredths

Warm Up   Write a decimal to tell how much is shaded.

1.
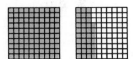

2.

3.

Write a decimal to tell how much is shaded.

1.

2.

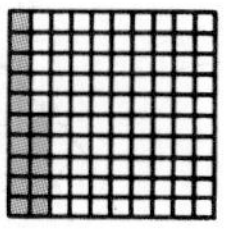

3.

4.

5.

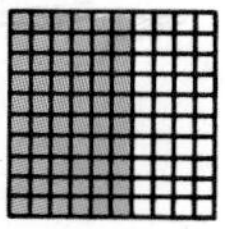

6.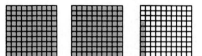

Write a decimal for each of the following.

7. one and sixty-five hundredths

8. two and forty-eight hundredths

9. seventy-five hundredths

10. nine hundredths

11. eight and forty-six hundredths

12. four and eighty hundredths

13. 2 ones
3 tenths
6 hundredths

14. 7 ones
5 tenths
8 hundredths

15. 9 hundredths
3 ones
6 tenths

16. 0 tenths
5 hundredths
1 one

SKILLKEEPER

Divide.

1. $4\overline{)8}$ **2.** $3\overline{)9}$ **3.** $20\overline{)80}$ **4.** $30\overline{)60}$ **5.** $7\overline{)35}$

6. $9\overline{)72}$ **7.** $4\overline{)32}$ **8.** $5\overline{)45}$ **9.** $20\overline{)140}$ **10.** $40\overline{)83}$

Decimals and Measurement

Centimeter rulers usually show tenths of a centimeter.

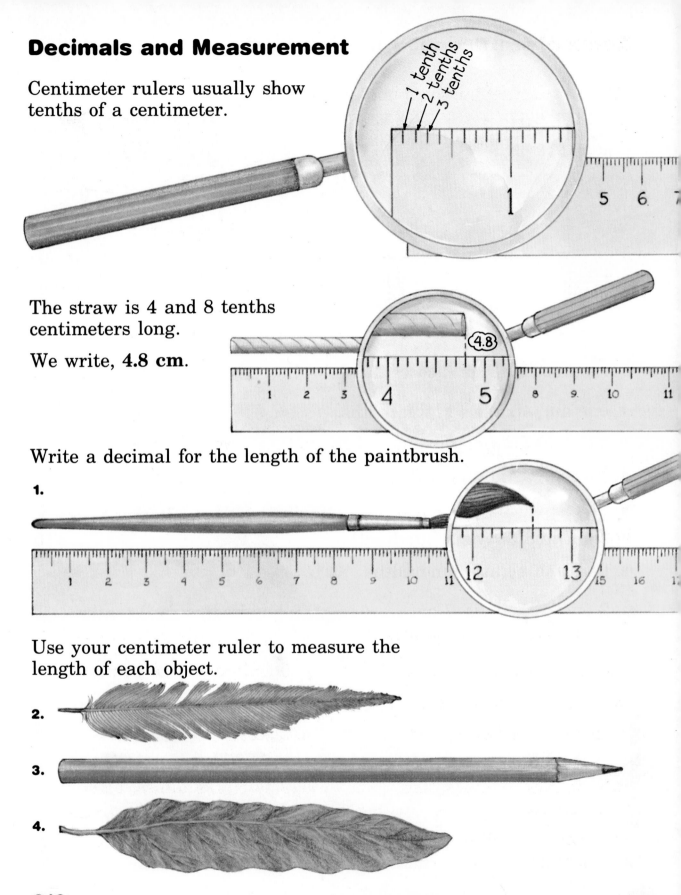

The straw is 4 and 8 tenths centimeters long.

We write, **4.8 cm**.

Write a decimal for the length of the paintbrush.

1.

Use your centimeter ruler to measure the length of each object.

2.

3.

4.

346

Decimals and Money

100 pennies will buy as much as 1 dollar.

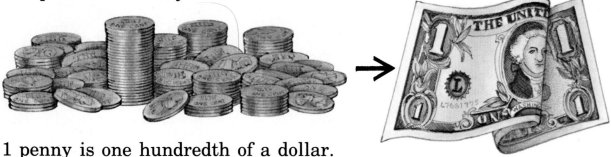

1 penny is one hundredth of a dollar.

$\frac{1}{100}$ dollar   We write, **$0.01.**

3 pennies are three hundredths of a dollar.

$\frac{3}{100}$ dollar   We write, **$0.03.**

For 3 dollars and 27 pennies,

We think, **"three and twenty-seven hundredths dollars."**
We write, **$3.27.**
We read, **"three dollars and twenty-seven cents."**

Write each amount using the dollar sign and a decimal point.

1. 2 dollars and 25 pennies

2. 7 dollars and 78 pennies

3. 5 dollars and 7 pennies

4. 6 dollars and 10 pennies

5. 9 dollars and 1 dime

6. 4 dollars and 2 dimes

7. 1 dollar, 3 dimes, and 4 pennies

8. 3 dollars, 6 dimes, and 7 pennies

9. 8 dollars, 7 dimes, and 9 pennies

10. 5 dollars, 4 dimes, and 0 pennies

11. 7 dollars, 0 dimes, and 6 pennies

12. 9 dollars, 3 dimes, and 6 pennies

Comparing Decimals

A horse ran at a speed of 69.3 km/h (kilometers per hour). A dog ran at a speed of 69.1 km/h. Which animal was faster?

Compare the speeds to see which is faster.

Line up the decimal points.

→

Start at the left. Find the first place where the digits are different.

→

Compare these digits.

→

The numbers compare the same way the digits compare.

69.3
69.1

69.3
69.1

{is greater than}
3 > 1

69.3 > 69.1

The horse was faster than the dog.

Other Examples

{is less than}

0.26 < 0.29   **0.40 > 0.04**   **2.47 < 2.59**
24.0 = 24   **32.4 > 32**   **0.6 = 0.60**

Warm Up   Give >, <, or = for each ▦.

1. 0.35 ▦ 0.37

2. 0.80 ▦ 0.8

3. 2.38 ▦ 2.46

4. 3.40 ▦ 3.4

5. 24 ▦ 24.3

6. 0.08 ▦ 0.70

7. 3.82 ▦ 3.78

8. 2.30 ▦ 2.06

9. 2.4 ▦ 2.40

10. 0.56 ▦ 0.59

11. 5.06 ▦ 5.60

12. 65.4 ▦ 65

Give >, <, or = for each .

1. 0.56 ⬤ 0.52   **2.** 2.56 ⬤ 2.51   **3.** 0.20 ⬤ 0.02

4. 24 ⬤ 24.1   **5.** 3.6 ⬤ 3.60   **6.** 0.65 ⬤ 0.68

7. 3.81 ⬤ 3.76   **8.** 0.20 ⬤ 0.02   **9.** 0.7 ⬤ 0.70

10. 0.60 ⬤ 0.6   **11.** 0.37 ⬤ 0.73   **12.** 0.07 ⬤ 0.70

13. 4.8 ⬤ 4.80   **14.** 4.38 ⬤ 4.4   **15.** 8.20 ⬤ 8.2

16. 6.28 ⬤ 6.30   **17.** 32.6 ⬤ 32   **18.** 0.29 ⬤ 0.32

19. 0.1 ⬤ 0.10   **20.** 0.41 ⬤ 0.35   **21.** 0.61 ⬤ 6.1

22. Which number is greater, 2.87 or 2.91?

23. Which number is less, 0.30 or 0.03?

24. Which number is greater, 0.29 or 0.3?

25. Which number is less, 32.4 or 32.6?

Give each set of decimals in order, from smallest to largest.

26. 3.6, 2.8, 4.1   **27.** 5.6, 5.2, 5.4   **28.** 0.37, 0.41, 0.34

Solve.

29. A rabbit ran 48.2 km/h. A fox ran 48.1 km/h. Which one ran faster?

30. A bird flew 72.2 km/h. Was this faster or slower than the dog's speed given on page 348?

THINK

Ordering Decimals

Put the numbers in order from smallest to largest.
Write the letter for each number above that number.
You will have the name of one of the fastest animals.

t	e	c	h	e	a	h
1.20	0.98	0.87	1.3	1.02	1.27	0.91

MATH

Adding Decimals

The chef mixed the two cans of juice together. How many liters of juice did he have?

Since we want the total amount, we add.

Line up the decimal points.	Add the hundredths. Trade if necessary.	Add the tenths. Trade if necessary.	Add the whole numbers. Place the decimal point.
0.83 + 0.95	0.83 + 0.95 8	1 0.83 + 0.95 78	1 0.83 + 0.95 1.78

The chef had 1.78 liters of juice.

17 tenths is 1 whole and 7 tenths.

Other Examples

1 27.6 + 38.9 66.5	1 13.27 + 62.56 75.83	1 1 $6.56 + 9.85 16.41	1 0.36 + 0.29 0.65

13 hundredths is 1 tenth and 3 hundredths.

Warm Up Add.

1.	48.3 + 17.8	2.	6.47 + 0.38	3.	23.78 + 37.69	4.	$3.76 + 9.38	5.	0.78 + 0.92

Add.

1.	78.3 + 16.8	**2.**	27.6 + 32.9	**3.**	7.60 + 1.83
4.	8.32 + 9.16	**5.**	3.78 + 1.99	**6.**	0.95 + 0.81

7.	0.67 + 0.85	**8.**	42.8 + 76.9	**9.**	3.85 + 4.76	**10.**	30.68 + 42.39	**11.**	74.83 + 60.67
12.	$3.95 + 2.69	**13.**	$4.38 + 2.76	**14.**	7.95 + 8.69	**15.**	$3.85 + 1.88	**16.**	$54.67 + 31.28

17. 3.62 + 4.81

18. 76.3 + 81.9

19. 46.28 + 18.75

20. 9.6 + 8.9

21. 0.36 + 0.89

22. $2.95 + $3.79

23. Add 3.75 to 2.80.

24. Add 6.78 to 0.95.

Solve.

25. One can had 0.83 L. Another had 1.74 L. How many liters were in both cans?

27. DATA BANK See page 383. The cook mixed a No. 2 can of juice with a No. 1 tall can of juice. How many liters of juice was this in all?

26. DATA HUNT Find the number of liters in each of two different sizes of canned fruit juice. Find the total number of liters for the two cans.

┌─ **THINK** ─┐

🖩 **Using a Calculator**

1. Show 8.0 on your calculator. Now show 8.7 by adding one number to 8.0.
2. Show 3.00 on your calculator. Now show 3.67 by adding one number to 3.00.

➤ **MATH** ◀

Subtracting Decimals

A serving of roast beef contains 23.40 grams of protein. The same size serving of turkey contains 28.13 grams of protein. How much more protein does the turkey have?

Since we want to find out how much more, we subtract.

Line up the decimal points.	Subtract the hundredths. Trade if necessary.	Subtract the tenths. Trade if necessary.	Subtract the whole numbers. Place the decimal point.

$$
\begin{array}{r} 28.13 \\ -\ 23.40 \\ \hline \end{array}
\qquad
\begin{array}{r} 28.13 \\ -\ 23.40 \\ \hline 3 \end{array}
\qquad
\begin{array}{r} {}^{7}\ {}^{11} \\ 28.\cancel{1}3 \\ -\ 23.40 \\ \hline 73 \end{array}
\qquad
\begin{array}{r} {}^{7}\ {}^{11} \\ 2\cancel{8}.\cancel{1}3 \\ -\ 23.40 \\ \hline 4.73 \end{array}
$$

A turkey has 4.73 grams more protein.

Other Examples

$$
\begin{array}{r} {}^{7}\ {}^{12} \\ 7.\cancel{8}\cancel{2} \\ -\ 3.56 \\ \hline 4.26 \end{array}
\qquad
\begin{array}{r} {}^{8}\ {}^{11}\ {}^{14} \\ \cancel{9}.\cancel{2}\cancel{4} \\ -\ 1.67 \\ \hline 7.57 \end{array}
\qquad
\begin{array}{r} {}^{6}\ {}^{12} \\ 6\cancel{7}.\cancel{2} \\ -\ 26.7 \\ \hline 40.5 \end{array}
\qquad
\begin{array}{r} {}^{2}\ {}^{11}\ {}^{16} \\ \$\cancel{3}\cancel{2}.\cancel{6}3 \\ -\ 28.93 \\ \hline \$\ 3.70 \end{array}
$$

Warm Up   Subtract.

1. $\begin{array}{r} 6.71 \\ -\ 3.28 \\ \hline \end{array}$
2. $\begin{array}{r} 5.39 \\ -\ 1.62 \\ \hline \end{array}$
3. $\begin{array}{r} 3.54 \\ -\ 2.69 \\ \hline \end{array}$
4. $\begin{array}{r} 48.23 \\ -\ 39.50 \\ \hline \end{array}$
5. $\begin{array}{r} \$43.27 \\ -\ \$17.36 \\ \hline \end{array}$

Subtract.

1. 9.24 − 3.70	**2.** 6.85 − 2.39	**3.** 4.48 − 1.24	**4.** 3.37 − 1.69	**5.** 2.43 − 1.58
6. 67.2 − 34.3	**7.** 6.25 − 5.75	**8.** 38.6 − 9.8	**9.** 27.4 − 14.9	**10.** 2.86 − 1.95
11. 32.46 − 17.83	**12.** 26.41 − 14.82	**13.** 13.40 − 6.17	**14.** 28.65 − 19.82	**15.** 67.62 − 53.46
16. $3.95 − 1.98	**17.** $2.76 − 0.98	**18.** $4.65 − 1.95	**19.** $32.45 − 17.60	**20.** $49.25 − 17.69

21. 32.4 − 17.9   **22.** 3.28 − 1.75   **23.** 2.76 − 1.90

24. $83.42 − $76.04   **25.** $29.75 − $19.95   **26.** $38.27 − $6.95

27. Subtract 3.75 from 6.82.   **28.** Subtract 37.50 from 62.35.

Solve.

29. There are 17.9 grams of protein in a serving of lamb. The same size serving of white fish has 25.2 grams of protein. How much more protein does the fish have?

30. Look at the data below. Choose one meat and one vegetable. Find the difference in grams of protein between them.

Veal—23.0, chicken—28.1, broccoli—3.3, spinach—2.3.

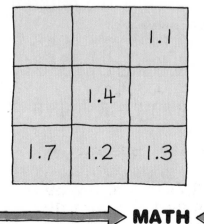

THINK

Magic Squares

Complete this magic square. Remember, the sums in all directions (→ ↑ ↗ ↖) must be the same. In this square, the sum is 4.2.

		1.1
	1.4	
1.7	1.2	1.3

MATH

More Adding and Subtracting Decimals

Marlo's time in the race was 52.15 seconds. Dawn's time was 54.8 seconds. How many seconds' difference was there?

Since we want the difference in the two times, we subtract.

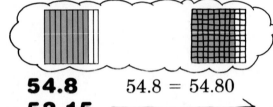

$$\begin{array}{r} 54.8 \\ -\ 52.15 \end{array} \qquad 54.8 = 54.80 \qquad \begin{array}{r} {}^{7\ 10} \\ 54.8\cancel{0} \\ -\ 52.15 \\ \hline 2.65 \end{array}$$

The difference in times was 2.65 seconds.

Other Examples

$$\begin{array}{r} 4.76 \\ +\ 2.8 \end{array} \rightarrow \begin{array}{r} 4.76 \\ +\ 2.80 \\ \hline 7.56 \end{array} \qquad\qquad \begin{array}{r} 79 \\ -\ 26.38 \end{array} \rightarrow \begin{array}{r} {}^{8\ \ 9\ 10} \\ 79.0\cancel{0} \\ -\ 26.38 \\ \hline 52.62 \end{array}$$

Find the sums and differences.

1. $\begin{array}{r} 42.7 \\ +\ 8.69 \end{array}$	**2.** $\begin{array}{r} 64.8 \\ -\ 21.34 \end{array}$	**3.** $\begin{array}{r} 2.69 \\ +\ 8 \end{array}$	**4.** $\begin{array}{r} 64 \\ -\ 18.3 \end{array}$	**5.** $\begin{array}{r} 93 \\ -\ 75.46 \end{array}$
6. $\begin{array}{r} 6.82 \\ +\ 57 \end{array}$	**7.** $\begin{array}{r} 48.6 \\ -\ 15.37 \end{array}$	**8.** $\begin{array}{r} 28.4 \\ +\ 17.67 \end{array}$	**9.** $\begin{array}{r} 56.2 \\ +\ 75 \end{array}$	**10.** $\begin{array}{r} 13.0 \\ -\ 7.23 \end{array}$

11. $14.3 + 32$ **12.** $16.4 - 3.25$ **13.** $75 + 16.4$

14. $58 - 13.43$ **15.** $18.35 + 9.6$ **16.** $76.1 - 2.85$

More Practice, page 416, Set B

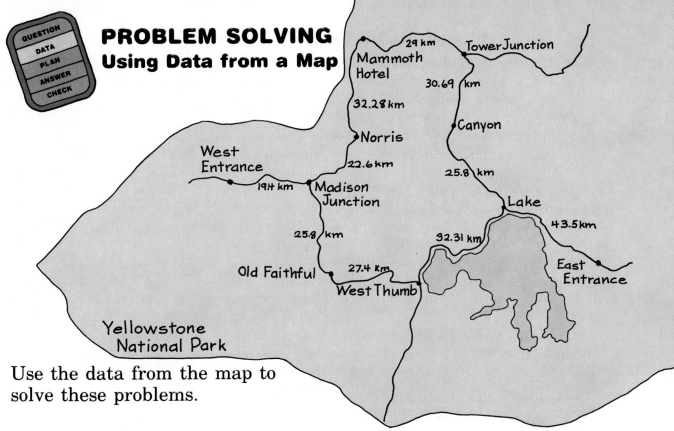

PROBLEM SOLVING
Using Data from a Map

QUESTION
DATA
PLAN
ANSWER
CHECK

Mammoth Hotel   29 km   Tower Junction

30.69 km

32.28 km

Norris

Canyon

West Entrance

22.6 km

25.8 km

19.4 km   Madison Junction

Lake

43.5 km

25.8 km

32.31 km

Old Faithful   27.4 km

East Entrance

West Thumb

Yellowstone National Park

Use the data from the map to solve these problems.

1. How far is it from Madison Junction to Mammoth Hotel?

2. How much farther is it from Lake to West Thumb than from Lake to Canyon?

3. How far is it from West Thumb to Madison Junction?

4. How much closer is it from Canyon to Lake than from Canyon to Tower Junction?

5. How far would you drive if you made 4 one-way trips between Mammoth Hotel and Tower Junction?

6. Which is farther, Madison Junction to Mammoth Hotel or Madison Junction to West Thumb?

★ 7. A group on bicycles took 3 hours to go from the West Entrance to Norris. About how far did they travel each hour?

8. *Try This* Some visitors started at Madison Junction and drove to one place and back. They traveled 45.2 km. Where did they go?

PROBLEM SOLVING
Using a Calculator

Use your calculator to **find the answer** to these problems.

1. Mr. Fry needed carpet for a room that was 7.4 m long and 5.8 m wide. How many square meters of carpet are needed?

2. Mr. Johnson bought a house for $75,600. He had to have $\frac{1}{4}$ of that amount in cash. How much cash did he have to have?

3. Joel paid $985.00 for a couch. He bought a matching chair for $495.50. How much more was the couch?

4. Mr. Lee has 5 water heaters for his apartments. Their total weight is 158.76 kg. How much does each one weigh?

5. Ms. Lopez has 3 houses for sale at $69,500, $72,950, and $68,750. What is the average of the houses?

6. Ms. Lee sold two houses for $59,790 and $68,900. She makes $0.02 on each dollar. How much did she make for selling these two houses? Hint: Multiply the total sales by 0.02.

7. *Try This* Mr. Jensen sells houses. He is supposed to sell the amounts listed below.

March	April	May
$39,500	$40,250	$41,000
June	July	August
$41,750	$42,500	

How much should he sell in August?

Decimal Practice

Find the sums.

1.	8.6 + 7.5	**2.**	27.3 + 58.9	**3.**	128.2 + 276.4	**4.**	58.7 + 65.9	**5.**	378.4 + 126.7
6.	3.42 + 1.86	**7.**	0.27 + 0.58	**8.**	28.75 + 19.82	**9.**	4.67 + 2.88	**10.**	0.76 + 0.95

Find the differences.

11.	3.8 − 2.6	**12.**	7.2 − 1.8	**13.**	24.3 − 10.6	**14.**	82.3 − 17.6	**15.**	42.7 − 17.8
16.	3.67 − 1.28	**17.**	0.36 − 0.18	**18.**	26.35 − 9.82	**19.**	4.60 − 1.88	**20.**	24.82 − 8.95

Find the sums and differences.

21.	26.1 − 17.35	**22.**	54 + 8.76	**23.**	35 − 4.8	**24.**	0.8 − 0.36	**25.**	13.8 + 6.75
26.	42.83 + 75	**27.**	26.1 − 9.75	**28.**	58.3 + 75	**29.**	86.7 + 19.38	**30.**	58 − 29.4

31. $27.6 + 35.8$

32. $83.2 - 16.7$

33. $7.86 + 9.27$

34. $4.86 - 2.39$

35. $84.83 + 26.75$

36. $76.34 - 28.09$

37. $38 + 19.2$

38. $69.24 + 27.9$

39. $7.8 - 2.36$

40. $54 - 7.6$

41. $38 - 27.67$

42. $75 + 28.63$

43. $96.1 - 27.87$

44. $67.2 + 96$

45. $56.1 - 29.36$

Solve these problems about the weather.

1. Hawaii has an average of 177.6 cm of rain per year. Nevada has an average of 18.8 cm. How much more rain does Hawaii average than Nevada?

2. Chicago had 85.12 cm of rain one year. The following year 96.62 cm of rain fell. How much rain did Chicago have in the two years?

3. The highest temperature ever for Alaska and Hawaii is the same, 37.78°C. The highest temperature for anywhere in the United States is 18.87°C higher. What is this highest temperature?

4. Dry snow is 10 times as deep as water. How deep would the snow be for 12 cm of water?

5. Wind moving 9 km/h is called a light breeze. A wind of 85 km/h is called a strong gale. How much faster is the gale?

6. In Tahoe, California, about 272 cm of snow fell in 4 days. If the same amount fell each day, how much snow fell each day?

7. In Juneau, Alaska, the average July temperature is 13°C. The average for July in Phoenix, Arizona, is about 32°C. How many degrees cooler is Juneau?

8. Dallas had 46.74 cm of snow one year. The next year only 6.35 cm of snow fell. What was the difference in snowfall in the two years?

9. A wind of 14 km/h is called a gentle breeze. A wind 5 times that fast is called a fresh gale. How fast is that?

10. One January, Seattle had 15 cm of rain. If that same amount had fallen as moist snow, it would have been 6 times that deep. How deep is that?

11. The average temperature in Boston in July is 24°C. The average temperature in March in Boston is only $\frac{1}{6}$ of that. What is the average for March?

12. The average wind speed for Salt Lake City is 14 km/h. The highest wind in Salt Lake City was 16 km/h faster than 7 times the average. How fast was that?

13. The wind was a gentle breeze of 14 km/h. A storm came up and the wind grew to 5 times what it was. Then it decreased by 25 km/h. How fast was it then?

14. **DATA HUNT** Find out what the difference in temperature is inside your classroom and outside your school.

15. **DATA BANK** See page 385. What is the difference in average rainfall between Seattle and Cincinnati?

16. *Try This* One year a city had 8 cm of snow for each 5 cm of rain. How much snow did they have if they had 40 cm of rain that year? Complete the table.

Rain	5	10	15
Snow	8	16	24

359

APPLIED PROBLEM SOLVING

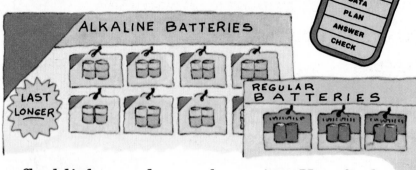

Your flashlight needs new batteries. You find two kinds of batteries at the store. One kind is alkaline, which costs $2.75 a pair. The other is regular, which costs $0.95 a pair. Both kinds fit your flashlight. Which pair of batteries will you buy?

Some Things to Consider

- You have $5.00 but there are some other things you would like to buy.

- The store clerk tells you that alkaline batteries will last 3 to 4 times as long as regular batteries.

- The flashlight will give the same amount of light using either pair of batteries.

Some Questions to Answer

1. Do you want to spend as much as $2.75 for batteries at this time?

2. About how many pair of regular batteries can you buy for $2.75?

3. What is $3 \times \$0.95$?

4. What is $4 \times \$0.95$?

What Is Your Decision?

Will you buy the regular batteries or the alkaline batteries?

Write a decimal for each picture.

1.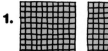

2.

3.

Use your centimeter ruler. Write a decimal
for the length of each rod.

4. ▭

5. ▭

Write each amount using a dollar sign and a decimal point.

6. 3 dollars and 37 pennies

7. 2 dollars and 3 dimes

8. 1 dollar, 5 dimes, and 7 pennies

9. 6 dollars, 0 dimes, and 4 pennies

Give the sign >, <, or = for each ▒ .

10. 4.8 ▒ 3.9

11. 6.27 ▒ 6.29

12. 45.20 ▒ 45.2

Find the sums and differences.

13.
$$\begin{array}{r} 0.86 \\ + 0.37 \\ \hline \end{array}$$

14.
$$\begin{array}{r} 24.5 \\ + 56.8 \\ \hline \end{array}$$

15.
$$\begin{array}{r} 27.65 \\ + 13.84 \\ \hline \end{array}$$

16.
$$\begin{array}{r} \$9.87 \\ + 4.95 \\ \hline \end{array}$$

17.
$$\begin{array}{r} 28.24 \\ - 13.61 \\ \hline \end{array}$$

18.
$$\begin{array}{r} 6.74 \\ - 1.36 \\ \hline \end{array}$$

19.
$$\begin{array}{r} 47.2 \\ - 19.8 \\ \hline \end{array}$$

20.
$$\begin{array}{r} 7.38 \\ + 47 \\ \hline \end{array}$$

21.
$$\begin{array}{r} 74.6 \\ - 16.28 \\ \hline \end{array}$$

22.
$$\begin{array}{r} 67.2 \\ + 13.86 \\ \hline \end{array}$$

Solve.

23. How far is it from Nome to Bend?

24. How much farther is it from Bend to Hope than from Hope to Nome?

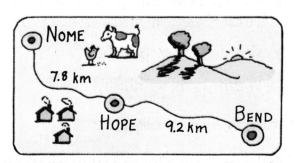

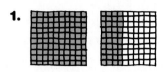

Write a decimal.

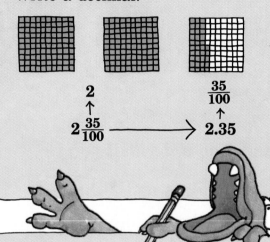

$$2$$
$$\uparrow$$
$$\frac{35}{100}$$
$$\uparrow$$
$$2\frac{35}{100} \longrightarrow 2.35$$

Write a decimal for each picture.

1.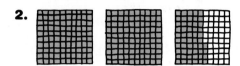

2.

Compare.

35.62 ● 35.64

The whole numbers are equal. The tenths are equal. The second number has more hundredths.

35.62 < 35.64

Write >, <, or = for each ●.

3. 2.6 ● 2.5   **4.** 8.2 ● 7.9

5. 0.35 ● 0.41   **6.** 0.67 ● 0.71

7. 0.7 ● 0.70   **8.** 3.60 ● 3.6

9. 5.82 ● 5.9   **10.** 4.6 ● 4.59

11. 7.86 ● 7.68   **12.** 5.9 ● 6

13. 37 ● 36.9   **14.** 28.1 ● 27.9

Add or subtract.

$$
\begin{array}{r}
{\scriptstyle 1\ 1\ 1} \\
36.28 \\
+\ 47.96 \\
\hline
84.24
\end{array}
\qquad
\begin{array}{r}
{\scriptstyle 6\ 1114} \\
7.24 \\
-\ 1.76 \\
\hline
5.48
\end{array}
$$

Add the whole numbers. Write the decimal point between the ones and tenths.

Add or subtract.

15.
$$\begin{array}{r} 3.8 \\ +\ 2.7 \\ \hline \end{array}$$
16.
$$\begin{array}{r} 5.86 \\ +\ 3.95 \\ \hline \end{array}$$
17.
$$\begin{array}{r} 16.82 \\ +\ 23.67 \\ \hline \end{array}$$

18.
$$\begin{array}{r} 48.1 \\ -\ 17.6 \\ \hline \end{array}$$
19.
$$\begin{array}{r} 3.85 \\ -\ 1.69 \\ \hline \end{array}$$
20.
$$\begin{array}{r} 27.83 \\ -\ 12.95 \\ \hline \end{array}$$

21.
$$\begin{array}{r} 26.75 \\ +\ 13.93 \\ \hline \end{array}$$
22.
$$\begin{array}{r} 48.96 \\ -\ 16.34 \\ \hline \end{array}$$
23.
$$\begin{array}{r} 75.96 \\ -\ 6.83 \\ \hline \end{array}$$

Negative and Positive Numbers

The number line below shows how **negative** and **positive** numbers can be used to describe the seconds **before** and **after** a rocket blast-off.

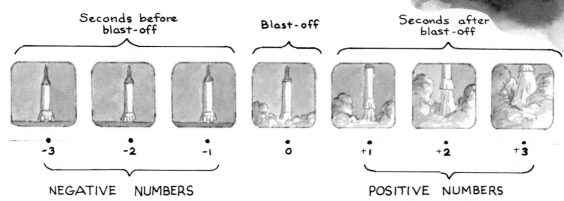

Seconds before blast-off   Blast-off   Seconds after blast-off

-3   -2   -1   0   +1   +2   +3

NEGATIVE NUMBERS   POSITIVE NUMBERS

We read ⁻3 as **"negative three."** We read ⁻2 as **"negative two."**

The graph below shows the changes in speed of a jet airplane during lift-off. Negative numbers show seconds before lift-off and positive numbers show seconds after lift-off.

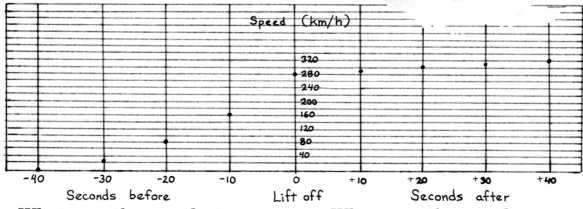

1. What was the speed at ⁻20 seconds?

2. What was the speed at lift-off?

3. When was the speed 80 km/h?

4. How many seconds was it from 0 to 300 km/h?

TECHNOLOGY

Using GOTO

Another important word the computer understands is GOTO. In the program below, GOTO 40 tells the computer to jump to line 40.

Program

```
10 PRINT "GOOD"
20 GOTO 40
30 PRINT "NIGHT."
40 PRINT "MORNING."
50 END
```

Screen

```
RUN
GOOD
MORNING.
```

Notice that the computer jumped over line 30.

Program A

```
10 PRINT "WHAT'S"
20 GOTO 40
30 PRINT "OLD?"
40 PRINT "NEW?"
50 END
```

Program B

```
10 PRINT "HAVE"
20 GOTO 50
30 PRINT "DAY."
40 GOTO 70
50 PRINT "A NICE"
60 GOTO 30
70 END
```

RUN A

```
RUN
WHAT'S
NEW?
```

RUN B

```
RUN
HAVE
A NICE
DAY.
```

1. What line did the computer jump over in Program A?

2. What did the computer do after printing HAVE in Program B?

3. What did the computer do after printing DAY in Program B?

Write the RUN for each program.

1.
```
10 PRINT "HOW OLD "
20 GOTO 40
30 PRINT "IS SHE?"
40 PRINT "ARE YOU?"
50 END
```

2.
```
10 PRINT "24 TIMES 6
   EQUALS"
20 GOTO 40
30 PRINT 24/6
40 PRINT 24 * 6
50 END
```

3.
```
10 PRINT "HOW"
20 GOTO 50
30 PRINT "YOU?"
40 GOTO 70
50 PRINT "ARE"
60 GOTO 30
70 END
```

4.
```
10 PRINT "54 DIVIDED
   BY 9"
20 GOTO 50
30 PRINT 54/9
40 GOTO 70
50 PRINT "EQUALS"
60 GOTO 30
70 END
```

5.
```
10 PRINT "TWINKLE
   TWINKLE"
20 GOTO 70
30 PRINT "HOW I"
40 PRINT "WONDER"
50 PRINT "WHERE
   YOU ARE."
60 GOTO 90
70 PRINT "LITTLE
   STAR"
80 GOTO 30
90 END
```

6.
```
10 PRINT "IF YOU
   KNOW"
20 GOTO 70
30 PRINT "ALSO
   KNOW"
40 GOTO 90
50 PRINT "THEN
   YOU"
60 GOTO 30
70 PRINT "9 * 7 = ";
   9 * 7
80 GOTO 50
90 PRINT "7 * 9 = ";
   7 * 9
100 END
```

★ 7. Write a program of your own using GOTO. Give the RUN.

Give the letter for the correct answer.
Which are right angles?

1. a.   **A** figure a
   B figure b
   b.   **C** figures a and b
   D not given

2. c.   **A** figure c
   B figure d
   d.   **C** figures c and d
   D not given

Which figure is congruent to the first?

3.   **A**
   B
   C
   D not given

4.   **A**
   B
   C
   D not given

Which is a line of symmetry?

5. **A** ⊦------⊣ **B**
   C **D** not given

6. **A**   **B**
   C   **D** not given

7. 20)‾35‾   **A** 1 R15 **B** 1 R5
   C 1 R51 **D** not given

8. 40)‾77‾   **A** 1 R7 **B** 1 R37
   C 1 R40 **D** not given

9. 23)‾88‾   **A** 3 R18 **B** 3 R9
   C 3 R19 **D** not given

10. 43)‾250‾   **A** 5 R35 **B** 6 R2
    C 5 R45 **D** not given

11. 36)‾290‾   **A** 8 R20 **B** 8 R2
    C 8 R52 **D** not given

12. 23)‾$2.07‾   **A** $0.90 **B** $0.09
    C $9.00 **D** not given

13. Tammy's soccer team practices for 45 minutes each time they meet. The team practiced 405 minutes in April. How many times did they meet?
    A 9   **B** 7
    C 6   **D** not given

14. A package of 32 rubber bands costs $2.24. How much is it for each rubber band?
    A $2.56   **B** $71.68
    C $0.07   **D** not given

MEASUREMENT: Customary Units

The clouds were low and dark. The wind was growing stronger. The temperature had dropped. So had the air pressure. Sean and Brian had made weather instruments. They used them to take exact readings. Then they made a decision. They guessed it would snow in the next hour. They were right. It soon began to snow. The next day the snowfall stopped. They used a measuring stick to find how deep the snow was. It came up to about their knees. The two boys ran home. They met again at the hill. This time they had their sleds.

Customary Units for Length

The pictures help you think about **customary** units for measuring length.

This is an **inch** (in.) unit.

1 **foot** (ft) = 12 inches.

1 **yard** (yd) = 36 inches or 3 feet.

1 **mile** (mi) = 1,760 yards or 5,280 feet.

A train with 120 boxcars is about 1 mile long.

Warm Up Which unit would you use?
Write **inches, feet, yards,** or **miles.**

1. The pencil is 7 __?__ long.

2. It is 128 __?__ to Detroit.

3. The football field is 100 __?__ long.

4. Tommy is 4 __?__ tall.

5. The ceiling is 3 __?__ high.

6. The teacher's desk is 27 __?__ high.

7. It is 3 __?__ across the lake.

8. The door is 7 __?__ high.

Which unit would you use?
Write inches, feet, yards, or miles.

1. The basketball player is 6 _?_ tall.

2. Mr. Calvo's car is about 2 _?_ long.

3. The classroom is 5 _?_ wide.

4. The jet is flying 6 _?_ high.

5. Teri's foot is 8 _?_ long.

6. Ryan can reach 8 _?_ high.

7. Ms. Soto drove 48 _?_ .

8. It is 275 _?_ to Dallas.

Choose the better estimate.

9. How wide is the desk?
   A 1 foot   **B** 1 yard

10. How long is the street?
    A 4 yards   **B** 4 miles

11. How tall is the school?
    A 16 inches   **B** 16 feet

12. How wide is the river?
    A 120 yards   **B** 120 miles

Copy and complete the tables.

13.
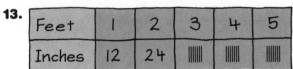

Feet	1	2	3	4	5
Inches	12	24	‖‖‖	‖‖‖	‖‖‖

14.
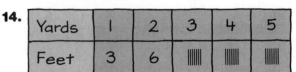

Yards	1	2	3	4	5
Feet	3	6	‖‖‖	‖‖‖	‖‖‖

THINK

Estimation

If the blue rod is 8 units long,

then the red rod is how many units long?

MATH

Using Fractions in Measurement

Robin and Sharon are building a tree house. They need nails that have different lengths. They are also using boards of many different sizes.

Examples

The length of this nail is $2\frac{1}{4}$ inches.

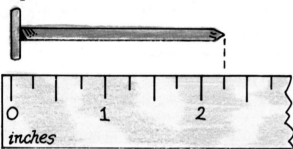

This board is $1\frac{3}{4}$ inches wide.

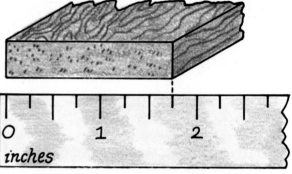

The length of this nail is $2\frac{1}{2}$ inches to the nearest quarter inch.

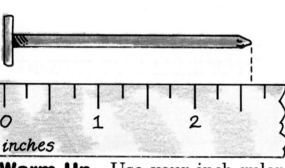

This board is 2 inches wide to the nearest quarter inch.

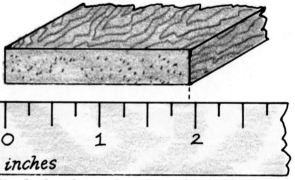

Warm Up Use your inch ruler. Find the length of each nail.

1.

2.

Find the width of each board to the nearest quarter inch.

3.

4.

370

Find the length or width.

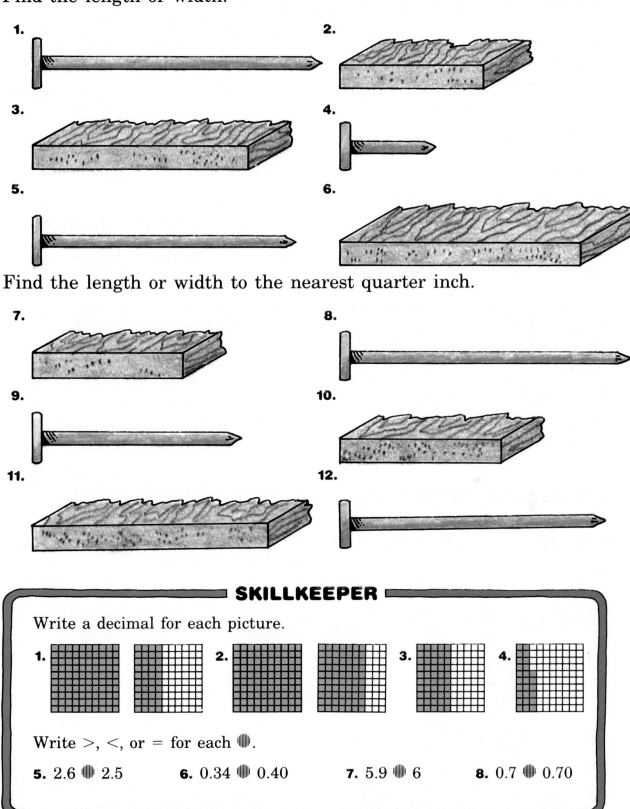

1.

2.

3.

4.

5.

6.

Find the length or width to the nearest quarter inch.

7.

8.

9.

10.

11.

12.

Perimeter

Elisa framed her butterfly collection with yarn. How much yarn did she use?

Since we want the total distance around, we add the lengths of the sides.

$$\begin{array}{r} 27 \\ 12 \\ 27 \\ + 12 \\ \hline 78 \end{array}$$ Elisa used 78 inches of yarn.

The **distance around** a figure is the **perimeter** of the figure.

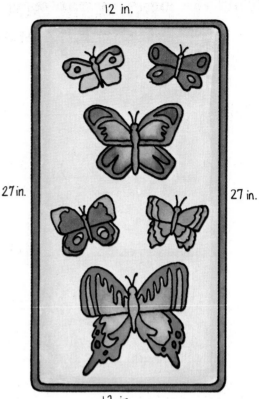

12 in.

27 in.   27 in.

12 in.

Find the perimeter of each figure.

1.

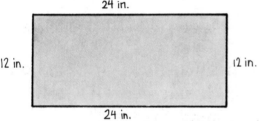
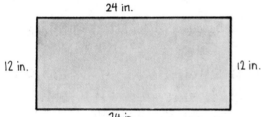

24 in.

12 in.   12 in.

24 in.

2.

56 ft

41 ft   41 ft

56 ft

3.

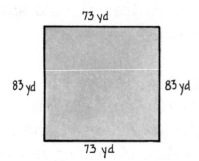

73 yd

83 yd   83 yd

73 yd

4.

18 in.   16 in.

20 in.

PROBLEM SOLVING
Length and Perimeter

Solve.

1. Joe ran around the edge of the field. How far did he run?

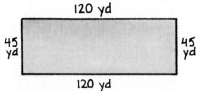

120 yd

45 yd   45 yd

120 yd

2. Jan ran 880 yd. How much farther must she run to run a mile? (1 mile = 1,760 yd)

3. The distance around the track is 440 yd. Leon ran around the track 3 times. How far did he run?

4. How far do baseball players run when they run all the way around the diamond?

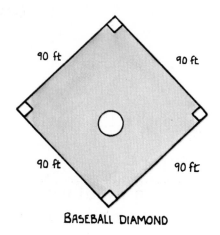

90 ft   90 ft

90 ft   90 ft

BASEBALL DIAMOND

5. Joy hiked 54 mi in 3 days. If she walked the same number of miles each day, how far did she hike each day?

6. How far is it from Hillview to Center to Upton to Hillview?

UPTON

62 mi

38 mi

HILLVIEW   40 mi   CENTER

7. A square field is 87 yd on each side. How far is it around the field?

8. Marta walked $5\frac{1}{4}$ mi in the morning and $6\frac{1}{2}$ mi in the afternoon. How far did she walk that day?

9. *Try This* A rectangle has a perimeter of 28 in. The length is 4 in. more than the width. How long is the rectangle?

Cups, Pints, Quarts, and Gallons

The milk comes in half-pint containers at Jim's school. Each half pint is 1 **cup**. Jim drinks 5 containers each week. Is that more or less than a quart?

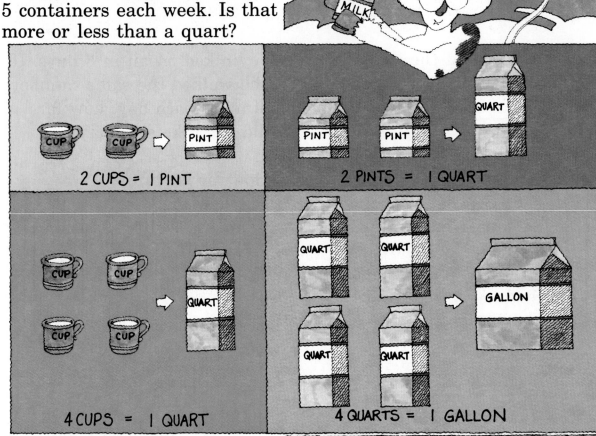

2 CUPS = 1 PINT

2 PINTS = 1 QUART

4 CUPS = 1 QUART

4 QUARTS = 1 GALLON

Since 4 cups equal 1 quart, 5 cups is more than a quart.

Give the missing numbers.

1. 1 pint = __?__ cups.

2. 2 pints = __?__ cups.

3. 1 quart = __?__ cups.

4. 2 quarts = __?__ cups.

5. 1 gallon = __?__ quarts.

6. 5 gallons = __?__ quarts.

Choose the better estimate.

7. Water in a tub
   A 8 pints   B 8 gallons

8. Gasoline in a full car tank
   A 15 quarts   B 15 gallons

PROBLEM SOLVING
Capacity

Solve.

1. The cook made 8 quarts of fruit punch for a party. How many cups is this?

2. The cook made 5 gallons of vegetable soup. How many quarts is this?

3. Half-pint containers of milk come in boxes of 24. How many quarts of milk are in a box? (1 half pint = 1 cup)

4. One day 225 containers of milk were used. The next day only 196 containers were used. How many more containers were used the first day?

5. How many quarts of milk were used on the day 196 containers were used? (4 containers = 1 quart)

6. The cook used 2 gallons of milk to make soup. How many pints of milk is this?

7. There are 16 cups in a gallon. How many cups of soup can a cook get from 25 gallons?

8. A recipe for fruit punch calls for 7 cups of pineapple juice and 9 cups of orange juice. How many cups of juice would it take to make 5 recipes?

9. The school ordered 15 boxes of milk. In each box there were 24 containers. On the first day 295 containers were used. How many were left?

10. *Try This* The cook uses 5 cups of whole-wheat flour for each 2 cups of white flour. How many cups of white flour are needed to go with 35 cups of whole-wheat flour? Complete the table.

Whole-wheat flour	5	10	15
White flour	2	4	6

Weight: Ounces, Pounds, and Tons

The **ounce** (oz), **pound** (lb), and **ton** (T) are customary units of weight.

5 nickels
about 1 ounce

pint of milk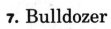
about 1 pound

compact car
about 1 ton

16 ounces = 1 pound   2,000 pounds = 1 ton

Write **ounces, pounds,** or **tons** for each weight.

1. Hand calculator

10 __?__

2. Roasting chicken

$3\frac{1}{2}$ __?__

3. Elephant

3 __?__

4. Typewriter

8 __?__

5. Truck

4 __?__

6. Small box of paper clips

2 __?__

7. Bulldozer

12 __?__

8. Portable TV

20 __?__

9. Orange

8 __?__

Temperature

The customary unit for measuring temperature is the **degree Fahrenheit** (°F). The thermometer shows some common temperatures.

Choose the best estimate.

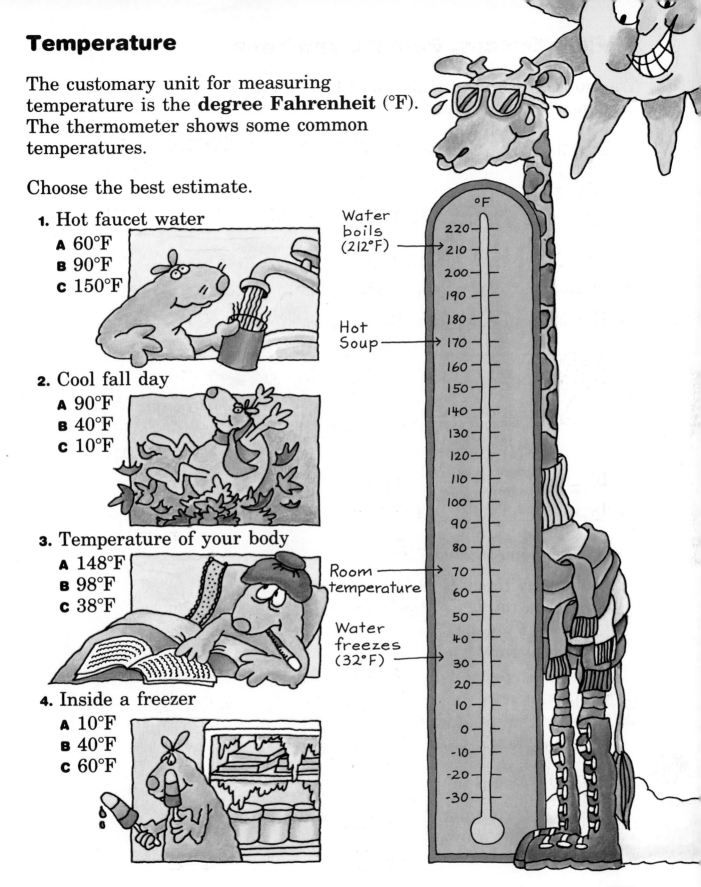

1. Hot faucet water
   - A 60°F
   - B 90°F
   - c 150°F

2. Cool fall day
   - A 90°F
   - B 40°F
   - c 10°F

3. Temperature of your body
   - A 148°F
   - B 98°F
   - c 38°F

4. Inside a freezer
   - A 10°F
   - B 40°F
   - c 60°F

Water boils (212°F)

Hot Soup

Room temperature

Water freezes (32°F)

°F
220
210
200
190
180
170
160
150
140
130
120
110
100
90
80
70
60
50
40
30
20
10
0
-10
-20
-30

377

APPLIED PROBLEM SOLVING

You want to plant a small vegetable garden. Your garden area is 9 feet by 12 feet. You have decided to plant tomatoes, summer squash, and green peppers. How many of each plant should you buy?

ROWS

12 FEET

9 FEET

QUESTION
DATA
PLAN
ANSWER
CHECK

Some Things to Consider

- You want 1 or more rows of each plant.
- You don't want to plant closer than 1 foot from the edge.
- You want only one row of squash.
- You don't want more than 2 rows of peppers.
- Amount of space needed between plants: tomatoes—2 to 3 ft, squash—2 to 3 ft, peppers—1 ft

Some Questions to Answer

1. How many tomato plants should you plant in a row?
2. How many squash plants should you plant in a row?
3. How many pepper plants should you plant in a row?
4. What is the greatest number of peppers you will plant?

What is Your Decision

How many of each plant will you buy? Draw a picture to show how you are planning your garden.

Which unit would you use? Write inches, feet, yards, or miles.

1. The baby was 18 __?__ long.

2. Mr. White drove 125 __?__ before stopping.

3. The basketball player was 2 __?__ tall.

4. Jo jumped across a creek that was 10 __?__ wide.

Find the length of each nail to the nearest quarter inch.

5.

6.

Find the perimeter of each figure.

7.
126 ft
42 ft   42 ft
126 ft

8.
14 yd
14 yd   14 yd
14 yd

Give the missing number.

9. 1 quart = __?__ cups

10. 1 gallon = __?__ quarts

11. 1 pint = __?__ cups

12. 1 quart = __?__ pints

Write ounces, pounds, or tons for each weight.

13. pickup truck

2 __?__

14. wrist watch

$1\frac{1}{2}$ __?__

15. 3 books

6 __?__

Choose the best estimate.

16. Hot summer day
A 90°F   **B** 10°F   **C** 30°F

17. Ice water
A 60°F   **B** 33°F   **C** 0°F

Solve.

18. A square field is 175 ft on each side. How far is it around the field?

19. The tank holds 72 gallons of water. How many quarts is this? 1 gallon = 4 quarts.

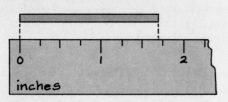

$1\frac{1}{2}$ inches to the nearest half inch.
$1\frac{3}{4}$ inch to the nearest quarter inch.

Find the length to the nearest half inch.

1.

2.

to the nearest quarter inch.

3.

4.

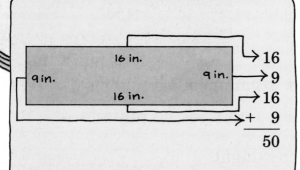

The perimeter of the rectangle is 50 inches.

Find the perimeter.

5.
14 yd
8 yd   8 yd
14 yd

6.
25 ft
15 ft
20 ft

7.
25 in.
25 in.   25 in.
25 in.

8.
15 yd
15 yd
17 yd
9 yd

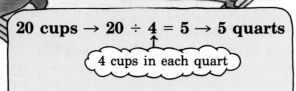

20 cups → 20 ÷ 4 = 5 → 5 quarts

4 cups in each quart

4 quarts → 4 × 2 = 8 → 8 pints

2 pints in each quart

Find the missing numbers.

9. 12 cups = __?__ quarts

10. 2 quarts = __?__ pints

11. 6 gallons = __?__ quarts

12. 16 quarts = __?__ gallons

Estimating Area

The example below shows how you can count squares and parts of squares to **estimate** area.

Estimate the area of this circle.

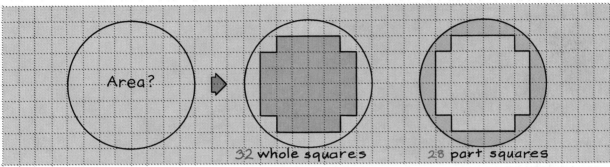

Estimate that the part squares **average** $\frac{1}{2}$ unit per square.

$\frac{1}{2}$ of 28 = 14

Area of the red region $\longrightarrow$ 32 square units

Estimated area of the blue region $\longrightarrow$ 14 square units

Estimated area of the circle $\longrightarrow$ 46 square units

Estimate the area of each region.

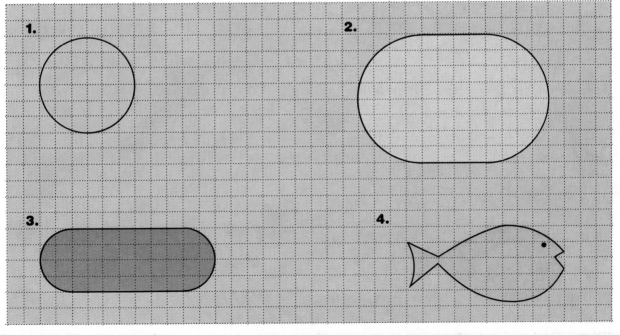

1.

2.

3.

4.

CUMULATIVE REVIEW

Give the letter for the correct answer.

Give the decimal shown.

1.
   - **A** 27.0 **B** 2.3
   - **C** 2.7   **D** not given

2.
   - **A** 4.4
   - **B** 0.44
   - **C** 4.04
   - **D** not given

Which amount is correct?

3. 2 dollars and 26 pennies
   - **A** $2.26 **B** $2.62
   - **C** $200.26 **D** not given

4. 1 dollar, 0 dimes, and 4 pennies
   - **A** $1.40 **B** $14.00
   - **C** $1.04 **D** not given

Which answer is correct?

5. 5.24 ▦ 5.26
   - **A** >   **B** <
   - **C** =   **D** not given

6. 32.7 ▦ 32.70
   - **A** >   **B** <
   - **C** =   **D** not given

7. 3.85   **A** 8.61 **C** 7.61
   + 4.76   **B** 8.51 **D** not given

What is the best unit?

8. The pencil is 7 __?__ long.
   - **A** inches **B** yards
   - **C** feet   **D** not given

9. The boy is 4 __?__ tall.
   - **A** inches **B** yards
   - **C** miles **D** not given

10. It is 275 __?__ to Dallas
   - **A** inches **B** yards
   - **C** miles **D** not given

11. Give the perimeter.

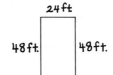

   - **A** 72 ft
   - **B** 96 ft
   - **C** 144 ft
   - **D** not given

12. 1 quart is equal to
   - **A** 4 cups   **B** 4 pints
   - **C** 4 gallons **D** not given

13. A square field is 54 yards on each side. How far is it around the field?
   - **A** 108 yards **B** 216 yards
   - **C** 206 yards **D** not given

14. A tank holds 20 gallons of water. How many quarts is this? (1 gallon = 4 quarts)
   - **A** 5 quarts   **B** 24 quarts
   - **C** 80 quarts **D** not given

Appendix

Canning and Freezing Cookbook

STANDARD CAN SIZES

CAN	SIZE	CAN	SIZE
No. 1	0.30 L	No. 2½	0.83 L
No. 300	0.41 L	No. 3	0.95 L
No. 1 tall	0.47 L	No. 5	1.74 L
No. 2	0.59 L	No. 10	3.08 L
No. 3 squat	0.65 L		

Recipe for Finger Paint

Materials:

125 mL cornstarch
250 mL cold water
1 envelope unflavored gelatin
500 mL boiling water
Food coloring

Directions:

1. Mix cornstarch with 185 mL cold water in a saucepan.
2. Soak gelatin in 65 mL cold water in a bowl.
3. Stir the boiling water into the cornstarch mixture. Cook over medium heat. Bring to boil. Mixture should be clear.
4. Remove from heat. Stir in the gelatin mixture.
5. Cool. Put small amounts of mixture into various containers. Each container will be a different color. Stir in enough drops of food coloring into each jar until desired color is reached.

PYRAMIDS
Perimeters of Square Bases and Heights

Giza

3rd Pyramid
Perimeter: 436 m
Height: 66 m

Great Pyramid
Perimeter: 920 m
Height: 137 m

2nd Pyramid
Perimeter: 864 m
Height: 144 m

North Stone Pyramid
Perimeter: 880 m
Height: 99 m

Dashur

South Stone Pyramid
Perimeter: 760 m
Height: 101 m

Nile

Pyramid of Senwosret I
Perimeter: 420 m
Height: 61 m

Pyramid of Maidum
Perimeter: 576 m
Height: 92 m

Maidum

TYPES OF RAINFALL

TYPE	AMOUNT
Trace	Unmeasurable
Light rain	About $\frac{1}{10}$ inch per hour
Moderate rain	About $\frac{3}{10}$ inch per hour
Heavy rain	Greater than $\frac{3}{10}$ inch per hour

PARK FOLDER

Volcanoes

Name	State	Height
Mt. Baker	WA	3,285 m
Glacier Peak	WA	3,213 m
Mt. Rainier	WA	4,392 m
Mt. Adams	WA	3,751 m
Mt. St. Helens	WA	2,547 m
Mt. Hood	OR	3,424 m
Mt. Jefferson	OR	3,199 m
Crater Lake	OR	2,486 m
Mt. Shasta	CA	4,317 m
Lassen Peak	CA	3,187 m
Mauna Loa	HI	4,169 m
Mt. Katmai	AK	2,047 m

Great Trees of the American Forest

Name	Maximum Height	Maximum Diameter
Douglas fir	76 m	244 cm
Loblolly pine	30 m	91 cm
Slash pine	30 m	91 cm
Shortleaf pine	30 m	91 cm
Longleaf pine	37 m	76 cm
Yellow poplar	37 m	182 cm
Sugar maple	30 m	121 cm
White oak	30 m	121 cm

Travelers' Guide to Average Annual Rainfall

City	Rainfall
Atlanta, GA	123 cm
Boston, MA	108 cm
Chicago, IL	87 cm
Cincinatti, OH	102 cm
Cleveland, OH	89 cm
Denver, CO	39 cm
Detroit, MI	79 cm
Honolulu, HI	58 cm
Houston, TX	122 cm
Juneau, AK	139 cm
Miami, FL	152 cm
New York, NY	106 cm
St. Louis, MO	91 cm
San Francisco, CA	50 cm
Seattle, WA	99 cm
Washington, DC	99 cm

—Registry of Ships—

FERRYBOATS

Name	Location	Number of Cars	Length of Boat
Elwha	Seattle, WA	162	116 m
Illahee	Seattle, WA	75	78 m
Tillikum	Seattle, WA	100	94 m
Kittitas	Seattle, WA	100	100 m
Columbia	Vancouver, B.C.	180	127 m
Malastina	Vancouver, B.C.	132	124 m
Taku	Vancouver, B.C.	105	107 m

OCEANS OF THE WORLD

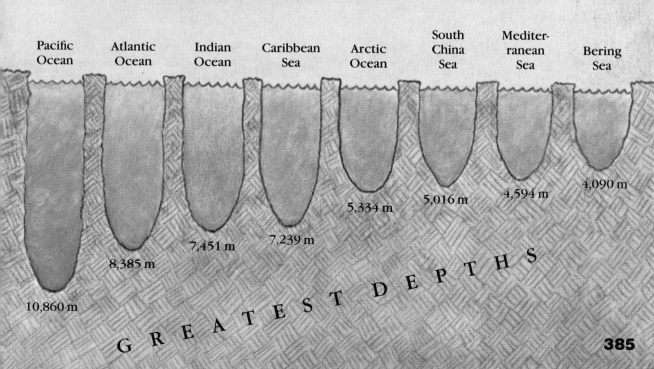

Pacific Ocean	Atlantic Ocean	Indian Ocean	Caribbean Sea	Arctic Ocean	South China Sea	Mediterranean Sea	Bering Sea
10,860 m	8,385 m	7,451 m	7,239 m	5,334 m	5,016 m	4,594 m	4,090 m

GREATEST DEPTHS

· ARTHUR'S ANIMAL ALMANAC ·

Record Ages of Animals

Name	Age
Elephant	61 years
Horse	54 years
Hippopotamus	41 years
Rhinoceros	40 years
Bear	34 years
Monkey	25 years
Cat	23 years
Dog	22 years

Animal Heartbeats in 1 Minute

Animal	Heartbeat
Bat	750
Cat	120
Dog	90
Elephant	33
Goat	90
Hamster	450
Lion	44
Monkey	192
Mouse	534
Rat	328
Sheep	75
Skunk	166
Squirrel	249

SPORTS PAGE

1980 WINTER OLYMPICS SPEED SKATING WOMEN'S EVENTS

500-METER RACE

	Seconds*
1. Karin Enke, East Germany	
2. Leah Mueller, U.S.A.	42
3. Natalia Petruseva, U.S.S.R.	42
	43

1,000-METER RACE

1. Natalia Petruseva, U.S.S.R.	
2. Leah Mueller, U.S.A.	84
3. Silvia Albrecht, East Germany	86
	87

1,500-METER RACE

1. Annie Borckink, Netherlands	
2. Ria Visser, Netherlands	131
3. Sabine Becker, East Germany	133
	133

3,000-METER RACE

1. Bjoerg Eva Jensen, Norway	
2. Sabine Becker, East Germany	272
3. Beth Heiden, U.S.A.	273
	274

*Race time to nearest second

AIRPLANE SEATING CAPACITY

AIRPLANE	NUMBER OF PERSONS
DC-10	380
L-1011	400
727	189
747	550
757	237
767	289

MAJOR WORLD AIRPORTS

NAME	NUMBER OF PASSENGERS (IN A RECENT YEAR)
Chicago O'Hare	44,238,000
Atlanta International	29,977,000
Los Angeles International	28,361,000
London Heathrow	23,775,000
Tokyo Haneda	23,190,000
JFK, New York	22,545,000
San Francisco International	20,249,000
Dallas-Ft. Worth	17,318,000
Denver Stapleton	15,281,000
La Guardia, New York	15,087,000

More Practice

Set A   For use after page 3

Add.

1. $\begin{array}{r} 5 \\ +\ 6 \\ \hline 11 \end{array}$	2. $\begin{array}{r} 7 \\ +\ 4 \\ \hline 11 \end{array}$	3. $\begin{array}{r} 4 \\ +\ 4 \\ \hline 8 \end{array}$	4. $\begin{array}{r} 0 \\ +\ 8 \\ \hline 0 \end{array}$	5. $\begin{array}{r} 9 \\ +\ 1 \\ \hline 10 \end{array}$	6. $\begin{array}{r} 3 \\ +\ 5 \\ \hline 8 \end{array}$	7. $\begin{array}{r} 5 \\ +\ 0 \\ \hline 5 \end{array}$
8. $\begin{array}{r} 6 \\ +\ 6 \\ \hline 12 \end{array}$	9. $\begin{array}{r} 8 \\ +\ 9 \\ \hline 17 \end{array}$	10. $\begin{array}{r} 4 \\ +\ 6 \\ \hline 10 \end{array}$	11. $\begin{array}{r} 3 \\ +\ 9 \\ \hline 12 \end{array}$	12. $\begin{array}{r} 1 \\ +\ 6 \\ \hline 7 \end{array}$	13. $\begin{array}{r} 7 \\ +\ 8 \\ \hline 15 \end{array}$	14. $\begin{array}{r} 6 \\ +\ 7 \\ \hline 15 \end{array}$
15. $\begin{array}{r} 7 \\ +\ 7 \\ \hline 14 \end{array}$	16. $\begin{array}{r} 3 \\ +\ 0 \\ \hline 3 \end{array}$	17. $\begin{array}{r} 7 \\ +\ 9 \\ \hline 16 \end{array}$	18. $\begin{array}{r} 3 \\ +\ 2 \\ \hline 5 \end{array}$	19. $\begin{array}{r} 4 \\ +\ 3 \\ \hline 7 \end{array}$	20. $\begin{array}{r} 8 \\ +\ 8 \\ \hline 16 \end{array}$	21. $\begin{array}{r} 2 \\ +\ 4 \\ \hline 6 \end{array}$
22. $\begin{array}{r} 2 \\ +\ 9 \\ \hline 10 \end{array}$	23. $\begin{array}{r} 2 \\ +\ 0 \\ \hline 2 \end{array}$	24. $\begin{array}{r} 8 \\ +\ 6 \\ \hline 14 \end{array}$	25. $\begin{array}{r} 4 \\ +\ 9 \\ \hline 13 \end{array}$	26. $\begin{array}{r} 9 \\ +\ 6 \\ \hline 15 \end{array}$	27. $\begin{array}{r} 3 \\ +\ 8 \\ \hline 10 \end{array}$	28. $\begin{array}{r} 3 \\ +\ 3 \\ \hline 6 \end{array}$
29. $\begin{array}{r} 7 \\ +\ 8 \\ \hline 15 \end{array}$	30. $\begin{array}{r} 0 \\ +\ 9 \\ \hline 9 \end{array}$	31. $\begin{array}{r} 7 \\ +\ 7 \\ \hline 14 \end{array}$	32. $\begin{array}{r} 9 \\ +\ 4 \\ \hline 13 \end{array}$	33. $\begin{array}{r} 7 \\ +\ 9 \\ \hline 16 \end{array}$	34. $\begin{array}{r} 1 \\ +\ 8 \\ \hline 9 \end{array}$	35. $\begin{array}{r} 4 \\ +\ 5 \\ \hline 9 \end{array}$

Set B   For use after page 5

Subtract.

1. $\begin{array}{r} 15 \\ -\ 7 \\ \hline 6 \end{array}$	2. $\begin{array}{r} 11 \\ -\ 8 \\ \hline 3 \end{array}$	3. $\begin{array}{r} 5 \\ -\ 5 \\ \hline 0 \end{array}$	4. $\begin{array}{r} 8 \\ -\ 6 \\ \hline 3 \end{array}$	5. $\begin{array}{r} 18 \\ -\ 9 \\ \hline 2 \end{array}$	6. $\begin{array}{r} 7 \\ -\ 3 \\ \hline 4 \end{array}$	7. $\begin{array}{r} 9 \\ -\ 3 \\ \hline 6 \end{array}$
8. $\begin{array}{r} 17 \\ -\ 8 \\ \hline 1 \end{array}$	9. $\begin{array}{r} 15 \\ -\ 9 \\ \hline 2 \end{array}$	10. $\begin{array}{r} 9 \\ -\ 5 \\ \hline 6 \end{array}$	11. $\begin{array}{r} 12 \\ -\ 7 \\ \hline 5 \end{array}$	12. $\begin{array}{r} 7 \\ -\ 0 \\ \hline 7 \end{array}$	13. $\begin{array}{r} 10 \\ -\ 7 \\ \hline 3 \end{array}$	14. $\begin{array}{r} 13 \\ -\ 4 \\ \hline 9 \end{array}$
15. $\begin{array}{r} 16 \\ -\ 8 \\ \hline 4 \end{array}$	16. $\begin{array}{r} 13 \\ -\ 5 \\ \hline 8 \end{array}$	17. $\begin{array}{r} 11 \\ -\ 7 \\ \hline 4 \end{array}$	18. $\begin{array}{r} 14 \\ -\ 9 \\ \hline 3 \end{array}$	19. $\begin{array}{r} 8 \\ -\ 5 \\ \hline 3 \end{array}$	20. $\begin{array}{r} 12 \\ -\ 8 \\ \hline 3 \end{array}$	21. $\begin{array}{r} 14 \\ -\ 6 \\ \hline 5 \end{array}$
22. $\begin{array}{r} 11 \\ -\ 10 \\ \hline 1 \end{array}$	23. $\begin{array}{r} 7 \\ -\ 2 \\ \hline 5 \end{array}$	24. $\begin{array}{r} 10 \\ -\ 6 \\ \hline 3 \end{array}$	25. $\begin{array}{r} 8 \\ -\ 8 \\ \hline 0 \end{array}$	26. $\begin{array}{r} 13 \\ -\ 8 \\ \hline 3 \end{array}$	27. $\begin{array}{r} 14 \\ -\ 7 \\ \hline 7 \end{array}$	28. $\begin{array}{r} 6 \\ -\ 5 \\ \hline 1 \end{array}$

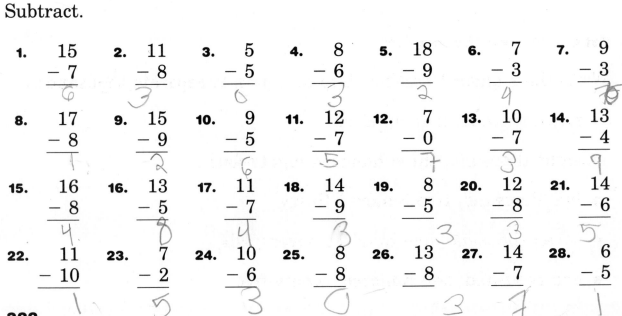

Set A   For use after page 13

Add.

1. 5	**2.** 7	**3.** 4	**4.** 3	**5.** 7	**6.** 1	**7.** 4
2	1	5	3	3	9	4
+ 6	+ 4	+ 5	+ 7	+ 2	+ 1	+ 4

8. 5	**9.** 4	**10.** 2	**11.** 1	**12.** 2	**13.** 6	**14.** 4
4	6	6	5	3	4	2
+ 0	+ 3	+ 2	+ 3	+ 6	+ 6	+ 1

Set B   For use after page 25

Write the standard number.

1. five hundred eighty nine

2. one hundred seventy

3. three hundred four

4. six hundred thirty-six

5. seven hundred forty

6. four hundred seventy-one

7. two hundred sixty

8. nine hundred sixty-four

Set C   For use after page 27

Write the standard number. Use a comma to separate thousands.

1. five thousand, four hundred

2. eight thousand, three hundred eighty-four

3. two thousand, five hundred thirty

4. seven thousand, one hundred seventy-six

5. one thousand, two hundred twenty-five

Set A   For use after page 29

Write > or < for each ▥ .

1.   73 ▥ 64

2.   46 ▥ 48

3.   676 ▥ 667

4.   538 ▥ 358

5.   312 ▥ 318

6. 2,000 ▥ 1,999

7. 5,267 ▥ 5,270

8. 8,363 ▥ 8,636

9. 3,450 ▥ 3,440

Set B   For use after page 31

Round to the nearest ten.

1. 28 → ▥

2. 83 → ▥

3. 65 → ▥

4. 34 → ▥

5. 71 → ▥

6. 46 → ▥

7. 17 → ▥

8. 52 → ▥

Round to the nearest hundred.

1. 285

2. 3,796

3. 733

4. 5,806

5. 461

6. 6,055

7. 866

8. 150

Set C   For use after page 33

Round to the nearest thousand.

1. 4,499

2. 8,207

3. 2,600

4. 5,653

5. 6,233

6. 7,492

7. 9,010

8. 6,874

Round to the nearest dollar.

1. $1.79

2. $68.16

3. $13.49

4. $72.28

5. $2.55

6. $64.95

7. $3.18

8. $87.32

Write the standard number. Use a comma to separate thousands.

1. thirty-six thousand

2. five hundred seventy-nine thousand

3. two hundred eight thousand, four hundred thirteen

4. nine hundred three thousand, two hundred twenty

5. three hundred one thousand, four hundred

Set B   **For use after page 36**

Write > or < for each ▨ .

1. 37,530 ▨ 36,351   **2.** 21,568 ▨ 21,658   **3.** 89,709 ▨ 100,000

4. 413,268 ▨ 413,260   **5.** 75,200 ▨ 85,200   **6.** 586,490 ▨ 86,490

7. 15,600 ▨ 16,500   **8.** 610,000 ▨ 609,000   **9.** 55,783 ▨ 55,800

Set C   **For use after page 39**

Write the standard number.

1. eight million, seven hundred twelve thousand

2. forty-nine million

3. five hundred sixty-eight million, three hundred sixty-five thousand

4. seven hundred million, five hundred thousand

5. sixty-three million

Find the sums.

1. 38 + 9	2. 35 + 44	3. 342 + 80	4. 36 + 53	5. 475 + 92	6. 747 + 14
7. 810 + 528	8. 661 + 70	9. 52 + 63	10. 8 + 46	11. 920 + 654	12. 95 + 51
13. 805 + 621	14. 628 + 54	15. 418 + 750	16. 39 + 39	17. 632 + 241	18. 266 + 451
19. 22 + 48	20. 265 + 205	21. 605 + 821	22. 26 + 57	23. 123 + 94	24. 200 + 847

Find the sums.

1. 715 + 916	2. 685 + 77	3. 263 + 98	4. 702 + 859	5. 457 + 382	6. 375 + 829
7. 316 + 607	8. 67 + 285	9. 447 + 285	10. 918 + 836	11. 607 + 798	12. 288 + 554
13. 307 + 21	14. 18 + 16	15. 279 + 111	16. 81 + 47	17. 714 + 600	18. 369 + 41
19. $3.26 + 2.97	20. $9.05 + 0.36	21. $2.17 + 6.84	22. $6.75 + 9.50	23. $3.88 + 2.55	24. $2.82 + 8.54
25. $1.96 + 2.37	26. $5.25 + 3.83	27. $4.59 + 2.45	28. $8.20 + 0.98	29. $7.39 + 3.26	30. $5.56 + 8.67

Set A   For use after page 55

Find the sums.

1.	2,964 + 5,682	**2.**	6,587 + 2,744	**3.**	4,532 + 1,607	**4.**	16,518 + 8,385	**5.**	3,358 + 3,692
6.	55,295 + 64,968	**7.**	64,615 + 34,607	**8.**	36,395 + 44,120	**9.**	3,643 + 5,818	**10.**	36,385 + 24,120
11.	$15.85 + 8.65	**12.**	$21.80 + 23.93	**13.**	$47.36 + 16.87	**14.**	$58.65 + 27.40	**15.**	$29.52 + 63.75
16.	$58.40 + 3.66	**17.**	$46.15 + 46.07	**18.**	$78.11 + 18.29	**19.**	$18.54 + 6.83	**20.**	$48.12 + 39.68

Set B   For use after page 57

Estimate by rounding to the nearest ten.

1.	75 + 34	**2.**	33 + 59	**3.**	46 + 21	**4.**	56 + 37	**5.**	98 + 43

Estimate by rounding to the nearest hundred or dollar.

6.	242 + 757	**7.**	$5.95 + 1.39	**8.**	618 + 333	**9.**	$8.11 + 2.95

Estimate by rounding to the nearest thousand.

10.	1,684 + 7,450	**11.**	5,258 + 7,500	**12.**	3,277 + 1,584	**13.**	4,623 + 2,418	**14.**	7,681 + 2,154

Add.

1. 16	**2.** 236	**3.** 37	**4.** 6,520	**5.** 335	**6.** 5,625
4	425	26	831	26	2,910
+ 59	+ 237	+ 17	+ 1,272	+ 796	+ 3,335

7. 64	**8.** $3.83	**9.** 746	**10.** 563	**11.** $1.95	**12.** 52
47	5.35	75	87	6.28	43
28	7.68	434	412	1.39	18
+ 35	+ 0.54	+ 8	+ 29	+ .97	+ 77

13. $8.84	**14.** 7,965	**15.** 2,746	**16.** $5.24	**17.** 1,039	**18.** $6.75
3.29	4,208	318	7.12	5,762	2.94
5.92	1,860	7,852	6.18	2,834	.66
+ 1.99	+ 3,222	+ 67	+ 4.70	+ 4,220	+ 2.82

Subtract.

1. 43	**2.** 30	**3.** 81	**4.** 56	**5.** 80	**6.** 77
− 8	− 18	− 36	− 17	− 26	− 25

7. 62	**8.** 50	**9.** $6.24	**10.** 138	**11.** 640	**12.** $3.79
− 48	− 36	− 1.30	− 85	− 326	− 1.45

13. 146	**14.** 629	**15.** 512	**16.** $6.70	**17.** 314	**18.** 327
− 72	− 149	− 190	− 2.34	− 181	− 85

19. 476	**20.** 559	**21.** $3.50	**22.** 859	**23.** 750	**24.** $4.11
− 228	− 167	− 1.24	− 384	− 370	− 2.70

25. 62	**26.** 158	**27.** $3.89	**28.** 473	**29.** 146	**30.** 341
− 24	− 92	− 1.79	− 57	− 72	− 281

Set A   For use after page 65

Find the differences.

1. 227 − 139	2. 244 − 87	3. 365 − 79	4. $6.41 − 3.97	5. 885 − 693	6. 720 − 388
7. 213 − 144	8. 351 − 267	9. $8.13 − 2.28	10. 644 − 356	11. 904 − 578	12. $5.68 − 1.79
13. 851 − 285	14. 513 − 175	15. 439 − 281	16. 518 − 269	17. $3.26 − 1.48	18. 540 − 288
19. 842 − 264	20. $5.36 − 0.78	21. 355 − 196	22. $7.61 − 3.95	23. 533 − 184	24. 866 − 278

Set B   For use after page 69

Find the differences.

1. 904 − 361	2. 701 − 646	3. 203 − 186	4. $4.00 − 1.61	5. 805 − 377	6. 300 − 85
7. 601 − 388	8. 400 − 168	9. $3.07 − 1.48	10. 801 − 44	11. 606 − 57	12. 107 − 78
13. 703 − 58	14. 904 − 718	15. 500 − 239	16. 200 − 97	17. 508 − 329	18. $3.05 − 2.86
19. 100 − 77	20. $7.08 − 3.99	21. 606 − 138	22. 903 − 357	23. 404 − 98	24. 208 − 155
25. 207 − 44	26. 907 − 249	27. $5.08 − 4.09	28. 400 − 231	29. 706 − 29	30. 809 − 679

Set A   For use after page 71

Subtract.

1. 4,430 − 726	**2.** 6,429 − 5,161	**3.** 5,000 − 2,435	**4.** $72.28 − 14.16	**5.** 84,520 − 15,635

6. $32.77 − 14.84	**7.** 2,628 − 879	**8.** 4,036 − 2,154	**9.** $36.64 − 8.36	**10.** 63,560 − 18,684

11. 77,252 − 44,683	**12.** 52,941 − 34,356	**13.** $24.36 − 10.85	**14.** 35,721 − 9,845	**15.** 8,826 − 5,471

16. 94,714 − 6,836	**17.** 49,267 − 25,074	**18.** 19,234 − 11,655	**19.** 89,165 − 22,618	**20.** $92.58 − 50.64

Set B   For use after page 73

Estimate by rounding to the nearest ten.

1. 42 − 33	**2.** 63 − 38	**3.** 84 − 16	**4.** 59 − 24	**5.** 72 − 46

Estimate by rounding to the nearest hundred or dollar.

6. 318 − 186	**7.** 683 − 321	**8.** $8.71 − 2.56	**9.** 442 − 276

Estimate by rounding to the nearest thousand.

10. 6,980 − 2,140	**11.** 5,825 − 2,066	**12.** 3,912 − 1,510	**13.** 7,258 − 4,517	**14.** 8,245 − 2,058

Set A   For use after page 83

Multiply.

1. $\begin{array}{r} 2 \\ \times\,8 \\ \hline \end{array}$
2. $\begin{array}{r} 3 \\ \times\,2 \\ \hline \end{array}$
3. $\begin{array}{r} 2 \\ \times\,5 \\ \hline \end{array}$
4. $\begin{array}{r} 3 \\ \times\,7 \\ \hline \end{array}$
5. $\begin{array}{r} 3 \\ \times\,9 \\ \hline \end{array}$
6. $\begin{array}{r} 2 \\ \times\,6 \\ \hline \end{array}$
7. $\begin{array}{r} 2 \\ \times\,7 \\ \hline \end{array}$

8. $\begin{array}{r} 3 \\ \times\,5 \\ \hline \end{array}$
9. $\begin{array}{r} 3 \\ \times\,7 \\ \hline \end{array}$
10. $\begin{array}{r} 2 \\ \times\,2 \\ \hline \end{array}$
11. $\begin{array}{r} 3 \\ \times\,8 \\ \hline \end{array}$
12. $\begin{array}{r} 2 \\ \times\,1 \\ \hline \end{array}$
13. $\begin{array}{r} 3 \\ \times\,3 \\ \hline \end{array}$
14. $\begin{array}{r} 3 \\ \times\,4 \\ \hline \end{array}$

Set B   For use after page 85

Multiply.

1. $\begin{array}{r} 4 \\ \times\,8 \\ \hline \end{array}$
2. $\begin{array}{r} 5 \\ \times\,8 \\ \hline \end{array}$
3. $\begin{array}{r} 5 \\ \times\,1 \\ \hline \end{array}$
4. $\begin{array}{r} 4 \\ \times\,6 \\ \hline \end{array}$
5. $\begin{array}{r} 5 \\ \times\,5 \\ \hline \end{array}$
6. $\begin{array}{r} 4 \\ \times\,5 \\ \hline \end{array}$
7. $\begin{array}{r} 5 \\ \times\,6 \\ \hline \end{array}$

8. $\begin{array}{r} 4 \\ \times\,7 \\ \hline \end{array}$
9. $\begin{array}{r} 5 \\ \times\,2 \\ \hline \end{array}$
10. $\begin{array}{r} 4 \\ \times\,9 \\ \hline \end{array}$
11. $\begin{array}{r} 5 \\ \times\,3 \\ \hline \end{array}$
12. $\begin{array}{r} 4 \\ \times\,2 \\ \hline \end{array}$
13. $\begin{array}{r} 4 \\ \times\,4 \\ \hline \end{array}$
14. $\begin{array}{r} 5 \\ \times\,9 \\ \hline \end{array}$

15. $\begin{array}{r} 4 \\ \times\,1 \\ \hline \end{array}$
16. $\begin{array}{r} 4 \\ \times\,0 \\ \hline \end{array}$
17. $\begin{array}{r} 5 \\ \times\,4 \\ \hline \end{array}$
18. $\begin{array}{r} 5 \\ \times\,7 \\ \hline \end{array}$
19. $\begin{array}{r} 1 \\ \times\,5 \\ \hline \end{array}$
20. $\begin{array}{r} 4 \\ \times\,3 \\ \hline \end{array}$
21. $\begin{array}{r} 5 \\ \times\,0 \\ \hline \end{array}$

Set C   For use after page 91

Multiply.

1. $\begin{array}{r} 6 \\ \times\,9 \\ \hline \end{array}$
2. $\begin{array}{r} 7 \\ \times\,8 \\ \hline \end{array}$
3. $\begin{array}{r} 6 \\ \times\,0 \\ \hline \end{array}$
4. $\begin{array}{r} 7 \\ \times\,4 \\ \hline \end{array}$
5. $\begin{array}{r} 6 \\ \times\,4 \\ \hline \end{array}$
6. $\begin{array}{r} 7 \\ \times\,5 \\ \hline \end{array}$
7. $\begin{array}{r} 7 \\ \times\,2 \\ \hline \end{array}$

8. $\begin{array}{r} 7 \\ \times\,7 \\ \hline \end{array}$
9. $\begin{array}{r} 6 \\ \times\,2 \\ \hline \end{array}$
10. $\begin{array}{r} 7 \\ \times\,1 \\ \hline \end{array}$
11. $\begin{array}{r} 6 \\ \times\,6 \\ \hline \end{array}$
12. $\begin{array}{r} 6 \\ \times\,3 \\ \hline \end{array}$
13. $\begin{array}{r} 6 \\ \times\,1 \\ \hline \end{array}$
14. $\begin{array}{r} 7 \\ \times\,0 \\ \hline \end{array}$

15. $\begin{array}{r} 5 \\ \times\,6 \\ \hline \end{array}$
16. $\begin{array}{r} 3 \\ \times\,7 \\ \hline \end{array}$
17. $\begin{array}{r} 8 \\ \times\,6 \\ \hline \end{array}$
18. $\begin{array}{r} 4 \\ \times\,7 \\ \hline \end{array}$
19. $\begin{array}{r} 4 \\ \times\,6 \\ \hline \end{array}$
20. $\begin{array}{r} 5 \\ \times\,7 \\ \hline \end{array}$
21. $\begin{array}{r} 8 \\ \times\,7 \\ \hline \end{array}$

Find the products.

1. 8 × 5 = 40
2. 9 × 3 = 27
3. 9 × 6 = 54
4. 8 × 7 = 56
5. 8 × 1 = 8
6. 9 × 5 = 45
7. 9 × 7 = 63
8. 8 × 9 = 72
9. 9 × 9 = 81
10. 8 × 3 = 24
11. 9 × 2 = 18
12. 9 × 8 = 72
13. 8 × 2 = 16
14. 8 × 8 = 64

53 sec.

Set B   For use after page 99

Find these factors.

1. 4 × [7] = 28
2. [9] × 9 = 81
3. [3] × 7 = 21
4. 5 × [0] = 0
5. 8 × [9] = 72
6. [8] × 5 = 40
7. 4 × [8] = 32
8. 7 × [8] = 56
9. [6] × 9 = 54
10. 9 × [5] = 45
11. 8 × [2] = 16
12. 4 × [4] = 16
13. 7 × [6] = 42
14. [3] × 9 = 27
15. [2] × 9 = 36
16. 6 × [8] = 48

30 sec.

Set C   For use after page 109

Find the quotients.

1 min 5 sec.

1. 8 ÷ 2 = 4
2. 24 ÷ 3 = 7
3. 14 ÷ 2 = 7
4. 15 ÷ 3 = 5
5. 18 ÷ 3 = 6
6. 10 ÷ 2 = 5
7. 4 ÷ 2 = 2
8. 9 ÷ 3 = 3

9. 2)16 = 8
10. 3)21 = 7
11. 2)12 = 6
12. 2)16 = 8
13. 3)27 = 9
14. 3)12 = 4
15. 2)14 = 7
16. 3)15 = 5
17. 3)6 = 2
18. 2)18 = 9
19. 2)12 = 6
20. 3)15 = 5
21. 2)10 = 5
22. 3)3 = 1
23. 3)9 = 3
24. 2)8 = 4
25. 3)18 = 6
26. 2)4 = 2
27. 2)2 = 1
28. 3)24 = 7

Set A   **For use after page 111**

Divide. Think about fact families or missing factors.

1. $20 \div 5 =$ **2.** $16 \div 4 =$ **3.** $10 \div 5 =$ **4.** $8 \div 4 =$

5. $40 \div 5 =$ **6.** $12 \div 4 =$ **7.** $25 \div 5 =$ **8.** $36 \div 4 =$

9. $4\overline{)20}$ **10.** $5\overline{)30}$ **11.** $4\overline{)24}$ **12.** $5\overline{)40}$ **13.** $5\overline{)15}$

14. $5\overline{)45}$ **15.** $4\overline{)28}$ **16.** $4\overline{)36}$ **17.** $5\overline{)35}$ **18.** $4\overline{)8}$

19. $6\overline{)30}$ **20.** $4\overline{)24}$ **21.** $8\overline{)64}$ **22.** $7\overline{)49}$ **23.** $6\overline{)42}$

24. $5\overline{)25}$ **25.** $4\overline{)28}$ **26.** $3\overline{)27}$ **27.** $7\overline{)63}$ **28.** $4\overline{)12}$

Set B   **For use after page 117**

Find the quotients.

1. $35 \div 7 =$ **2.** $54 \div 6 =$ **3.** $12 \div 6 =$ **4.** $21 \div 7 =$

5. $30 \div 6 =$ **6.** $42 \div 7 =$ **7.** $28 \div 7 =$ **8.** $18 \div 6 =$

9. $7\overline{)14}$ **10.** $6\overline{)24}$ **11.** $7\overline{)49}$ **12.** $7\overline{)63}$ **13.** $6\overline{)36}$

14. $6\overline{)42}$ **15.** $7\overline{)28}$ **16.** $6\overline{)6}$ **17.** $6\overline{)48}$ **18.** $7\overline{)56}$

Set C   **For use after page 119**

Divide.

1. $8 \div 8 =$ **2.** $27 \div 9 =$ **3.** $56 \div 8 =$ **4.** $81 \div 9 =$

5. $32 \div 8 =$ **6.** $63 \div 9 =$ **7.** $40 \div 8 =$ **8.** $16 \div 8 =$

9. $8\overline{)72}$ **10.** $9\overline{)36}$ **11.** $8\overline{)48}$ **12.** $9\overline{)18}$ **13.** $9\overline{)54}$

14. $8\overline{)24}$ **15.** $8\overline{)64}$ **16.** $9\overline{)45}$ **17.** $9\overline{)72}$ **18.** $9\overline{)9}$

Find these products. Use the grouping shown.

1. $(2 \times 3) \times 3 = \square$ **2.** $(4 \times 1) \times 10 = \square$ **3.** $5 \times (4 \times 2) = \square$

4. $4 \times (2 \times 100) = \square$ **5.** $5 \times (2 \times 3) = \square$ **6.** $(3 \times 3) \times 10 = \square$

7. $7 \times (1 \times 10) = \square$ **8.** $3 \times (3 \times 2) = \square$ **9.** $(1 \times 8) \times 800 = \square$

Find these products. Use any grouping you want.

1. $4 \times 2 \times 2 = \square$ **2.** $5 \times 1 \times 9 = \square$ **3.** $7 \times 1 \times 5 = \square$

4. $2 \times 3 \times 100 = \square$ **5.** $6 \times 1 \times 10 = \square$ **6.** $5 \times 2 \times 50 = \square$

7. $3 \times 3 \times 100 = \square$ **8.** $2 \times 2 \times 10 = \square$ **9.** $2 \times 3 \times 1{,}000 = \square$

Multiply.

1. $\begin{array}{r} 21 \\ \times\ 3 \\ \hline \end{array}$ **2.** $\begin{array}{r} 27 \\ \times\ 3 \\ \hline \end{array}$ **3.** $\begin{array}{r} 15 \\ \times\ 5 \\ \hline \end{array}$ **4.** $\begin{array}{r} 32 \\ \times\ 3 \\ \hline \end{array}$ **5.** $\begin{array}{r} 46 \\ \times\ 2 \\ \hline \end{array}$

6. $\begin{array}{r} 12 \\ \times\ 7 \\ \hline \end{array}$ **7.** $\begin{array}{r} 19 \\ \times\ 4 \\ \hline \end{array}$ **8.** $\begin{array}{r} 25 \\ \times\ 3 \\ \hline \end{array}$ **9.** $\begin{array}{r} 24 \\ \times\ 4 \\ \hline \end{array}$ **10.** $\begin{array}{r} 15 \\ \times\ 4 \\ \hline \end{array}$

11. $\begin{array}{r} 18 \\ \times\ 3 \\ \hline \end{array}$ **12.** $\begin{array}{r} 27 \\ \times\ 3 \\ \hline \end{array}$ **13.** $\begin{array}{r} 16 \\ \times\ 6 \\ \hline \end{array}$ **14.** $\begin{array}{r} 38 \\ \times\ 2 \\ \hline \end{array}$ **15.** $\begin{array}{r} 12 \\ \times\ 5 \\ \hline \end{array}$

16. $\begin{array}{r} 13 \\ \times\ 7 \\ \hline \end{array}$ **17.** $\begin{array}{r} 33 \\ \times\ 2 \\ \hline \end{array}$ **18.** $\begin{array}{r} 17 \\ \times\ 4 \\ \hline \end{array}$ **19.** $\begin{array}{r} 46 \\ \times\ 2 \\ \hline \end{array}$ **20.** $\begin{array}{r} 13 \\ \times\ 4 \\ \hline \end{array}$

21. $\begin{array}{r} 23 \\ \times\ 3 \\ \hline \end{array}$ **22.** $\begin{array}{r} 30 \\ \times\ 2 \\ \hline \end{array}$ **23.** $\begin{array}{r} 42 \\ \times\ 2 \\ \hline \end{array}$ **24.** $\begin{array}{r} 12 \\ \times\ 2 \\ \hline \end{array}$ **25.** $\begin{array}{r} 17 \\ \times\ 5 \\ \hline \end{array}$

Set A   For use after page 169

Find the products.

1. $\begin{array}{r} 53 \\ \times\ 4 \\ \hline \end{array}$
2. $\begin{array}{r} 72 \\ \times\ 5 \\ \hline \end{array}$
3. $\begin{array}{r} 24 \\ \times\ 4 \\ \hline \end{array}$
4. $\begin{array}{r} 45 \\ \times\ 6 \\ \hline \end{array}$
5. $\begin{array}{r} 86 \\ \times\ 5 \\ \hline \end{array}$
6. $\begin{array}{r} 12 \\ \times\ 8 \\ \hline \end{array}$

7. $\begin{array}{r} 62 \\ \times\ 3 \\ \hline \end{array}$
8. $\begin{array}{r} 22 \\ \times\ 7 \\ \hline \end{array}$
9. $\begin{array}{r} 88 \\ \times\ 2 \\ \hline \end{array}$
10. $\begin{array}{r} 76 \\ \times\ 8 \\ \hline \end{array}$
11. $\begin{array}{r} 36 \\ \times\ 3 \\ \hline \end{array}$
12. $\begin{array}{r} 57 \\ \times\ 6 \\ \hline \end{array}$

13. $\begin{array}{r} 16 \\ \times\ 9 \\ \hline \end{array}$
14. $\begin{array}{r} 70 \\ \times\ 5 \\ \hline \end{array}$
15. $\begin{array}{r} 49 \\ \times\ 2 \\ \hline \end{array}$
16. $\begin{array}{r} 34 \\ \times\ 5 \\ \hline \end{array}$
17. $\begin{array}{r} 63 \\ \times\ 4 \\ \hline \end{array}$
18. $\begin{array}{r} 15 \\ \times\ 6 \\ \hline \end{array}$

19. $\begin{array}{r} 74 \\ \times\ 6 \\ \hline \end{array}$
20. $\begin{array}{r} 18 \\ \times\ 3 \\ \hline \end{array}$
21. $\begin{array}{r} 77 \\ \times\ 4 \\ \hline \end{array}$
22. $\begin{array}{r} 82 \\ \times\ 8 \\ \hline \end{array}$
23. $\begin{array}{r} 92 \\ \times\ 7 \\ \hline \end{array}$
24. $\begin{array}{r} 56 \\ \times\ 2 \\ \hline \end{array}$

25. $\begin{array}{r} 63 \\ \times\ 4 \\ \hline \end{array}$
26. $\begin{array}{r} 37 \\ \times\ 3 \\ \hline \end{array}$
27. $\begin{array}{r} 14 \\ \times\ 7 \\ \hline \end{array}$
28. $\begin{array}{r} 49 \\ \times\ 6 \\ \hline \end{array}$
29. $\begin{array}{r} 15 \\ \times\ 9 \\ \hline \end{array}$
30. $\begin{array}{r} 63 \\ \times\ 8 \\ \hline \end{array}$

Set B   For use after page 171

Find the products.

1. $\begin{array}{r} 130 \\ \times\ \ 4 \\ \hline \end{array}$
2. $\begin{array}{r} 161 \\ \times\ \ 7 \\ \hline \end{array}$
3. $\begin{array}{r} 128 \\ \times\ \ 3 \\ \hline \end{array}$
4. $\begin{array}{r} 116 \\ \times\ \ 5 \\ \hline \end{array}$
5. $\begin{array}{r} 411 \\ \times\ \ 8 \\ \hline \end{array}$

6. $\begin{array}{r} 314 \\ \times\ \ 4 \\ \hline \end{array}$
7. $\begin{array}{r} 601 \\ \times\ \ 5 \\ \hline \end{array}$
8. $\begin{array}{r} 232 \\ \times\ \ 4 \\ \hline \end{array}$
9. $\begin{array}{r} 81 \\ \times\ 7 \\ \hline \end{array}$
10. $\begin{array}{r} 183 \\ \times\ \ 3 \\ \hline \end{array}$

11. $\begin{array}{r} 206 \\ \times\ \ 2 \\ \hline \end{array}$
12. $\begin{array}{r} 512 \\ \times\ \ 5 \\ \hline \end{array}$
13. $\begin{array}{r} 721 \\ \times\ \ 6 \\ \hline \end{array}$
14. $\begin{array}{r} 681 \\ \times\ \ 2 \\ \hline \end{array}$
15. $\begin{array}{r} 92 \\ \times\ 6 \\ \hline \end{array}$

16. $\begin{array}{r} 59 \\ \times\ 2 \\ \hline \end{array}$
17. $\begin{array}{r} 74 \\ \times\ 8 \\ \hline \end{array}$
18. $\begin{array}{r} 115 \\ \times\ \ 6 \\ \hline \end{array}$
19. $\begin{array}{r} 532 \\ \times\ \ 3 \\ \hline \end{array}$
20. $\begin{array}{r} 63 \\ \times\ 8 \\ \hline \end{array}$

Find the products.

1. 636 × 4	**2.** 254 × 6	**3.** 842 × 5	**4.** 312 × 8	**5.** 69 × 9
6. 605 × 3	**7.** 250 × 7	**8.** 708 × 2	**9.** 435 × 8	**10.** 582 × 5
11. 751 × 9	**12.** 320 × 5	**13.** 491 × 4	**14.** 88 × 3	**15.** 286 × 7
16. 164 × 6	**17.** 487 × 2	**18.** 185 × 3	**19.** 625 × 9	**20.** 125 × 4

Find the products.

1. 4,512 × 7	**2.** 1,475 × 6	**3.** 7,004 × 5	**4.** 2,351 × 3	**5.** 5,267 × 8
6. 3,418 × 4	**7.** 2,358 × 2	**8.** 1,059 × 9	**9.** 4,289 × 6	**10.** 1,286 × 7
11. 8,537 × 3	**12.** 4,230 × 5	**13.** 2,006 × 8	**14.** 944 × 4	**15.** 3,172 × 8
16. 867 × 5	**17.** 5,616 × 2	**18.** 5,009 × 6	**19.** 6,031 × 9	**20.** 3,548 × 2
21. 6,009 × 3	**22.** 242 × 7	**23.** 2,071 × 4	**24.** 319 × 3	**25.** 1,428 × 6

Multiply. Write the answers with dollars and cents.

1. $0.45 × 7	2. $5.26 × 8	3. $3.02 × 4	4. $8.59 × 9	5. $0.78 × 5
6. $10.62 × 6	7. $0.32 × 8	8. $15.16 × 3	9. $9.33 × 5	10. $41.50 × 7
11. $55.35 × 8	12. $60.07 × 6	13. $7.89 × 2	14. $75.36 × 3	15. $20.06 × 5
16. $19.83 × 9	17. $67.38 × 2	18. $35.18 × 4	19. $25.16 × 7	20. $85.42 × 6

Find the quotients and remainders.

1. $2\overline{)3}$ 2. $3\overline{)6}$ 3. $3\overline{)8}$ 4. $8\overline{)4}$ 5. $6\overline{)21}$

6. $5\overline{)6}$ 7. $4\overline{)9}$ 8. $7\overline{)46}$ 9. $9\overline{)41}$ 10. $8\overline{)36}$

11. $2\overline{)17}$ 12. $5\overline{)36}$ 13. $4\overline{)0}$ 14. $9\overline{)78}$ 15. $7\overline{)6}$

16. $6\overline{)30}$ 17. $8\overline{)61}$ 18. $9\overline{)47}$ 19. $3\overline{)16}$ 20. $5\overline{)14}$

21. $2\overline{)13}$ 22. $4\overline{)22}$ 23. $7\overline{)16}$ 24. $6\overline{)15}$ 25. $8\overline{)65}$

26. $9\overline{)39}$ 27. $5\overline{)47}$ 28. $2\overline{)9}$ 29. $3\overline{)22}$ 30. $7\overline{)38}$

31. $4\overline{)35}$ 32. $6\overline{)49}$ 33. $5\overline{)28}$ 34. $8\overline{)15}$ 35. $3\overline{)10}$

36. $4\overline{)29}$ 37. $3\overline{)33}$ 38. $6\overline{)50}$ 39. $7\overline{)60}$ 40. $9\overline{)85}$

41. $7\overline{)37}$ 42. $6\overline{)22}$ 43. $8\overline{)42}$ 44. $3\overline{)20}$ 45. $9\overline{)50}$

Set A   **For use after page 195**

Find the quotients and remainders.

1. $2\overline{)21}$ 2. $4\overline{)88}$ 3. $5\overline{)91}$ 4. $5\overline{)86}$ 5. $6\overline{)80}$

6. $3\overline{)35}$ 7. $9\overline{)99}$ 8. $7\overline{)36}$ 9. $2\overline{)34}$ 10. $8\overline{)75}$

11. $5\overline{)68}$ 12. $8\overline{)94}$ 13. $2\overline{)91}$ 14. $6\overline{)53}$ 15. $4\overline{)79}$

16. $3\overline{)55}$ 17. $7\overline{)81}$ 18. $9\overline{)86}$ 19. $3\overline{)92}$ 20. $8\overline{)82}$

21. $4\overline{)65}$ 22. $6\overline{)70}$ 23. $2\overline{)69}$ 24. $7\overline{)88}$ 25. $5\overline{)59}$

26. $9\overline{)96}$ 27. $3\overline{)64}$ 28. $8\overline{)84}$ 29. $4\overline{)45}$ 30. $2\overline{)53}$

31. $7\overline{)74}$ 32. $6\overline{)92}$ 33. $4\overline{)55}$ 34. $5\overline{)62}$ 35. $3\overline{)88}$

Set B   **For use after page 199**

Find the quotients and remainders.

1. $3\overline{)416}$ 2. $5\overline{)681}$ 3. $8\overline{)994}$ 4. $2\overline{)625}$ 5. $6\overline{)818}$

6. $4\overline{)727}$ 7. $7\overline{)925}$ 8. $3\overline{)640}$ 9. $6\overline{)934}$ 10. $4\overline{)551}$

11. $2\overline{)750}$ 12. $8\overline{)941}$ 13. $5\overline{)704}$ 14. $7\overline{)808}$ 15. $5\overline{)593}$

16. $3\overline{)700}$ 17. $4\overline{)791}$ 18. $6\overline{)788}$ 19. $2\overline{)547}$ 20. $8\overline{)892}$

21. $7\overline{)796}$ 22. $5\overline{)839}$ 23. $3\overline{)334}$ 24. $4\overline{)633}$ 25. $7\overline{)799}$

26. $6\overline{)677}$ 27. $8\overline{)937}$ 28. $2\overline{)248}$ 29. $5\overline{)909}$ 30. $3\overline{)587}$

31. $7\overline{)884}$ 32. $6\overline{)893}$ 33. $4\overline{)450}$ 34. $2\overline{)335}$ 35. $8\overline{)884}$

36. $6\overline{)696}$ 37. $4\overline{)510}$ 38. $2\overline{)392}$ 39. $5\overline{)718}$ 40. $2\overline{)221}$

41. $3\overline{)987}$ 42. $9\overline{)998}$ 43. $8\overline{)916}$ 44. $3\overline{)753}$ 45. $4\overline{)893}$

Divide and check.

1. $3\overline{)124}$ 2. $7\overline{)810}$ 3. $6\overline{)200}$ 4. $2\overline{)137}$ 5. $4\overline{)543}$

6. $9\overline{)425}$ 7. $5\overline{)663}$ 8. $8\overline{)383}$ 9. $3\overline{)707}$ 10. $7\overline{)400}$

11. $4\overline{)564}$ 12. $2\overline{)845}$ 13. $5\overline{)109}$ 14. $6\overline{)507}$ 15. $9\overline{)377}$

16. $8\overline{)178}$ 17. $3\overline{)573}$ 18. $7\overline{)306}$ 19. $4\overline{)326}$ 20. $6\overline{)728}$

21. $9\overline{)267}$ 22. $5\overline{)586}$ 23. $8\overline{)977}$ 24. $2\overline{)479}$ 25. $7\overline{)918}$

26. $3\overline{)278}$ 27. $6\overline{)805}$ 28. $5\overline{)285}$ 29. $4\overline{)629}$ 30. $9\overline{)840}$

31. $8\overline{)893}$ 32. $2\overline{)197}$ 33. $7\overline{)243}$ 34. $3\overline{)359}$ 35. $5\overline{)427}$

Divide.

1. $7\overline{)636}$ 2. $6\overline{)604}$ 3. $9\overline{)98}$ 4. $2\overline{)801}$ 5. $5\overline{)750}$

6. $3\overline{)91}$ 7. $4\overline{)431}$ 8. $7\overline{)846}$ 9. $8\overline{)819}$ 10. $3\overline{)901}$

11. $5\overline{)502}$ 12. $9\overline{)365}$ 13. $6\overline{)744}$ 14. $2\overline{)81}$ 15. $4\overline{)823}$

16. $8\overline{)480}$ 17. $3\overline{)32}$ 18. $7\overline{)721}$ 19. $5\overline{)450}$ 20. $9\overline{)995}$

21. $4\overline{)83}$ 22. $2\overline{)612}$ 23. $8\overline{)721}$ 24. $6\overline{)62}$ 25. $3\overline{)311}$

26. $9\overline{)546}$ 27. $7\overline{)75}$ 28. $5\overline{)52}$ 29. $2\overline{)416}$ 30. $4\overline{)203}$

31. $8\overline{)325}$ 32. $6\overline{)363}$ 33. $3\overline{)272}$ 34. $5\overline{)203}$ 35. $7\overline{)354}$

36. $3\overline{)61}$ 37. $4\overline{)363}$ 38. $8\overline{)882}$ 39. $3\overline{)306}$ 40. $5\overline{)505}$

41. $7\overline{)216}$ 42. $9\overline{)814}$ 43. $2\overline{)507}$ 44. $6\overline{)612}$ 45. $5\overline{)900}$

Set A   For use after page 205

Divide.

1. $5)\overline{\$0.30}$ 2. $8)\overline{\$1.44}$ 3. $2)\overline{\$0.18}$ 4. $4)\overline{\$7.56}$ 5. $7)\overline{\$0.56}$

6. $3)\overline{\$4.56}$ 7. $6)\overline{\$7.86}$ 8. $9)\overline{\$0.72}$ 9. $5)\overline{\$6.40}$ 10. $2)\overline{\$1.60}$

11. $4)\overline{\$0.92}$ 12. $7)\overline{\$4.41}$ 13. $8)\overline{\$8.00}$ 14. $3)\overline{\$0.78}$ 15. $6)\overline{\$2.70}$

16. $9)\overline{\$5.67}$ 17. $2)\overline{\$8.06}$ 18. $5)\overline{\$4.60}$ 19. $4)\overline{\$3.88}$ 20. $7)\overline{\$8.61}$

21. $6)\overline{\$8.04}$ 22. $3)\overline{\$1.50}$ 23. $8)\overline{\$9.76}$ 24. $2)\overline{\$0.90}$ 25. $9)\overline{\$8.46}$

26. $3)\overline{\$6.00}$ 27. $4)\overline{\$0.36}$ 28. $6)\overline{\$0.48}$ 29. $5)\overline{\$8.90}$ 30. $7)\overline{\$2.59}$

31. $2)\overline{\$2.02}$ 32. $6)\overline{\$0.36}$ 33. $7)\overline{\$9.17}$ 34. $8)\overline{\$3.28}$ 35. $4)\overline{\$2.80}$

36. $3)\overline{\$9.30}$ 37. $5)\overline{\$0.50}$ 38. $5)\overline{\$9.25}$ 39. $4)\overline{\$8.04}$ 40. $2)\overline{\$9.18}$

Set B   For use after page 206

Find the averages of these numbers.

1. 88, 36, 14   2. 16, 11, 14, 15   3. 10, 13, 15, 22

4. 55, 74, 39   5. 115, 149, 108, 132   6. 121, 84, 66, 109

7. 19, 10, 7, 8   8. 37, 15, 29   9. 137, 111, 124

10. 13, 9, 17, 6, 15   11. 37, 17, 9, 21   12. 64, 35, 12

13. 43, 12, 8   14. 15, 7, 12, 5, 21   15. 72, 46, 26

16. 32, 65, 24, 47   17. 40, 16, 7   18. 17, 23, 36, 12

19. 33, 22, 17   20. 16, 34, 8, 2   21. 112, 39, 5

22. 56, 12, 8, 24   23. 17, 6, 73   24. 61, 25, 21, 5

Multiply the numerator and denominator by
2, 3, and 4 to find a set of equivalent fractions.

1. $\frac{1}{4} = \frac{}{} = \frac{}{} = \frac{}{}$

2. $\frac{1}{3} = \frac{}{} = \frac{}{} = \frac{}{}$

3. $\frac{2}{5} = \frac{}{} = \frac{}{} = \frac{}{}$

4. $\frac{3}{8} = \frac{}{} = \frac{}{} = \frac{}{}$

5. $\frac{3}{4} = \frac{}{} = \frac{}{} = \frac{}{}$

6. $\frac{5}{9} = \frac{}{} = \frac{}{} = \frac{}{}$

7. $\frac{1}{6} = \frac{}{} = \frac{}{} = \frac{}{}$

8. $\frac{1}{2} = \frac{}{} = \frac{}{} = \frac{}{}$

9. $\frac{4}{5} = \frac{}{} = \frac{}{} = \frac{}{}$

Reduce each fraction to lowest terms.

1. $\frac{6}{8}$ **2.** $\frac{3}{9}$ **3.** $\frac{4}{16}$ **4.** $\frac{18}{24}$ **5.** $\frac{8}{12}$ **6.** $\frac{3}{9}$

7. $\frac{2}{10}$ **8.** $\frac{4}{6}$ **9.** $\frac{6}{15}$ **10.** $\frac{25}{45}$ **11.** $\frac{6}{12}$ **12.** $\frac{6}{24}$

13. $\frac{4}{8}$ **14.** $\frac{6}{9}$ **15.** $\frac{18}{60}$ **16.** $\frac{15}{24}$ **17.** $\frac{2}{8}$ **18.** $\frac{10}{15}$

19. $\frac{2}{20}$ **20.** $\frac{3}{15}$ **21.** $\frac{6}{30}$ **22.** $\frac{15}{18}$ **23.** $\frac{3}{24}$ **24.** $\frac{12}{16}$

Write $>$, $<$, or $=$, for each ●.

1. $\frac{1}{5}$ ● $\frac{1}{3}$ **2.** $\frac{1}{2}$ ● $\frac{1}{3}$ **3.** $\frac{1}{10}$ ● $\frac{1}{5}$ **4.** $\frac{1}{4}$ ● $\frac{1}{5}$ **5.** $\frac{2}{4}$ ● $\frac{5}{10}$

6. $\frac{1}{3}$ ● $\frac{1}{10}$ **7.** $\frac{2}{5}$ ● $\frac{1}{2}$ **8.** $\frac{3}{4}$ ● $\frac{5}{8}$ **9.** $\frac{1}{5}$ ● $\frac{3}{10}$ **10.** $\frac{1}{5}$ ● $\frac{2}{10}$

11. $\frac{3}{4}$ ● $\frac{2}{3}$ **12.** $\frac{3}{5}$ ● $\frac{6}{10}$ **13.** $\frac{7}{10}$ ● $\frac{4}{5}$ **14.** $\frac{5}{10}$ ● $\frac{4}{5}$ **15.** $\frac{8}{10}$ ● $\frac{4}{5}$

16. $\frac{1}{2}$ ● $\frac{2}{3}$ **17.** $\frac{2}{3}$ ● $\frac{2}{5}$ **18.** $\frac{4}{10}$ ● $\frac{3}{5}$ **19.** $\frac{2}{5}$ ● $\frac{1}{4}$ **20.** $\frac{9}{10}$ ● $\frac{4}{5}$

Set A   **For use after page 233**

Find the missing numbers.

1. $\frac{1}{2}$ of 8

2. $\frac{1}{3}$ of 21

3. $\frac{1}{5}$ of 10

4. $\frac{1}{4}$ of 8

5. $\frac{1}{8}$ of 16

6. $\frac{1}{4}$ of 12

7. $\frac{1}{2}$ of 10

8. $\frac{1}{3}$ of 3

9. $\frac{1}{5}$ of 25

10. $\frac{1}{8}$ of 32

11. $\frac{1}{4}$ of 16

12. $\frac{1}{2}$ of 20

13. $\frac{1}{8}$ of 8

14. $\frac{1}{4}$ of 24

15. $\frac{1}{3}$ of 9

16. $\frac{1}{2}$ of 14

Set B   **For use after page 235**

Find the missing numbers.

1. $\frac{2}{3}$ of 9

2. $\frac{2}{5}$ of 10

3. $\frac{3}{8}$ of 8

4. $\frac{2}{4}$ of 8

5. $\frac{5}{8}$ of 16

6. $\frac{2}{3}$ of 12

7. $\frac{2}{5}$ of 5

8. $\frac{3}{4}$ of 24

9. $\frac{4}{5}$ of 15

10. $\frac{2}{4}$ of 16

11. $\frac{3}{8}$ of 24

12. $\frac{3}{4}$ of 16

Set C   **For use after page 239**

Write as a whole number or mixed number.
Reduce all fraction parts to lowest terms.

1. $\frac{8}{4}$

2. $\frac{5}{2}$

3. $\frac{6}{3}$

4. $\frac{26}{4}$

5. $\frac{10}{2}$

6. $\frac{41}{8}$

7. $\frac{17}{3}$

8. $\frac{16}{4}$

9. $\frac{47}{5}$

10. $\frac{18}{6}$

11. $\frac{40}{6}$

12. $\frac{12}{2}$

13. $\frac{11}{4}$

14. $\frac{15}{2}$

15. $\frac{9}{3}$

16. $\frac{18}{3}$

17. $\frac{8}{3}$

18. $\frac{24}{8}$

19. $\frac{20}{8}$

20. $\frac{22}{5}$

Find the sums.

1. $\frac{2}{5} + \frac{2}{5}$ 2. $\frac{1}{4} + \frac{2}{4}$ 3. $\frac{4}{6} + \frac{1}{6}$ 4. $\frac{4}{8} + \frac{2}{8}$

5. $\frac{3}{10} + \frac{3}{10}$ 6. $\frac{3}{5} + \frac{1}{5}$ 7. $\frac{1}{3} + \frac{1}{3}$ 8. $\frac{4}{10} + \frac{5}{10}$

9. $\begin{array}{r} \frac{1}{8} \\ + \frac{2}{8} \\ \hline \end{array}$ 10. $\begin{array}{r} \frac{1}{5} \\ + \frac{2}{5} \\ \hline \end{array}$ 11. $\begin{array}{r} \frac{1}{10} \\ + \frac{3}{10} \\ \hline \end{array}$ 12. $\begin{array}{r} \frac{2}{6} \\ + \frac{2}{6} \\ \hline \end{array}$ 13. $\begin{array}{r} \frac{1}{10} \\ + \frac{8}{10} \\ \hline \end{array}$ 14. $\begin{array}{r} \frac{3}{8} \\ + \frac{1}{8} \\ \hline \end{array}$

Find the differences.

1. $\frac{9}{10} - \frac{6}{10}$ 2. $\frac{7}{8} - \frac{2}{8}$ 3. $\frac{6}{8} - \frac{2}{8}$ 4. $\frac{4}{5} - \frac{2}{5}$

5. $\frac{12}{8} - \frac{6}{8}$ 6. $\frac{11}{10} - \frac{6}{10}$ 7. $\frac{4}{4} - \frac{1}{4}$ 8. $\frac{5}{6} - \frac{1}{6}$

9. $\begin{array}{r} \frac{4}{6} \\ - \frac{2}{6} \\ \hline \end{array}$ 10. $\begin{array}{r} \frac{3}{5} \\ - \frac{2}{5} \\ \hline \end{array}$ 11. $\begin{array}{r} \frac{5}{4} \\ - \frac{3}{4} \\ \hline \end{array}$ 12. $\begin{array}{r} \frac{8}{10} \\ - \frac{6}{10} \\ \hline \end{array}$ 13. $\begin{array}{r} \frac{4}{8} \\ - \frac{1}{8} \\ \hline \end{array}$ 14. $\begin{array}{r} \frac{5}{5} \\ - \frac{1}{5} \\ \hline \end{array}$

Find the sums and differences.

1. $\frac{3}{8} + \frac{6}{8}$ 2. $\frac{8}{10} + \frac{8}{10}$ 3. $\frac{3}{4} + \frac{2}{4}$ 4. $\frac{4}{6} + \frac{4}{6}$

5. $\begin{array}{r} 2\frac{2}{3} \\ + 1\frac{1}{3} \\ \hline \end{array}$ 6. $\begin{array}{r} 6\frac{2}{4} \\ - 1\frac{1}{4} \\ \hline \end{array}$ 7. $\begin{array}{r} 4\frac{1}{6} \\ + 3\frac{2}{6} \\ \hline \end{array}$ 8. $\begin{array}{r} 12\frac{6}{8} \\ - 6\frac{2}{8} \\ \hline \end{array}$ 9. $\begin{array}{r} 5\frac{3}{10} \\ + 1\frac{4}{10} \\ \hline \end{array}$ 10. $\begin{array}{r} 8\frac{1}{2} \\ - 4\frac{1}{2} \\ \hline \end{array}$

11. $\begin{array}{r} 3\frac{1}{2} \\ + 2\frac{1}{2} \\ \hline \end{array}$ 12. $\begin{array}{r} 4\frac{5}{8} \\ + 4\frac{2}{8} \\ \hline \end{array}$ 13. $\begin{array}{r} 8\frac{6}{10} \\ - 7\frac{3}{10} \\ \hline \end{array}$ 14. $\begin{array}{r} 2\frac{2}{3} \\ - 1\frac{1}{3} \\ \hline \end{array}$ 15. $\begin{array}{r} 2\frac{1}{4} \\ + 3\frac{1}{4} \\ \hline \end{array}$ 16. $\begin{array}{r} 9\frac{4}{6} \\ - 3\frac{3}{6} \\ \hline \end{array}$

Add.

1. $\frac{5}{8}$
$+ \frac{2}{4}$

2. $\frac{2}{10}$
$+ \frac{2}{5}$

3. $\frac{2}{9}$
$+ \frac{1}{3}$

4. $\frac{1}{2}$
$+ \frac{4}{6}$

5. $\frac{3}{4}$
$+ \frac{1}{2}$

6. $\frac{1}{6}$
$+ \frac{2}{3}$

7. $\frac{6}{10}$
$+ \frac{3}{5}$

8. $\frac{2}{8}$
$+ \frac{2}{4}$

9. $\frac{1}{3}$
$+ \frac{5}{6}$

10. $\frac{3}{10}$
$+ \frac{3}{5}$

Subtract.

1. $\frac{6}{8}$
$- \frac{1}{4}$

2. $\frac{2}{3}$
$- \frac{2}{9}$

3. $\frac{4}{5}$
$- \frac{3}{10}$

4. $\frac{3}{4}$
$- \frac{3}{8}$

5. $\frac{1}{3}$
$- \frac{1}{6}$

6. $\frac{5}{8}$
$- \frac{1}{2}$

7. $\frac{1}{2}$
$- \frac{1}{8}$

8. $\frac{2}{3}$
$- \frac{2}{6}$

9. $\frac{6}{8}$
$- \frac{1}{2}$

10. $\frac{7}{8}$
$- \frac{3}{4}$

Multiply.

1. $\begin{array}{r} 63 \\ \times\ 80 \\ \hline \end{array}$

2. $\begin{array}{r} 48 \\ \times\ 30 \\ \hline \end{array}$

3. $\begin{array}{r} 75 \\ \times\ 40 \\ \hline \end{array}$

4. $\begin{array}{r} 43 \\ \times\ 10 \\ \hline \end{array}$

5. $\begin{array}{r} 27 \\ \times\ 60 \\ \hline \end{array}$

6. $\begin{array}{r} 38 \\ \times\ 20 \\ \hline \end{array}$

7. $\begin{array}{r} 12 \\ \times\ 40 \\ \hline \end{array}$

8. $\begin{array}{r} 16 \\ \times\ 70 \\ \hline \end{array}$

9. $\begin{array}{r} 97 \\ \times\ 50 \\ \hline \end{array}$

10. $\begin{array}{r} 64 \\ \times\ 30 \\ \hline \end{array}$

11. $\begin{array}{r} 77 \\ \times\ 90 \\ \hline \end{array}$

12. $\begin{array}{r} 58 \\ \times\ 80 \\ \hline \end{array}$

Set A   For use after page 301

Find the products.

1. $\begin{array}{r} 12 \\ \times\, 23 \\ \hline \end{array}$	2. $\begin{array}{r} 31 \\ \times\, 42 \\ \hline \end{array}$	3. $\begin{array}{r} 43 \\ \times\, 11 \\ \hline \end{array}$	4. $\begin{array}{r} 30 \\ \times\, 24 \\ \hline \end{array}$	5. $\begin{array}{r} 14 \\ \times\, 12 \\ \hline \end{array}$	6. $\begin{array}{r} 44 \\ \times\, 34 \\ \hline \end{array}$
7. $\begin{array}{r} 10 \\ \times\, 42 \\ \hline \end{array}$	8. $\begin{array}{r} 40 \\ \times\, 14 \\ \hline \end{array}$	9. $\begin{array}{r} 24 \\ \times\, 31 \\ \hline \end{array}$	10. $\begin{array}{r} 22 \\ \times\, 43 \\ \hline \end{array}$	11. $\begin{array}{r} 41 \\ \times\, 21 \\ \hline \end{array}$	12. $\begin{array}{r} 32 \\ \times\, 13 \\ \hline \end{array}$
13. $\begin{array}{r} 22 \\ \times\, 43 \\ \hline \end{array}$	14. $\begin{array}{r} 33 \\ \times\, 24 \\ \hline \end{array}$	15. $\begin{array}{r} 24 \\ \times\, 22 \\ \hline \end{array}$	16. $\begin{array}{r} 34 \\ \times\, 41 \\ \hline \end{array}$	17. $\begin{array}{r} 21 \\ \times\, 32 \\ \hline \end{array}$	18. $\begin{array}{r} 11 \\ \times\, 20 \\ \hline \end{array}$

Set B   For use with page 303

Multiply.

1. $\begin{array}{r} 16 \\ \times\, 83 \\ \hline \end{array}$	2. $\begin{array}{r} 33 \\ \times\, 46 \\ \hline \end{array}$	3. $\begin{array}{r} 52 \\ \times\, 70 \\ \hline \end{array}$	4. $\begin{array}{r} 25 \\ \times\, 41 \\ \hline \end{array}$	5. $\begin{array}{r} 64 \\ \times\, 15 \\ \hline \end{array}$	6. $\begin{array}{r} 72 \\ \times\, 39 \\ \hline \end{array}$
7. $\begin{array}{r} 55 \\ \times\, 27 \\ \hline \end{array}$	8. $\begin{array}{r} 63 \\ \times\, 52 \\ \hline \end{array}$	9. $\begin{array}{r} 75 \\ \times\, 42 \\ \hline \end{array}$	10. $\begin{array}{r} 86 \\ \times\, 62 \\ \hline \end{array}$	11. $\begin{array}{r} 37 \\ \times\, 43 \\ \hline \end{array}$	12. $\begin{array}{r} 44 \\ \times\, 56 \\ \hline \end{array}$
13. $\begin{array}{r} 18 \\ \times\, 26 \\ \hline \end{array}$	14. $\begin{array}{r} 38 \\ \times\, 21 \\ \hline \end{array}$	15. $\begin{array}{r} 42 \\ \times\, 35 \\ \hline \end{array}$	16. $\begin{array}{r} 24 \\ \times\, 84 \\ \hline \end{array}$	17. $\begin{array}{r} 43 \\ \times\, 19 \\ \hline \end{array}$	18. $\begin{array}{r} 46 \\ \times\, 66 \\ \hline \end{array}$

Set C   For use after page 307

Multiply.

1. $\begin{array}{r} 300 \\ \times\, 21 \\ \hline \end{array}$	2. $\begin{array}{r} 642 \\ \times\, 53 \\ \hline \end{array}$	3. $\begin{array}{r} 684 \\ \times\, 15 \\ \hline \end{array}$	4. $\begin{array}{r} 259 \\ \times\, 36 \\ \hline \end{array}$	5. $\begin{array}{r} 135 \\ \times\, 47 \\ \hline \end{array}$
6. $\begin{array}{r} 407 \\ \times\, 63 \\ \hline \end{array}$	7. $\begin{array}{r} 500 \\ \times\, 28 \\ \hline \end{array}$	8. $\begin{array}{r} 76 \\ \times\, 52 \\ \hline \end{array}$	9. $\begin{array}{r} 384 \\ \times\, 18 \\ \hline \end{array}$	10. $\begin{array}{r} 708 \\ \times\, 24 \\ \hline \end{array}$

Find the amounts.

1.	$2.79 × 32	**2.**	$1.15 × 46	**3.**	$8.08 × 29	**4.**	$0.68 × 15	**5.**	$5.27 × 24
6.	$4.73 × 36	**7.**	$9.06 × 53	**8.**	$5.61 × 42	**9.**	$8.34 × 16	**10.**	$3.10 × 45
11.	$4.50 × 57	**12.**	$0.72 × 13	**13.**	$8.65 × 31	**14.**	$6.72 × 26	**15.**	$5.98 × 78

Divide.

1. $20\overline{)80}$ 2. $60\overline{)180}$ 3. $10\overline{)90}$ 4. $40\overline{)240}$ 5. $90\overline{)360}$

6. $70\overline{)420}$ 7. $30\overline{)90}$ 8. $70\overline{)280}$ 9. $30\overline{)120}$ 10. $50\overline{)450}$

11. $20\overline{)100}$ 12. $40\overline{)200}$ 13. $40\overline{)80}$ 14. $80\overline{)640}$ 15. $10\overline{)10}$

16. $50\overline{)350}$ 17. $60\overline{)540}$ 18. $20\overline{)80}$ 19. $50\overline{)400}$ 20. $30\overline{)60}$

Divide.

1. $30\overline{)78}$ 2. $70\overline{)92}$ 3. $40\overline{)333}$ 4. $80\overline{)266}$

5. $60\overline{)153}$ 6. $40\overline{)178}$ 7. $30\overline{)56}$ 8. $50\overline{)122}$

9. $50\overline{)285}$ 10. $30\overline{)95}$ 11. $90\overline{)508}$ 12. $60\overline{)185}$

13. $20\overline{)99}$ 14. $70\overline{)383}$ 15. $80\overline{)490}$ 16. $20\overline{)53}$

Divide and check.

1. $15\overline{)48}$ **2.** $47\overline{)96}$ **3.** $33\overline{)47}$ **4.** $25\overline{)56}$

5. $39\overline{)34}$ **6.** $14\overline{)30}$ **7.** $22\overline{)92}$ **8.** $52\overline{)67}$

9. $23\overline{)32}$ **10.** $16\overline{)71}$ **11.** $37\overline{)75}$ **12.** $26\overline{)85}$

13. $46\overline{)73}$ **14.** $64\overline{)60}$ **15.** $36\overline{)87}$ **16.** $63\overline{)79}$

17. $56\overline{)90}$ **18.** $74\overline{)65}$ **19.** $45\overline{)90}$ **20.** $18\overline{)95}$

21. $27\overline{)39}$ **22.** $34\overline{)61}$ **23.** $41\overline{)89}$ **24.** $24\overline{)89}$

25. $18\overline{)38}$ **26.** $25\overline{)77}$ **27.** $12\overline{)80}$ **28.** $27\overline{)89}$

                                           5 R6
29. $35\overline{)79}$ **30.** $17\overline{)91}$ **31.** $11\overline{)96}$ **32.** $36\overline{)56}$

Divide and check.

1. $23\overline{)100}$ **2.** $14\overline{)\$1.26}$ **3.** $42\overline{)376}$ **4.** $36\overline{)61}$

5. $64\overline{)504}$ **6.** $31\overline{)300}$ **7.** $73\overline{)467}$ **8.** $24\overline{)123}$

9. $12\overline{)\$1.08}$ **10.** $74\overline{)457}$ **11.** $86\overline{)735}$ **12.** $52\overline{)232}$

13. $45\overline{)258}$ **14.** $27\overline{)\$2.43}$ **15.** $62\overline{)388}$ **16.** $16\overline{)\$1.28}$

17. $29\overline{)180}$ **18.** $32\overline{)74}$ **19.** $56\overline{)400}$ **20.** $76\overline{)342}$

21. $46\overline{)235}$ **22.** $41\overline{)\$2.87}$ **23.** $22\overline{)185}$ **24.** $18\overline{)151}$

25. $32\overline{)100}$ **26.** $13\overline{)\$5.20}$ **27.** $62\overline{)190}$ **28.** $56\overline{)240}$

29. $17\overline{)145}$ **30.** $22\overline{)204}$ **31.** $42\overline{)\$1.68}$ **32.** $66\overline{)462}$

Set A   For use after page 331

Divide and check.

1. $30\overline{)536}$ 2. $10\overline{)324}$ 3. $40\overline{)687}$ 4. $50\overline{)650}$

5. $40\overline{)748}$ 6. $60\overline{)700}$ 7. $20\overline{)435}$ 8. $10\overline{)462}$

9. $20\overline{)\$7.00}$ 10. $70\overline{)955}$ 11. $30\overline{)812}$ 12. $40\overline{)579}$

13. $50\overline{)805}$ 14. $10\overline{)\$4.60}$ 15. $30\overline{)\$8.70}$ 16. $40\overline{)475}$

17. $10\overline{)143}$ 18. $30\overline{)421}$ 19. $90\overline{)963}$ 20. $20\overline{)787}$

21. $20\overline{)666}$ 22. $40\overline{)563}$ 23. $80\overline{)988}$ 24. $50\overline{)\$9.00}$

25. $30\overline{)427}$ 26. $40\overline{)\$4.80}$ 27. $70\overline{)960}$ 28. $10\overline{)196}$

29. $20\overline{)\$3.80}$ 30. $60\overline{)863}$ 31. $50\overline{)550}$ 32. $80\overline{)872}$

Set B   For use after page 333

Divide and check.

1. $14\overline{)279}$ 2. $22\overline{)354}$ 3. $41\overline{)892}$ 4. $35\overline{)961}$

5. $46\overline{)703}$ 6. $57\overline{)665}$ 7. $11\overline{)\$7.92}$ 8. $64\overline{)828}$

9. $42\overline{)622}$ 10. $36\overline{)504}$ 11. $23\overline{)490}$ 12. $39\overline{)400}$

13. $73\overline{)\$8.76}$ 14. $81\overline{)857}$ 15. $45\overline{)786}$ 16. $86\overline{)946}$

17. $12\overline{)277}$ 18. $37\overline{)395}$ 19. $18\overline{)388}$ 20. $26\overline{)\$4.68}$

21. $34\overline{)414}$ 22. $44\overline{)\$8.36}$ 23. $27\overline{)344}$ 24. $38\overline{)667}$

25. $22\overline{)436}$ 26. $31\overline{)961}$ 27. $47\overline{)549}$ 28. $55\overline{)\$9.90}$

29. $67\overline{)843}$ 30. $37\overline{)999}$ 31. $43\overline{)\$6.45}$ 32. $91\overline{)932}$

Set A   For use after page 349

Give $>$, $<$, or $=$ for each ▦ .

1. 0.27 ▦ 0.30   2. 7.60 ▦ 7.6   3. 0.03 ▦ 0.30

4. 4.8 ▦ 3.9   5. 6.27 ▦ 6.29   6. 2.5 ▦ 2.6

7. 0.41 ▦ 0.35   8. 0.72 ▦ 0.68   9. 0.8 ▦ 0.80

10. 45.20 ▦ 45.2   11. 4.50 ▦ 4.5   12. 6.8 ▦ 5.72

13. 5.6 ▦ 5.59   14. 7.67 ▦ 7.76   15. 4.9 ▦ 5

16. 34.9 ▦ 35   17. 24.1 ▦ 23.9   18. 5.5 ▦ 5.48

19. 0.39 ▦ 0.4   20. 38 ▦ 38.1   21. 0.1 ▦ 0.10

22. 0.30 ▦ 0.03   23. 0.51 ▦ 5.1   24. 36.4 ▦ 36.6

25. 0.27 ▦ 0.72   26. 6.80 ▦ 6.8   27. 0.20 ▦ 0.2

Set B   For use after page 351

Add.

1.	3.68 + 4.19	2.	42.7 + 69.1	3.	4.83 + 1.47	4.	58.26 + 17.35	5.	8.3 + 7.2
6.	6.85 + 5.93	7.	$78.23 + 12.85	8.	28.61 + 76.32	9.	84.1 + 67.3	10.	5.38 + 1.96
11.	75.62 + 33.91	12.	98.46 + 13.53	13.	69.75 + 3.86	14.	$0.68 + 0.73	15.	54.2 + 86.5
16.	56.72 + 31.84	17.	$8.73 + 47.00	18.	47.6 + 16	19.	27.6 + 12.73	20.	$7.89 + 5.94

Set A   For use after page 353

Subtract.

1. 14.0 − 9.6	2. 56.8 − 24.5	3. 27.65 − 13.84	4. 9.87 − 4.95	5. 38.42 − 16.31
6. 7.64 − 3.16	7. $47.20 − 19.80	8. 47.52 − 8.73	9. 47.60 − 17.82	10. 32.75 − 12.08
11. 42.7 − 15.8	12. 2.83 − 1.57	13. 4.76 − 3.85	14. $42.39 − 30.68	15. 32.9 − 27.6
16. $6.45 − 2.81	17. 8.32 − 4.60	18. 76.54 − 43.38	19. 76.28 − 35.64	20. $42.35 − 16.10

Set B   For use after page 354

Find the sums and differences.

1. 0.6 − 0.27	2. 43 + 6.78	3. 12.7 + 5.67	4. 67.43 − 29.08	5. 68 − 34.9
6. 8.62 + 75	7. 15.38 − 6.9	8. 14.0 + 3.27	9. 48.2 + 16.77	10. 49.62 − 39.7
11. 78 − 14.33	12. 6.92 + 9	13. 73.74 − 27.65	14. 67.1 + 8.52	15. 17.53 − 6.9
16. 75 + 68.23	17. 3.75 + 4.93	18. 15.8 − 6.6	19. 48 − 17.76	20. 6.3 + 1.6
21. 21.3 + 13.6	22. 17.8 − 8	23. 63.1 + 4.3	24. 54 − 12.8	25. 11 + 14.9

Table of Measures

Metric System		**Customary System**	

Length

Metric System		Customary System	
1 centimeter (cm)	10 millimeters (mm)	1 foot (ft)	12 inches (in.)
1 decimeter (dm)	$\begin{cases} 100 \text{ millimeters (mm)} \\ 10 \text{ centimeters (cm)} \end{cases}$	1 yard (yd)	$\begin{cases} 36 \text{ inches (in.)} \\ 3 \text{ feet (ft)} \end{cases}$
1 meter (m)	$\begin{cases} 1{,}000 \text{ millimeters (mm)} \\ 100 \text{ centimeters (cm)} \\ 10 \text{ decimeters (dm)} \end{cases}$	1 mile (m)	$\begin{cases} 5{,}280 \text{ feet (ft)} \\ 1{,}760 \text{ yards (yd)} \end{cases}$
1 kilometer (km)	1,000 meters (m)		

Area

Metric System		Customary System	
1 square meter (m^2)	$\begin{cases} 100 \text{ square} \\ \quad \text{decimeters (dm}^2) \\ 10{,}000 \text{ square} \\ \quad \text{centimeters (cm}^2) \end{cases}$	1 square foot (ft^2)	$\begin{cases} 144 \text{ square inches} \\ \quad (\text{in.}^2) \end{cases}$

Volume

Metric System		Customary System	
1 cubic decimeter (dm^3)	$\begin{cases} 1{,}000 \text{ cubic centimeters} \\ \quad (\text{cm}^3) \\ 1 \text{ liter (L)} \end{cases}$	1 cubic foot (ft^3)	$\begin{cases} 1{,}728 \text{ cubic inches} \\ \quad (\text{in.}^3) \end{cases}$

Capacity

Metric System		Customary System	
		1 cup (c)	8 fluid ounces (fl oz)
		1 pint (pt)	$\begin{cases} 16 \text{ fluid ounces (fl oz)} \\ 2 \text{ cups (c)} \end{cases}$
1 teaspoon	5 milliliters (mL)	1 quart (qt)	$\begin{cases} 32 \text{ fluid ounces (fl oz)} \\ 4 \text{ cups (c)} \\ 2 \text{ pints (pt)} \end{cases}$
1 tablespoon	12.5 milliliters (mL)		
1 liter (L)	$\begin{cases} 1{,}000 \text{ milliliters (mL)} \\ 1{,}000 \text{ cubic centimeters} \\ \quad (\text{cm}^3) \\ 1 \text{ cubic decimeter (dm}^3) \\ 4 \text{ metric cups} \end{cases}$	1 gallon (gal)	$\begin{cases} 128 \text{ fluid ounces} \\ \quad (\text{fl oz}) \\ 16 \text{ cups (c)} \\ 8 \text{ pints (pt)} \\ 4 \text{ quarts (qt)} \end{cases}$

Weight

Metric System		Customary System	
1 gram (g)	1,000 milligrams (mg)	1 pound (lb)	16 ounces (oz)
1 kilogram (kg)	1,000 grams (g)		

Time

Metric System		Customary System	
1 minute (min)	60 seconds (s)	1 year (yr)	$\begin{cases} 365 \text{ days} \\ 52 \text{ weeks} \\ 12 \text{ months} \end{cases}$
1 hour (h)	60 minutes (min)		
1 day (d)	24 hours (h)		
1 week (w)	7 days (d)	1 decade	10 years
1 month (mo)	about 4 weeks	1 century	100 years

Glossary

a.m. A way to indicate the times from 12:00 midnight to 12:00 noon.

addend One of the numbers to be added.

Example:

angle Two rays from a single point.

area The measure of a region, expressed in square units.

average The quotient obtained when the sum of the numbers in a set is divided by the number of addends.

capacity The volume of a space figure given in terms of liquid measurement.

centimeter (cm) A unit of length in the metric system. 100 centimeters equal 1 meter.

circle A plane figure in which all the points are the same distance from a point called the center.

congruent figures Figures that have the same size and shape.

congruent triangles

cube A space figure that has squares for all of its faces.

cup (c) A unit for measuring liquids. 1 quart equals 4 cups.

cylinder A space figure that has a circle for a face.

cylinder

decimal A number that shows tenths by using a decimal point.

3.2 ← decimal
↑
decimal point

degree Celsius (°C) A unit for measuring temperature in the metric system.

degree Fahrenheit (°F) A unit for measuring temperature in the customary system of measurement.

denominator The number below the line in a fraction.

$\frac{3}{4}$ ← denominator

difference The number obtained by subtracting one number from another.

digits The symbols used to write numerals: 0, 1, 2, 3, 4, 5, 6, 7, 8, and 9.

dividend A number to be divided.

$\overset{4}{7\overline{)28}}$ ← dividend

divisor The number by which a dividend is divided.

divisor → $7\overline{)28}$

edge One of the segments making up any of the faces of a space figure.

edge

END An instruction in a computer program that tells the computer to stop.

equation A number sentence involving the use of the equality symbol.

Examples: $9 + 2 = 11$
$8 - 4 = 4$

equivalent fractions Fractions that name the same amount.

Example: $\frac{1}{2}$ and $\frac{2}{4}$

estimate To find an answer that is close to the exact answer.

even number A whole number that has 0, 2, 4, 6, or 8 in the ones' place.

face One of the plane figures (regions) making up a space figure.

face

factors Numbers that are multiplied together to form a product.

factors → $6 \times 7 = 42$

flowchart A chart that shows a step-by-step way of doing something.

foot (ft) A unit for measuring length. 1 foot equals 12 inches.

fraction A number that expresses parts of a whole or a set.

Example: $\frac{3}{4}$

gallon (gal) A unit of liquid measure. 1 gallon equals 4 quarts.

GOTO An instruction in a computer program that tells the computer to jump to a specified line.

gram (g) The basic unit for measuring weight in the metric system. A paper clip weighs about 1 gram.

graph A picture that shows information in an organized way.

grouping property When the grouping of addends or factors is changed, the sum or product is the same.

greater than The relationship of one number being larger than another number.

Example: 6 > 5, read "6 is greater than 5."

hexagon A polygon with six sides.

inch (in.) A unit for measuring length. 12 inches equal 1 foot.

intersecting lines Lines that have one common point.

kilogram (kg) A unit of weight in the metric system. 1 kilogram is 1,000 grams.

kilometer (km) A unit of length in the metric system. 1 kilometer is 1,000 meters.

length The measure of distance from one end to the other end of an object.

less than The relationship of being smaller than another number.

Example: 5 < 6, read "5 is less than 6."

line A straight path that is endless in both directions.

line of symmetry A line on which a figure can be folded so that the two parts fit exactly.

line of symmetry

liter (L) A metric unit used to measure liquids. 1 liter equals 1,000 cubic centimeters.

Logo A special computer language that is used for computer graphics.

lowest terms A fraction is in lowest terms if the numerator and denominator have no common factor greater than 1.

meter (m) A unit of length in the metric system. 1 meter is 100 centimeters.

mile (mi) A unit for measuring length. 1 mile equals 5,280 feet.

milliliter (mL) A metric unit for measuring capacity. 1,000 milliliters equal 1 liter.

mixed number A number that has a whole number part and a fractional part, such as $2\frac{3}{4}$.

multiple A number that is the product of a given number and a whole number.

negative number A number that is less than zero.

number pair Two numbers that are used to give the location of a point on a graph.

Example: (3,2)

numeral A symbol for a number.

numerator The number above the line in a fraction. $\frac{3}{4}$ ◄—— numerator

octagon A polygon with eight sides.

odd number A whole number that has 1, 3, 5, 7, or 9 in the ones' place.

one property In multiplication, when either factor is 1, the product is the other factor. In division, when 1 is the divisor, the quotient is the same as the dividend.

order property When the order of addends or factors is changed, the sum or product is the same.

ordinal number A number that is used to tell order.

Example: first, fifth

ounce (oz) A unit for measuring weight. 16 ounces equal 1 pound.

p.m. A way to indicate the times from 12:00 noon to 12:00 midnight.

parallel lines Lines in the same plane that do not intersect.

pentagon A polygon with five sides.

perimeter The distance around a figure.

pint (pt) A unit for measuring liquid. 2 pints equal 1 quart.

place value The value given to the place a digit occupies in a number.

Example:

3 5 6

hundreds' place
tens' place
ones' place

plane figures Figures that lie on a flat surface.

Examples:

square   triangle   circle

point A single, exact location, often represented by a dot.

polygon A closed figure formed by line segments.

pound (lb) A customary unit for measuring weight. 1 pound equals 16 ounces.

prime number A whole number greater than 1, whose only factors are itself and 1.

PRINT An instruction in a computer program that tells the computer to print something.

product The result of the multiplication operation.

$$6 \times 7 = 42 \longleftarrow \text{product}$$

program The set of instructions that tells a computer what to do.

quadrilateral A polygon with four sides.

quart (qt) A unit for measuring liquids. 1 quart equals 4 cups.

quotient The number (other than the remainder) that is the result of the division operation.

$$45 \div 9 = 5 \qquad \qquad 6 \longleftarrow \text{quotient}$$
$$\uparrow \qquad \qquad 7\overline{)45}$$
$$\text{quotient} \qquad -42$$
$$\overline{3}$$

ray A part of a line having only one endpoint.

ray

rectangle A plane figure with four sides and four right angles.

rectangular prism A space figure with six faces. It has the shape of a box.

remainder The number less than the divisor that remains after the division process is completed.

Example:
$$6$$
$$7\overline{)47}$$
$$-42$$
$$\overline{5} \longleftarrow \text{remainder}$$

right angle An angle that has the same shape as the corner of a square.

rounding Replacing a number with a number that tells about how many.

Example: 23 rounded to the nearest 10 is 20.

RUN What appears on the video screen when a computer program is used.

segment A straight path from one point to another.

similar figures Two or more figures having the same shape but not necessarily the same size.

space figure A figure that is not flat but that has volume.

cube   cylinder

sphere A space figure that has the shape of a round ball.

square A plane figure that has four equal sides and four equal corners.

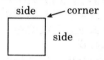

side   corner
side

sum The number obtained by adding numbers.

Example:
$$3$$
$$+\,2$$
$$\overline{5} \longleftarrow \text{sum}$$

symmetric figure A plane figure that can be folded in half so that the two halves match.

ton A unit for measuring weight. 1 ton equals 2,000 pounds.

trading To make a group of ten from one of the next highest place value, or one from ten of the next lowest place value.

Examples: 1 hundred can be traded for 10 tens; 10 ones can be traded for 1 ten.

triangle A plane figure with three segments as sides.

unit An amount or quantity used as a standard of measurement.

vertex (vertices) The common point of any two sides of a polygon.

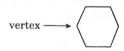

vertex ⟶

volume The number of units of space that a space figure holds.

yard (yd) A unit for measuring length. 1 yard equals 3 feet.

zero property In addition, when one addend is 0, the sum is the other addend. In multiplication, when either factor is 0, the product is 0.

Index